Reproduction Reborn

REPRODUCTION REBORN

How Science, Ethics, and Law Shape
Mitochondrial Replacement Therapies

Edited by Diana M. Bowman, Karinne Ludlow,
and Walter G. Johnson

OXFORD
UNIVERSITY PRESS

Oxford University Press is a department of the University of Oxford. It furthers
the University's objective of excellence in research, scholarship, and education
by publishing worldwide. Oxford is a registered trade mark of Oxford University
Press in the UK and certain other countries.

Published in the United States of America by Oxford University Press
198 Madison Avenue, New York, NY 10016, United States of America.

CIP data is on file at the Library of Congress
ISBN 978–0–19–761620–8 (pbk.)
ISBN 978–0–19–761619–2 (hbk.)

DOI: 10.1093/oso/9780197616192.001.0001

This material is not intended to be, and should not be considered, a substitute for medical or
other professional advice. Treatment for the conditions described in this material is highly
dependent on the individual circumstances. And, while this material is designed to offer accurate
information with respect to the subject matter covered and to be current as of the time it was
written, research and knowledge about medical and health issues is constantly evolving and
dose schedules for medications are being revised continually, with new side effects recognized
and accounted for regularly. Readers must therefore always check the product information and
clinical procedures with the most up-to-date published product information and data sheets
provided by the manufacturers and the most recent codes of conduct and safety regulation.
The publisher and the authors make no representations or warranties to readers, express or
implied, as to the accuracy or completeness of this material. Without limiting the foregoing, the
publisher and the authors make no representations or warranties as to the accuracy or efficacy
of the drug dosages mentioned in the material. The authors and the publisher do not accept,
and expressly disclaim, any responsibility for any liability, loss, or risk that may be claimed or
incurred as a consequence of the use and/or application of any of the contents of this material.

CONTENTS

ACKNOWLEDGMENTS

Never, in our wildest dreams, would we have imagined that we would be creating this edited volume against the backdrop of a global pandemic, one that has touched every single one of us in one way or another. We are incredibly grateful to our contributing authors who, despite the challenges and juggles they faced personally and professionally during this period, generously gave their time and intellectual insights to create this collection. As international leaders in their respective fields, it is their understandings, experience, and expertise that make this volume not only timely but also thought provoking. As the editors of this volume, we would like to thank our authors for their unwavering support and express our deep appreciation for saying yes to our invitation to contribute to this volume.

We would also like to thank our home universities and the respective universities of our contributing authors, without whose support projects like these would not happen. We would also like to express our thanks to our extraordinary reviewers, who provided insightful comments, and to the team at Oxford University Press for their professionalism and support from the proposal stage through to publication.

CONTRIBUTORS

Eli Y. Adashi, former (fifth) Dean of Medicine and Biological Sciences at Brown University and academic physician-executive, is a graduate of Tel Aviv University School of Medicine (MD, 1973) and the Harvard T. H. Chan School of Public Health program in Health Care Management (MS, 2005). An elected member of the National Academy of Medicine, Dr Adashi is a former president of the Society for Reproductive Endocrinologists, the Society for Gynecologic Investigation, and the American Gynecological and Obstetrical Society. Dr Adashi also served as Examiner and Director of the Division of Reproductive Endocrinology of the American Board of Obstetrics and Gynecology.

Deepak Adhikari career in reproductive biology began with his PhD from Umea University, Sweden, in 2014, in which he studied molecular mechanisms underlying primordial ovarian follicle activation. In 2015, he moved to Professor John Carroll's group at Monash University, Australia, on a postdoctoral fellowship. Subsequently, he was awarded a Peter Doherty Early Career Fellowship from the National Health and Medical Research Council. Dr Adhikari's work focuses on mitochondrial regulation of oocyte function, in particular, the effect of mitochondrial dysfunction during oogenesis on subsequent embryonic development. He is actively involved in supervising postgraduate students.

Diana M. Bowman is Associate Dean and Professor in the Sandra Day O'Connor College of Law and Professor in the College of Global Futures at Arizona State University. Dr Bowman's research primarily focuses on the legal and policy issues associated with emerging technologies and public health. Over the past 15 years she has worked extensively with governments and other organizations, including the World Economic Forum and the Organisation for Economic Cooperation and Development, on shaping the governance framework for new technologies. In 2018, Dr Bowman was named an Andrew Carnegie Fellow by the Carnegie Corporation of New York. This award has supported her research on MRT.

John Carroll is Director of the Monash Biomedicine Discovery Institute and Dean of Biomedical Sciences at Monash University. He moved to Monash from the United Kingdom in 2012, where he was Director of the Division of Biosciences at University College London. Dr Carroll leads a research team focused on understanding mitochondrial biology in oocytes and embryos. By utilizing imaging, genetic, and cell biology approaches, the team aims to obtain insights that may improve fertility and minimise genetic disease. Dr Carroll collaborates with Monash in vitro fertilisation (IVF) for translational research and holds an Ideas Grant from the National Health and Medical Research Council to investigate aspects of mitochondrial donation.

I. Glenn Cohen is Deputy Dean and James A. Attwood and Leslie Williams Professor of Law, Harvard Law School and the Faculty Director, Petrie-Flom Center for Health Law Policy, Biotechnology & Bioethics. He is the author or co-author of more than 200 articles and book chapters in law, medicine, science, public health, bioethics, and business journals and books. Cohen is the author, co-author, editor, or co-editor of more than 18 books. For the public he created the free online Harvard X Class Bioethics: The Law, Medicine, and Ethics of Reproductive Technologies and Genetics, which has been taken by more than 97,000 students so far.

Rebecca Dimond is a lecturer and researcher in medical sociology at the School of Social Sciences, Cardiff University. Her research interests include classification of genetic syndromes and their consequences; reproductive technologies; sociology of donation; and patient, family and professional perspectives. Dr Dimond's research on the development and legalization of MRT and patient experiences used semi-structured interviews with patients, professionals, and stakeholders; ethnographic observation of meetings and conferences; and documentary analysis and was funded through an ESRC Future Research Leaders grant.

Kevin Doxzen is an André Hoffmann Fellow, holding joint affiliations with Arizona State University's Thunderbird School of Global Management and Sandra Day O'Connor College of Law, and the World Economic Forum's Shaping the Future of Health and Healthcare platform. Dr Doxzen researches the societal impact, ethical considerations, and agile governance of emerging biotechnologies, with a primary focus on precision medicine. Kevin received a BA in biophysics from Johns Hopkins University and a PhD in biophysics from UC Berkeley.

Sandra P. González-Santos is Associate Researcher at the Bioethics Faculty, Universidad Anáhuac, México. Her work focuses on the study of reproduction from a science and technology studies perspective. She is currently looking at the circulation of knowledge between clinicians and basic science researchers and at the role of women in the development of the field of reproductive medicine in Mexico. Dr González-Santos's latest book is *A Portrait of Assisted Reproduction in México: Scientific, Political and Cultural Interactions* (Palgrave, 2020).

Mary Herbert is Professor of Reproductive Biology at Newcastle University and Honorary Consultant Embryologist/Scientific Director at Newcastle Fertility Centre. She leads a closely integrated team of research and clinical scientists. Her work in the field of mammalian reproductive cell biology is focused on understanding the mechanisms governing transmission of the maternal genomes (nuclear and mitochondrial) and on developing clinically relevant methods to prevent disease transmission through the female germline. Dr Herbert was elected Fellow of the Academy of Medical Sciences in 2019.

Cathy Herbrand is a Reader in Medical Sociology and Deputy Director of the Centre for Reproduction Research at De Montfort University (UK). She is a member of the Belgian Advisory Council on Bioethics, where she currently leads the sub-committee on "Surrogacy Regulation." Dr Herbrand's research interests lie in the sociological and anthropological study of new family forms, reproductive technologies, health, and genetics. Her current work explores the interactions between scientific progress, policies, and patients' lives by looking at the social, political, and ethical issues surrounding mitochondrial donation techniques, egg donation, and expanded carrier screening.

Tetsuya Ishii is Professor in the Office of Health and Safety, Hokkaido University, teaching bioethics. He is interested in the ethics of biotechnology for human reproduction and food. Dr Ishii's recent works include reproduction via gamete donation, mitochondrial replacement, and genome editing, as well as plant and animal breeding by genome editing and DNA recombination technology. He is serving as an associate editor of the *Japan Medical Association Journal*, in addition to being an associate member of Science Council of Japan.

Walter G. Johnson is a PhD scholar at the School of Regulation and Global Governance (RegNet) at the Australian National University. His research covers topics around law and regulation for a variety of current and emerging technologies. Johnson was awarded a JD from the Sandra

Day O'Connor College of Law at Arizona State University and a Master of Science and Technology Policy from Arizona State University.

Julian Koplin is a lecturer at the Monash Bioethics Centre. Dr Koplin's research interests include reproductive ethics, moral status issues, and the ethics of emerging technologies.

Karinne Ludlow is Associate Professor in the Monash University Law Faculty. Dr Ludlow's research primarily focuses on regulation of, and legal challenges to, innovative technologies, particularly biotechnology. That research addresses biotechnology across all species and in applications including health, agriculture and food, and industrial purposes. Dr Ludlow has particular expertise in the regulation of reproductive technologies. Her research on MRT is supported by a joint Australian government ARC Discovery grant and Department of Health's Medical Research Future Fund grant.

Jeffrey R. Mann currently performs MRT research at Monash University. Previously he led laboratories researching the role of epigenetics in mammalian germ cell development at the City of Hope National Medical Center in Los Angeles, the University of Melbourne, and the Murdoch Children's Research Institute, Melbourne. He taught the Molecular Embryology of the Mouse course at the Cold Spring Harbor Laboratory, New York, and directed institutional facilities for making preclinical models of disease. He received his PhD from University College London.

Priyanka Menon is a second-year student at Harvard Law School, where she is concurrently pursuing a PhD in government from Harvard Graduate School of Arts and Sciences as a Presidential Scholar. Her writing and research have appeared in *Slate*, *Harvard Law Review*, and *Modern Asian Studies*, among other publications. Menon received her AB *magna cum laude* in mathematics from Harvard College.

Catherine Mills is Professor of Bioethics at Monash University. Her research primarily addresses ethical issues in human reproduction. She also has expertise in feminist philosophy and aspects of Continental philosophy. Dr Mills is the author of *Biopolitics* (Routledge, 2018), *Futures of Reproduction* (Springer, 2011), and *The Philosophy of Agamben* (Routledge, 2008), as well as numerous articles in her areas of research.

Abril Saldaña-Tejeda is Associate Professor of Sociology at the Department of Philosophy, Universidad de Guanajuato, Mexico. Her work focuses on the social determinants of health, genomics, and postgenomics. Dr Saldaña-Tejeda is currently exploring bioethical principles, practices, and regulations on human genome editing and stem cell research in Latin America. Her research was supported by a Small Grant in Humanities and Social Science, Wellcome Trust (Ref. 218699/Z/19/Z).

Robert Sparrow is Professor in the Philosophy Program at Monash University, where he works on ethical issues raised by new technologies. Dr Sparrow has published on topics as diverse as the ethics of military robotics, the moral status of artificial intelligence, human enhancement, stem cells, preimplantation genetic diagnosis, xenotransplantation, and migration.

Neil Stephens is an Associate Professor in Technology and Soicety at the University of Birmingham, School of Social Policy. He works with sociology and Science and Technology Studies to analyze innovations in biotechnology. Dr Stephen's Wellcome Trust Research Fellowship titled "Big Tissue and Society" focused on cultured skin, blood, and meat. Previous case studies include stem cell science, robotic surgery, and mitochondrial donation. With Dr Rebecca Dimond, he has co-authored the book, *Legalising Mitochondrial Donation: Enacting Ethical Futures in UK Biomedical Politics* (Palgrave, 2018).

Deirdre L. Zander-Fox is the Monash IVF Group Chief Scientific Officer as well as the Regional Scientific Director overseeing Monash IVF Victorian and Malaysian laboratories. In addition, she supervises PhD and honors students and holds Adjunct Associate Professor positions at two major Australian Universities (Monash University and University of Adelaide) as well as receiving joint funding from the National Health and Medical Research Council. Associate Professor Zander-Fox's research is primarily focused on improving in vitro fertilisation laboratory technology that will directly benefit infertile patients, including cryopreservation, microinjection technology, and culture media design.

ABBREVIATIONS

ADP	Adenosine diphosphate
AG	Artificial gametes
AGCMT	Autologous granular cell mitochondrial transfer
ATP	Adenosine triphosphate
ARTs	Assisted reproductive technologies
AUGMENT	Autologous germline mitochondrial energy transfer
BAC	Bioethics Advisory Committee (Singapore)
CBER	Center for Biologics Evaluation and Research (US)
CMOB	Chinese Ministry of Health
CORE	Campaign on Reproductive Ethics (UK)
CONBIOETICA	Comisión Nacional de Bioética (Mexico)
CRISPR	Clustered Regularly Interspaced Short Palindromic Repeats
DNA	Deoxyribonucleic acid
DoH	Department of Health (UK)
DSB	Double-stranded break
EC	European Commission
ECHR	European Court of Human Justice
ECJ	European Court of Justice
EMA	European Medicines Agency
ESCs	Embryonic stem cells
ESHRE	European Society of Human Reproduction and Embryology
EPIs	Extremely premature infants
ERLC	Embryo Research Licensing Committee (Australia)
EU	European Union
EUFI	Extrauterine fetal incubation
FDA	Food and Drug Administration (US)
FFD&C Act	Federal Food, Drug and Cosmetics Act (US)

GGE	Germline genome engineering
GMO	Genetically modified organism
HCT/Ps	Human cells, tissues, and cellular and tissue-based products
HDR	Homology-directed repair
HFE Act	Human Fertilisation and Embryology Act (2008) (UK)
HFEA	Human Fertilisation and Embryology Authority (UK)
HGA	Human Genetics Alert (UK)
HHGE	Human heritable genome editing
HIV	Human immunodeficiency viruses
HVJ	Hemagglutinating virus of Japan
ICSI	Intracytoplasmic sperm injection
iPSCs	Induced pluripotent stem cells
ISeV	Inactivated Sendai virus
ISSCR	International Society for Stem Cell Research
IVF	In vitro fertilisation
IVG	In vitro gametogenesis
Maeve's Law (Cth)	Mitochondrial Donation Law Reform (Maeve's Law) Bill 2021 (Commonwealth) (Australia)
MD	Mitochondrial disease
MOHW	Ministry of Health and Welfare (China)
MRT	Mitochondrial replacement therapies
MRT Regulations	Human Fertilisation and Embryology Regulations (2015) (UK)
MST	Maternal spindle transfer
mtDNA	Mitochondrial DNA
mtREs	Mitochondrial restriction endonuclease
NAM	National Academies of Medicine (US)
NAS	National Academies of Science (US)
NASEM	National Academies of Sciences, Engineering, and Medicine (or National Academies) (US)
NCoB	Nuffield Council on Bioethics (UK)
nDNA	Nuclear genome
NHEJ	Non-homologous end joining
NHMRC	National Health and Medical Research Council (Australia)
NHS	National Health Service (UK)
NIH	National Institute for Health (US)
NOA	Nonobstructive azoospermia
PBT	Polar body transplantation

PCOS	Polycystic ovary syndrome
PCT	Pronuclear transfer
PGCs	Primordial germ cells
PGD	Preimplantation genetic diagnosis
PND	Prenatal diagnosis
PNT	Pronuclear transfer
POHCR Act	Prohibition of Human Cloning for Reproduction Act 2002 (Commonwealth) (Australia)
RE	Restriction endonuclease
RIHE Act	Research Involving Human Embryos Act 2002 (Commonwealth) (Australia)
RNA	Ribonucleic acid
RS	Royal Society (UK)
RTAC	Reproductive Technology Accreditation Committee (Australia)
SCNT	Somatic cell nuclear transfer
TALENs	Transcription activator-like effector nucleases
ZFNs	Zinc finger nucleases

Introduction

DIANA M. BOWMAN, WALTER G. JOHNSON,
AND KARINNE LUDLOW

I.1 THE EVOLVING REPRODUCTIVE TECHNOLOGY LANDSCAPE

Advances in assisted reproductive technologies (ARTs) have always been controversial. From the birth of Louise Brown with in vitro fertilisation (IVF) in 1978, to the births of Lulu and Nana following heritable human genome editing 40 years later (Cyranoski and Ledford, 2018), emerging scientific breakthroughs challenge social views of reproduction and reproductive rights and can spark global policy debates (Alghrani, 2018; Brezina and Zhao, 2012; Vayena et al., 2002). Opponents and proponents draw from public health, ethics, religion, and law to shape their arguments, and those arguments in turn shape ARTs. The story of mitochondrial replacement therapies (MRT) both mirrors and adds to this rich and complex history, presenting novel treatment options but contextualised within the systems built around existing reproductive technologies.

In the past decade, MRT has entered the public awareness—reigniting debates around social values in human reproduction, as well as how legal and policy apparatuses should implement those values. Techniques for mitochondrial replacement offer the potential to prevent complex, heritable mitochondrial diseases and offer more families a chance at a healthy, genetically related child. These methods could avoid suffering for patients, families, and caretakers while relieving some strain on families, healthcare systems, and governments. Yet safety and effectiveness questions remain—both for children born from MRT techniques and for subsequent

Diana M. Bowman, Walter G. Johnson, and Karinne Ludlow, *Introduction* In: *Reproduction Reborn*. Edited by: Diana M. Bowman, Karinne Ludlow, and Walter G. Johnson, Oxford University Press. © Oxford University Press 2023. DOI: 10.1093/oso/9780197616192.003.0001 generations—alongside various social and ethical concerns and questions of regulatory design. Even the controversy over what to name these techniques (MRT, mitochondrial donation, "three-parent IVF," human nuclear genome transfer) reveals fractures over how different actors identify and mobilise social values in medicine, health policy, biotechnology regulation, and human reproduction. Inevitably, the shadow of heritable human genome editing looms in the background of these conversations.

This edited volume, which brings together the leading experts around the world, strives to weave together the scientific and regulatory histories of MRT, particularly in those jurisdictions and regions that were, and continue to be, groundbreakers in the field. Given the importance of reproduction in family life, culture, and community, it will look at the influences of patients and their families, public debate, the media, religion, and governmental and expert inquiries regarding MRT on the evolving shape of the technologies themselves and their regulation across these jurisdictions and regions. This exploration offers important insights into the ethics and social concerns of several different countries, cultures, and religions (as well as regulatory schemes) which can inform future policy positions on MRT and other advanced ARTs. In doing so, this collection attempts to identify the ethical, legal, and societal norms that need to be addressed by policymakers and communities as an increasing number of people seek to gain access to these technologies—whether in their home country or across borders.

I.2 MITOCHONDRIAL REPLACEMENT THERAPIES ARE CURRENTLY IN USE

A small group of patients and practitioners, along with advocacy groups such as the United Kingdom's Lily Foundation, have shown strong interest in moving forward with MRT over the past 10 years. With no curative options and costly treatments with limited efficacy, mitochondrial diseases can sharply reduce length and quality of life (McFarland et al., 2007). Current evidence strongly suggests that a small number of individuals will always pass these conditions on to their biological children through mitochondrial DNA (mtDNA), even when preimplantation genetic diagnostics are available. It is, arguably, these patients who could benefit most from MRT (Pickett et al., 2019). A subset of experts also believes these techniques could improve on the success rates of standard fertility treatments, especially for patients of advanced age, although available data show limited benefits at this time. For some non-heteronormative family structures, such as lesbian couples or people in polyamorous relationships, MRT could also be used to create genetic links between a child and each parent.

Reproductive technologies manipulating mitochondria, including MRT, have been in use since the turn of the millennium. The late 1990s saw the first successful births resulting from cytoplasmic transfer in the United States, while the first pregnancy from an MRT that would come to be called *pronuclear transfer* was reported in 2003, in the People's Republic of China (Barritt et al., 2001; Zhang et al., 2003). The techniques were used not to prevent mitochondrial diseases but rather to treat infertility. Against the backdrop of concerns over reproductive human cloning, the United States and China responded quickly with regulatory barriers—although some clinics continued to offer, or at least advertise, mitochondria-based reproductive services (Ishii and Hibino, 2018). In 2016, the first child was born through MRT in a clinic located in New York, after the embryo transfer was performed in Guadalajara, for the purpose of preventing mitochondrial disease (Zhang et al., 2017). The following year, a clinic in Ukraine announced the first birth of a child from MRT performed to treat the mother's complex infertility (Coghlan, 2017).

These clinical applications of MRT have emerged into a diverse set of national regulatory and healthcare systems, each coloured by a unique history and sociocultural experience with existing ARTs and human embryo research (Jasanoff and Metzler, 2020). These backgrounds have translated into different policy approaches for MRT (Cohen et al., 2020). In 2012, the United Kingdom took the unprecedented step of commissioning an expert group to examine the ethical, legal, and social issues associated with clinical MRT, which resulted in the world's first MRT legislation in 2015.[1] The novel, strict regulatory regime permitted licenced clinics the ability to employ certain MRT for the prevention of mitochondrial diseases.

Novel regulation in the United Kingdom and several births reported globally have accelerated the consideration by policymakers around the world of potential legislative and oversight responses to MRT. In 2016, Greek regulators quietly approved a very small clinical trial of MRT to treat infertility rather than prevent disease (Costa-Borges et al., 2020). The trial concluded in 2020, with Costa-Borges et al. (2020) reporting limited success. Lawmakers in the United States considered permitting the techniques to move to human trials in 2019, but ultimately allowed their policy apparatus to continue to block clinical applications of MRT. The announcement in 2021 by Australian lawmakers of their intent to introduce legislation similar to the United Kingdom's and its subsequent passage in 2022, with Singapore considering similar moves, will only hasten policy conversations around the world.

1.3 GOVERNANCE CHALLENGES

While the complex public debates around the role and regulation of advanced ARTs like MRT are far from settled, clinical applications and technological advancements continue. By 2021, an estimated 10–20 babies had been born with MRT, with a minimum of three additional births following heritable human genome editing techniques. These estimates are extremely difficult to confirm as many clinics do not share outcome data. However, they illustrate the desire for scientists and patients to participate in these treatments despite regulatory status. In parallel, would-be parents may now be able to travel abroad to countries such as Ukraine and Greece to access MRT not available in their own countries. As with other emerging technologies, MRT raise issues of "legal lag" or the "pacing problem" in which law is unable to respond to an emerging technology in a timely manner (Marchant et al., 2011). But more importantly, the shape of evolving MRT regulatory regimes has been moulded by (often unseen) past responses to technologies that play a role in reproduction.

Regulatory and policy frameworks at various levels of government will need to address complex challenges posed by MRT with global repercussions. In conjunction with broader ethical and religious discourse surrounding the sanctity of human life (including, e.g., experimenting with human embryos), the scientific and societal developments around MRT present a myriad of moral, ethical, and political questions with which governments and policymakers must grapple. Consultation with the public on these issues will likely provide significant information to both guide and legitimate policy decisions on whether to approve MRT and, if so, how to effectively oversee these technologies.

Should jurisdictions move to expressly permit MRT, how to use regulatory tools to set, monitor, and enforce safety and effectiveness standards within their clinics will become one of the most important and immediate issues to address. Options for implementing these standards can range from establishing novel MRT regulation, as in the United Kingdom, to adjusting existing ART frameworks or other regulatory systems (Johnson and Bowman, 2022a). Part of these decisions will require policymakers to consider which intended uses of MRT to approve, since only preventing mitochondrial diseases provides direct health benefits to the resulting child. Since the efficacy and health impacts, if any, of these techniques in humans are still understudied, policy instruments will need to facilitate longitudinal and likely multigenerational human studies to inform regulatory decision-making over time. As the techniques become more common and more families seek these services, jurisdictions must determine how to provide equitable access to MRT services within their own national health-care systems.

Current regulatory frameworks also struggle to cope with transnational conduct, such as MRT medical tourism, which complicates the potential for longitudinal study and would require considerable global coordination. Achieving equitable access to MRT and other ARTs in lower- and middle-income countries will present further challenges requiring global cooperation. Global governance for MRT—a comprehensive version of which, at least in our view, is unrealistic—would need to effectively resolve such issues while respecting the varied and nuanced sets of values present across states and regions.

I.4 STRUCTURE OF THE BOOK

In light of these governance challenges and ongoing clinical applications that transcend jurisdictional borders, this volume aims to gather insights from across disciplines and jurisdictions provide a cutting-edge and comprehensive look at the issues surrounding MRT in real time. The science, ethics, and law undergirding developments in MRT influence each other and the policy process in subtle and overt ways. Public opinion, social values, technical possibility, law already applicable to ARTs, and models of other jurisdictions will all shape what is possible and preferred in MRT governance, whether in designing the broad structure of regulatory and coverage frameworks or making more granular decisions on the requirements of technical standards. By placing these accounts and analyses in dialogue with one another, this book strives to better outline, contextualise, and compare the successes and failures observed thus far.

The chapters of this collection offer various perspectives pertaining to MRT governance and are organised into three sections. Part I, Untangling the Development of Science and Public Opinion Around MRT (Chapters 1–3) begins by exploring the scientific, social, and ethical dimensions of MRT.

In Chapter 1, "Development of Mitochondrial Replacement Therapies," Jeffrey R. Mann, Mary Herbert, Deirdre L. Zander-Fox, Deepak Adhikari, and John Carroll trace the evolution of MRT, exploring the foundational research that provided the "frontier therapy for treating human mitochondrial DNA disease" (p. 20). The authors review the major strands of biomedical research, dating back to the 1980s, which supported the development of clinical interventions, and consider the clinical role of MRT compared to other relevant techniques. While highlighting the significance of the technique being used within the clinical environment, the authors do not shy away from addressing the scientific unknowns associated with the use of MRT. In their words, "these unknowns are particularly significant because the procedure will be performed at the first stage of human development and produce a new individual" (p. 20). Mann et al. set out four discrete areas of concern, each of which is underpinned by questions around safety or effectiveness. While each is important and requires additional research, it is the possibility of "carryover of mutant mitochondrial DNA" (p. 20) which, for Mann et al., carries the greatest degree of risk. In their eyes, though, the benefits of MRT—"the potential to greatly reduce the risk of devastating disease" (p. 26)—far outweighs the risks.

Robert Sparrow, Julian Koplin, and Catherine Mills provide an in-depth exploration of the philosophical and ethical questions raised by MRT in Chapter 2. In "Mitochondrial Replacement Techniques: A Critical Review of the Ethical Issues," the authors systematically tackle a suite of thought-provoking questions that range from, for example, identity, through to those relating to parenthood, resource allocation, risk, and social impact and have been raised in response to the scientific advancements. Sparrow et al. eloquently explore the claim that MRT is therapeutic and the implications of this framing for justifying clinical intervention. The relationship of the donor and the child are similarly explored by the authors, who note that parenthood is an evolving social construct and that other scientific advances have already complicated the notion of what it means to reproduce and be a parent. As Sparrow et al. unpack questions regarding ethical objections to a child having "three parents," the small population of people who will potentially benefit from MRT, and the potential physical and social risks posed by the technique to parent and child, we are reminded that many of these questions are not new and have been raised in relation to each advance with reproductive technologies. What is new here, though, is whether MRT is viewed as a form of germline editing and what the implications of that framing may be given the "relatively widespread (though not universal) opposition to [its] clinical use" (p. 45). While this remains an ongoing and controversial global debate, Sparrow et al. conclude that the implications are likely to be significant in terms of legislative activity and social acceptance to other forms of germline modification.

Part I of the book concludes with a chapter by Cathy Herbrand focused on the perspectives of individuals and families within the United Kingdom who are personally impacted by mitochondrial disorders and are actively engaged in reproductive decision-making. Chapter 3, "Reproductive Decisions and Mitochondrial Disease: Disruption, Risk, and Uncertainty," begins with a very poignant point: the voices and insights of those intimately impacted by the scientific and political discussions on mitochondrial donation are largely absent from the debates. Herbrand seeks to change this with her contribution. The chapter draws on the voices of 24 English women whom Herbrand interviewed as part of a larger study (the Mitofamily study) to provide in-depth accounts of "the perceptions and choices with respect to reproductive options" (p. 65). Of these women, 10 had "lost a child from a mitochondrial disorder and 8 of them had an affected child" (p. 66). Through the voices of these women Herbrand documents the multilevel impact of diagnosis, the realisation of transmissibility of mitochondrial disease to their child, and the ways in which these individuals—and, in some cases their partners—grappled with coming to terms with what this diagnosis means around risk to future children and their exploration of other options. In bringing the voices and experiences of these women to life, Herbrand shows the complexities and weight of the decision-making process. Every story was different. Every story brought with it different challenges ranging from the high costs—personal, emotional, and financial—of caring for an ill child or family member through to their ability to access different forms of reproductive technologies. But every story was underpinned by greater uncertainty. The importance of having children who "were healthy *and* biologically related" to the women is also addressed, with Herbrand reporting an overwhelming desire on the part of her participants to achieve this result. The drive of achieving this twin goal was so important to those women interviewed that many of them were willing to use "some kind of reproductive or screening technologies in order to have children and avoid transmitting the disorder to them" (p. 77).

Part II, "The Evolution of Regulatory Frameworks for MRT: How Regulation Got from There to Here (and Everywhere In-Between)" (Chapters 4–9), reviews the regulatory histories and strategies on MRT across multiple jurisdictions and regions before examining the international framework into which MRT have emerged.

In Chapter 4, "Legalising MRT in the United Kingdom," Rebecca Dimond and Neil Stephens document how the United Kingdom became the pioneer in passing legislation in 2015 that establishes a comprehensive regulatory regime for MRT. As Dimond and Stephens highlight, history played an important role in creating the enabling conditions for what they describe as the "MRT debates," with UK scientists having been at the forefront of IVF advances in the 1970s and the jurisdiction being one of the earliest to establish a regulatory regime for embryo research following the birth of Louise Brown in the United Kingdom in 1978. Dimond and Stephens detail the prominent role of institutions such as the Human Fertilisation and Embryology Authority (HFEA), the Nuffield Council on Bioethics, and Wellcome Trust in framing the narrative and providing the scientific evidence for public and parliamentary debates. In relation to the former, Dimond and Stephens note that the debates "were inherently adversarial" (p. 96), involving a sophisticated cluster of individuals, including patients, and institutions arguing in favour of the legislation, against a much smaller and chaotic cluster of parties opposed to the legislation. The authors suggest that the framing of hope and the patient voice were particularly persuasive in the debates and resonated strongly with members within the House of Commons and the House of Lords. Importantly, as Dimond and Stephens articulate, the significance of the United Kingdom's experience with MRT extends not only to other jurisdictions grappling with the questions and concerns associated with the technology but also to the next emerging technology, CRISPR-Cas9, that will challenge regulatory regimes and public attitudes and demand a regulatory response.

Australia has long been at the forefront of medical research into ARTs, as explained by Karinne Ludlow in Chapter 5, "MRT in Australia," with the "world's first reported IVF pregnancy (but not birth)" (p. 112) having occurred in Melbourne. The country was also the first to enact the "world's first IVF and associated embryo research regulation" (p. 113) in response to the ethical and societal concerns raised by these advances. This history, as discussed by Ludlow, established the pathway on which the Australian government began to consider reviewing the national regulatory framework that oversees human embryo research and, subsequently, "permit clinical MRT" (p. 115) without broad regulatory reform. As Ludlow's chapter highlights, patient advocacy groups and experts have played a key role in advancing legislative reform, stressing not only the promise of circumventing debilitating illness and the pain associated with mitochondrial disease, but also the economic advantages of allowing for MRT for individuals and the community more generally. These themes appear to have resonated loudly with the legislature, with Ludlow noting the passing of the Mitochondrial Donation Law Reform (Maeve's Law) Act 2021 in March 2022. Of particular note is the role that the Australian Prime Minister, Scott Morrison, played in bringing the bill to the floor: he is, as Ludlow explains, "the patron of the Mito Foundation, the advocacy group behind the moves to make MRT available in Australia" (p. 118). The new legislation sets out a regulatory framework not too dissimilar to that adopted in the United Kingdom, only allowing for licenced clinicians to use MRT in the case of disease prevention. The passage of the legislation makes Australia the second jurisdiction to have expressly approved the technique, setting up new opportunities for medical tourism. The passage of Maeve's Law will not, however, address some of the broader concerns with the overarching regulatory framework for human embryos within the country nor address other potential advances in ARTs including, for example, germline modifications, which will raise further ethical and legal challenges for Australian governance.

The contradictions offered up by the United States in relation to reproductive technologies and MRT is discussed by I. Glenn Cohen, Priyanka Menon, and Eli Y. Adashi in Chapter 6, "MRT in the United States." The United States is generally considered, as explained by the authors, the "Wild West" (p. 129) when it comes to access to reproductive technologies; unlike a number of countries, the United States does not have a central regulatory body for the use of reproductive technologies, with this power instead falling to subnational governments. As explained by Cohen et al., federal legislation is, instead, focused on the funding of research involving human embryos, which has, as the authors note, become a significant "regulatory technique that has been used to regulate other cutting-edge technologies in the reproductive and genetics space" (p. 131). MRT have, however, been framed for regulatory purposes as a therapeutic product, thus bringing them under the regulatory scope of the Food and Drug Administration (FDA) without the need for additional regulatory authority. This approach is not new for the FDA, with the Administration having previously asserted its authority "over reproductive technologies such as human cloning, cytoplasmic transfer, etc." (p. 132) in this way. As explained by Cohen et al., while the FDA was proactive in drawing together experts to discuss the potential path for MRT, it has been Congress—through the enactment of a 2016 rider—that has played the most significant role in shaping the US response: "whatever the congressional intent behind the rider, the rider's effect has been to stifle completely attempts at clinical development of MRT in the United States" (p. 135). This is despite, as Cohen et al. suggest, questions over whether or not this was their actual intent, causing the authors to reiterate their call for a "more targeted amendment to the rider the next time it is up for renewal—one that directly distinguishes MRT from gene editing" (p. 137). Cohen et al. conclude by mapping out pathways for MRT in the United States, noting, though, that even if the current de facto ban is lifted, significant other ethical and legal questions will still need to be overcome.

As widely reported, the first live birth of a child conceived through MRT occurred after the embryo transfer stage of treatment took place in a Mexican clinic in 2016. In Chapter 7, "Contesting the 'No Rules' Label: ARTs in Mexico Before and After the First MRT Baby," Sandra González-Santos and Abril Saldaña-Tejeda paint a picture of Mexico's evolving reproductive technologies landscape and describe the research and market conditions that gave rise to the baby boy's birth. González-Santos and Saldaña-Tejeda explore the social influence of religion and science in Mexico, highlighting the different spheres of influence that they have on trust and public perception around issues such a reproductive technologies and rights. Importantly, the authors dispel the media headlines and unsubstantiated claims that the MRT procedure took place in an unregulated jurisdiction, free from any federal or state oversight. The framework articulated by González-Santos and Saldaña-Tejeda (2022) shows a multilayered governance framework involving not only federal and state government, but also non-state actors such as professional associations that have developed nonbinding recommendations and best practice guidance. As such, the absence of a central regulatory body for reproductive technologies—despite attempts to rectify this situation—raises questions of efficacy of the regulatory regimes rather than a complete absence of regulatory oversight for MRT activities.

The activities of an Athens-based clinic have similarly propelled Greece and the European Union into the forefront of both scientific and broader societal debates. In Chapter 8, "Medical Tourism and Multi-Level Regulation for MRT in the European Union," Walter G. Johnson and Diana M. Bowman examine why the EU and closely related states, including Ukraine, have been able to position themselves at the forefront for delivering advanced reproductive services to those seeking fertility assistance. As explained by Johnson and Bowman, while the EU's governance structure has evolved over time to minimise regulatory barriers between member states, individual countries have retained significant control over their health care systems. EU residents have the right to seek healthcare outside of their home country within the block, which actively encourages medical tourism within the market and arguably encourages some countries to specialise in the provision of certain treatments or care. The absence of supranational regulation in the European Union that would prohibit MRT has, as explained by Johnson and Bowman, enabled certain countries with favourable domestic governance frameworks for ARTs (such as Greece) to be pioneers within the field, potentially opening up new opportunities for EU residents seeking infertility treatments. Opportunities to cross borders in search of treatment are not limited, as pointed out by Johnson and Bowman, to EU member states: Ukraine, for example, has a favourable regulatory environment for advanced ARTs including MRT and the necessary clinical expertise. The authors go on to argue that while fragmentation in the regulatory approach for MRT appears to have drawn very little concern from the European Commission or members of the EU community, the general ambivalence to these advanced techniques and their legality may shift should "other advanced ARTs such as human heritable genome editing (HHGE) enter clinics or policy conversations" (p. 183).

In Chapter 9, "Asia," Tetsuya Ishii traces the history of reproductive experimentation involving mitochondrial manipulation in four prominent Asian countries—China, Japan, Singapore, and Taiwan—painting a picture of the different clinical activities that have been performed and the subsequent responses they have garnered upon becoming public. In doing so, Ishii highlights the fast-moving nature of these activities, noting, for example, that Taiwanese scientists were performing cytoplasmic transfer in 1999, followed by autologous granular cell mitochondrial transfer in 2001. By documenting the range of activities taking place across the jurisdictions including, for example, the "more radical mitochondrial manipulation" (p. 197) by Chinese scientists in 2003, Ishii highlights the heterogenous nature of the advanced reproductive landscape within the region and the subsequent regulatory frameworks that have been enacted as a result of such experimentation. Ishii's observation that, within the Asian countries reviewed for his chapter, "all mitochondrial manipulations were implemented for the purposes of having genetically related offspring without directly using donor eggs" (p. 206) is radically different from the regulatory approach adopted by United Kingdom (Chapter 4) and Australia (Chapter 5) and more in line with the clinical study conducted in Greece (Chapter 8). Ishii argues that while religion may play a role in family planning decision-making, it is likely to have played a negligible role in the regulatory responses: politics and the progressive opening up of the economies of these jurisdictions appear to have been more influential.

Part III, "Looking Forward" (Chapters 10–11), explores the ways in which cutting edge technologies are being used to push the boundaries of ARTs. In Chapter 10, "Future Technological Advancements," Kevin Doxzen traces the history of three promising technologies—genome engineering, in vitro gametogenesis, and artificial wombs—for advancing the field of ARTs, providing insights into active areas of research being undertaken by scientists around the globe. While Doxzen's chapter focuses primarily on the cutting-edge advances that scientists from, for example, China to the United States are making, it also highlights the potential ethical questions that the three technologies may raise as scientists refine their experiments and explore potential clinical applications. Doxzen notes, for example, that experimentation on germline genome engineering (GGE) will raise questions of how to ethically regulate its use that will be of "central concern for international scientific and political communities" (p. 221). By incorporating both realistic future applications and more fanciful interventions, Doxzen sets out a human reproduction landscape that looks very different from that of today. The need for experimentation, therefore, is not just in relation to the science but also the regulatory frameworks underpinning it and in the ways in which family structures are framed.

1.5 CONCLUSION

Even if MRT only provide direct health benefits to a relatively small number of families, how policy for these techniques develops around the world will illuminate social values and set the stage for the governance of other advanced ARTs. This edited collection seeks to advance a broader conversation on how to structure regulation around cutting-edge reproductive technological advancements that must fit in a global context, one with complex multistakeholders, countries holding predictably different ethical and moral considerations, and the safety, health, and the well-being of future generations at the core. Further, as the world begins to grapple with heritable human genome editing, lessons from the emerging governance of MRT should prove informative and instructive.[2] As governments and stakeholders continue policy conversations on emerging reproductive technologies, the chapters of this volume may provide valuable starting points to inform policy positions on MRT and other advanced ARTs.

NOTES

1. Human Fertilisation and Embryology: The Human Fertilisation and Embryology (Mitochondrial Donation) Regulations 2015. 2015. Stat. Instr. No. 572. https://www.legislation.gov.uk/uksi/2015/572/made.
2. Already, the US National Academies of Sciences, Engineering, and Medicine and the UK Royal Society (2020) have looked to the novel UK regulatory framework for MRT and the public consultation used to arrive there as a potential model for approaching the oversight of heritable human genome editing.

REFERENCES

Alghrani, Amel. *Regulating Assisted Reproductive Technologies: New Horizons.* Cambridge University Press, 2018.
Barritt, Jason A., Steen Willadsen, Carol Brenner, and Jacques Cohen. 'Cytoplasmic transfer in assisted reproduction.' *Human Reproduction Update* 7, no. 4 (2001): 428–435.
Brezina, Paul R., and Yulian Zhao. 'The ethical, legal, and social issues impacted by modern assisted reproductive technologies.' *Obstetrics and Gynecology International* (2012): 686253.

Coghlan, Andy. 'First baby born using 3-parent technique to treat infertility.' *New Scientist*, 18 January 2017. https://www.newscientist.com/article/2118334-first-baby-born-using-3-parent-technique-to-treat-infertility/.

Cohen, I. Glenn, Eli Y. Adashi, Sara Gerke, César Palacios-González, and Vardit Ravitsky. 'The regulation of mitochondrial replacement techniques around the world.' *Annual Review of Genomics and Human Genetics* 21 (2020): 565–586.

Costa-Borges, Nuno, Eros Nikitos, Katharina Spath, Klaus Rink, Konstantinos Kostaras, Ioannis Zervomanolakis, George Kontopoulos et al. 'First registered pilot trial to validate the safety and effectiveness of maternal spindle transfer to overcome infertility associated with poor oocyte quality.' *Fertility and Sterility* 114, no. 3 (2020): e71–e72.

Cyranoski, David, and Heidi Ledford. 'Genome-edited baby claim provokes international outcry.' *Nature* 563, no. 7733 (2018): 607–608.

Dimond, Rebecca, and Neil Stephens. *Legalising Mitochondrial Donation: Enacting Ethical Futures in UK Biomedical Politics.* Springer, 2018.

Ishii, Tetsuya, and Yuri Hibino. 'Mitochondrial manipulation in fertility clinics: Regulation and responsibility.' *Reproductive Biomedicine and Society Online* 5 (2018): 93–109.

Jasanoff, Sheila, and Ingrid Metzler. 'Borderlands of life: IVF embryos and the law in the United States, United Kingdom, and Germany.' *Science, Technology, and Human Values* 45, no. 6 (2020): 1001–1037.

Johnson, Walter G., and Diana M. Bowman. 'Inherited regulation for advanced ARTs: Comparing jurisdictions' applications of existing governance regimes to emerging reproductive technologies.' *Journal of Law and the Biosciences* 9, no. 1 (2022a): lsab034.

Marchant, Gary E., Braden R. Allenby, and Joseph R. Herkert, eds. *The Growing Gap Between Emerging Technologies and Legal-Ethical Oversight: The Pacing Problem.* Vol. 7. Springer Science and Business Media, 2011.

McFarland, R., R. W. Taylor, and D. M. Turnbull. 'Mitochondrial disease: Its impact, etiology, and pathology.' *Current Topics in Developmental Biology* 77 (2007): 113–155.

Pickett, Sarah J., Alasdair Blain, Yi Shiau Ng, Ian J. Wilson, Robert W. Taylor, Robert McFarland, Doug M. Turnbull, and Gráinne S. Gorman. 'Mitochondrial donation: Which women could benefit?' *New England Journal of Medicine* 380, no. 20 (2019): 1971–1972.

United States National Academies of Sciences, Engineering, and Medicine and United Kingdom Royal Society. *Heritable Human Genome Editing.* National Academies Press, 2020. https://www.nap.edu/catalog/25665/heritable-human-genome-editing.

Vayena, Effy, Patrick J. Rowe, and P. David Griffin. *Current Practices and Controversies in Assisted Reproduction: Report of a Meeting on Medical, Ethical and Social Aspects of Assisted Reproduction, Held at WHO Headquarters in Geneva, Switzerland.* World Health Organization, 2002.

Zhang, John, Guanglun Zhuang, Yong Zeng, Carlo Acosta, Yimin Shu, and Jamie Grifo. 'Pregnancy derived from human nuclear transfer.' *Fertility and Sterility* 80 (2003): 56.

Zhang, John, Hui Liu, Shiyu Luo, Zhuo Lu, Alejandro Chávez-Badiola, Zitao Liu, Mingxue Yang et al. 'Live birth derived from oocyte spindle transfer to prevent mitochondrial disease.' *Reproductive Biomedicine Online* 34, no. 4 (2017): 361–368.

PART I

*Untangling the Development of Science
and Public Opinion Around MRT*

1
Development of Mitochondrial Replacement Therapies

JEFFREY R. MANN, MARY HERBERT,
DEIRDRE L. ZANDER-FOX, DEEPAK ADHIKARI,
AND JOHN CARROLL

1.1 MITOCHONDRIA: ENERGY, DISEASE, AND INHERITANCE

Mitochondria are cytoplasmic membrane-bound organelles which produce most of the body's energy requirements. This energy is stored within the energy carrier molecule adenosine triphosphate (ATP), the end product of a complex biochemical process known as oxidative phosphorylation in which oxygen is used to convert adenosine diphosphate (ADP) back to its triphosphate form. Newly synthesized ATP is transported from mitochondria to where it is required, with energy for fuelling metabolic events released on the breakdown of ATP back to its diphosphate form. Muscle contraction and neural activity are large users of this stored chemical energy.

The mitochondrion is about the same size as a typical bacterium, and most cells contain well over a thousand. Mitochondria also contain DNA in the form of a tiny circular genome which is approximately 200,000 times smaller than the nuclear genome in terms of DNA base count. Its 37 tightly packed genes compare to at least 50,000 genes (Salzberg, 2018), along with a vast repertoire of interspersed regulatory and structural sequences comprising the nuclear genetic material. The human egg, the largest cell, contains more than 200,000 copies of mitochondrial DNA (Hashimoto et al., 2017). Because a mitochondrion can harbour more than one DNA

Jeffrey R. Mann, Mary Herbert, Deirdre L. Zander-Fox, Deepak Adhikari, and John Carroll, *Development of Mitochondrial Replacement Therapies* In: *Reproduction Reborn*. Edited by: Diana M. Bowman, Karinne Ludlow, and Walter G. Johnson, Oxford University Press. © Oxford University Press 2023. DOI: 10.1093/oso/9780197616192.003.0002 molecule, the number of mitochondria in an egg is likely to be less than the mitochondrial DNA copy number. Mitochondria contain more than a thousand unique proteins, the large majority encoded by nuclear genes and imported. A small number of mitochondrial proteins—13 to be precise— are encoded by the corresponding genes in mitochondrial DNA and form part of the oxidative phosphorylation machinery. Mitochondrial DNA also contains two ribosomal and 22 tiny transfer RNA genes required to produce these 13 proteins (Calvo and Mootha, 2010; Craven et al., 2017).

The mitochondrion is devoid of the sophisticated DNA repair mechanisms present in the nucleus. This, together with the high free radical environment resulting from oxidative phosphorylation, leads to frequent and persistent mutations in mitochondrial DNA. In turn, these mutations can lead to defects in oxidative phosphorylation and disease. A pathogenic mitochondrial DNA mutation can be present in all mitochondria in a cell, a condition known as *homoplasmy*. Often, a mutation is present in only some mitochondria—known as *heteroplasmy*. Generally, disease does not develop until a heteroplasmy level of at least 50 percent is attained (Gorman et al., 2016; Craven et al., 2017; Frazier et al., 2019).

Mitochondria are inherited from the mother through the egg (Giles et al., 1980). The small number of sperm mitochondria which enter the egg at fertilisation are selectively eliminated soon after (Shitara et al., 2000; Sutovsky et al., 2000). Mitochondrial DNA– disease is therefore propagated through the maternal parent. Whether a child develops disease depends on the inherited heteroplasmic load in the egg, and later in developing tissues, and this can vary between children from the same mother (Otten et al., 2018).

1.2 MITOCHONDRIAL REPLACEMENT THERAPY

While there are no cures for mitochondrial DNA disease, preimplantation genetic testing, which is a well-established procedure for detecting genetic lesions in nuclear DNA, has been used in human embryos to determine mitochondrial DNA heteroplasmy levels. By identifying embryos with low heteroplasmy, this testing can reduce the risk of transmission of serious mitochondrial DNA disease (Richardson et al., 2015; Smeets et al., 2015). However, preimplantation genetic testing is not suitable in cases of high heteroplasmy or homoplasmy of pathogenic mitochondrial DNA mutations (Richardson et al., 2015). In these cases, mitochondrial replacement therapy (MRT) offers the potential for an affected woman to conceive her own biological child with a substantially reduced risk of developing serious disease (Russell et al., 2020). This therapy is performed at the ovulated unfertilised egg, or fertilised egg (zygote) stage, and involves the transplantation of the nuclear genetic material from an egg with affected mitochondria into a donor egg which contains only normal mitochondria. For this to work, the nuclear genetic material of the donor egg must first be removed. The methodology was first developed in laboratory mice several decades ago by James McGrath and Davor Solter of the Wistar Institute in Philadelphia, United States (McGrath and Solter, 1983) (see Figure 1.1). This technological development was revolutionary in facilitating pronuclear transplantation or transfer (PNT) between zygotes, avoiding rupture

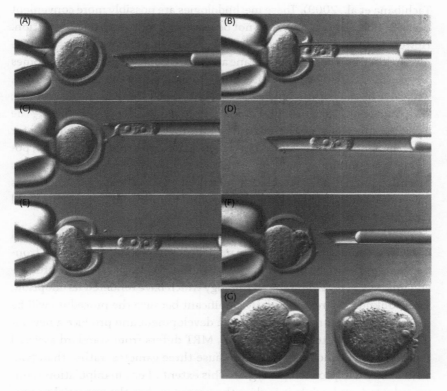

Figure 1.1 Mitochondrial donation in mouse zygotes by PNT.
(A–C) The maternal (egg) and paternal (sperm) haploid pronuclei are extracted from a fertilised egg (zygote) with the egg membrane pinching off and remaining sealed after extraction. This forms a karyoplast inside the pipette, with the pronuclei being surrounded by a small amount of ooplasm containing carryover mitochondria and surrounded by an intact cell membrane. (D) A small amount of fusogen—inactivated Sendai virus—is taken into the pipette. (E,F) The karyoplast is ejected onto the surface of a mitochondrial donor egg from which the pronuclei have previously been removed by the same method used in Steps A–C. (G) The karyoplast fuses with the donor egg within 30 minutes of culture. The pronuclei eventually migrate back to the centre of the egg. The egg then divides—marking the beginning of embryogenesis in terms of current Australian legislation.

of the egg membrane which often results in cell death. The method was first used to study nuclear-cytoplasmic interactions in mouse zygotes and led to the development of the field of genomic imprinting (Mann and Lovell-Badge, 1984; McGrath and Solter, 1984a, 1984b; Surani et al., 1984). More recently, PNT has been adopted for MRT (Craven et al., 2010; Hyslop et al., 2016).

Variant technologies for MRT involve meiotic spindle transplantation (MST) or polar body transplantation (PBT) from an unfertilised egg with affected mitochondria into an unfertilised egg with normal mitochondria. This is then followed by fertilisation of the reconstituted egg in vitro, generally by intracytoplasmic sperm injection (ICSI) (Wang et al., 2001, 2014; Tachibana et al., 2009). These methodologies are possibly more convenient than PNT because zygotes need not be sourced prior to micromanipulation. However, it is possible that the spindle, which is a microtubular structure not enclosed by a nuclear membrane and on which condensed chromosomes are attached, could be more susceptible to damage by the procedure. Also, while live births in mice can be obtained from PBT (Wakayama et al., 1997; Wakayama and Yanagimachi, 1998; Wang et al., 2014), polar bodies are the redundant products of asymmetric meiotic division, and the possibility for an accumulation of genetic and epigenetic damage within these bodies, potentially beginning at the time of their extrusion from the egg, requires careful examination. The relative merits of these alternative procedures have not been thoroughly investigated, and it remains unknown if one will ultimately be preferable.

While MRT methodology is well developed and, at least in animal models, is compatible with overtly normal development, it remains a frontier therapy for treating human mitochondrial DNA disease. There are several unknowns regarding the technology which have hindered its adoption. These unknowns are particularly significant because the procedure will be performed at the first stage of human development and produce a new individual (see Chapter 2, this volume). MRT differs from standard assisted reproductive technology practice because three gametes, rather than two, are combined in producing a zygote. This extent of egg manipulation is unprecedented, and, while it is clear the procedure has the potential to produce a new person free of debilitating mitochondrial genetic disease, the unknowns naturally lead to safety concerns (Newson et al., 2019; National Health and Medical Research Council, 2019). These concerns relate to (1) the effect of the procedure alone, (2) the presence of carryover mutant mitochondrial DNA, (3) the potential for genetic consequences other than those of carryover, and (4) the potential for epigenetic consequences. Each of these is now discussed.

1.2.1 Effect of the Procedure Alone

Compared to ICSI and preimplantation embryo biopsy—as performed o in the artificial reproduction technology clinic—MRT appears particularly invasive. A wide-bore pipette is advanced into the egg, without breaking the egg membrane, to draw the nuclear material into the pipette. The pipette is then retracted to pinch off the egg membrane, allowing it to remain sealed. This resulting egg fragment within the pipette is termed a *karyoplast*, being comprised of the cellular genetic material surrounded by a narrow band of egg cytoplasm (ooplasm) encapsulated in a sealed egg membrane. The karyoplast is deposited on, then fused with, the enucleated donor egg (see Figure 1.1). The potential for breakage of the egg membrane is reduced by adding reagents to collapse the cytoskeletal architecture and reduce ooplasm rigidity. In PNT, cytochalasin and nocodazole are added to inhibit actin filament and microtubule structures, respectively. The reagents are washed out when the procedure is complete, after which the cytoskeletal architecture reforms. Removal of the reagents well before the first cleavage division should minimise the possibility of the mitotic spindle being affected, which could result in abnormal chromosome segregation. Also, there is no evidence for any form of polarity in the egg which could be disturbed. In MST, nocodazole is omitted, otherwise the microtubular spindle would be destroyed. While cytochalasin might not be immediately suspected of affecting the spindle, this requires careful examination given the role of actin filaments in chromosome segregation and polar body extrusion (Mogessie and Schuh, 2017; Uraji et al., 2018). There is no reason to suspect that the physical manoeuvring of the ooplasm by the pipette would lead to any permanent disturbance of subcellular structure.

In mice, the complete micromanipulation procedure for PNT, MST, and PBT can be performed successfully at a very high frequency—approximately 90 percent of attempts—and the large majority of successfully reconstituted eggs and zygotes are able to progress to the blastocyst stage (McGrath and Solter, 1983; Wang et al., 2014; Costa-Borges et al., 2020). For PNT, the frequency of development to term is generally at least 65 percent when robust zygotes from hybrid mice are used, and at least when the stage of zygotic development is closely matched between the two zygotes used (Mann and Lovell-Badge, 1984, 1987). This frequency approaches that of non-manipulated controls, therefore it appears the PNT procedure per se has little detrimental effect on overall viability in the mouse. There is some evidence that this frequency can drop when the two zygotes used are not closely matched in developmental stage (McGrath and Solter, 1984b; Mann and Lovell-Badge, 1987). Use of human zygotes at an early stage of pronuclear development, along with adjustments to culture conditions and fusogen concentration, allowed for development to the blastocyst stage at nearly the same frequency as controls. Also, the quality of these reconstituted zygotes was similar to controls in terms of cell number and global gene expression assessed by RNA sequencing (Hyslop et al., 2016). For MST in mice, survival frequencies to term of reconstituted eggs fertilised by ICSI were low in two studies (Wang et al., 2001; Costa-Borges et al., 2020) and high in another study, including for PBT (Wang et al., 2014), although the data were limited. Results for MST in a rhesus monkey model were also comparable to controls (Tachibana et al., 2009) although, again, the data were limited.

For fusion of the karyoplast with the donor egg, the two alternatives of inactivated Sendai virus (iSeV), also known as haemagglutinating virus of Japan (HVJ) (Okada, 1993), and electrofusion have been used in animal eggs, while iSeV has generally been used in experiments with human eggs. The viral envelope contains glycoproteins which facilitate the fusion or melding of the karyoplast egg membrane with the donor egg membrane, thereby allowing the nuclear material in the karyoplast to enter the donor egg (as illustrated in Figure 1.1G). In electrofusion, this melding is achieved by controlled electrical pulses. Electrofusion is less convenient than iSeV because it is an additional procedure applied after the micromanipulation step. For PNT, both methods appear to be suitable. For MST, electrofusion has been problematic. The method artificially activated the donor egg, resulting in failed pronuclear development in a rhesus monkey model, while meiotic defects were observed in human eggs (Paull et al., 2013; Tachibana et al., 2013). By contrast, iSeV-induced fusion caused no such problems in the monkey model and resulted in live births (Tachibana et al., 2009). Furthermore, iSeV-induced fusion has also been successful in human MST. For manipulated eggs—those that underwent karyoplast fusion—subsequent frequencies of fertilisation by ICSI and preimplantation development were comparable to non-manipulated controls (Kang et al., 2016).

1.2.2 Mutant Mitochondrial DNA Carryover

Probably the most significant concern for MRT is the possibility for adverse consequences resulting from the carryover of mutant mitochondrial DNA. Using current technology, it is impossible to avoid transplanting some mitochondria along with the nuclear genetic material regardless of whether PNT, MST, or PBT is used. An advantage of polar bodies is that they contain considerably less mitochondrial DNA than pronuclear or spindle karyoplasts (Wang et al., 2014). When manipulating mouse zygotes, in terms of the volume of ooplasm, the amount in a pronuclear karyoplast is typically 5 percent that of the donor ooplasm. If desired, this amount can be reduced substantially if care is taken to exclude as much ooplasm as possible (JRM, unpublished observations). Given that mitochondria are not necessarily distributed evenly in the cytoplasm and may be concentrated near the pronuclei (Bavister and Squirrell, 2000; Van Blerkom et al., 2000) and that mitochondrial DNA copy number varies between eggs, the carryover of mitochondrial DNA can show considerable variability between individual transplantations (Craven et al., 2010). Carryover of mitochondria after mitochondrial donation is depicted under fluorescence confocal microscopy (see Figure 1.2).

In practice, the amount of carryover of mitochondrial DNA can be reduced to less than 2 percent, and in some cases to undetectable amounts, after PNT in human zygotes (Craven et al., 2010; Hyslop et al., 2016); after MST in human, monkey, and mouse eggs (Tachibana et al., 2009, 2013; Paull et al., 2013; Costa-Borges et al., 2020), and after PBT in mice (Wang et al., 2014). While these amounts of carryover are substantially less than the amount leading to disease, any carryover could be considered problematic because of the potential for tissue-specific amplification of mutant mitochondrial DNA during fetal development and after birth. Such effects can be substantial, for example (Sato et al., 2005), and the contribution of stochastic or selective forces to this amplification has been reviewed (Lawless et al., 2020; Yamada et al., 2020). Of particular concern is the potential for a substantial heteroplasmic load developing in the egg because of the bottleneck effect in their precursors known as *primordial germ cells* (Cao et al., 2009; Otten et al., 2018). This effect can lead to familial reemergence of the disease in subsequent generations.

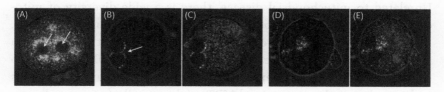

Figure 1.2 Visualisation of carryover in mitochondrial donation.
(A) Zygote with pronuclei to be transplanted (arrows) and containing unwanted mitochondria (green). Before karyoplast fusion: (B) pronuclei from zygote in A have been placed on the surface of the mitochondrial donor egg. The carryover mitochondria in the karyoplast are seen surrounding the pronuclei (green, arrow). (C) Merge with B, with donor mitochondria (red) and carryover mitochondria (yellow). After karyoplast fusion: (D) the carryover mitochondria are dispersing into the donor ooplasm. (E) Merge with D, with donor mitochondria (red) and carryover mitochondria (yellow).
From DA and JRM, unpublished data.

Given these concerns, the ideal solution would be to consistently eliminate carryover completely. Various strategies have been employed to selectively degrade mutant mitochondrial DNAs through the targeting of nucleases to mitochondria which can degrade mitochondrial DNAs based on sequence specificity. These include restriction enzymes, transcription activator-like effector nucleases (TALENs), and zinc finger nucleases (ZFNs) (Bayona-Bafaluy et al., 2005; Reddy et al., 2015; Bacman et al., 2018; Gammage et al., 2018b). Unfortunately, the more recent CRISPR system appears restricted for this purpose because, while CRISPR nuclease can be imported into mitochondria, the essential guide RNA is left behind by the transport machinery (Gammage et al., 2018a). Mitochondria do have mechanisms to import RNA, and eventually it may be possible to exploit these mechanisms to obtain efficient CRISPR-mediated editing or degradation of mitochondrial DNA (Hussain et al., 2021; see also Chapter 10, this volume). The application of gene editing technologies, together with MRT, could eventually reduce carryover to levels low enough to obviate amplification of unwanted mitochondrial DNA molecules. The gene editing nucleases are appended with mitochondrial localisation signal sequences and therefore should be active only in mitochondria. Nevertheless, it is conceivable that some nuclease molecules may find their way to nuclear DNA, and the potential for nuclear off-target effects requires careful examination. For example, such events may result if mitochondrial import is not 100 percent efficient regardless of the expression level of the nuclease or if the nuclease is expressed in excess of the capacity for mitochondrial import.

1.2.3 Potential for Genetic Consequences

Unrelated to mitochondrial disease, there is a wide diversity of mitochondrial DNA sequence types, or *haplotypes*, in the human population. Even so, these haplotypes are similar enough to indicate that all of them originated from a single ancestor living in Africa up to 200,000 years ago (Cann et al., 1987; van Oven and Kayser, 2009). Various observations and experiments have suggested MRT might contribute to new disease because of incompatibilities between the nuclear DNA haplotype and the donor mitochondrial DNA haplotype. First, the distinct geographical distribution of human mitochondrial DNA haplotypes (van Oven and Kayser, 2009) is consistent with nuclear and mitochondrial DNA sequence co-adaptation to the environment following early human migration (Wallace, 2015). Second, an influence of mitochondrial haplotype on phenotype has been shown in conplastic mice. These mice are produced by several generations of backcrossing to the maternal parent so they have the same nuclear but different mitochondrial genome (Latorre-Pellicer et al., 2016; Nagao et al., 1998; Yu et al., 2009). And, third, deviations in gene expression and global DNA methylation patterns have been described in conplastic mouse cell lines (Lee et al., 2017). On the other hand, it has been noted that population genetic theory predicts that nuclear and mitochondrial DNA haplotype incompatibility, should it exist, is likely to be similar in degree in persons born with and without MRT (Eyre-Walker, 2017), with this prediction supported by the available experimental evidence in a range of species (Eyre-Walker, 2017; Vaught et al., 2020). Indeed, an extensive human population study has shown that a person's health, at least at a superficial level, is not affected if the nuclear and mitochondrial DNA haplotypes are divergent and therefore potentially incompatible (Rishishwar and Jordan, 2017). It is also noted that, today, estimates of geographical ancestry as assessed by nuclear DNA haplotype vary widely between individuals with the same mitochondrial DNA haplotype (Emery et al., 2015), presumably because of recent human migration. These various observations and studies indicate there are few if any significant incompatibilities between nuclear and mitochondrial DNA haplotypes in the human population, and the possibility that such incompatibilities are a risk factor in MRT remains predominantly theoretical.

1.2.4 Potential for Epigenetic Consequences

While it is established that mitochondrial DNA haplotype can affect phenotype—at least in conplastic studies in mice—the possibility remains that new or different epigenetic effects on phenotype, even disease, will be induced by MRT. These are in addition to some increased risk, at least historically, of epigenetic genomic imprinting disorders resulting from artificial reproduction technology procedures such as in vitro culture (Watkins et al., 2008; Kopca and Tulay, 2021). This is because mitochondrial donation is in fact ooplasmic donation, meaning that, in addition to mitochondria, all other ooplasmic components are donated, such as transcription factors, other organelles, cytoskeletal components, etc., with these being produced and stored during egg growth. Preimplantation embryo development is completely dependent on these factors, and a lasting maternal epigenetic influence on phenotype by foreign non-mitochondrial DNA egg components is conceivable.

An effect on phenotype could be negative, in which case the procedure is a safety concern. Alternatively, a somewhat different yet still healthy phenotype could result, in which case the issue is perhaps mostly an ethical one.

While again this concern is largely theoretical, a small number of experiments in mice have shown that phenotypic alterations—for example, effects on growth and altered gene expression patterns—can result from PNT between different strains of mice (Latham and Solter, 1991; Reik et al., 1993; Fetterman et al., 2013). While an epigenetic cause of the phenotypic effects has been suggested (Latham and Solter, 1991; Reik et al., 1993), in none of these studies was it discerned if the effects were caused by an exposure to a foreign mitochondrial DNA haplotype or to foreign ooplasmic factors. Furthermore, some of the findings have been difficult to replicate (Cheng et al., 2009). The possibility that foreign non-mitochondrial DNA egg components might have epigenetic consequences for phenotype requires further investigation.

1.3 CONCLUSION

The technologies required for mitochondrial donation have been used for various experimental purposes in animal models for decades and are compatible with normal developmental outcomes. While there remains concern about the effects of carryover in the micromanipulation procedure, all other things being equal, it is clearly of health benefit to commence development from the zygote stage with a greatly increased load of normal mitochondrial DNA—which is achieved by MRT. Other potential health risks, such as an incompatibility between mitochondrial and nuclear DNA haplotypes, and for epigenetic effects resulting from exposure to foreign ooplasm, continue to be investigated in animal models. It seems clear from these ongoing studies that changing mitochondrial haplotype can affect phenotype, although not necessarily in ways that are detrimental. Also, studies in human populations have yet to reveal any serious health concerns based on the combination of nuclear and mitochondrial DNA haplotype. Nevertheless, it is axiomatic that mitochondrial DNA genotypes which are as benign as possible in terms of health risk should, as far as possible, be used for MRT. MRT offers the potential to greatly reduce the risk of devastating disease in children of women who carry high loads of pathogenic mitochondrial DNA mutations and for whom preimplantation genetic testing may be unsuitable.

REFERENCES

Bacman, Sandra R., Johanna H. K. Kauppila, Claudia V. Pereira, Nadee Nissanka, Maria Miranda, Milena Pinto, Sion L. Williams, Nils-Göran Larsson, James B. Stewart, and Carlos T. Moraes. 'MitoTALEN reduces mutant mtDNA load and restores tRNAAla levels in a mouse model of heteroplasmic mtDNA mutation.' *Nature Medicine* 24, no. 11 (2018): 1696–1700.

Bavister, Barry D., and Jayne M. Squirrell. 'Mitochondrial distribution and function in oocytes and early embryos.' *Human Reproduction* 15, no. suppl. 2 (2000): 189–198.

Bayona-Bafaluy, Maria Pilar, Bas Blits, Brendan J. Battersby, Eric A. Shoubridge, and Carlos T. Moraes. 'Rapid directional shift of mitochondrial DNA heteroplasmy in animal tissues by a mitochondrially targeted restriction endonuclease.' *Proceedings of the National Academy of Sciences* 102, no. 40 (2005): 14392–14397.

Calvo, Sarah E., and Vamsi K. Mootha. 'The mitochondrial proteome and human disease.' *Annual Review of Genomics and Human Genetics* 11 (2010): 25–44.

Cann, Rebecca L., Mark Stoneking, and Allan C. Wilson. 'Mitochondrial DNA and human evolution.' *Nature* 325, no. 6099 (1987): 31–36.

Cao, Liqin, Hiroshi Shitara, Michihiko Sugimoto, Jun-Ichi Hayashi, Kuniya Abe, and Hiromichi Yonekawa. 'New evidence confirms that the mitochondrial bottleneck is generated without reduction of mitochondrial DNA content in early primordial germ cells of mice.' *PLoS Genetics* 5, no. 12 (2009): e1000756.

Cheng, Yong, Kai Wang, Lori D. Kellam, Young S. Lee, Cheng-Guang Liang, Zhiming Han, Namdori R. Mtango, and Keith E. Latham. 'Effects of ooplasm manipulation on DNA methylation and growth of progeny in mice.' *Biology of Reproduction* 80, no. 3 (2009): 464–472.

Costa-Borges, N., K. Spath, I. Miguel-Escalada, E. Mestres, R. Balmaseda, A. Serafín, M. Garcia-Jiménez, I. Vanrell, J. González, K. Rink, and D. Wells. 'Maternal spindle transfer overcomes embryo developmental arrest caused by ooplasmic defects in mice.' *eLife* 9 (2020): e48591.

Craven, Lyndsey, Charlotte L. Alston, Robert W. Taylor, and Doug M. Turnbull. 'Recent advances in mitochondrial disease.' *Annual Review of Genomics and Human Genetics* 18 (2017): 257–275.

Craven, Lyndsey, Helen A. Tuppen, Gareth D. Greggains, Stephen J. Harbottle, Julie L. Murphy, Lynsey M. Cree, Alison P. Murdoch, et al. 'Pronuclear transfer in human embryos to prevent transmission of mitochondrial DNA disease.' *Nature* 465, no. 7294 (2010): 82–85.

Emery, Leslie S., Kevin M. Magnaye, Abigail W. Bigham, Joshua M. Akey, and Michael J. Bamshad. 'Estimates of continental ancestry vary widely among individuals with the same mtDNA haplogroup.' *American Journal of Human Genetics* 96, no. 2 (2015): 183–193.

Eyre-Walker, Adam. 'Mitochondrial replacement therapy: Are mito-nuclear interactions likely to be a problem?' *Genetics* 205, no. 4 (2017): 1365–1372.

Fetterman, Jessica L., Blake R. Zelickson, Larry W. Johnson, Douglas R. Moellering, David G. Westbrook, Melissa Pompilius, Melissa J. Sammy, et al. 'Mitochondrial genetic background modulates bioenergetics and susceptibility to acute cardiac volume overload.' *Biochemical Journal* 455, no. 2 (2013): 157–167.

Frazier, Ann E., David R. Thorburn, and Alison G. Compton. 'Mitochondrial energy generation disorders: Genes, mechanisms, and clues to pathology.' *Journal of Biological Chemistry* 294, no. 14 (2019): 5386–5395.

Gammage, Payam A., Carlos T. Moraes, and Michal Minczuk. 'Mitochondrial genome engineering: The revolution may not be CRISPR-Ized.' *Trends in Genetics* 34, no. 2 (2018a): 101–110

Gammage, Payam A., Carlo Viscomi, Marie-Lune Simard, Ana S. H. Costa, Edoardo Gaude, Christopher A. Powell, Lindsey Van Haute, et al. 'Genome editing in mitochondria corrects a pathogenic mtDNA mutation in vivo.' *Nature Medicine* 24, no. 11 (2018b): 1691–1695.

Giles, Richard E., Hugues Blanc, Howard M. Cann, and Douglas C. Wallace. 'Maternal inheritance of human mitochondrial DNA.' *Proceedings of the National Academy of Sciences* 77, no. 11 (1980): 6715–6719.

Gorman, Gráinne S., Patrick F. Chinnery, Salvatore DiMauro, Michio Hirano, Yasutoshi Koga, Robert McFarland, Anu Suomalainen, David R. Thorburn, Massimo Zeviani, and Douglass M. Turnbull. 'Mitochondrial diseases.' *Nature Reviews Disease Primers* 2, no. 1 (2016): 1–22.

Hashimoto, Shu, Naoharu Morimoto, Masaya Yamanaka, Hiroshi Matsumoto, Takayuki Yamochi, Hiroya Goto, Masayasu Inoue, Yoshiharu Nakaoka, Hiroaki Shibahara, and Yoshiharu Morimoto. 'Quantitative and qualitative changes of mitochondria in human preimplantation embryos.' *Journal of Assisted Reproduction and Genetics* 34, no. 5 (2017): 573–580.

Hussain, Syed-Rehan A., Mehmet E. Yalvac, Benedict Khoo, Sigrid Eckardt, and K. John McLaughlin. 'Adapting CRISPR/Cas9 system for targeting mitochondrial genome.' *Frontiers in Genetics* 12 (2021): 627050.

Hyslop, Louise A., Paul Blakeley, Lyndsey Craven, Jessica Richardson, Norah M. E. Fogarty, Elpida Fragouli, Mahdi Lamb, et al. 'Towards clinical application of pronuclear transfer to prevent mitochondrial DNA disease.' *Nature* 534, no. 7607 (2016): 383–386.

Kang, Louise A., Paul Blakeley, Lyndsey Craven, Jessica Richardson, Norah M. E. Fogarty, Elpida Fragouli, Mahdi Lamb, et al. 'Towards clinical application of pronuclear transfer to prevent mitochondrial DNA disease.' *Nature* 534, no. 7607 (2016): 383–386.

Kopca, T., and Pinar Tulay. 'Association of assisted reproductive technology treatments with imprinting disorders.' *Global Medical Genetics* 8, no. 1 (2021): 1–6.

Latham, Keith E., and Davor Solter. 'Effect of egg composition on the developmental capacity of androgenetic mouse embryos.' *Development* 113, no. 2 (1991): 561–568.

Latorre-Pellicer, Ana, Raquel Moreno-Loshuertos, Ana Victoria Lechuga-Vieco, Fátima Sánchez-Cabo, Carlos Torroja, Rebeca Acín-Pérez, Enrique Calvo, et al. 'Mitochondrial and nuclear DNA matching shapes metabolism and healthy ageing.' *Nature* 535, no. 7613 (2016): 561–565.

Lawless, Conor, Laura Greaves, Amy K. Reeve, Doug M. Turnbull, and Amy E. Vincent. 'The rise and rise of mitochondrial DNA mutations.' *Open Biology* 10, no. 5 (2020): 200061.

Lee, William T., Xin Sun, Te-Sha Tsai, Jacqueline L. Johnson, Jodee A. Gould, Daniel J. Garama, Daniel J. Gough, Matthew McKenzie, Ian A. Trounce, and Justin C. St John. 'Mitochondrial DNA haplotypes induce differential patterns of DNA methylation that result in differential chromosomal gene expression patterns.' *Cell Death Discovery* 3, no. 1 (2017): 1–11.

Mann, Jeff R., and Robin H. Lovell-Badge. 'Inviability of parthenogenones is determined by pronuclei, not egg cytoplasm.' *Nature* 310, no. 5972 (1984): 66–67.

Mann, Jeff R. and Robin H. Lovell-Badge. 'The development of XO gynogenetic mouse embryos.' *Development* 99, no. 3 (1987): 411–416.

McGrath, James, and Davor Solter. 'Nuclear transplantation in the mouse embryo by microsurgery and cell fusion.' *Science* 220, no. 4603 (1983): 1300–1302.

McGrath, James, and Davor Solter. 'Maternal Thp lethality in the mouse is a nuclear, not cytoplasmic, defect.' *Nature* 308, no. 5959 (1984a): 550–551.

McGrath, James, and Davor Solter. 'Completion of mouse embryogenesis requires both the maternal and paternal genomes.' *Cell* 37, no. 1 (1984b): 179–183.

Mogessie, Binyam, and Melina Schuh. 'Actin protects mammalian eggs against chromosome segregation errors.' *Science* 357, no. 6353 (2017): eaal1647.

Nagao, Yasumitsu, Yoshikazu Totsuka, Yoriko Atomi, Hideki Kaneda, Kirsten Fischer Lindahl, Hiroshi Imai, and Hiromichi Yonekawa. 'Decreased physical performance of congenic mice with mismatch between the nuclear and the mitochondrial genome.' *Genes and Genetic Systems* 73, no. 1 (1998): 21–27.

National Health and Medical Research Council. *Mitochondrial Donation Issues Paper: Ethical and Social Issues for Community Consultation*. NHMRC, 2019.

Newson, A. J., S. De Lacey, D. K. Dowling, S. Murray, C. M. Sue, David R. Thorburn, L. Gillam, and C. Degeling. 'Public attitudes towards novel reproductive technologies: A citizens' jury on mitochondrial donation.' *Human Reproduction* 34, no. 4 (2019): 751–757.

Okada, Yoshio. '[3] Sendai virus-induced cell fusion.' In *Methods in Enzymology*, vol. 221, pp. 18–41. Academic Press, 1993.

Otten, uke B. C., Suzanne C. E. H. Sallevelt, Phillippa J. Carling, Joseph C. F. M. Dreesen, Marion Drüsedau, Sabine Spierts, Aimee D. C. Paulussen, et al. 'Mutation-specific effects in germline transmission of pathogenic mtDNA variants.' *Human Reproduction* 33, no. 7 (2018): 1331–1341.

Paull, Daniel, Valentina Emmanuele, Keren A. Weiss, Nathan Treff, Latoya Stewart, Haiqing Hua, Matthew Zimmer, et al. 'Nuclear genome transfer in human oocytes eliminates mitochondrial DNA variants.' *Nature* 493, no. 7434 (2013): 632–637.

Reddy, Pradeep, Alejandro Ocampo, Keiichiro Suzuki, Jinping Luo, Sandra R. Bacman, Sion L. Williams, Atsushi Sugawara, et al. 'Selective elimination of mitochondrial mutations in the germline by genome editing.' *Cell* 161, no. 3 (2015): 459–469.

Reik, Wolf, I. Romer, Sheila C. Barton, M. Azim Surani, Sarah K. Howlett, and Joachim Klose. 'Adult phenotype in the mouse can be affected by epigenetic events in the early embryo.' *Development* 119, no. 3 (1993): 933–942.

Richardson, Jessica, Laura Irving, Louise A. Hyslop, Meenakshi Choudhary, Alison Murdoch, Douglass M. Turnbull, and Mary Herbert. 'Concise reviews: Assisted reproductive technologies to prevent transmission of mitochondrial DNA disease.' *Stem Cells* 33, no. 3 (2015): 639–645.

Rishishwar, Lavanya, and I. King Jordan. 'Implications of human evolution and admixture for mitochondrial replacement therapy.' *BMC Genomics* 18, no. 1 (2017): 1–11.

Russell, Oliver M., Gráinne S. Gorman, Robert N. Lightowlers, and Doug M. Turnbull. 'Mitochondrial diseases: Hope for the future.' *Cell* 181, no. 1 (2020): 168–188.

Salzberg, Steven L. 'Open questions: How many genes do we have?' *BMC Biology* 16, no. 1 (2018): 1–3.

Sato, Akitsugu, Tomohiro Kono, Kazuto Nakada, Kaori Ishikawa, Shin-Ichi Inoue, Hiromichi Yonekawa, and Jun-Ichi Hayashi. 'Gene therapy for progeny of mito-mice carrying pathogenic mtDNA by nuclear transplantation.' *Proceedings of the National Academy of Sciences* 102, no. 46 (2005): 16765–16770.

Shitara, Hiroshi, Hideki Kaneda, Akitsugu Sato, Kimiko Inoue, Atsuo Ogura, Hiromichi Yonekawa, and Jun-Ichi Hayashi. 'Selective and continuous elimination of mitochondria microinjected into mouse eggs from spermatids, but not from liver cells, occurs throughout embryogenesis.' *Genetics* 156, no. 3 (2000): 1277–1284.

Smeets, Hubert J. M., Suzanne C. E. H. Sallevelt, Jos C. F. M. Dreesen, Christine E. M. de Die-Smulders, and Irenaeus F. M. de Coo. 'Preventing the transmission of mitochondrial DNA disorders using prenatal or preimplantation genetic diagnosis.' *Annals of the New York Academy of Sciences* 1350, no. 1 (2015): 29–36.

Surani, M. A. H., Sheila C. Barton, and M. L. Norris. 'Development of reconstituted mouse eggs suggests imprinting of the genome during gametogenesis.' *Nature* 308, no. 5959 (1984): 548–550.

Sutovsky, Peter, Ricardo D. Moreno, João Ramalho-Santos, Tanja Dominko, Calvin Simerly, and Gerald Schatten. 'Ubiquitinated sperm mitochondria, selective proteolysis, and the regulation of mitochondrial inheritance in mammalian embryos.' *Biology of Reproduction* 63, no. 2 (2000): 582–590.

Tachibana, Masahito, Paula Amato, Michelle Sparman, Joy Woodward, Dario Melguizo Sanchis, Hong Ma, Nuria Marti Gutierrez, et al. 'Towards germline gene therapy of inherited mitochondrial diseases.' *Nature* 493, no. 7434 (2013): 627–631.

Tachibana, Masahito, Michelle Sparman, Hathaitip Sritanaudomchai, Hong Ma, Lisa Clepper, Joy Woodward, Ying Li, Cathy Ramsey, Olena Kolotushkina, and Shoukhrat Mitalipov. 'Mitochondrial gene replacement in primate offspring and embryonic stem cells.' *Nature* 461, no. 7262 (2009): 367–372.

Uraji, Julia, Kathleen Scheffler, and Melina Schuh. 'Functions of actin in mouse oocytes at a glance.' *Journal of Cell Science* 131, no. 22 (2018): jcs218099.

Van Blerkom, Jonathan, Patrick Davis, and Samuel Alexander. 'Differential mitochondrial distribution in human pronuclear embryos leads to disproportionate inheritance between blastomeres: Relationship to microtubular organization, ATP content and competence.' *Human Reproduction* 15, no. 12 (2000): 2621–2633.

van Oven, Mannis, and Manfred Kayser. 'Updated comprehensive phylogenetic tree of global human mitochondrial DNA variation.' *Human Mutation* 30, no. 2 (2009): E386–E394.

Vaught, Rebecca C., Susanne Voigt, Ralph Dobler, David J. Clancy, Klaus Reinhardt, and Damian K. Dowling. 'Interactions between cytoplasmic and nuclear genomes confer sex-specific effects on lifespan in Drosophila melanogaster.' *Journal of Evolutionary Biology* 33, no. 5 (2020): 694–713.

Wakayama, Teruhiko, Y. Hayashi, and A. Ogura. 'Participation of the female pronucleus derived from the second polar body in full embryonic development of mice.' *Reproduction* 110, no. 2 (1997): 263–266.

Wakayama, Teruhiko, and R. Yanagimachi. 'The first polar body can be used for the production of normal offspring in mice.' *Biology of Reproduction* 59, no. 1 (1998): 100–104.

Wallace, Douglas C. 'Mitochondrial DNA variation in human radiation and disease.' *Cell* 163, no. 1 (2015): 33–38.

Wang, Min-Kang, Da-Yuan Chen, Ji-Long Lui, Guang-Peng Li, and Qing-Yuan Sun. 'In vitro fertilisation of mouse oocytes reconstructed by transfer of metaphase II chromosomes results in live births.' *Zygote* 9, no. 1 (2001): 9–14.

Wang, Tian, Hongying Sha, Dongmei Ji, Helen L. Zhang, Dawei Chen, Yunxia Cao, and Jianhong Zhu. 'Polar body genome transfer for preventing the transmission of inherited mitochondrial diseases.' *Cell* 157, no. 7 (2014): 1591–1604.

Watkins, Adam J., Tom Papenbrock, and Tom P. Fleming. 'The preimplantation embryo: Handle with care.' *Seminars in Reproductive Medicine*, vol. 26, no. 2 (2008): 175–185.

Yamada, Mitsutoshi, Kazuhiro Akashi, Reina Ooka, Kenji Miyado, and Hidenori Akutsu. 'Mitochondrial genetic drift after nuclear transfer in oocytes.' *International Journal of Molecular Sciences* 21, no. 16 (2020): 5880.

Yu, Xinhua, Ulrike Gimsa, Lena Wester-Rosenlöf, Ellen Kanitz, Winfried Otten, Manfred Kunz, and Saleh M. Ibrahim. 'Dissecting the effects of mtDNA variations on complex traits using mouse conplastic strains.' *Genome Research* 19, no. 1 (2009): 159–165.

2

Mitochondrial Replacement Techniques

A Critical Review of the Ethical Issues

ROBERT SPARROW, JULIAN KOPLIN, AND
CATHERINE MILLS

2.1 INTRODUCTION

Mitochondria are found in most of the cells of the human body. Often
described as the 'powerhouse of the cell' (Siekevitz, 1957), mitochondria
are involved in supplying energy to cells, among other tasks. Mutations in
mitochondrial DNA (mtDNA) can cause a wide range of medical problems,
affecting the brain, muscle, cochlea, liver, and/or kidney, amongst other
things, with symptoms that can range from mild to severe (Molnar and
Kovacs, 2018). Mitochondria have their own DNA. Unlike nuclear DNA
(nDNA), which is transmitted by both genetic parents, mtDNA is inherited
only via the maternal line. Mitochondrial replacement techniques (MRT)
offer a new strategy for avoiding the transmission of certain forms of
mtDNA disorders from genetic mothers to their offspring.

Two different techniques to achieve mitochondrial replacement are
widely discussed in the biomedical and bioethical literature on MRT
(Chapter 1, this volume). Maternal spindle transfer (MST) involves
reconstructing a single egg, which can then be fertilised, from two
sources: an egg from the intending mother (which contributes the spindle
of chromosomes) and a donor egg (which contributes the rest of the cellular material, including the donor's healthy mitochondria). Pronuclear

Robert Sparrow, Julian Koplin, and Catherine Mills, *Mitochondrial Replacement Techniques* In: *Reproduction Reborn.*
Edited by: Diana M. Bowman, Karinne Ludlow, and Walter G. Johnson, Oxford University Press.
© Oxford University Press 2023. DOI: 10.1093/oso/9780197616192.003.0003

transfer (PNT) involves reconstructing an embryo from two sources: an embryo created using sperm and egg from the intending parents (which contributes the pronuclei) and an embryo created using a donor egg and sperm from the intending father (which is denucleated and then injected with the pronuclei from the first embryo).[1] Both these techniques result in the creation of an embryo whose nDNA comes from the intending parents and mtDNA from a separate donor. In this way, mitochondrial donation provides a novel means for women with mitochondrial disorders to have children who are genetically related to them and who have a reduced risk of being born with a mitochondrial disorder.

In this chapter we review the philosophical and ethical questions raised by MRT and by decisions regarding the regulation of MRT. We begin, in Section 2.2 by considering the strength of the 'therapeutic' case for MRT, arguing that it is much weaker than the medical literature presupposes and that MRT is most appropriately understood as a technology to facilitate the securing of a relationship of 'genetic relatedness' where a mother would otherwise only be able to give birth to a child unaffected by mitochondrial disease by the use of donor oocytes. In Section 2.3 we discuss the implications of mtDNA for identity as well as the question of whether the genetic relationship that MRT establishes between the donor and the child is appropriately thought of as 'genetic parenthood' such that the technology involves bringing children into existence who would have 'three parents.' Although, we argue, *contra* many of the early discussions of MRT, it is false that mtDNA plays less of a role in determining identity than does nDNA, whether the genetic relationship between the mtDNA donor and the child conceived as a result of the procedure should be called 'parenthood' or not is ultimately a matter of social choice. We argue that concerns about parenthood are unlikely to count as a substantial objection to MRT given the diversity of parental relationships that already exist. This section also includes discussion of a novel feature of the genetic relationship established by MRT that has previously been unremarked upon and also notes the potential of this technology to serve the desires of lesbian couples for both women to achieve a genetic relationship with a child. Section 2.4 briefly discusses concerns about resource allocation in the context of MRT. We suggest that although concerns about the appropriate use of financial resources provide only weak and generic grounds for reservations about MRT, concerns about the best use of the scarce resource of oocytes in the context of assisted reproductive technology (ART) represent a significant ethical barrier to the use of MRT. In Section 2.5 we raise the question of whether MRT should be prohibited by virtue of being a form of germline gene editing. We conclude that, where female embryos are conceived using this technique, it is at least a form of germline genetic modification. The extent to which that should be counted as an objection to MRT, though, will turn on one's stance on any of a number of issues in the larger debate about germline genetic modification. Section 2.6 surveys the risks involved in MRT, including to the parents (and ova donor), physical health of the future child, psychological health of the future child, and future generations. We suggest that the easy availability of various arguments for discounting such risks means that they are unlikely to hold back the development and application of MRT. In Section 2.7, we turn to the social impacts of MRT: the adoption of MRT seems likely to subtly transform social attitudes towards genetic parenthood in various ways and might also work to undermine public hostility to germline genetic modification of human beings more generally. Again, however, whether this provides reasons to restrict access to this technology turns on larger questions about the sorts of reasons that might justify legislation by liberal states. Consequently, in Section 2.8, we consider whether reference to the influential idea of a 'right to reproductive liberty' is sufficient to establish that it would be wrong for the state to limit access to MRT. We argue that although a concern for reproductive liberty may provide some reasons against preventing couples from accessing this technique once it exists, it does not suffice to establish either that states should fund the development of this technology or that they must enact a regulatory framework to facilitate its use. The final two sections consider questions that will arise for jurisdictions that *do* decide to permit MRT: whether couples undergoing MRT should be permitted, or even required, to select male embryos in order to reduce the risk to future generations involved in MRT (Section 2.9) and whether children conceived via MRT have a right to know the identity of the donor of the oocyte used in the procedure (Section 2.10).

2.2 IS MRT THERAPEUTIC?

Any account of the ethics of MRT must begin with an accurate understanding of what the technique makes possible and thus of the strength of the case for its use. MRT has been developed and advertised as a treatment for mitochondrial disorders or a treatment for a form of infertility characterised by the inability to have a genetically related child. That is to say, MRT is often advertised as a therapy, perhaps even a 'life-saving therapy' (Herbrand, 2017). For instance, when the Australian government announced its Mitochondrial Donation Law Reform Bill (also known as

Maeve's Law, named after a young girl with a severe form of mitochondrial disease), the Minister for Health and Aged Care suggested that

> [Mitochondrial donation] means that young children who would otherwise be born with an inherited genetic condition and have either a terminal or an utterly debilitating condition, might be able to live a rich, full life, and that's the gift of life. (Australian Government Department of Health, 2021: x)

However, there are reasons to doubt both that resort to MRT can really be justified with reference to the desire to have a healthy child and whether the intervention itself is therapeutic.

2.2.1 Use of Donor Gametes as an Alternative to MRT

That the use of MRT can be justified with reference to the desire to have a healthy child alone is called into question by the fact that an existing, simpler, and safer technique—the use of donor gametes—allows prospective parents with a relevant history of mitochondrial disease to bring into existence a child with a greatly reduced risk of mitochondrial disease. If couples are willing to use an egg from a donor without a history of mitochondrial disorders, their children will not inherit a mitochondrial disorder (although there is a small chance that they will develop one *de novo*).[2] Given that the birth of a healthy baby can be achieved using donor gametes, the case for MRT must rest on the fact that, unlike the use of donor gametes, MRT allows prospective parents to conceive and raise a child who is the genetic offspring of the mother but who will not inherit a mitochondrial disorder (Herbrand, 2017; Chapter 3, this volume). That is to say, the justification of MRT ultimately relies on the desire of (a relatively small number of) individuals who have mitochondrial disorders to become genetic parents, and not just gestational or social parents, of a healthy child.[3]

2.2.2 Missing Patients and the Non-Identity Problem

That MRT is therapeutic is called into question by the difficulty involved in identifying the individual treated and the benefit they receive.

When it comes to the question of whom MRT treats, there seems to be two possible answers: MRT treats (prospective) parents; or, MRT treats children who have (or who might otherwise have) mitochondrial disease. There are problems with both answers.

As we noted above, the ultimate justification of the use of MRT seems to rest on the desire of a prospective mother to conceive a genetically related child who is unlikely to be affected by her mitochondrial disease. However, it stretches credulity to describe MRT as 'treating' any condition of the mother. Although, insofar as it involves in vitro fertilisation (IVF), MRT does involve medical interventions into the body of the mother, those that are distinctive to MRT are actually manipulations of her gametes or of an embryo outside of her body. It is hard to see how manipulating these entities could count as treating her. Moreover, MRT does not treat infertility, as ordinarily conceived (cf., Chapter 9, this volume). At the end of the 'treatment,' the capacity of the mother to have genetically related children who are unaffected by mitochondrial disease is unchanged.

Although MRT involves manipulation of gametes or embryos to reduce the chance that an individual is born who suffers from mitochondrial disease, there are significant barriers to understanding it as treating the child who will be born as a result of the procedure. As Tina Rulli (2017) has observed, we usually hold that a therapy or cure 'treats an existing person with disease' (Rulli, 2017: 372). However, MST involves manipulation of the oocyte, before any identifiable person actually exists. More generally, and more fundamentally—insofar as, were MRT not available, women with mitochondrial diseases might choose instead to adopt a child, use a donor egg, or to abstain from having children altogether—the availability of MRT will often affect whether a child is brought into existence at all, while—regardless of the technique used for MRT—the decision to use it (or not) will determine *which* individual comes into existence. Rather than treating an existing person with a disease, then, MRT attempts to bring into existence a child without mitochondrial disease.

In cases where women who are affected by mitochondrial disease do undertake to have a child, the fact that the decision to use (or not use) MRT determines which child comes into existence also calls into question the extent to which it may properly be described as therapeutic by problematising the claim that it delivers a benefit to the child. As is the case with many other ARTs, MRT raises a philosophical conundrum known as the 'non-identity problem' (Parfit, 1984: 351–379). Ordinarily, we determine whether an action has harmed or benefited a given individual by asking what their welfare would have been (a 'counterfactual') had we not performed that action. In the case of MRT, though—had the parents made a different decision—a different child would have come into existence. In Parfit's terminology, the decision whether or not to use MRT is 'identity affecting' rather than 'person affecting.' Asking whether the decision harmed or benefited the child therefore requires a comparison with what the child's welfare would have been had they not existed.[4] Most critics have concluded that this comparison is impossible (Brock, 1995; Glover, 2006: 50; Robertson, 1994: 76; Savulescu, 2002; Strong, 2005).

The significance of the non-identity problem for debates about the ethics of reproduction is contested and the literature surrounding it voluminous and complex. Even if identity-affecting interventions do not harm or benefit those whom they bring into existence, it is difficult to think that we don't have some reason to prefer to bring children with higher expected welfare into existence over children with lower expected welfare—although, notoriously, this thought has counterintuitive implications (Parfit, 1984). In the current context, it suffices to observe that the identity-affecting nature of MRT significantly undercuts the argument that it is therapeutic. Importantly, as we discuss further below, it also has implications for arguments about the risks involved in the technology.

2.2.3 Public Health Justifications for MRT

Even if MRT does not treat or cure specific, existing, persons with disease, it might still be argued that it is justified by public health considerations of a sort that have traditionally been part of the practice of medicine. MRT could potentially reduce the overall incidence of mitochondrial disease in the community if mitochondrial disease carriers opt for MRT where they would otherwise resist the use of donor gametes and conceive a child naturally (Schaefer, 2020).

A noteworthy feature of this justification for the development, funding, and use of MRT is that it is 'eugenic' in a stronger sense than is true of the prospective parents' desire to conceive a healthy child. The mobilisation, *by the parents*, of the science of genetics in the service of the desire to provide future individuals with a 'good life' already risks being described as eugenic (Sparrow, 2011). The development and rollout of a genetic technology *by the state* with the goal of promoting the health of the population clearly needs to be situated in the context of a longer—and morally troubling—history of state interest in population genetics (Kevles, 1995). Given that any insistence that the 'natural' distribution of MRT disorders is to be preferred over the lower prevalence of these disorders that might be produced through the use of MRT is equally concerned with the distribution of genes in a population, it cannot be the case that 'public health' considerations should play no role in our thinking about the appropriate uses of reproductive technology (Sparrow, 2015). Nevertheless, the more weight an argument for the value of MRT places on the goal of reducing the number of 'defective' mitochondria circulating in the population, the more it behooves us to pay close attention to the value judgments implicit in state support for MRT and the risk of coercion—and other subtle and not so subtle pressures—that may emerge once the technology is widely available.

In this context it is striking that, as far as we are aware, a 'disability critique' of the use of MRT as being motivated by the desire to 'get rid of' people suffering from mitochondrial disease or as expressing the idea that the lives of people suffering from mitochondrial disease are less worthwhile than the lives of healthy people is yet to receive much of an airing in the debate around MRT. We suspect that this is because the voices that have been most heard in this debate are the voices of those who desire to access MRT, who identify as suffering from a mitochondrial *disease* (or disorder), rather than a 'disability', and who, *ex hypothesi*, don't believe that there is anything morally problematic about preferring to bring into existence a child without mitochondrial disease (Chapters 3, 4, and 5, this volume). It may also reflect the fact that descriptions of the technology typically emphasise its positive and creative aspects, wherein scientists create new, healthy, embryos, rather than its nature as a technology which determines what sort of people are brought into existence. Both the accuracy of these speculations and the normative significance of the considerations which they highlight are, we believe, topics that are highly deserving of future research.

2.3 MRT AND GENETIC PARENTHOOD

MRT brings into existence children with a genetic link to three progenitors: the commissioning mother, whose nDNA is used in the procedure, a genetic father (who is usually the partner of the commissioning mother, but might also be a sperm donor), and the mitochondrial donor. For this reason, media coverage of mitochondrial donation frequently refers to the resulting children as 'three-parent babies.' Unsurprisingly, then, in the public discourse, much of the opposition to mitochondrial donation seems to have been driven by discomfort at the creation of children with three genetic parents (Dimond and Stephens, 2018a; Chapter 4, this volume).

2.3.1 Three-Parent Babies?

Perhaps because of this, proponents of mitochondrial donation have resisted the characterisation of mitochondrial donation as producing 'three-parent embryos.' One common response in the United Kingdom is to deny that mtDNA contributes meaningfully to personal characteristics or to the 'identity' of the child.

One rhetorical strategy for denying this involves the use of what Turkmendag (2018) has described as the 'battery pack analogy' which suggests that mitochondria are, like batteries, entirely separate from the make-up of the system they power and essentially fungible. As Dimond and Stephens (2018b: 251) also observe,

> positioning the mitochondria as a battery . . . performs this work of underplaying the social meaning of the donor's genetic contribution. The replicability, and with it disposability, of a battery that only powers, but does not alter the form of that which it powers, creates a disconnect between mitochondrial DNA and the identity of the child.

Another strategy, which played a major role in the UK policy debate (Scott and Wilkinson, 2017), is to insist that mtDNA makes a 'negligible' contribution to the identity of the individual born as a result of MRT (Harris, 2016; Savulescu, 2015). For example, in its response to submissions to a public consultation on the drafting of regulations to enable clinical uses of MRT under the UK Human Fertilisation and Embryology Act 2008, the UK Department of Health held that

> the resulting child will have nuclear DNA (99.9 per cent) from their father and mother and healthy mitochondrial DNA (0.1 per cent) from a female donor. Genetically, the child will, indeed, have DNA from three individuals but all available scientific evidence indicates that the genes contributing to personal characteristics and traits come solely from the nuclear DNA, which will only come from the proposed child's mother and father. The donated mitochondrial DNA will not affect those characteristics. (UK Department of Health, 2014: 15–16)

In a similar vein, an Australian Senate Report into mitochondrial donation rejected concerns that MRT could lead to children having three genetic parents. Importantly, the Report holds that mtDNA does not affect traits that would be relevant to parenthood.

> mtDNA does not contribute to a person's genetic identity because mtDNA only provides energy to the cells. Nuclear DNA is responsible for a person's physical, cognitive and behavioural characteristics. A recipient of donated mtDNA will not resemble the donor. (Community Affairs References Committee of the Senate of Australia, 2018: 3)

Others have attempted to defuse concerns about three-parent babies by emphasising that the genetic contribution made by mitochondrial donors is much smaller than that made by the individuals who contribute the nDNA in MRT (Thorburn and Christodoulou, 2019). For example, in an early paper on MRT—based on an article published in the UK paper *The Guardian* in 2012—when the public consultation on MRT was announced in the United Kingdom and a presentation made to the UK Parliament on the eve of the vote that gave the go-ahead to MRT in the United Kingdom, John Harris (2016: 11) wrote,

> The 'three genetic parents' label that has been applied by many commentators is also grossly misleading. The third-party DNA contained in the donated mitochondria makes up much less than 1 percent of the total genetic contribution and does not transmit any of the traits that confer the usual family resemblances and distinctive personal features in which both parents and children are interested. The mitochondria provide energy to cells and when they are diseased cause inheritable harm—hence the need for mitochondria replacement therapy [*sic*]. No identity conferring features are transmitted by the mitochondria.

One difficulty for such claims is that, while the science remains unsettled, there are some indications that mtDNA does contribute to traits that are usually considered 'personal characteristics,' including athleticism, fertility, intelligence, health (Dupras-Leduc et al., 2018: 4), and even personality (Cruz et al., 2019).

The fundamental problem with both these lines of argument, though, is that they presume that it is possible to separate out the implications of different genes for phenotype in an individual case and that each gene makes the same amount of contribution to the phenotype. Neither of these things is true. Genes—including genes transmitted in the mitochondria—interact with each other, in complex networks of influence, and with the environment to generate phenotype (Kampourakis, 2017). Changing even a single gene may have large implications for phenotype in a given environment; because each gene contributes to phenotype in a developmental process that is shaped by every other gene, strictly speaking it is not possible to say which gene is responsible for the phenotype of any particular individual or how much each gene contributes to that phenotype. For these reasons, the relative number of genes contained in mitochondria versus nuclear DNA tells us nothing about how much either contributes to the characteristics or 'identity' of an individual organism.

Finally, attempts to deny the importance of mitochondria in the context of MRT run afoul of the fact that it is precisely because the mitochondria can be so significant for the phenotype—and life prospects—of the child that the procedure is being considered at all (Bredenoord et al., 2011; Mills, 2021; Sparrow et al., 2021). If, as seems reasonable, the presence or absence of genetic disease counts as a personal characteristic, then mitochondrial donors *do* make a *significant contribution to the identity of the resulting child.*

2.3.2 Is It Parenthood?

What is less clear, given the novel nature of this technology and contribution, is whether this is sufficient to make the mitochondrial donor one of the child's 'parents'? That is to say, is the relationship that mitochondrial donation establishes between the donor and the child such that the former becomes a 'genetic parent' of the latter?

There are two significant reasons to doubt that the mitochondrial donor is appropriately conceived of as a parent, which are, we suspect at least part of what has motivated the various tortuous attempts to deny that mitochondrial donors make a meaningful contribution to the characteristics or identity of the child.

First, unlike nDNA, the mitochondrial genome is not subject to recombination at fertilisation, which means that the mitochondria that come to us from our mothers are also present in our grandmothers. If we think of genes as encoding or transmitting 'information,' then, whatever relationship exists between the mitochondrial donor and the child also exists between the mitochondrial donor's (genetic) mother and the child. If the mitochondrial donor is a parent by virtue of this relationship, then so, too, is the mitochondrial donor's mother. Yet we don't normally think of our grandparents as themselves being our genetic parents.

Second, because the mitochondrial genome is not subject to genetic reshuffling, there is actually only a relatively small number of mitochondrial types (haplogroups) present in the community (Van Oven and Kayser, 2009). We 'share' our mtDNA not only with all our maternal ancestors but also with many other people to whom we are otherwise genetically unrelated. This means that there is an important informational homology that exists between the genes of the child and the donor, which also exists between the child and many others in the community. However, again, we don't typically think of the other people who share our mitochondrial haplogroup as our parents in any sense. The existence of mitochondrial haplogroups also means that difference between the contribution to the phenotype of the child made by the actual mitochondrial donor and that which might have been made by any other person in the same mitochondrial haplogroup as the donor is negligible. This is the sense in which mitochondria might be held to be 'fungible.' By comparison, in most circumstances, there is no other individual who could have made the same contribution to the nDNA—and thus phenotype—as the child's genetic father and/or (nuclear) genetic mother.

However, the force of these objections is, in turn, undercut by their relying on an 'informational' account of genetic relatedness at the expense of a concern for the causal processes involved in the creation of an embryo. While we might share almost all our mitochondrial genes with our grandmothers, our grandmothers did not provide the gametes that are the reason why we have those genes. While any number of other people in the same mitochondrial haplogroup might have made the same contribution to the phenotype of the child, only the mitochondrial donor actually made this contribution—and, as we have seen, this act of donation was highly significant for the identity and life prospects of the resulting child. If the mere existence of other people who might have made the 'same' genetic contribution to the child is corrosive of genetic parenthood, this would imply that identical twins are less capable of achieving genetic parenthood than are individuals without identical twins.

Given that, as Sparrow's (and others') work elsewhere (Kolers, 2003; Sparrow, 2006, 2009) has demonstrated, our folk concept of genetic parenthood encompasses intuitions about the significance of both informational homologies and causal processes, the arguments canvassed above underdetermine the question of whether the genetic relationship created by transmission of mitochondria is a parental relationship. Ultimately, this seems to be a matter of social choice. Do we want to acknowledge mitochondrial donation as constituting a new way of becoming a (genetic) parent?

Adoption, gamete donation, and gestational surrogacy have already complicated the matter of defining who, precisely, is a child's parent. Accordingly, it is now common to distinguish between different kinds of parenthood, such as social, gestational, and genetic parenthood (Bayne and Kolers, 2003). Perhaps genetic parenthood should itself be broken down into *nuclear genetic parenthood* and *mitochondrial genetic parenthood* (Mills, 2021)? To the extent that being a parent is a matter of social practice, it may be that mitochondrial parenthood is yet to emerge as a relationship that structures people's interactions, but it does not seem impossible that it might. Cultural and legal understandings of parenthood have already evolved to accommodate other new ways of reproducing; presumably they could also evolve to accommodate MRT.

2.3.3 Is Three Parents Too Many?

While concerns about three-parent babies seem to have played a major role in public debate, concerns about extending parenthood to three parties have played a comparatively modest role in the ethics literature on MRT. Most of the ethical objections to MRT seem to stand or fall independently of whether the child has three parents.

One exception is the idea that allowing the possibility of having more than two genetic parents will lead to moral confusion about the relationships between the individuals involved in MRT and about the relation between the gamete donors and the child: we treat this in our discussion of the risk that MRT might have negative social impacts below. The other is that the creation of three-parent babies per se would be morally problematic in and of itself by virtue of being 'unnatural.' The weight of such arguments from nature, which can—and have—been mounted about every innovation in reproductive technology, is unclear (Ball, 2014; Kaebnick, 2008; Harris, 2016; Kass, 1997; Smajdor et al., 2018). They are notoriously difficult to express and evaluate in the context of a secular approach to bioethics. For this reason alone, they seem unlikely to carry the day in debates about the moral permissibility of MRT.

2.3.4 New Opportunities for Women Who Wish to Have Genetically Related Offspring?

It is worth observing that there is at least one group of potential users of MRT who might prefer that the genetic relationship established by contributing mitochondria to the genome of a child is recognised as a form of genetic parenthood. As Cavaliere and Palacios-González (2018) have argued, MRT provides a means for lesbian couples to have children who share a genetic connection with both parents—in this case, nDNA from one mother and mtDNA from the other. Granting that this would constitute a form of genetic parenthood might increase the attractiveness of this reproductive option for female same-sex couples.

2.4 RESOURCE ALLOCATION CONCERNS

One argument often made against new reproductive technologies, including MRT, is that investment in the development of such technologies represents an ethically indefensible (mis)use of resources given the existence of more urgent unmet medical needs elsewhere, including in the Global South (Baylis, 2013: 534). While this line of criticism has some intuitive force, especially given that, as we have argued here, MRT is really a technology to allow a relatively small cohort of potential parents to have genetically related children without mitochondrial disease rather than a cure for mitochondrial disease, it is also clear that this argument is too powerful: it is true of all but the most basic of preventative health measures in wealthy Northern nations that resources dedicated to improving the welfare of citizens could be spent more effectively, and deliver greater benefits, especially in the Global South. While governments continue to spend money on defence, sports stadiums, or subsidies for high culture, singling out MRT as immoral because the money it costs could be better used elsewhere seems unprincipled.

However, a more troubling version of this argument highlights the opportunity costs of MRT associated with the use of donor eggs for MRT. In all likelihood, achieving a live birth from MRT will require multiple oocytes. In many countries, oocytes are a scarce resource. Using numerous oocytes to achieve a live birth in a pregnancy using MRT will mean that there are even fewer available for other fertility procedures, including procedures with much higher success rates of achieving live birth from an oocyte. This may be a particular problem in countries that rely on a donation system for procuring oocytes, such as Australia. Until the techniques involved in MRT are efficient enough that it requires no more donated oocytes than ordinary IVF—or artificial gametogenesis (Hayashi et al., 2021; Chapter 10, this volume) eliminates scarcity of oocytes—it will be difficult to justify MRT while other prospective parents could make better use of donated oocytes to secure the birth of a child via IVF.

2.5 IS MRT GERMLINE GENETIC MODIFICATION?

The development of MRT has taken place against the backdrop of relatively widespread (though not universal) opposition to the clinical use of germline gene editing, at least given the current state of the science. When applied to female (but not male) embryos, MRT constitutes a form of heritable genetic modification. In this respect, it resembles forms of germline gene editing, such as the use of technologies like CRISPR/Cas9 to modify human embryos. A legal prohibition, or blanket moral rejection, of germline gene editing therefore poses an obstacle to MRT (Cohen et al., 2019; Chapters 5 and 6, this volume).[5]

There are, however, a number of significant *dis*analogies between MRT and other forms of germline gene editing (Newson and Wrigley, 2017). In particular, where proposed uses of CRISPR/Cas9, or related systems, for germline gene editing would typically involve making a small number of precisely targeted changes to the nuclear genome of the embryo (Chapter 10, this volume), MRT involves substituting a large number of genes in the form of healthy mitochondria for another similarly large bundle of genes—calling into question the appropriateness of describing the latter as 'gene editing,' even if the term 'genome modification' is appropriate (Chapter 6, this volume).[6] MRT does not rely on the process of homologous recombination that plays a central role in genome editing using CRISPR/Cas9 (and other similar systems) and, as such, might be held to be less disruptive of the 'integrity' or 'structure' of the genome than the latter. Relatedly, there is arguably now more data available regarding the risks to the health of the future child involved in MRT than is available for other forms of genome editing (although see below for some sceptical reflections on the ultimate significance of such claims about risk).

Whether these differences are sufficient to exempt MRT from concerns about the ethics of germline genetic modification will depend on the grounds on which the larger category is held to be morally problematic. This is a topic of ongoing controversy (see, for instance, Savulescu and Sparrow, 2013; Sparrow, 2021).

2.6 RISKS

For better or worse (Winner, 1986: 138–154; Rothman, 1986), debates about new reproductive technologies are typically framed in terms of their risks and benefits—and MRT is no exception in this regard. We have already observed that the benefits of MRT are much harder to characterise than is usually assumed. In this section we consider those implications of MRT that might be conceptualised as risks—although we will also emphasise, in the following section, the extent to which some of these may be understood as concerns about the meaning of reproduction and parenting.

2.6.1 Risks to Parents

As is the case with any reproductive technology—or, indeed, as does reproduction itself—MRT involves a number of risks to the health and happiness of the adults—and especially the gestational mother—who undergo the procedure. The hormonal and surgical procedures required to source ova for IVF involve a certain degree of risk to the health of the mother (and the egg donor), as does giving birth itself. These risks involved in pregnancy may be higher for women who themselves suffer from mitochondrial disease. Prospective parents may experience psychological stress during the procedure and, especially, if they do not succeed in giving birth to a healthy child. These risks don't seem different in nature, or to differ greatly in degree, to the risks that we typically hold that it is ethical to allow parents to incur in the course of trying to give birth to a healthy child. Nevertheless, it is important to acknowledge them.

2.6.2 Physical Health of the Future Child

The risks to the physical health of children conceived using MRT have been a central focus of the debate about the ethics of the procedure (Chapter 1, this volume). Will children suffer any ill effects from the cytoplasmic manipulations involved in MRT? How safe is the procedure, which will remain essentially experimental for the foreseeable future?

2.6.3 Psychological Health of the Future Child

MRT may also involve risks to the *psychological* health of the future child. For the most part, discussion of the risks to the psychological health of the future child involved in being conceived via MRT have concentrated on the possibility that children may struggle with having 'three genetic parents' or with feeling as though they do even if that is not the case (National Academies of Sciences, Engineering, and Medicine, 2016: 101): these risks may be thought to be higher or lower depending on whether or not children conceived via MRT have access to information about the identities of the individuals who donated the gametes used in the procedure.[7] However, it is worth observing that individuals conceived via MRT might also suffer harm from worrying about the long-term consequences of being conceived via an experimental procedure or as a result of differences in parental attitudes towards them associated with the difficulties involved in conceiving them.

2.6.4 Risks to Future Generations

Because mtDNA is transmitted along the maternal line, the mitochondria present in the embryos produced in MRT will be inherited by a significant portion of the descendants (if any) of the children born as a result of this procedure. In an early article on the topic, Annelein Bredenoord and colleagues (2010) note that mitochondrial donation may not fully eliminate mitochondria with harmful mutations. Although a low-level mutant load is unlikely to harm the child conceived through mitochondrial donation, it could rise to harmful levels in subsequent generations. Alternatively, if transplantation causes alteration to the genes in the mitochondria (or to their patterns of expression) that are associated with negative impacts on human health, there is a chance that these could be transmitted to future generations.

2.6.5 How Safe Is 'Safe Enough'?

Scientific research, in the form of animal models and in vitro human studies, offers one means to try to address these risks (Chapter 1, this volume). The results of such studies have brought many authorities to conclude that the risks involved in MRT are low. However, notoriously, we cannot *know* the implications of being conceived via MRT for the psychological or physical health of the person so conceived until a sufficiently large number of children have been conceived via MRT and sufficient time has passed for it to be plausible to hold that any problems that might emerge should have emerged. It will be several decades *at least* before we know whether MRT is safe or not: until that time, the procedure will remain essentially experimental. Similarly, we cannot know the impact of MRT on future generations for at least a generation. It seems, then, that we cannot gain the information needed to accurately gauge the risks involved in MRT except by incurring them.

Given this, it is perhaps fortunate for enthusiasts for MRT that they have easy recourse to a number of other arguments to claim that concerns about risk should not stand as a barrier to trialling the technology.

First, ordinary reproduction involves risks to the parents, to the physical and mental well-being of the child, and to future generations. Giving birth involves risks to the mother. As David Benatar (2006) has argued, the one thing of which one can be certain when one brings a new child into the world is that they will suffer and die. With any conception, there is a chance of a de novo mutation that might impact on the health of future generations. Our willingness to tolerate such risks undercuts any suggestion that the mere presence of a risk to the health of the child or to the health of future generations renders MRT unethical.

Second, whatever risks are involved in MRT, they are unlikely to be greater than those involved in the reproductive choices of people who carry genes for genetic disorders but who wish to conceive using their own gametes and without using preimplantation genetic diagnosis (PGD). Unless we are prepared to argue that it is unethical for parents who carry genes for genetic disorders (including women who suffer from mitochondrial disorders) to attempt to have children via natural conception, it is hard to see how the risk involved in MRT could make it unethical (Harris, 2016).

Third, the non-identity problem means that it is possible to insist that even if there is some risk that children conceived via MRT will suffer some ill effects as a result of the procedure, as long as these children will have 'lives worth living,' they will not be harmed by the procedure and thus that the procedure involves no risk of harm.

Finally, the history of the development and trialling of other ARTs establishes a high threshold of tolerance of risk for those who wish to refer to this history. All reproductive technologies are necessarily highly experimental when first trialled; other reproductive technologies have been trialled with much less information about the risks involved than is available for MRT. For instance, IVF was developed and trialled in the context of an understanding of the science of embryogenesis and the impact of cell culture media on gametes and embryos that seems woefully primitive by today's standards. Indeed, given that the oldest person conceived using this technology is yet to turn 50 (at the time of writing), there is a sense in which we *still* don't know whether there are any negative impacts of being conceived via IVF across the full course of the human lifespan. Unless we are willing to say that it was unethical to proceed to human trials of IVF at the time at which this technology was developed, we will struggle to conclude that the risks involved in MRT render it unethical.

Thus, although arguments about risk and safety have been at the forefront of the debate about the ethics of MRT, the relative ease with which such arguments can be—and often are—discounted along the lines canvassed here is a reason for a certain scepticism about the role they play in debate about this technology.

2.7 SOCIAL IMPACTS

Some of the most interesting and provocative arguments regarding the ethics of MRT concern the impacts of the development and use of the technology on our understandings of reproduction and parenthood and its implications for our future choices about other reproductive technologies, that is, its *social* impacts.

While, as we observed above, other reproductive technologies have complexified our understanding of what it means to be the parent of a child, until recently, *genetic* parenthood has followed a familiar mould; children have one (genetic) mother and one (genetic) father. The reproductive use of MRT might create a kind of 'moral confusion' about who counts as a genetic parent of the child.[8]

How seriously one takes this concern is likely to depend on how committed one is to the idea that children should only have two genetic parents. Even if one recognises the mitochondrial donor as a third genetic parent of the child, there is no reason to think that people would not be able to maintain a distinction between the nuclear genetic parents of an individual and their mitochondrial genetic parents. Nor does it seem likely that recognising this new relationship would lead to any more confusion than has been generated by the diversification of our concept of parenthood that has resulted from the widespread use of IVF, surrogacy, and gamete donation (Ball, 2014; Garasic and Sperling, 2015). For that matter, parents, children, and the broader society seem to be able to cope reasonably well with a diversity of social arrangements for the raising of children. The claim MRT will generate 'confusion' about genetic parenthood, then, seems to trade on an equivocation between mistake and uncertainty: the version of the claim based on reading confusion as 'mistake' relies on a contestable intuition that the only 'correct' number of genetic parents is 'two,' while the version based on reading confusion as 'uncertainty' relies on tendentious speculation about empirical matters.

It is also worth noting that a number of other reproductive technologies that might be developed in the coming decades would also challenge our understanding of genetic parenthood. For instance: it is unclear whether a clone of one individual should be described as having a single genetic parent (the person who was cloned) or two (the clone's parents); genome editing raises the possibility of designing children with a genome that partly resembles that of any number of existing individuals, as does the eventual possibility of synthesizing a bespoke human genome using the techniques of synthetic biology; and, advances in stem cell science may soon make it possible to create 'synthetic' embryos out of three or more stem cell lines that contribute to different parts of the body (Bowman-Smart, 2021). It may be, therefore, that we will be forced to rethink the meaning of genetic parenthood regardless of whether MRT is adopted more widely or not. Conversely, any rejection of MRT on the basis of concerns about it promoting moral confusion about genetic parenthood would have implications for the ethics of the development and use of these other technologies.

Perversely, concerns about the impacts of MRT on our concept of genetic parenthood themselves risk exacerbating the impacts of MRT when it comes to our ideas about parenthood more generally. As we noted above, given that the use of donor gametes would allow parents with a family history of mitochondrial disorders to reduce the chance of bringing into existence a child who suffers from mitochondrial disease, the case for MRT rests on the importance that some prospective parents place on conceiving a child who is genetically related to them. The choice to pursue MRT arguably reflects and expresses a judgment about the value of genetic parenthood (Schaefer and Labude, 2017). The amount of time, money, and effort devoted by scientists and regulators to make it possible for a relatively small cohort of patients to secure genetic parenthood seems to constitute a strong endorsement of the idea that genetic parenthood is better, perhaps even more 'real,' than social parenthood.

It is not unreasonable to suspect that the broader social implications of this shift in cultural understandings of parenthood are politically salient. Emphasising the importance of genetic parenthood at the expense of social parenthood may be expected to impact negatively on those who are adopted, those who have chosen to adopt, stepparents and their children, those who have had children using donor gametes and those children, and those who might be unable to become a genetic parent using any of our available reproductive technologies. This shift towards genetic understandings of parenthood has also been criticised for failing to recognise women's reproductive labour. For example, Barbara Katz Rothman (1989, 1995) has argued that the idea that 'real' parenthood is genetic parenthood, which is also promoted by the development and use of many—but not all—other ARTs, fundamentally reconfigures our understanding of the role of men and women in relation to reproduction by implying that men contribute just as much to the creation of children as do women and reducing the role of the mother's body to a 'foetal container'.[9] The valorisation of genetic parenthood implied by MRT may also contribute to a morally problematic 'geneticisation' of social and political questions more generally (Lippman, 1992; Sparrow et al., 2021; ten Have, 2001).

Finally, where societies embrace MRT, this may be anticipated to have implications for the public's attitudes towards other novel reproductive technologies. In particular, as we noted above, given that MRT is a form of germline genetic modification, public acceptance of MRT may establish a precedent with regards to the other such technologies. While there is no necessary contradiction between licencing MRT and prohibiting germline genome editing using (for instance) CRISPR/Cas9, it is not unreasonable to think that doing the former might undermine the current public consensus that germline genome editing is a step too far or that advocates of germline gene editing might refer to the use of MRT to argue that this line has already been crossed (Adashi and Glenn, 2016; Harris, 2016). Of course, whether the possibility of such social consequences counts as an argument against or for MRT will depend on one's prior sense of the ethics of germline gene editing.

We think that there is a real possibility that MRT would reshape our so-cial understandings of what it means to be a parent towards genetic ideas of parenthood and that it would make it more likely that societies will eventually embrace germline gene editing. However, the ultimate signifi-cance of these considerations for decisions about regulation and licencing of MRT turns on deeper questions in the philosophy of law and political philosophy about the sorts of goals it is appropriate for the state to pursue through legislation.

2.8 MRT AND REPRODUCTIVE LIBERTY

Even if one believes that MRT is morally problematic, it does not follow that the state should prohibit it. As a number of eminent authorities have argued, decisions around reproduction are, for many people at least, highly significant when it comes to the answer to larger questions about the nature of a good human life (Robertson, 1994: 22–42; Dworkin, 1993: 157–160). Preventing individuals from having children when they wish to, forcing people to become parents against their will, or restricting with whom individuals can have children, all frustrate projects about which people tend to care deeply. For this reason, it is widely held that such choices are protected by a right to 'reproductive liberty' or 'procreative freedom' (Brock, 1994; Robertson, 1994). One way to attempt to resolve the debate about the legalisation of MRT, then, is to insist that the choice to use MRT is included within the scope of reproductive liberty, such that it would be profoundly wrong for the state to limit access to the technology (Schaefer and Labude, 2017).

However, whether the right to reproductive liberty includes a right to access novel reproductive technologies is itself contested (Sparrow, 2008; Robertson, 2003). While it is plausible to think that preventing someone from having a child is wrong, it is less clear that preventing them from (for instance) cloning themselves is wrong. One might concede that people have a right to reproduce without conceding that they have the right to reproduce however they like and/or to shape the genetics of their child in ways that are historically unprecedented. Nor is it clear what the right to reproductive liberty implies when it comes to the obligations, if any, that governments have to *fund* the development of reproductive technologies or to facilitate the use of new reproductive technologies by establishing a regulatory framework that resolves the social and legal uncertainties such technologies tend to generate (Sparrow, 2008). It is one thing to say that it would be wrong for the state to prevent couples from accessing a reproductive technology once it exists, it is another to say that the state has an obligation to fund its development or to change the law to allow the technology to be commercially viable.

While the importance of reproductive liberty suggests that the onus should be on critics of MRT to justify restrictions on individuals accessing this technology where it exists, then, it is not possible to resolve the policy questions surrounding MRT simply by invoking a right to reproductive liberty.

2.9 SEX SELECTION

Unlike nDNA, mitochondria are maternally inherited. This means that only female offspring would pass on their mtDNA to future generations. This feature of mtDNA has led to calls to utilise sex selection in mitochondrial donation, particularly in early trials while the risks remain poorly understood, at least in cases where it would not be too costly or impose additional risks to the embryo.[10] Appleby (2015) recommends the use of sperm sorting technology to select 'male' sperm cells, since such technology—while not fully reliable—would increase the probability of having male offspring without requiring additional manipulation of the embryo. A 2016 report from the US National Academies of Sciences, Engineering, and Medicine (2016) goes further and recommends that initial clinical investigations be restricted to male embryos, selected via preimplantation diagnosis, to limit health risks to future generations.[11]

The suggestion that parents should be prohibited from conceiving female embryos using MRT has been criticised on the grounds that the benefits are arguably too speculative and/or too modest to warrant such a highly intrusive policy. As Reuven Brandt (2018) points out, we do not require individuals with recessive genetic abnormalities to use preimplantation genetic diagnosis to avoid creating asymptomatic carriers, even though such a policy would tangibly reduce health risks to future generations.

Even if sex selection should not be mandatory in the context of MRT, there is the further question of whether voluntary sex selection (of male embryos) should be permitted. This question does not map neatly onto existing debates about the moral permissibility of medical and non-medical sex selection. The selection of male embryos in MRT differs from standard cases of medical sex selection in that the aim is not to avoid genetic illness in the child being conceived, but rather to reduce the possibility of illness in future generations. It also differs from standard cases of non-medical sex selection in that the aim is not to satisfy the parents' preference for a child of one sex over another; accordingly, many common objections to non-medical selection, such as those grounded in concerns about reflecting or reinforcing sexism, seem not to apply. Many people (and jurisdictions) accept medical sex selection while rejecting non-medical sex selection. For those who hold such a view, sex selection in the context of MRT poses an ethical challenge

2.10   DONOR ANONYMITY AND THE 'RIGHT TO KNOW'

Like traditional forms of donor conception, MRT involves the use of donor gametes. For standard forms of donor conception, there is live debate about whether donor-conceived people have a moral right to learn identifying information about their donors, which is often termed the 'right to know' (Frith, 2007). According to a number of authors, and some donor-conceived individuals themselves, information about one's genetic origins can be important for donor-conceived people's well-being and/or sense of identity (Ravitsky, 2014). Some jurisdictions, including the United Kingdom and several states in Australia, have effectively established a legal right to know in the context of donor conception by prohibiting anonymous gamete donation and establishing systems to help donor-conceived people learn the identity of their donor(s) (Blyth and Frith, 2009).

Discussions of whether the right to know extends to include the right to know the identity of those who have contributed the mtDNA to one's genetic makeup have arguably been distorted by reliance on implausible claims about the role of mtDNA in determining the identity of children conceived using MRT. For instance, the Nuffield Council on Bioethics (2012) and Human Fertilisation and Embryology Authority (2015) hold, roughly, that because mitochondrial donation egg donors do not make a meaningful contribution to the resulting child's phenotype, they do not have the kind of genetic connection to the child that undergirds the right to know.[12] Even discussions that are more sympathetic to the idea that the right to know might include the right to know the identity of MRT donors, such as those of Reuven Brandt (2016) and John Appleby (2018), tend to grant that mtDNA makes less of a contribution to identity than does nDNA. However, as we argued above, these claims are false: a difference in mtDNA can make the difference between having a serious illness or not; and, phenotype is always the product of the *interaction* of genes (and environment) so that, strictly speaking, it is not possible to identify which genes are responsible for an organism having the phenotype that it does.

If the right to know is founded in the importance of knowing how one's identity has been shaped by those to whom one is genetically related or by whether one shares particular characteristics with one's gamete donor, which some donor-conceived children claim is important for their sense of self, then it seems that it should extend to include the right to know the identity of MRT donors. Moreover, as John Appleby has argued, curiosity about their genetic origins is only one of many possible reasons why donor-conceived children might want identifying information about their gamete donor(s). Some of these reasons are also relevant to mitochondrial donation, such as a desire to understand the donor's motivation and/or to thank them (Appleby, 2018: 272). Other possible motivations are unique to MRT. In the United Kingdom, parents who use MRT are advised to disclose this to their children while their children are young and to encourage their children to participate in long-term medical monitoring and follow-up by clinicians and researchers. Children who are aware that they were conceived via MRT will grow up among media and cultural attention to mitochondrial donation. Appleby argues these factors might create a desire to learn identifying information about their donors; as in donor conception more generally, some children born via MRT might feel such information is important for their sense of self (Appleby, 2018).

The right to know is ethically controversial (Harris, 2016), with some feminist critics, especially, arguing that it overemphasises the importance of genetic information (Rothman, 1998; Melo-Martín, 2014). However, if there is a right to know, the considerations surveyed here suggest that it should extend to include the right to know the identity of gamete donors who provided the mtDNA involved in one's conception.

2.11 CONCLUSION

MRT is the latest reproductive technology to offer new options to parents hoping to achieve the 'Platonic Ideal' of parenthood: the birth of a healthy, genetically related baby. It is unlikely to be the last. We have argued that the therapeutic case for this technology is weak and that the involvement of a third party, in the form of the mitochondrial donor, establishes a relationship between the donor and the child that strays from this ideal. MRT dedicates scarce resources to a relatively rare problem that might be addressed in other ways, involves unknown risks, and is itself likely to reinforce the ideal of genetic parenthood at the same time as it destabilises it. However, in these, and in many other ways, MRT is very much akin to other ARTs. Insofar as, at least when used to create female embryos, MRT is a form of germline modification, legalisation and public acceptance of MRT is also likely to have implications for social attitudes towards other technologies of germline modification, including germline gene editing. We hope our discussion here might help inform future deliberation about these questions as well as contemporary social debates about the development, regulation, and application of MRT.

ACKNOWLEDGEMENTS

Sparrow would like to thank Nick Agar and Ainsley Newson for comments and discussions that have improved this chapter and Marcy Darnovsky and Justin Oakley for assistance in locating relevant sources. This research was supported by the Australian government through the Australian Research Council's Discovery Projects funding scheme (project DP170100919) and the Department of Health's Medical Research Future Fund (project 76744). The views expressed herein are those of the authors and are not necessarily those of Monash University, the Australian Government, the Department of Health, or the Australian Research Council.

NOTES

1. Given that both of these techniques are most naturally described as involving the transfer of *nuclear* material into a denucleated egg or zygote, the appropriateness of labelling them as *mitochondrial* replacement techniques has been contested (Baylis, 2017; Newman, 2015; Newson and Wrigley, 2017; Nisker, 2015). We continue to use the term "MRT" solely because it has become dominant in the literature.
2. Couples could also avoid bringing into existence a child likely to inherit a mitochondrial disorder by sourcing a donor embryo and implanting it into the commissioning mother's (or a surrogate's) womb. However, where a child conceived using a donor oocyte would typically be the genetic offspring of the commissioning father, if not the commissioning mother, a child brought into existence using a donor embryo would not be the genetic offspring of either of the commissioning parents.
3. For an informative discussion of the "use case" for MRT, see Herbrand (2017).

4. Wrigley et al. (2015) make the more restricted claim that MST (which takes place pre-fertilisation, and will therefore likely affect which sperm fertilises which egg) affects who comes into existence, whereas PNT (which takes place post-fertilisation) does not. This, they claim, provides reasons to prefer PNT over MST. However, as Rulli (2017) points out, even in the case of PNT, were MRT not available, prospective parents would most likely have had a different child—if they chose to have a child at all. Identifying the relevant counterfactual is one of the key challenges involved in thinking through the implications of the non-identity problem for the ethics of decisions around reproduction (Douglas and Devolder, 2021; Sparrow, 2021).

5. The United Kingdom is the first—and currently only—country to change its laws and regulations to explicitly allow mitochondrial donation, though mitochondrial donation has also been performed in countries that lack explicit regulation of mitochondrial donation techniques or assisted reproduction more generally (Cohen et al., 2020; Ishii and Hibino, 2018). Other countries—including Australia—are currently deciding whether to follow the United Kingdom's lead (Koplin, 2021; Nicol and Richards, 2020).

6. Alternatively, one might describe MRT as involving "clumsy" or "crude" editing or the making of "large" edits. It is striking how what is normally portrayed as a virtue of the new genome editing systems—their relative "precision"—is here abjured for the sake of claiming that the relatively large genetic changes involved in MRT are less morally troubling.

7. We discuss the question of whether the donors of ova used in MRT should be permitted to remain anonymous or not below.

8. Writing in a different context, Jason Scott Robert and Françoise Baylis (2003) have raised the concern that novel technologies can introduce "moral confusion" that disrupts existing social and moral categories.

9. Interestingly, insofar as it draws attention to the role of mitochondria (as we have seen, discourses around MRT also try to downplay the significance of mitochondria), MRT does imply that women contribute "more" to the constitution of children than do men. However, as two of the authors have argued elsewhere, in highlighting the role of mitochondrial DNA, the development of, and discourses around MRT also contribute to the dynamic identified by Katz Rothman by neglecting and obscuring the contribution made by the cytoplasm of the mitochondrial donor and of the body of the woman who gives birth to the child (Sparrow et al., 2021).

10. Accordingly, there is a much stronger case for undertaking sex selection when PGD is already being performed than for introducing PGD purely for the purpose of sex selection.

11. The Report suggests that mandatory sex selection could eventually be dropped once the safety of mitochondrial donation is better established. The United Kingdom has not provided provisions for sex selection in its model of MRT. Indeed, MRT sex selection in the context of MRT would be inconsistent with UK legislation on sex selection, which is permitted only when there is a risk that the woman will give birth to a child at risk of a serious gender-related disability, illness, or medical condition (Human Fertilisation and Embryology [HFE] Act 1990, Schedule II, Section 1ZB (3)). The Human Fertilisation and Embryology Authority has, however, recommended that girls born following MRT be informed of the risk of transmitting mitochondrial disease to their own children (Human Fertilisation and Embryology Authority, 2014).

12. Consequently, in the United Kingdom, MRT egg donors are able to donate anonymously, whereas standard gamete donors are not (de Campos and Milo, 2018).

REFERENCES

Adashi, Eli Y., and I. Glenn Cohen. 'Going germline: Mitochondrial replacement as a guide to genome editing.' *Cell* 164, no. 5 (2016): 832–835.

Appleby, John B. 'The ethical challenges of the clinical introduction of mitochondrial replacement techniques.' *Medicine, Health Care and Philosophy* 18, no. 4 (2015): 501–514.

Appleby, John B. 'Should mitochondrial donation be anonymous?' *Journal of Medicine and Philosophy: A Forum for Bioethics and Philosophy of Medicine* 43, no. 2 (2018): 261–280.

Australian Government Department of Health. 'Press conference in Canberra about Maeve's Law, COVID-19 vaccine rollout, and assistance to Papua New Guinea.' Australian Government Department of Health, 24 March 2021. https://www. health.gov.au/ministers/the-hon-greg-hunt-mp/media/press-conference-in-canberra-about-maeves-law-covid-19-vaccine-rollout-and-assistance-to-papua-new-guinea.

Ball, Philip. 'Unnatural reactions.' *Lancet* 383, no. 9933 (2014): 1964–1965.

Baylis, Françoise. 'The ethics of creating children with three genetic parents.' *Reproductive Biomedicine Online* 26, no. 6 (2013): 531–534.

Baylis, Françoise. 'Human nuclear genome transfer (so-called mitochondrial replacement): Clearing the underbrush.' *Bioethics* 31, no. 1 (2017): 7–19.

Baylis, Françoise. '"No" to lesbian motherhood using human nuclear genome transfer.' *Journal of Medical Ethics* 44, no. 12 (2018): 865–867.

Bayne, Tim, and Avery Kolers. 'Toward a pluralist account of parenthood.' *Bioethics* 17, no. 3 (2003): 221–242.

Benatar, David. *Better Never to Have Been: The Harm of Coming into Existence*. Oxford University Press, 2006.

Blyth, Eric, and Lucy Frith. 'Donor-conceived people's access to genetic and biographical history: An analysis of provisions in different jurisdictions permitting disclosure of donor identity.' *International Journal of Law, Policy and the Family* 23, no. 2 (2009): 174–191.

Bowman-Smart, Hilary. 'Orphans by design: The future of genetic parenthood.' *Bioethics* 35, no. 1 (2021): 23–30.

Brandt, Reuven. 'Mitochondrial donation and "the right to know".' *Journal of Medical Ethics* 42, no. 10 (2016): 678–684.

Brandt, Reuven. 'Mandatory sex selection and mitochondrial transfer.' *Bioethics* 32, no. 7 (2018): 437–444.

Bredenoord, Annelien L., Wybo Dondorp, Guido Pennings, and Guido De Wert. 'Avoiding transgenerational risks of mitochondrial DNA disorders: A morally acceptable reason for sex selection?' *Human Reproduction* 25, no. 6 (2010): 1354–1360.

Bredenoord, Annelien L., Wybo Dondorp, Guido Pennings, and Guido De Wert. 'Ethics of modifying the mitochondrial genome.' *Journal of Medical Ethics* 37, no. 2 (2011): 97–100.

Brock, Dan W. 'Reproductive freedom: Its nature, bases and limits.' In *Health Care Ethics: Critical Issues*, edited by David C. Thomasma and John F. Monagle, pp. 43–61. Aspen Publishers, 1994.

Brock, Dan W. 'The non-identity problem and genetic harms–The case of wrongful handicaps.' *Bioethics* 9, no. 3 (1995): 269–275.

Cavaliere, Giulia, and César Palacios-González. 'Lesbian motherhood and mitochondrial replacement techniques: Reproductive freedom and genetic kinship.' *Journal of Medical Ethics* 44, no. 12 (2018): 835–842.

Cohen, I. Glenn, Eli Y. Adashi, Sara Gerke, César Palacios-González, and Vardit Ravitsky. 'The regulation of mitochondrial replacement techniques around the world.' *Annual Review of Genomics and Human Genetics* 21 (2020): 565–586.

Cohen, I. Glenn, Eli Y. Adashi, and Vardit Ravitsky. 'How bans on germline editing deprive patients with mitochondrial disease.' *Nature Biotechnology* 37, no. 6 (2019): 589–592.

Community Affairs References Committee of the Senate of Australia. '*Science of mitochondrial donation and related matters.*' Parliament of Australia, 27 June 2018. https://apo.org.au/node/180206.

Cruz, Ana Carolina P., Adriano Ferrasa, Alysson R. Muotri, and Roberto H. Herai. 'Frequency and association of mitochondrial genetic variants with neurological disorders.' *Mitochondrion* 46 (2019): 345–360.

De Campos, Thana C., and Caterina Milo. 'Mitochondrial donations and the right to know and trace one's genetic origins: An ethical and legal challenge.' *International Journal of Law, Policy and the Family* 32, no. 2 (2018): 170–183.

Dimond, Rebecca, and Neil Stephens. 'Contesting mitochondrial donation: The cluster against.' In *Legalising Mitochondrial Donation: Enacting Ethical Futures in UK Biomedical Politics*, edited by Rebecca Dimond and Neil Stephens, pp. 47–67. Springer International Publishing, 2018a.

Dimond, Rebecca, and Neil Stephens. 'Three persons, three genetic contributors, three parents: Mitochondrial donation, genetic parenting and the immutable grammar of the 'three x'.' *Health* 22, no. 3 (2018b): 240–258.

Douglas, Thomas, and Katrien Devolder. 'Gene editing, identity and benefit.' *The Philosophical Quarterly* (2021): pqab029. doi:10.1093/pq/pqab029.

Dupras-Leduc, Raphaëlle, Stanislav Birko, and Vardit Ravitsky. 'Mitochondrial/ nuclear transfer: A literature review of the ethical, legal and social issues.' *Canadian Journal of Bioethics/Revue canadienne de bioéthique* 1, no. 2 (2018): 1–17.

Dworkin, R. *Life's Dominion*. Alfred A. Knopf, 1993.

Frith, Lucy. 'Gamete donation, identity, and the offspring's right to know.' *AMA Journal of Ethics* 9, no. 9 (2007): 644–648.

Garasic, Mirko Daniel, and Daniel Sperling. 'Mitochondrial replacement therapy and parenthood.' *Global Bioethics* 26, no. 3–4 (2015): 198–205.

Glover, Jonathan. *Choosing Children: Genes, Disability, and Design*. Oxford University Press, 2006.

Harris, John. 'Germline modification and the burden of human existence.' *Cambridge Quarterly of Healthcare Ethics* 25, no. 1 (2016): 6–18.

Hayashi, Katsuhiko, Cesare Galli, Sebastian Diecke, and Thomas B. Hildebrandt. 'Artificially produced gametes in mice, humans and other species.' *Reproduction, Fertility and Development* 33, no. 2 (2021): 91–101.

Herbrand, Cathy. 'Mitochondrial replacement techniques: Who are the potential users and will they benefit?' *Bioethics* 31, no. 1 (2017): 46–54.

Human Fertilisation and Embryology (HFE) Act (United Kingdom). 1990. https://www.legislation.gov.uk/en/ukpga/1990/37.

Human Fertilisation and Embryology Authority (HFEA). 'Third scientific review of the safety and efficacy of methods to avoid mitochondrial disease through assisted conception: 2014 update.' Human Fertilisation and Embryology Authority, 2014. https://www.aph.gov.au/DocumentStore.ashx?id=bd2f664c-c87e-4da0-a119-6b71c78bc73a.

Human Fertilisation and Embryology Authority (HFEA). 'Explanatory memorandum to the human fertilisation and embryology (mitochondrial donation) regulations 2015.' Human Fertilisation and Embryology Authority, 2015. http://www.legislation.gov.uk/ukdsi/2015/9780111125816/pdfs/ukdsiem_9 780111125816_en.pdf.

Ishii, Tetsuya, and Yuri Hibino. 'Mitochondrial manipulation in fertility clinics: Regulation and responsibility.' Reproductive Biomedicine & Society Online 5 (2018): 93–109.

Kaebnick, Gregory E. 'Emotion, rationality, and the "wisdom of repugnance".' Hastings Center Report 38, no. 4 (2008): 36–45.

Kampourakis, Kostas. Making Sense of Genes. Cambridge University Press, 2017.

Kass, Leon R. 'The wisdom of repugnance.' New Republic, June 2 (1997): 17–26.

Kevles, Daniel J. In the Name of Eugenics: Genetics and the Uses of Human Heredity. Harvard University Press, 1995.

Kolers, Avery. 'Cloning and genetic parenthood.' Cambridge Quarterly of Healthcare Ethics 12, no. 4 (2003): 401–410.

Koplin, Julian J. 'How should mitochondrial donation operate in Australia?' BioNews, 12 April 2021. https://www.bionews.org.uk/page_155799.

Lippman, Abby. 'Led (astray) by genetic maps: The cartography of the human genome and health care.' Social Science & Medicine 35, no. 12 (1992): 1469–1476.

Melo-Martín, Inmaculada De. 'The ethics of anonymous gamete donation: Is there a right to know one's genetic origins?' Hastings Center Report 44, no. 2 (2014): 28–35.

Mills, Catherine. 'Nuclear families: Mitochondrial replacement techniques and the regulation of parenthood.' Science, Technology, & Human Values 46, no. 3 (2021): 507–527.

Molnar, Maria J., and Gabor G. Kovacs. 'Mitochondrial diseases.' In Handbook of Clinical Neurology, edited by Gabor G. Kovacs and Irina Alafuzoff, pp. 147–155. Elsevier, 2018.

National Academies of Sciences, Engineering, and Medicine. Mitochondrial Replacement Techniques: Ethical, Social, and Policy Considerations. National Academies Press, 2016.

Newman, Stuart A. 'Deceptive labeling of a radical embryo construction technique.' Huffington Post, 31 January 2015. https://www.huffpost.com/entry/deceptive-labeling-of-a-r_b_6213320.

Newson, Ainsley J., and Anthony Wrigley. 'Is mitochondrial donation germ-line gene therapy? Classifications and ethical implications.' Bioethics 31, no. 1 (2017): 55–67.

Nicol, Dianne, and Bernadette Richards. 'Mitochondrial donation: The Australian story.' Journal of Bioethical Inquiry 17, no. 2 (2020): 161–164.

Nisker, Jeff. 'The latest thorn by any other name: Germ-line nuclear transfer in the name of "mitochondrial replacement".' Journal of Obstetrics and Gynaecology Canada/Journal d'obstetrique et gynecologie du Canada 37, no. 9 (2015): 829–831.

Nuffield Council on Bioethics. 2012. 'Novel techniques for the prevention of mitochondrial DNA disorders: An ethical review.' Nuffield Council on Bioethics, 2012. https://www.nuffieldbioethics.org/publications/mitochondrial-dna.

Parfit, Derek. *Reasons and Persons*. Clarendon Press, 1984.

Ravitsky, Vardit. 'Autonomous choice and the right to know one's genetic origins.' *Hastings Center Report* 44, no. 2 (2014): 36–37.

Robert, Jason Scott, and Françoise Baylis. 'Crossing species boundaries.' *American Journal of Bioethics* 3, no. 3 (2003): 1–13.

Robertson, John. A. *Children of Choice: Freedom and the New Reproductive Technologies*. Princeton University Press, 1994.

Robertson, John A. 'Procreative liberty in the era of genomics.' *American Journal of Law & Medicine* 29, no. 4 (2003): 439–487.

Rothman, Barbara Katz. *The Tentative Pregnancy: Prenatal Diagnosis and the Future of Motherhood*. Viking, 1986.

Rothman, Barbara Katz. *Recreating Motherhood: Ideology and Technology in a Patriarchal Society*. W. W. Norton & Company, 1989.

Rothman, Barbara Katz. 'Daddy plants a seed: Personhood under patriarchy.' *Hastings Law Journal* 47 (1995): 1241–1248.

Rothman, Barbara Katz. *Genetic Maps and Human Imaginations: The Limits of Science in Understanding Who We Are*. Norton & Co., 1998.

Rulli, Tina. 'The mitochondrial replacement "therapy" myth.' *Bioethics* 31, no. 5 (2017): 368–374.

Savulescu, Julian. 'Deaf lesbians, "designer disability," and the future of medicine.' *British Medical Journal* 325, no. 7367 (2002): 771–773.

Savulescu, Julian. 'Mitochondrial disease kills 150 children a year. A micro-transplant can cure it.' *The Guardian*, 2 February 2015. https://www.theguardian.com/science/2015/feb/02/mitochondrial-transfer-micro-transplant-parliamentary-debate.

Savulescu, Julian, and Robert Sparrow. 'Making better babies: Pro and con.' *Monash Bioethics Review* 31, no. 1 (2013): 36–59.

Schaefer, G. Owen. 'Can reproductive genetic manipulation save lives?' *Medicine, Health Care and Philosophy* 23, no. 3 (2020): 381–386.

Schaefer, G. Owen, and Markus K. Labude. 'Genetic affinity and the right to "three-parent IVF".' *Journal of Assisted Reproduction and Genetics* 34, no. 12 (2017): 1577–1580.

Scott, Rosamund, and Stephen Wilkinson. 'Germline genetic modification and identity: The mitochondrial and nuclear genomes.' *Oxford Journal of Legal Studies* 37, no. 4 (2017): 886–915.

Siekevitz, Philip. 'Powerhouse of the cell.' *Scientific American* 197, no. 1 (1957): 131–144.

Smajdor, Anna, Daniela Cutas, and Tuija Takala. 'Artificial gametes, the unnatural and the artefactual.' *Journal of Medical Ethics* 44, no. 6 (2018): 404–408.

Sparrow, Robert. 'Cloning, parenthood, and genetic relatedness.' *Bioethics* 20, no. 6 (2006): 308–318.

Sparrow, Robert. 'Is it 'every man's right to have babies if he wants them'?: Male pregnancy and the limits of reproductive liberty.' *Kennedy Institute of Ethics Journal* 18, no. 3 (2008): 275–299.

Sparrow, Robert. 'Therapeutic cloning and reproductive liberty.' *Journal of Medicine and Philosophy* 34, no. 2 (2009): 102–118.

Sparrow, Robert. 'Liberalism and eugenics.' *Australasian Journal of Philosophy* 89, no. 3 (2011): 499–517.

Sparrow, Robert. 'Imposing genetic diversity.' *The American Journal of Bioethics* 15, no. 6 (2015): 2–10.

Sparrow, Robert. 'Human germline genome editing: On the nature of our reasons to genome edit.' *American Journal of Bioethics* (2021): 1–12. Online first, 19 April 2021. doi:10.1080/15265161.2021.1907480.

Sparrow, Robert, Catherine Mills, and John Carroll. 'Gendering the seed: Mitochondrial replacement techniques and the erasure of the maternal.' *Bioethics* 35, no. 7 (2021)" 608-614.

Strong, Carson. 'Harming by conceiving: A review of misconceptions and a new analysis.' *Journal of Medicine and Philosophy* 30, no. 5 (2005): 491–516.

ten Have, Henk A. M. J. 'Genetics and culture: The geneticization thesis.' *Medicine, Health Care and Philosophy* 4, no. 3 (2001): 295–304.

Thorburn, David, and John Christodoulou. '3-parent IVF could prevent illness in many children (but it's really more like 2.002-parent IVF).' *The Conversation*, 11 November 2019. https://theconversation.com/3-parent-ivf-could-prevent-illn ess-in-many-children-but-its-really-more-like-2-002-parent-ivf-126591.

Turkmendag, Ilke. 'It is just a "battery": "Right" to know in mitochondrial replacement.' *Science, Technology, & Human Values* 43, no. 1 (2018): 56–85.

UK Department of Health. 'Draft regulations to permit the use of new treatment techniques to prevent the transmission of a serious mitochondrial disease from mother to child.' UK Department of Health, 2014. https://www.gov.uk/ government/uploads/system/uploads/attachment_data/file/332881/Consul tation_response.pdf.

Van Oven, Mannis, and Manfred Kayser. 'Updated comprehensive phylogenetic tree of global human mitochondrial DNA variation.' *Human Mutation* 30, no. 2 (2009): E386–E394.

Winner, Langdon. *The Whale and the Reactor: A Search for Limits in an Age of High Technology*. University of Chicago Press, 1986.

Wrigley, Anthony, Stephen Wilkinson, and John B. Appleby. 'Mitochondrial replacement: Ethics and identity.' *Bioethics* 29, no. 9 (2015): 631–638.

3

Reproductive Decisions and Mitochondrial Disease

Disruption, Risk, and Uncertainty

CATHY HERBRAND

3.1 INTRODUCTION

This chapter aims to provide insights into the experiences and challenges of having a family and making reproductive choices in the context of mitochondrial disorders, insights that are currently missing from debates on mitochondrial donation and, more broadly, from social science literature. Situating new mitochondrial donation techniques amidst the various decisions and options parents or prospective parents need to consider when family plans are disrupted by mitochondrial disease puts the potential benefits of this reproductive technology into perspective and provides context to understand its meaning in patients' lives.

'Mitochondrial disease' is an umbrella term that encompasses a set of complex genetic conditions that are highly variable and have very uncertain outcomes (Chinnery, 2000; Chapter 1, this volume). While the disease tends to severely affect children from early on, it may also affect adults of any age to various degrees. The symptoms and syndromes experienced are usually caused by dysfunctions of the cell energy production process, but they can vary greatly and cause, for instance, hearing loss, seizures, diabetes, myopathy, epilepsy, and heart problems. It is a degenerative

Cathy Herbrand, *Reproductive Decisions and Mitochondrial Disease* In: *Reproduction Reborn*. Edited by: Diana M. Bowman, Karinne Ludlow, and Walter G. Johnson, Oxford University Press. © Oxford University Press 2023. DOI: 10.1093/oso/9780197616192.003.0004 illness, which means that symptoms are likely to increase over time, possibly leading to death, particularly in young children. There is no cure or efficient treatment available. Women at risk of transmitting a mitochondrial disorder thus often face a number of difficult questions if they wish to have children, especially as their access to reproductive and screening technologies, such as prenatal diagnosis (PND) and preimplantation genetic testing (PGT), is conditioned on various factors. Yet little has been said about how women at risk of transmitting these disorders view and experience their situation and come to make difficult decisions regarding having children in the face of complex and uncertain medical information and limited reproductive options.

While families affected by mitochondrial disorders have negotiated reproductive issues for a long time, these issues were particularly brought to public attention by the public and parliamentary debates that took place around the legalisation of mitochondrial donation in the United Kingdom, mostly between 2012 and 2015 (Chapter 4, this volume). This set of new high-profile reproductive technologies aims to prevent the transmission of maternally inherited mitochondrial disorders by creating an embryo combining the genetic material from three different people (Chapter 1, this volume). During the years preceding the adoption of the Human Fertilisation and Embryology (Mitochondrial Donation) Regulations 2015, there was considerable media attention around the techniques themselves and the tragedy faced by the families they were intended to help. Typically, the women 'at risk' featured in the media were healthy women with seriously ill children or women who had lost a child and were desperate to have another. Mitochondrial donation was usually depicted as their only solution to have a healthy biological child, which, once legalised, would become quickly available for and requested by women at risk of transmitting mitochondrial diseases.

The accounts I collected during interviews with women at risk of transmitting mitochondrial disorders revealed a much more nuanced and complex picture than was presented in the media, where choices were not straightforward and decisions depended on a number of ideals, medical factors, and social constraints, which made each situation unique and the use of reproductive technologies simultaneously appealing, uncertain, and contingent. This was particularly the case for potential use of mitochondrial donation, as in reality this technology is only suitable for a very limited number of women carrying a faulty mutation (Herbrand, 2022, 2017). These accounts also highlighted the much more diverse profiles and situations of these at-risk women and the particular difficulties they may face when having to make reproductive choices in a context of considerable uncertainty due to the nature of these complex diseases.

While much discussion has been and is still dedicated to the ethical, legal, and medical aspects of mitochondrial donation, very little sociological data and analyses are available about what is happening to patients (with the exception of Dimond, 2013) and prospective parents who are at risk of transmitting mitochondrial disorders. For this reason, it also is important to shed light on what this technology means for patients and how it could fit into their lives amongst the various challenges they need to overcome to possibly have a(nother) child. This chapter aims to give a voice to the women at risk of transmitting mitochondrial disorders who want to have children, as these were the potential beneficiaries of mitochondrial donation as broadly described in the media and the UK public and parliamentary debates on this new technology.

The chapter begins by setting out the multilayered disruptions to their own biographies encountered by women finding themselves at risk of transmitting mitochondrial disorders. The second part then explains how the characteristics of the disease itself make reproductive choices in the context of mitochondrial disorders especially challenging and transform prospective parents' reproductive journey into a long 'obstacle race' with very uncertain outcomes. Five major difficulties faced by affected families are examined and illustrated via examples provided by participants. The third part describes how, despite the many problems to overcome, prospective parents showed a strong desire and persistent efforts to have healthy children who are biologically related to them. In this context, reproductive technologies were therefore invested with much hope and efforts as the most efficient means to reach this desirable outcome. The fourth part illustrates how, in this context, mitochondrial donation was a technology that empowered women with respect to mitochondrial disease in the present, but for whom reproductive hopes were oriented towards a further future.

This chapter draws on qualitative research exploring reproductive choices in the context of mitochondrial disorders (the Mitofamily study). It comprised in-depth interviews with 28 women, ranging from 18 to 51 years old, who were all at risk of transmitting the disorder. They all lived in England and were white, apart from one woman from a South-Asian background. As this chapter focuses on the perceptions and choices with respect to reproductive options, four women were excluded from the analysis because they were no longer able or willing to have children.[1] Among the 24 participants who had not yet completed their family,[2] 14 women were carrying a nuclear mutation (all have had a child affected by the disease) and 10 women were carrying a mitochondrial mutation and were physically affected by the disease themselves, at risk of developing it in the future, or asymptomatic carriers. Among these 10 women carrying a mitochondrial mutation, 6 were childless. In total, 10 of the 24 participants had lost a child from a mitochondrial disorder, and 8 of them had an affected child. Participants were recruited through the national patient cohort database held at Newcastle University and a national support group, and ethics approval was granted from De Montfort University and the London NRES Committee.

3.2 BEING AT RISK OF TRANSMITTING A DISEASE: BIOGRAPHICAL AND REPRODUCTIVE DISRUPTIONS

To understand reproductive choices in the context of mitochondrial disorders, it is first important to consider the multilevel biographical disruption (Becker, 1997) that constitutes the discovery of being at risk of transmitting a potentially severe genetic condition (i.e., how it threatens, questions, and impacts an individual's life, identity, and expectations on various levels). The women I interviewed happened to learn about this risk because they were themselves affected by it physically or after having a child or a relative diagnosed with a mitochondrial disorder. Women carrying a nuclear defect or asymptomatic carriers of a mitochondrial mutation are usually unaware of their reproductive risk until their child is diagnosed with the disorder. Most of the time, biological and genetic tests may provide a diagnosis of the condition after often experiencing disparate symptoms. This direct or indirect diagnosis often happened after months or years of questioning and was at times accompanied by the loss of a child or maternal relative. It usually constituted a profound biographical disruption in participants' life, not only in terms of their personal identity in becoming a carrier, a patient, or a 'patient-in-waiting' (Timmermans and Buchbinder, 2010), but also with respect to their family situations and expectations. It meant fearing and facing the implications of this diagnosis for their own health or that of a close relative, perhaps grieving the loss of a loved one, while realising they might have transmitted or were at risk of transmitting this condition to their offspring. Alice recalled the shock and numerous questions her brothers and she suddenly faced when their mother, who had encountered various mild and serious symptoms over the years, eventually was diagnosed with a maternally inherited mitochondrial disease.

It was a shock because with these conditions, we had done a bit of reading up on it, and we knew there were implications for the children. When they came back and said "yes, it's tested positive for this genetic mutation," it was like a huge shock for not only my mum but also myself and my two brothers. Because we thought "well, what is it for us? what is going to happen to us?" We had seen what happened with my mum and we were just so worried that something was going to happen the same to us. But, at the same time, we kind of felt relieved because we had a name for what had been going on.

Many participants told a story similar to Alice's. Often, the diagnosis of a mitochondrial disease in the family, followed by the news that they were at risk of transmitting this disease, came as a surprise. Most participants were not aware of having a family history of the condition. This contrasts with Dimond's study, which focused on patients with a known family history of maternally inherited mitochondrial disorders and who often anticipated the diagnosis as confirmation of their symptoms (Dimond, 2013).

Biographical disruption caused by the diagnosis and at times by the death of a close relative was further amplified if participants wanted to have a child or further children because they had to reconsider their family plans in light of the transmission risk and the impact that the disease could have on their current and future situation. For instance, Alice felt 'devastated' when she realised the implications, particularly around having a family.

All of a sudden, when we got this diagnosis and to learn of the implications of it, it kind of just hit me like a bus thinking "oh god, it's not going to be a normal life for you. This genetic mutation is part of your family and I know it may mean that you can't have your own children." And, up until that point, you always just think well I will get married and I will have children and I will just be like every-body else. And then all of a sudden, it's like well no you won't, it's not going to be like that for you. Oh, it was terrible.

Some women and couples I interviewed also had to put their plans on hold because they had an ill child and close relative to take care of, one whose condition was likely to deteriorate. This was the case of Amber and her husband, who were ready to have another child when they learnt that their first daughter had a mitochondrial disease.

I think had [our daughter] not got, you know, not ill, ill is the wrong word, but had she not had issues at that point, we'd probably . . ., we were quite keen to have three children. She was coming up to 2, it probably would have been around about the time we might have started thinking about having another one. So that definitely halted that process. It's like "ok, we need to understand more about this . . . before we go down that route."

All the women knew what the disease could be like and had faced it in one way or another, through either direct bodily experience, because they had or were developing the disease, or through close emotional ties with an ill relative they were caring for. Interestingly, despite this experiential knowledge of the disease (Boardman, 2017), which provided them with an understanding of the impacts of the disease in practice, they were still determined to have one or additional children. This desire seemed even more intense for those participants who had lost a child (10 out of 24).

As for the women who had symptoms of the disease and had been diagnosed, many were not in a position to have children yet but were hoping to become mothers in the future. Despite their medical difficulties, and perhaps because of their disease, the desire to have children constituted a great source of motivation, and several of these women were ready to go to great lengths to achieve this goal. Achieving parenthood was often experienced as an affirmation of their willingness to overcome their physical condition and create something positive, which helped them look to the future in an optimistic way.

3.3 UNDERSTANDING RISK AND REPRODUCTIVE OPTIONS

After realising that they were at risk of transmitting a mitochondrial disease, most women and couples I interviewed turned to the internet or medical specialists to try to figure out what the risks and their different reproductive options were. It is important to emphasise that, in the case of mitochondrial disorders, these options are specific to each medical situation and often complex to understand, involving much uncertainty and dependent on several factors. In particular, five overlapping elements related to the particular characteristics of the disease make reproductive decisions especially complicated for at-risk prospective parents: (1) the difficulty of determining and assessing the risk of transmission, (2) the uncertain and complex illness trajectory, (3) the potential necessity to take care of one's own or someone else's illness, (4) the limited and conditional access to reproductive techniques, and (5) the social isolation caused by heterogeneous experiences.

3.3.1 The Difficulty of Determining and Assessing the Risk of Transmission

While the women I interviewed had been identified as being at risk of transmitting a mitochondrial disorder, they did not necessarily know what their chance of transmission was because it depended on the type of mutation they carried. Not only are there hundreds of single mutations which can cause mitochondrial disorders, but these mutations can follow different inheritance patterns, which makes it especially complex to determine the transmission risks for this disease. The UK debate on mitochondrial donation highlighted the existence of *maternally inherited* mitochondrial disorders because the new technology under discussion aimed to prevent only these particular type of disorders by replacing the mutated mitochondria contained in the mother's egg or embryo. However, it needs to be remembered that these disorders can also be transmitted by both parents. The calculation of the risk of transmission depends on the location of the DNA mutation and possibly the mutation loads, as mutations can be situated either in the nuclear DNA or in the mitochondrial DNA. If the mutation is in the nuclear DNA and is transmitted by both parents, there is usually a one in four chance of transmitting the disorder,[3] but if the mutation is in the mitochondrial DNA, there is no precise way of calculating the risk of transmission. This risk is always present and depends on how the mitochondria multiply in the embryo, as small amounts in the egg can increase rapidly in the cells of the embryo or fetus, a process known as the *mitochondrial bottleneck* (Chapter 1, this volume). In practice, this means that women carrying a maternally inherited mitochondrial mutation (10 out of 25 participants) could only get a vague approximation of their chance of transmitting the disorder based on the biopsy of some of their tissues, which made future projections especially uncertain and stressful.

However, it is important to note that for those couples who had been told that they had a one in four chance of transmitting a severe disorder caused by a *nuclear* defect (14 out of 25 participants), the assessment of their risks was not easy either, especially if they already had an affected child. Mina, whose first child was affected, explained.

> I suppose if somebody had said to me before we had Maria [her daughter], it's one in four, I'd have been like "that's not bad odds" but she was the one in four. So then, when I think she was the one in four, it's quite easy that there could be another one in four. Where [her partner] was very: "oh that's better than I thought, I thought it was going to be like one in two or almost definitely." So he was very . . ., but he's like that all along, he still is now, he doesn't mind, he's just

like, if it is, it is, where I'm a bit more . . . I don't know if it's because I spend most of my time with her, I've always been a bit like "one in four." . . .

Mina's account illustrates how her experience of having an affected child and becoming a full-time caregiver has impacted the way she perceives the transmission risk. This experiential knowledge gained through her daughter's severe illness has made her more hesitant to take this risk, dreading the possibility of having to relive the suffering and difficulties she had already been through. Overall, it appeared difficult for many participants not only to know what their risks of transmission were, but also, when they knew this information, to make sense of it and base their reproductive decisions on this relative risk ratio or uncertain estimation.

3.3.2 The Uncertain and Complex Illness Trajectory

Because this chapter focuses on reproductive decisions, the ways in which the disease is experienced in daily life and across generations by patients and affected families are not developed here (see Dimond, 2013). It is important, however, to emphasise how uncertainty regarding the development, progression, and severity of mitochondrial disease made reproductive decisions especially challenging for at-risk women. The way the disease evolves over time is highly unpredictable, even within the same family. Many mitochondrial disorders have incomplete penetrance, meaning that siblings carrying the same faulty mutation may develop the disease very differently and at different ages. Some of them might not even develop the disease. That was the case in one of the families involved in the study. While the mother had not developed any symptoms, she had passed her mitochondrial mutation to her four children: one of them was severely affected by the disorder and died from it, another had started developing mild symptoms, and the others had no sign of the disease at all. It was therefore difficult for participants to anticipate what would happen if they conceived a child without medical assistance, not knowing whether the offspring would carry the mutation and, if they did, whether they would develop the disease, when, and to what extent. Participants then tried to imagine what their life and that of an affected child could be by relying on their personal experience of the disease or what they had observed in affected relatives or by considering the worse form of the condition affecting their family. Uncertainty around the illness trajectory meant that prognosis regarding mitochondrial disorders could not be considered as a solid and reliable criterion in participants' reproductive decision-making.

3.3.3 The Potential Necessity to Take Care of One's Own or Someone Else's Illness

Another factor which could further complicate decisions about having children for women at risk of transmitting mitochondrial disease related to the necessity for many of them to care for themselves or for currently ill children. This could indeed interfere with their capacity to raise a(nother) child. Seven participants were themselves at risk of developing the disease or were already affected by the disease. They knew that symptoms were likely to develop or deteriorate over the coming years, which raised the question of the extent to which they would be physically able to carry a pregnancy, manage their symptoms, and, later on, raise children and possibly take care of an ill child because the disease was likely to impact not only their everyday life but also their life expectancy. For instance, Beth, who was in her early 20s, childless and in a relationship for three years, was beginning to experience extreme fatigue and much lower energy levels. She told me,

> Well I don't want to have a child that has any [faulty] mitochondria at all, just
> because I think it would be hard for me showing symptoms and things like that.
> I think it would be hard for me to then deal with a child that has the same as
> what I have, you know, with my energy levels and things like that, it would be
> really hard for me to cope. I wouldn't want to have to go through what we went
> through with Tom again [her brother who died from mitochondrial disorders]
> and I just think it would be . . . I just would like a healthy baby [laughs].

Beth's account was embedded in her own experience of living with the increasing signs of the disease and that of her brother who was severely affected. She did not think she would be physically able to cope with a child who was disabled, as she often felt weak and could see how much energy it required when her mother had to take care of her brother. As other studies on decision-making in the context of a chronic illness have shown (Hudson and Law, 2022), it is interesting to see here 'how embodied uncertainty and reproductive desires intersect with symptom-management to produce a distinctive set of experiences.' Those participants who were already affected by the disorders had therefore to think carefully about the kind of extra support they could get if they were to have a child and what would happen if their health condition were to worsen in the future.

It is also worth mentioning that eight participants in my research had a severely ill child at the time of the interview, one who required a lot of time, attention, and resources. This situation was usually quite challenging, physically and emotionally, especially when they had more than one child, like Sarah, a mother of three children, with one child affected by a nuclear defect.

> It's so disrupting when you have got young children, a husband that needs to carry on working, children at school and a child that's in and out, and in and out of hospital. It's massive for the whole family. And having a very poorly little girl that we just didn't know where to go next because we just kept treating, her getting home, and bouncing back in and out again.

The day-and-night intensive care, the regular and often urgent visits to the hospitals, and the constant fears regarding the child's illness progression had prompted these mothers to stop working in order to dedicate all their time and efforts to taking care of their child. Mina explains the shock of learning that her child had a severe degenerative disease while also suddenly having to become a nurse for her.

> And then at the same time, they were throwing some drugs, some vitamins at us and said: "you need to give her these," and then we had to wait for the prescription to come from the pharmacy and then it arrives and the pill crusher arrives and I don't know how to use a pill crusher. So you're just kind of all of a sudden thrown into needing to be a nurse for your daughter as opposed to a mother, and there's no support for that really, in the early days, and you're not really in the right headspace to become a nurse for her when you just want to be a mum.

Some of these mothers strongly wanted another child but, given the special needs of their existing child and the financial impact and stress this was adding to their relationships, they were struggling to imagine how they could cope with another. Amanda had lost a child from a mitochondrial disease and reflected on how anxious she was about the future and the care of her other older healthy child when her child was ill.

> I just didn't know if I was going to be changing his nappies when he was 50, I just had no idea. That was the scariest thing, is just that it could go on forever or it could just get worse and he could be ill. I used to worry that if he gets more— because I read so many of the mitochondria stories—and if he gets more and more ill and weak, and what if he's in [hospital in London] for a year, you know, what about G. [older healthy child]? How does she get?

In some cases, the situation was further complicated by the fact that the interviewed couples knew that their ill child had little chance to survive beyond a few more years, which created a real dilemma for them as they wanted to have more children but found it difficult to do so in these circumstances and in light of what was coming up. Trying to conceive another child meant that they might find themselves having to care for a dying child and grieve his loss while simultaneously dealing with a pregnancy and welcoming a newborn into their family. Two couples in this particular situation nonetheless decided to go ahead with having another child. Overall, for women who had to care for either themselves or a close relative, this necessity was weighing on their reproductive decision as they had to consider how it would affect their parenting capacity and availability.

3.3.4 The Limited and Conditional Access to Reproductive Techniques

While several screening or reproductive technologies, such as PND and PGT, exist and may *potentially* prevent the transmission of a mitochondrial disorder, they have their own drawbacks: PND may lead to a selective termination, and PGT often proves costly and time-consuming. Moreover, access to these technologies is limited in practice by a number of factors. Above all, it depends on the type of mutation causing the disorder and whether it has been possible to identify it. It is important to emphasise that PND and PGT are most efficient for couples carrying a nuclear defect and for whom the faulty mutation has been identified. The particular faulty mutation must also be approved by the Human Fertilisation and Embryology Authority (HFEA) before a clinic may be licenced to use PGT or PND to test for it, a procedure which may prove quite lengthy. The fact that several women I interviewed were still in the process of seeking a licence for the nuclear mutation which had affected their child, with the hope of being able to use PGT or PND, indicates that scientific advances and reproductive possibilities in this field are rapidly evolving.

Moreover, current criteria to access National Health Service (NHS) funding for reproductive treatments are quite restrictive. For instance, in my study, several couples met the medical criteria for PGT but were not eligible for NHS funding because they did not meet the social eligibility criteria, such as not already having a healthy child from their current or previous relationship. They therefore had to forego the option of PGT and use PNT at 3 months of pregnancy because they could not afford private treatment.

It is also worth emphasising that 4 of the 24 women included in this analysis could use neither PND or PGT as their particular nuclear mutation had not yet been identified. The genetic diagnosis could indeed take years or might not even happen, as many nuclear defects causing mitochondrial disorder remain unidentified. They were therefore left with the possibilities of waiting for a genetic diagnosis, taking the risk of conceiving without medical assistance, or turning to adoption or gamete donation. This situation often created a real dilemma for these couples, who often felt left in limbo and torn between the risk of transmitting the disorder and an intense desire to have a biological child.

As for women carrying a maternally inherited mitochondrial disorder, it is usually possible to identify their faulty mutation since all the potential faulty mutations present in mitochondria are known. PGT is therefore possible but can only reduce the risk of transmission; it does not guarantee a child unaffected by the disorder because mitochondrial mutations, even in small amounts in the egg, can increase rapidly in the cells of the embryo or fetus. PGT is thus only suitable for women whose mutation load is low enough since they have better chance of producing an embryo with a very low mutation load to be implanted. The same uncertainty persists with PND as it can offer an indication of the fetus's mutation load, but it is difficult to assess how this mutation load will evolve and to what extent the future child will be affected. For women with a high mutation load, both technologies are therefore not advisable, and there is no other option for them than adoption or egg donation. It is for these cases that mitochondrial donation could provide, if all necessary conditions are met (Herbrand, 2017), an opportunity to have a healthy and biologically related child by transferring the mother's egg nucleus into a donated enucleated egg whose mitochondria are not affected.

3.3.5 Social Isolation and Uncertainty Caused by Heterogeneous Experiences

Because mitochondrial disorders are particularly diverse in terms of mutations, prognoses, inheritance patterns, and symptoms, medical treatments—including reproductive options—are often specific to prospective parents' particular situation. This contributes to making the search for relevant information and support more challenging. While most participants in my study had spent much time and effort consulting different sources of information on the topic, it often proved difficult to figure out what options were suitable and available for them. This required them, first, to find and understand a wide range of the complex and sometimes contradictory medical information regarding their own condition or that affecting their child or relative(s). Moreover, if they were ill or had an affected child, they often had to prioritise the consultation of various medical specialists regarding the management of the condition itself before being able to meet with a genetic counsellor. The information provided could then be quite intense and difficult to digest in one go.

This diversity of situations among people affected by mitochondrial disorders also meant that, while a number of patients and families were connected through and at times involved in patient support groups, it was often difficult for a particular individual or family to find other people who experienced a similar situation and with whom to share information and advice in terms of treatment or reproductive options. Amber recalled her first contacts with the main patients' group.

> That was it, we said "we want to get in touch to see what support you offer, to see if there are other families", and I think she [the head of the group], even in that first email back, said "I'd be hesitant to put you in touch with another family directly because everyone's experiences are so different." And I guess she couldn't very easily, it's not like you could match a family and say "ok, well you're quite similar to them so. . . . Even if the similar ones are similar, they're not the same.

Another consequence is that communicating clear and relevant information appears especially challenging for patient support groups, as each case would ideally require a tailored package of information.

To sum up, the particular nature of mitochondrial disease and its related consequences created uncertainty at many levels for at-risk prospective parents, which made reproductive decisions in this context particularly difficult. Often, the women I interviewed found themselves in complicated daily life situations where they had to manage their own condition or care for an ill relative. In this context, medical treatment for the condition might overcome reproduction considerations as seeking access to reproductive technologies seemed quite distant and removed from their everyday life. In addition to these possible practical challenges, which had be overcome in order to be in a position to consider having children, these women had to make important and detailed decisions while missing crucial information regarding their future health and that of their relatives. In this respect, the case of mitochondrial disorders is quite unique as the difficulties surrounding reproductive choices in this context often intersect, creating situations where the difficulties and risks related to the transmission of inherited a genetic condition with variable inheritance patterns and trajectories often overlap with those of living with a chronic and degenerative illness. Prospective parents therefore often faced dilemmas, torn between a limited number of options which were not straightforward and not without significant inconvenience. They learn to navigate uncertainty along the way, as explained by Ruth, who lost a child to a mitochondrial disorder and was seeking to have another child through PGT.

> It's trying to understand all the difficulties of going through this journey. Yes, it's trying to weigh up your options, trying to think what's going to be best for your family and what's going to be most successful without causing too much heartache. Yes, that's what the problem is [nervous laugh]. Yes, and also making decisions with all this uncertainty. If someone said "right, this is what you need to do and it's going to work," then you would go for it, without a doubt, wouldn't you? But when there's so much uncertainty and you don't know if it's going to work.

Ruth's words sum up well how planning for and having children in this context usually constituted a journey made of obstacles, often upsetting, and where prospective parents struggled to find the least damaging solution.

3.4 THE IMPORTANCE OF HAVING A HEALTHY BIOLOGICAL CHILD

Despite the challenging circumstances they found themselves in and the risk of transmitting the disorder, it was striking to observe how important it was for the participants in my study to have a child or subsequent children who were healthy *and* biologically related to them. This double imperative guided the reproductive decisions of most women and couples I interviewed.

It is first important to emphasise that, based on their experience of the disease, the vast majority of participants made clear that they would not take the risk of transmitting the disorder, as Mina explained.

> I wouldn't take the risk as don't want to see another child suffer that way. The thing for me is that it's not that I wouldn't cope or we wouldn't manage, it's because I feel for her because of everything that's happened. . . . It's me choosing to give that child that life, I know that it's my choice and I wouldn't wish what she's got on anybody.

Those who had the maternally inherited version were also categorical that they wanted to avoid transmission, like Alice, whose mother had developed various symptoms. At the time of interview, Alice was in her late 20s, had no children, and was the asymptomatic carrier of a mitochondrial mutation.

> But we both [her and her partner] decided together that if there is any chance at all that I could pass it on, then we don't want to take that risk. . . . Because I have seen what mitochondrial disease can do and on the scale of things, I think my mum's case is actually fairly mild. I have joined different groups on Facebook of people in similar situation and they appear much worse off. Many of them have lost children or miscarried or lost babies. . . . And I just think it's been so horrible to see what it's done to my mum, I couldn't possibly risk seeing that happen to my own baby. And possibly it be worse.

It is worth noting here that, unlike other inherited conditions, such as inherited deafness or spinal muscular atrophy, for which attitudes regarding the condition and its transmission are more ambivalent and diverse (Boardman, 2014; Scully, 2013), there was a general sense, in the accounts I collected, that mitochondrial disease had to be avoided by all means and if possible eradicated. It was never considered as a disability that could be an important element of one's identity (Chapter 2, this volume).

Although most at-risk women I interviewed were determined to avoid transmitting the disorder, they also firmly wanted to have a biological child. This desire was especially apparent in the way the majority of these women did not want to turn to or consider adoption or gamete donation, even when they could not access reproductive technologies. Having a child who was healthy and biologically connected to them appeared to be essential conditions for many participants in order achieve the family or the maternity they wanted, and this might explain why reproductive technologies appeared so appealing to them. Indeed, nearly all the women I interviewed, whether they were directly affected by the disorder or were asymptomatic carriers, said they were interested in using, now or in the future, some kind of reproductive or screening technologies in order to have children and avoid transmitting the disorder to them. In particular, nine women had an affected child and had their mutation identified were trying or had tried to access either PGT or PND.

Despite the physical and emotional difficulties involved, participants were persistent in their effort in trying to access selective reproductive technologies in order to achieve a healthy pregnancy. The example of Jess and Marc was quite striking in this respect: this couple had a first healthy child, followed by a second child who became ill and died aged one. While they initially wanted to use PGT, they realised they were not eligible for

NHS funding as they already had a healthy child. Unfortunately, they were not able to pay for PGT themselves, with a cost of around £10,000 per cycle. They then decided that they would use PND, so they tried conceiving naturally. Jess fell pregnant and had the test after three months. Unfortunately, the fetus was found to have the mitochondrial mutation and Jess had to go through a selective termination. She explained how painful and frustrating these first three months of waiting had been for them and how traumatic it had been to go through a selective termination. They hesitated to start again, but they were reluctant to turn to gamete donation and adoption as they really wanted to have another biological child. So, they tried again and went through another stressful 3 months of pregnancy; again, the fetus appeared affected after being tested and Jess had a second abortion. Despite their distress and frustration, they tried a third time. Fortunately, they were luckier this time and the fetus was found healthy; by chance I bumped into them a few months later at a patient event that they attended with their baby.

For would-be parents who could access reproductive technologies, it seemed that the way they approached reproductive options was similar to that shown in previous studies on infertility (Becker, 2000; Franklin, 1997): that 'patients are not able to consider alternatives to a biological child (such as adoption or living childless) until they have exhausted all their medical and financial resources' (Perrotta and Hamper, 2021). When people I interviewed knew they could access a reproductive technology which would offer them prevention, biological relatedness, and the experience of pregnancy, they wanted to use it and keep trying, sometimes for years and despite the considerable efforts, disappointment, and possible costs it could involve before considering alternative options (Appelton, 2004). In this respect, and all things considered, the case of Jess and Marc was a positive one, as, despite the horrendous experiences they had to go through, their journey ended well. Not every couple did manage to have a child at the end of the road though.

As for those women who had the disease themselves, either with mild or more severe symptoms, none of them had used or considered PND or PGT, mostly because they were not in a position to have children at the time of the interview. They either did not have a partner or did yet not feel ready. Because of this, they had not investigated further existing options, and most of them knew little regarding PND and PGT. However, as mentioned earlier, they all expressed the desire to have children in the future, in a way that made sure they did not transmit their disorder. The prospect of potentially having access to mitochondrial donation was therefore something which gave them much hope and that they entirely supported, although without knowing whether they would meet the conditions to use it (Herbrand and Dimond, 2018).

3.5 MITOCHONDRIAL DONATION AS A REPRODUCTIVE OPTION

At the time of my study, the legalisation of mitochondrial donation was discussed in the media and in Parliament. Most people I interviewed had heard of it and were overly in favour of it, many of them supporting the campaign for its legalisation in various ways. For example, many had contacted their Member of Parliament, attended the debates at the Parliament, shared their stories in the media, helped with the fund raising, etc. While most participants knew they would never be in a position to use mitochondrial donation themselves because of their particular genetic and medical situation, they thought that it was positive that the debate was drawing attention to families affected by mitochondrial disorders and that it might help get support for patients' groups, as reflected in the following exchange with Amanda, a woman who had a child affected with a nuclear defect:

Question: Going back to the debate on mitochondrial donation, have you seen that this has had any kind of impact on the way your friends knew about that or talked about mitochondrial disorders?
Yes, it definitely made, more people would say "oh, we've heard about that, that's what [your child]'s got, isn't it? We've heard about it on the. . . ." It definitely raised people's awareness of it, definitely. Because nobody, I mean we'd never heard of mitochondria, nobody had ever heard of it and it's only really in the last couple of years because it's been on the news and because people know about [my child] and things, that it's come out really, hasn't it. So I think it's made a big difference in terms of that, it's definitely raising a lot of awareness.

However, women with a child who was affected by a mitochondrial disease caused by a nuclear defect also recognised that the debate created some confusion among their relatives and friends as everyone assumed they could benefit from the technology to have unaffected children, whereas this was not the case.

The women who were carrying a nuclear defect were nonetheless hoping that mitochondrial donation would make a difference for women affected by a maternally inherited mutation.

People knew that I was excited about this happening, obviously not for our family, but we know other families it's going to have a massive impact on. And so friends that aren't mitochondrial disease related were congratulating me on the news, and that's lovely that they were able to see what a big step forward it was for people that we know.

In this respect, asymptomatic carriers of a maternally inherited mutation had often been presented in the media as the future beneficiaries of the technology, especially those who had lost a child from the disease. As they were healthy, their mutation load was likely to be relatively low, which meant they could also use PGT, though this was not mentioned or discussed in public debates (Herbrand, 2022). Presented with those two potential reproductions options, it was not always clear, however, what these women would prefer or be ready to try. For instance, Amber, an asymptomatic carrier with two daughters, explained that, despite being fully supportive of mitochondrial donation, PGT, in her view, was a cheaper and simpler option, which also appeared less experimental.

> I suppose as much as I'm hugely, hugely supportive of the legislation that's gone through, I'm not sure I'd want to be the first to do it is my honest view. For us, that was massively important for them [her daughters] when they're older, when, you know, in 20-odd years time, it will be more normal, more routine, they'll have a view of how babies who have been born via that method have progressed and stuff. Yes, so it just feels a bit scary to be first.

Kylie, another participant and an asymptomatic carrier and mother of two, who could potentially use both options shared similar concerns.

> Well, I think as PGD has now obviously been around for a little while, so it's been, I suppose, to a certain extent tried and tested. Mitochondrial replacement therapy is a new technique, so it's untrodden ground, you don't really know how things are going to progress.

While she might be reluctant to be the first one to use mitochondrial donation, Kylie was convinced of the importance of campaigning in favour of its legalisation as this fed into the wider awareness which needed to be raised around mitochondrial disorders.

> Even though it was mitochondrial donation, I still feel that it was still mitochondrial awareness. If you knew about mitochondrial donation, you must know about the disease. . . . If I was trying to push forward that technique, it

is still people understanding and knowing that there is something called mito-chondrial diseases out there, and I think that's one of the things that I was very much focused on. The more people we could speak to on the radio, the more newspaper pictures and interviews that we could do, and the more [TV shows] we could go and see, the better it was.

As for women who were already affected by the disease or at high risk of developing it because of their family history, PGT was unlikely to be an option as their mutation load had to be low enough if they were to have a chance of finding an embryo with a low percentage of mutated mitochondria. These women were therefore especially keen about the legalisation of mitochondrial donation and some of them, like Alice, were harbouring the hope that they could use it at some point.

> With everything being so doom and gloom about the diagnosis, it seemed like a bit of a ray of light at the end of the tunnel. Because it would give us the opportunity to live a normalish life, even though we are a family affected by mitochondrial disease, we will still be able to have a family and be normal. Knowing that our babies not going to be affected by it.

However, Alice, like the other women affected by disease or at risk of developing it, was in a situation where she was not considering having children immediately, so this prospect remained quite hypothetical and likely to depend on the progression of her medical condition and her future access to the technology.

Rebecca Dimond and I have explained elsewhere why only a minority of the women affected by mitochondrial disorders that we interviewed in our two separate studies had considered mitochondrial donation for personal use. However, the majority of them did support fervently the legalisation of mitochondrial donation, mostly in the hope that these techniques could help their daughters or other affected families to have healthy children in the future (Herbrand and Dimond, 2018). This was a huge source of motivation which prompted many participants to play a key role in the UK public and parliamentary debates by becoming advocates who shared their stories and supported the campaign in favour of the new technology. In this respect, the debates on mitochondrial donation and its legalisation empowered many patients and attracted attention to a complex and severe disease which often leaves patients and their families feeling devastated and isolated. The development of mitochondrial donation techniques has also constituted a significant scientific achievement which might generate further knowledge and techno-medical innovations in the future.

However, the current impact of these techniques in practice for families affected by mitochondrial disorders should not be overstated. In the United Kingdom so far, 7 years after the legalisation of these techniques, no child born through the use of mitochondrial donation has been made public yet, potentially demonstrating the specificity of the techniques and the barriers to its use (Herbrand, 2017).

3.6 CONCLUSION

In this chapter, mitochondrial donation techniques have been situated in the broader context of the reproductive decisions women at risk of transmitting mitochondrial disorders need to make if they want to have children while facing much uncertainty and a number of difficulties. By providing important and much needed contextual background information on the disease and its implications, this chapter helps us understand how the nature of mitochondrial disease makes reproductive choices particularly complicated for at-risk women. If they want to have a healthy and biological child, they often need to go through many questionings and a long road filled with obstacles whose outcome remains highly uncertain. Five elements which make their reproductive journey especially challenging have been considered in this chapter: (1) the difficulty of determining and assessing the risk of transmission, (2) the uncertain and complex illness trajectory, (3) the potential necessity to take care of one's own or someone else's illness, (4) the limited and conditional access to reproductive techniques, and (5) the social isolation caused by diverse experiences. These various difficulties at-risk women have to overcome means that their initial family plans end up being considerably challenged and need often to be postponed or reconsidered in the face of the disease.

However, the accounts of women at risk of transmitting mitochondrial disorder presented in this chapter show how many of them never considered giving up on having a child and deployed much effort to have a child who is *both* healthy and biologically related, these being two essential considerations in their reproductive decisions. The women I interviewed were all aware of the risks at stake and took them seriously, and nearly all of them sought actively not to transmit the disease. Technologies such as PND, PGT, or mitochondrial donation often appeared as the best way of achieving this, especially while maintaining a biological connection to the child. Many participants in my study deployed considerable effort to pursue having a child through PND and PGT and persisted despite experiencing several failures. In this context, mitochondrial donation was invested with very high hopes, especially by those who were directly affected by or at risk of developing the disease. These accounts also demonstrate that while reproductive technologies are increasingly considered as an easily accessible and efficient way of having a healthy biological child, they still raise numerous challenges in practice in terms of costs, risks, invasiveness, availability, and suitability.

Overall, this chapter has highlighted how women at risk of transmitting mitochondrial disorders face a number of difficulties which need to be carefully considered while attempting to improve patients' lives and reproductive options. Understanding more about the complexities of those who may seek treatment through mitochondrial donation remains imperative within this context. Moreover, there are significant medical and financial constraints which limit the applications not only of mitochondrial donation but also of PND and PGT in practice, and these need to be addressed together if the ultimate goal is to help families with mitochondrial disease have the children they wish.

NOTES

1. The research project also included interviews with UK experts in the field and the analysis of a wide range of publicly available documents relating to the UK public and parliamentary debates on the legalisation of mitochondrial donation. These were not included in the chapter.
2. Nine of the 24 women were interviewed with their partners, when they opted to participate. Only women's accounts are presented here.
3. In rarer cases, there are also possibilities for the nuclear mutation to be X-linked or autosomal dominant, which means that the couple would have a 50 percent chance of transmitting the mutation. The mutation might also be a spontaneous one which appeared in embryo.

REFERENCES

Appelton, Susan Frelich. 'Adoption in the age of reproductive technology.' *University of Chicago Legal Forum* (2004): 393–451.

Becker, Gay. *Disrupted Lives*. University of California Press, 1997.

Becker, Gay. *The Elusive Embryo: How Women and Men Approach New Reproductive Technologies*. University of California Press, 2000.

Boardman, Felicity Kate. 'The expressivist objection to prenatal testing: The experiences of families living with genetic disease.' *Social Science & Medicine* 107 (2014): 18–25.

Boardman, Felicity K. 'Experience as knowledge: Disability, distillation and (reprogenetic) decision-making.' *Social Science & Medicine* 191 (2017): 186–193.

Chinnery, Patrick F. 'Primary mitochondrial disorders overview.' *GeneReviews* (2000, updated 2021). In GeneReviews® [Internet], edited by M. P. Adam et al. Seattle, WA: University of Washington, 1993–2022. https://www.ncbi.nlm.nih.gov/books/NBK1224/.

Dimond, Rebecca. 'Patient and family trajectories of mitochondrial disease: Diversity, uncertainty, and genetic risk.' *Life Sciences, Society and Policy* 9, no. 1 (2013): 1–11.

Franklin, Sarah. *Embodied Progress: A Cultural Account of Reproduction.* Routledge, 1997.

Herbrand, Cathy. 'Mitochondrial replacement techniques: Who are the potential users and will they benefit?' *Bioethics* 31, no. 1 (2017): 46–54.

Herbrand, Cathy. 'Silences, omissions and oversimplification? The UK debate on mitochondrial donation.' *Reproductive Biomedicine & Society Online* 14 (2022): 53–62.

Herbrand, Cathy, and Rebecca Dimond. 'Mitochondrial donation, patient engagement and narratives of hope.' *Sociology of Health & Illness* 40, no. 4 (2018): 623–638.

Hudson, Nicky, and Caroline Law. 'Chronic uncertainty and modest expectations: Navigating fertility desires in the context of life with endometriosis.' In *Technologies of Reproduction Across the Lifecourse* (Emerald Studies in Reproduction, Culture and Society), edited by V. Boydell and K. Dow, pp. 83–99. Bingley: Emerald Publishing Ltd, 2022.

Perrotta, Manuela, and Josie Hamper. 'The crafting of hope: Contextualising add-ons in the treatment trajectories of IVF patients.' *Social Science & Medicine* 287 (2021): 114317.

Scully, Jackie Leach. 'Deaf identities in disability studies.' In *Routledge Handbook of Disability Studies*, edited by Nick Watson, Alan Roulstone, and Carol Thomas, pp. 109–121. Routledge, 2013.

Timmermans, Stefan, and Mara Buchbinder. 'Patients-in-waiting: Living between sickness and health in the genomics era.' *Journal of Health and Social Behavior* 51, no. 4 (2010): 408–423.

PART II

The Evolution of Regulatory Frameworks for MRT

4

Legalising MRT in the United Kingdom

REBECCA DIMOND AND NEIL STEPHENS

4.1 INTRODUCTION

In 2015, the United Kingdom became the first country to legalise mitochondrial replacement therapy (MRT), a complex reproductive technology using part of a donated egg to replace faulty mitochondria that
can cause severe disease. Legalisation followed an extensive review process, one focusing on safety and efficacy, ethical concerns, and assessing
public opinion and public support. This involved the work and resources
of key stakeholder institutions such as the Department of Health (DoH),
the Human Fertilisation and Embryology Authority (HFEA)—which is
the UK regulator for the research and use of human tissue and embryos—
and the Wellcome Trust, which resourced the core research conducted
at Newcastle, UK. This chapter explains how MRT moved towards the
clinic in the United Kingdom, in highly contested debates about its risks
and benefits. Most of the evidence collected from this range of activities
(which we collectively name 'the MRT debates') supported the dominant
view that MRT was at a stage of development appropriate to be considered
for clinical use, that there was clear patient need, and that the risks of
transmitting severe mitochondrial disease were higher than the risks of
using the technology. In this chapter, we first explain the UK historical context, the stringent yet liberal approach to supporting embryo research that
enables scientific development and through which the United Kingdom

Rebecca Dimond and Neil Stephens, *Legalising MRT in the United Kingdom* In: *Reproduction Reborn.* Edited by: Diana
M. Bowman, Karinne Ludlow, and Walter G. Johnson, Oxford University Press. © Oxford University Press 2023.
DOI: 10.1093/oso/9780197616192.003.0005

can claim several 'world firsts.' We then consider how safety, ethics, and public opinion were assessed, part of which involved mobilising an 'interpretive package' through which the techniques were given meaning and where those meanings were also contested. The UK debates were notable because they were adversarial in nature, and here we explore the power of the dominant view of the rightness of legalisation. We then consider how the work of review and debate were significant as they contributed to the production of an ethical future for MRT by making it knowable, desirable, ethical, and sanctionable. Finally, we conclude by considering the legacy of the MRT debates and how it might shape contestations around the latest technology, CRISPR/Cas9 gene editing.

4.2   MRT AND THE UNITED KINGDOM CONTEXT

Mitochondria are structures in the cytoplasm of a cell. Their main role is to produce energy for each cell, and each cell contains hundreds to thousands of mitochondria depending on its energy requirements. Mitochondrial disease is caused by the failure of mitochondria, and it can have wide-ranging implications, often of late onset; it can also lead to infant mortality (Chapter 1, this volume). While both sexes can inherit mitochondrial disease, diseases caused by mutations in mitochondrial DNA are transmitted through the female line, which means that only women are at risk of transmitting the disease to their offspring. The Wellcome Trust Centre for Mitochondrial Research in Newcastle, UK, has been at the forefront of developing techniques to prevent disease transmission. Two techniques have been their focus, using a reconstructed egg (before fertilisation) or embryo (after fertilisation), formed through the nuclear DNA from the intended mother and father and mitochondrial DNA from a woman known as the *donor*. In the United Kingdom, both techniques were legalised at the same time, despite ethical differences between the two (Gómez-Tatay et al., 2017; Palacios-González, 2017).

In the context of a potentially severe disease with little treatment options and no cure, reproductive technologies which can prevent transmission have been widely welcomed. Several other reproductive options are available. including egg donation, prenatal testing, and preimplantation genetic testing, but because of the complexity of mitochondria transmission these might not be suitable for all women. MRT has been represented as the only option for some women to have healthy, genetically related children.

One of the reasons why the United Kingdom was the first country to assess and legalise MRT was that it has a long and established history of reviewing and regulating embryo research. The UK approach is described as a permissive, yet highly scrutinised regime (Mikami and Stephens, 2016; Reubi, 2013). Formal regulation was developed and introduced following the birth of and concern about Louise Brown, the first 'test tube' baby, in 1978 (Strathern, 1992), and subsequently through the establishment of the HFEA. The HFEA regulates, monitors, and licences research and use involving human tissue and embryos in the United Kingdom under the Human Fertilisation and Embryology Act 1990 (HFE Act). The possibility that the transmission of mitochondrial disease can be prevented through assisted technologies was recognised in the United Kingdom following a DoH (2000) report on stem cell research, and the first research licence, using abnormally fertilised human eggs, was granted in 2005 by the HFEA to the research group in Newcastle.

As was the case for MRT, changes to the legal framework can only be achieved with the agreement of parliament. The UK Parliament is made up of the House of Commons for Members of Parliament (MPs) (locally elected political representatives) and the House of Lords, served by some who have inherited their position through land ownership and those who been invited in recognition of their skills or experience. In 2008, both Houses of Parliament agreed to an amendment of the 1990 HFE Act, part of which permitted discussion about future clinical use of MRT (Jones and Holme, 2013). Following the first successful proof of concept study in 2010, which confirmed the potential of MRT to prevent the transmission of mitochondrial disease (Craven et al., 2016), the government acted on the powers within this amendment and began the process of review and parliamentary vote which would lead to legalisation. What followed was a period of about five years during which safety, ethics, and public opinion were assessed in order to inform and persuade Parliament about the benefits and implications of their vote.

4.3 ASSESSING SAFETY, ETHICAL QUESTIONS, AND PUBLIC OPINION

Safety was assessed by an independent panel of scientists organised through the HFEA at the request of the DoH. Members of the panel were selected on the basis of 'broad-ranging scientific and clinical expertise' and with 'no direct interests in the outcome of the review' (Human Fertilisation and Embryology Authority [HFEA], 2011: 27), with additional members subsequently invited depending on specific technical expertise. They drew on evidence from United Kindgom and international experts to consider the current state of understanding of mitochondria research and note areas which were still in development. Following the publication of their initial findings, the panel requested further information to assess progress, and subsequent updates were published in 2013, 2014, and 2016. The panel concluded that 'the evidence it has seen does not suggest that these techniques are unsafe' (HFEA, 2014b: 4; see also HFEA, 2016). While the report suggested that MRT could be 'cautiously adopted' into clinical practice, it recommended that research continued in order to better understand the biology of mitochondria, including mito–nuclear interactions in humans. Those against legalisation, including religious groups such as Christian Action and the Roman Catholic academic institute the Anscombe Bioethics Centre, and secular groups such as the public interest watchdog Human Genetics Alert (HGA), the Scottish Council on Human Bioethics, and Campaign on Reproductive Ethics (CORE), were not satisfied with the review process, believing it to be rushed, and expressed particular concern about the inadequacy of its conclusions. There were calls for additional scientific reviews before clinical application to ensure greater certainty in terms of risk to the child and to future generations. However, for those supporting legalization, the review process was seen as extensive and thorough, and reports that no evidence had been found that would indicate a scientific reason why MRT should be prevented from further development was broadly welcomed (Greenfield, 2014). A degree of uncertainty was also seen as acceptable and inevitable as new scientific developments moved towards first clinical use. This is particularly so in the context of the '14-day rule,' which prevents research being conducted on embryos beyond 14 days. While this determines the extent of embryo research in the United Kingdom, as it has done in other countries, many scientists support its extension to further the possibilities of understanding human development. The International Society for Stem Cell Research (ISSCR) has relaxed this rule in its latest research guidelines in favour of a case-by-case consideration (Subbaraman, 2021).

Furthermore, additional layers of protection would be in place through licencing of each individual clinic and each individual clinical application (British Medical Association, 2015). Overall, the government accepted the final recommendations of the expert panel, that 'in specific circumstances, [MRT] are cautiously adopted in clinical practice where inheritance of the disease is likely to cause death or serious disease and where there are no acceptable alternatives' (HFEA, 2016: 3).

Alongside the scientific reviews was a process of consultation and public engagement. The Nuffield Council on Bioethics, which is the closest the United Kingdom has to a national bioethics institution, was one of the first to call for evidence. It reported on several issues identified as ethically contentious, including the rights and responsibilities of the mitochondrial donor, genetic parentage, the identity of the future child, the health implications for the child and future generations, how this will be monitored, and implications for society. The report concluded that it would be ethical to conduct further research to pursue clinical use, and it would be ethical for families to use MRT.

> Due to the health and social benefits to individuals and families of living free from mitochondrial disorders, and where potential parents express a preference to have genetically-related children, on balance we believe that if these novel techniques are adequately proven to be acceptably safe and effective as treatments, it would be ethical for families to use them, if they wish to do so and have been offered an appropriate level of information and support (Nuffield Council on Bioethics, 2012: xvi).

The prominent role of the Nuffield Council on Bioethics, in terms of their findings being used as evidence in subsequent reports and debates, is not surprising. Bioethics has played a historical and increasingly prominent role in the UK process of assessment and review in assisted reproductive technology. The initial conception of the HFEA recognised bioethics as an intermediary between politics, biomedicine, and the public, with the potential to enhance scientific credibility and transparency (Wilson, 2011). The Nuffield Council on Bioethics report was not just significant for its conclusions: it also established the parameters for ethical debate by excluding alternative questions about priority setting and resource allocation (Baylis, 2017), alternative uses such as the potential (yet currently prohibited) benefits for older women seeking fertility treatment and lesbian couples seeking a child genetically related to both (Dimond and Stephens, 2017), and further legitimising the boundary between science and ethics (Lewens, 2019).

Understanding public attitudes and valuing their opinion is now a familiar and expected part of the project of reviewing technology, particularly so in the early stages of technological development (see, e.g., Franklin, 2013; Kelty and Panofsky, 2014; Kerr et al., 2007; McNeil and Haran, 2013). A public consultation was launched by the HFEA based on a broad approach to engagement including workshops, focus groups, and questionnaires, with the aim to assess public understanding about MRT and attitudes towards legalisation. These explored issues such as modification of embryos, implication for identity, status of the mitochondrial donor, and general attitudes about legalising MRT. The HFEA concluded that

[o]ur advice to Government, set out in this report, is that there is general support for permitting mitochondria replacement in the UK, so long as it is safe enough to offer in a treatment setting and is done so within a regulatory framework. Despite the strong ethical concerns that some respondents to the consultation expressed, the overall view is that ethical concerns are outweighed by the arguments in favour of permitting mitochondria replacement (HFEA, 2013: 4).

The DoH also launched a public consultation which focused on the detail of the draft regulations (DoH, 2014). Although it included a section on costs, this was not explored further in the final report. Financial costs and benefits did not appear to be significant motivators during the UK debates. The economic impact of mitochondrial donation in the United Kingdom may not be significant in the long term due to its use for a small number of patients and where initial use is funded through the National Health Service (NHS) rather than private clinics. The conclusions from these multiple reviews all pointed towards the same direction, providing evidence of support for legalising MRT when the techniques were considered safe enough to be offered in a regulated clinical setting.

4.4 AN 'INTERPRETIVE PACKAGE': GENE MODIFICATION, 'THREE-PARENT' BABIES, AND MITOCHONDRIA AS BATTERY

Across the MRT debates, there was evidence of key themes and ideas and a set of vocabulary that were used to explain MRT. MRT is a complex technology, far beyond the experience of most people, which meant that part of the task of assessment was to make the techniques meaningful so that they and their implications could be understood. The choice of terminology matters, as it is through language that particular risks, benefits, and voices can be highlighted or silenced, and many of the tools used to explain MRT also became a site of contest. These interrelated sets of terminologies formed an 'interpretive package' (Gamson and Modigliani, 1989) which was used by those involved in the debates in different ways to assign a particular meaning to the techniques and what they represent.

As we will see, some aspects of the interpretive package were specific to MRT, particularly those describing mitochondria as battery, and in discussions about whether MRT results in a 'three-parent baby.' But some have relevance beyond MRT, such as employing a particular definition of genetic modification, where its use in the MRT debates might have significant implications for the regulation of future technologies. The DoH played an important role in not just assessing opinion about MRT, but also in establishing specific ways in which the technology should be known. An example of the definition of genetic modification in relation to MRT can be seen here, in the DoH report on the topic.

> While the Government accepts the techniques do result in germ-line modification, in that the result of mitochondrial donation—the avoidance of the transmission of a serious mitochondrial disease—will be passed down to future generations, it has consistently rejected claims that the techniques constitute genetic modification and remains firmly of that view. . . .
>
> There is no universally agreed definition of 'genetic modification' in humans—people who have organ transplants, blood donations or even gene therapy are not generally regarded as being "genetically modified." While there is no universally agreed definition, the Government has decided to adopt a working definition for the purpose of taking forward these regulations. The working definition that we have adopted is that genetic modification involves the germ-line modification of nuclear DNA (in the chromosomes) that can be passed on to future generations. This will be kept under review.
>
> On the basis of that working definition, the Government's view is that the proposed mitochondrial donation techniques do not constitute genetic modification (DoH, 2014: 15).

The words of the DoH are significant here and have considerable implications for the meaning that we attribute to MRT and its route to legalisation. First, it acknowledges that MRT constitutes germline modification (see e.g., Newson and Wrigley, 2017), addressing the implicit question of whether a technology which modifies the germline could be considered problematic. The DoH accepted that the techniques were germline, but describe this as having positive implications: avoiding the inheritance of serious disease. More contentious was the question and the conclusion of whether the techniques constituted genetic modification. Here the DoH perform important discursive work. Producing a definition of genetic modification was considered acceptable, even desirable, in the context that there is 'no universally agreed definition' and that this would be productive for the debate. Nuclear DNA is ruled into this definition, and, significantly, mitochondrial DNA is excluded. Although the DoH have extensively defended this approach, the practice of redefining the object of enquiry for the purpose of easing legalisation has been criticised.

The role of the mitochondrial donor was widely discussed within the MRT debates, with questions of biological accuracy of the 'three-parent baby' label (Baylis, 2013; Cohen and Alikani, 2013) and the implications for the child (Bredenoord et al., 2011; Scully, 2017). The status of the donor was important to clarify because of its legal significance, as the rights and responsibilities of egg donors towards any children born (and issues such as anonymity) are closely regulated by the HFEA. In the case of MRT however, the DoH concluded that

> Genetically, the child will, indeed, have DNA from three individuals but all available scientific evidence indicates that the genes contributing to personal characteristics and traits come solely from the nuclear DNA, which will only come from the proposed child's mother and father. The donated mitochondrial DNA will not affect those characteristics (DoH, 2014).

The conclusion of the DoH reflected the views of many of those involved in the debates, acknowledging that while the child would inherit DNA from the mitochondrial donor, this did not mean that the donor should be seen as a genetic parent. Part of the reason why this approach was considered acceptable was because of the way in which mitochondrial DNA was represented in terms of the quantity and quality of genetic material. First, mitochondria contribute a very small amount of DNA in total, and, second, only nuclear DNA is represented as contributing to a child's 'personal characteristics and traits' (see also, Chapters 2 and 5, this volume).

A key recurrent feature of the interpretative package was a set of phrases used to name the techniques, which took on the format of 'three-x,' with the main example being 'three-parent baby,' and other formulations including 'three-parent family,' 'three-person DNA,' and 'three-person IVF [in vitro fertilisation].' This became an immutable grammar with popular appeal (Dimond and Stephens, 2017). We can see its precedents as early as 2004, for example, in the newspaper headline 'Science Seeks to Deliver a Baby with Three Parents' (Haran et al., 2008: 127). More recently there has been an explicit recognition of the power of the 'three-x' label. Those who supported legalisation were much more likely to contest the biological accuracy of 'three-parent baby' and the genetic relationship that it implies, with calls by some individuals and organisations, such as Progress Educational Trust, for it to not be used by media because of its inaccurate yet persuasive appeal. It is important to consider what the 'three-parent' labels achieve, particularly in how they conceptualise a relationship between the child and mitochondrial donor, with the 'three-parent baby' suggesting a much closer genetic relationship than 'three-person IVF.' These labels, of donor, mother, or contributor, also have implications for how the physical and emotional labour of egg donation are represented in the process of MRT. Haimes and Taylor (2017) highlight an ambiguous role for egg donors, who are central to the MRT process yet rendered invisible in the debates. They suggest that this positioning was strategic in enabling MRT to follow a smoother pathway to legalisation, yet this 'othering' of egg donors could have a longer legacy in the form of detrimental impact on donor recruitment in the future.

Alongside the 'three-x' debate, the 'battery' metaphor was one of the most often used and contested devices for making sense of MRT and its implications. Its power is in its simplicity: if the role of mitochondria is as a battery, then MRT can be easily rendered unproblematic because it simply involves 'changing the batteries.' Part of this, of course, is that it also minimises the role of the donor and her genetic contribution (Turkmendag, 2018; Sparrow et al., 2021; Chapter 2, this volume). The battery metaphor has been used frequently throughout the United Kindom debates. For example, one of the scientists involved in the Newcastle group, when it received its first research licence, was quoted as saying, 'I would use the analogy of simply replacing the battery in a pocket radio to explain what we are doing. You are not altering the radio at all—just giving it a new power source' (Highfeld, 2005). The emphasis here is that changing a battery does not induce change in the product that it powers. The battery metaphor was also used by the DoH in explicitly stating how MRT replaces rather than alters.

> The proposed mitochondrial donation techniques only allow for unaltered nuclear DNA to be transferred to an egg or embryo that has unaltered healthy mitochondria. The key consideration is that these techniques only replace, rather than alter, a small number of unhealthy genes in the 'battery pack' of the cells with healthy ones. Most importantly, mitochondrial donation techniques do not alter personal characteristics and traits of the person (DoH, 2014: 15).

Again, the DoH is doing important discursive work here. The battery metaphor is used to explain the process of MRT: that it is just replacing the power source rather than altering anything of significance and where identity (defined here as 'personal characteristics and traits of the person') is reduced to nuclear DNA and therefore remains intact. The battery metaphor has been identified as a useful tool to represent the main role of mitochondria as the 'powerhouse of the cell.' However, this approach can be questioned as reductionist. Other biological components within the cytoplasm are transferred in the process, and a complex relationship between nuclear DNA and mitochondrial DNA might be affected by MRT (Hyslop et al., 2016; see also Dimond and Stephens, 2018; Chapter 1, this volume).

We have seen how the MRT debates link to particular images, such as the three-parent baby, but there were also images in use which suggested that a different future should MRT be legalised. Mention of a 'slippery slope' towards 'designer babies' reflects a rhetoric of fear, as identified by Mulkay (1993) in work exploring the 1990 HFE Act debates. However, what was interesting about the MRT debates was that this rhetoric of fear was not used only by those campaigning against legalisation, but also by those in support. For example, in one parliamentary debate, Baroness Warwick used these concepts to support her own case.

> All the evidence I have seen and the arguments I have heard reassure me that this is not a slippery slope or an open door, or any other cliché. Nuclear DNA is not altered, so donation will not affect the child's appearance or personality, or its uniqueness. It will simply allow parents to choose to have children who are genetically related to them but who are free from potentially devastating disease (House of Lords debate, 2015: col. 1608).

This approach was used numerous times, mostly by those in support of the technology, such as by Lord Turnberg who argued that,

> suggestions that mitochondrial transfer techniques . . . are on the slippery slope to genetic manipulation and designer babies when there is no conceivable link between them, are very unhelpful. (House of Lords debate, 2015: col. 1583)

It is significant to note that, in the parliamentary debates, only those arguing for legalisation used the term 'designer babies.' Thus, these terms, which are central to a rhetoric of fear, are actually used as a resource by those in favour of legalisation.

4.5 AN ADVERSARIAL YES–NO CAMPAIGN

The legalisation of MRT occurred within debates which were inherently adversarial, with supporters and opposers of legalisation frequently sharing a stage (whether in meetings or through publications) to debate their differences. Thus, the MRT debates required and relied on the intense investment of the two sides (which we call 'clusters') who were fighting for or against legalisation.

Ultimately, those supporting legalisation produced a stronger campaign. The for-cluster had representation from key institutions, including explicit institutional support from the Wellcome Trust that was funding the technologies, and more implicit encouragement from the DoH and Nuffield Council on Bioethics. Such institutional power was supplemented by the work of a broad range of institutions and individuals. The accounts of members of this cluster highlight how this was a well-organised campaign directed by those with experience of the UK process of assessment. Key stakeholders met frequently to consult and coordinate their activities. This group had access to significant resources, which they could use to support their work and provide training where necessary. Patients and spokespeople were offered media training when needed.

But importantly, this group represented the dominant perspective of the appropriateness of legalising MRT as a reproductive technology. Those in support were able to draw on the sense of hope that it brought patients, and patients themselves were willing to contribute to the campaigns and advocate for the technology even if they might not use it themselves.

Herbrand and Dimond (2017) identified how hope played an important role within the UK debates, through an 'affective economy' (Buchbinder and Timmermans, 2014) in which the debates operated (Chapter 3, this volume). Patient narratives focusing on child suffering were powerfully used to encourage investment in MRT on behalf of patients, producing a simplified account of both patient experience and reproductive decision-making (Dimond, 2013). It is important to note—and is a testament to the power of the rhetoric of hope—that patient perspectives and the benefits of MRT for patient choice and life enhancement were not contested by those who opposed MRT. Indeed, most were keen to explicitly express their support for preventing patient suffering. This was the case in one of the parliamentary debates, where Fiona Bruce, a keen opponent of legalisation explained her position in the context of support for patients.

> Human mitochondrial disease is a dreadful condition and, as a caring society, we must do all we can to address it, and do so as sensitively as we can for those families affected by it. As a caring society, however, we must also do so in an ethical manner and with proper regard for safety. I believe that the regulations we are considering today fail on both counts—ethics and safety—and that they are inextricably interlinked. (House of Commons debate, 2015: col. 168)

In contrast to the strong and collaborative approach of those in support of legalisation, the campaigning work of those in the against-cluster was much less powerful and, ultimately, unable to offer a persuasive account against legalisation. Those speaking out against legalisation were a much smaller number of people within the UK, with access to far fewer resources. But importantly, they were much less well-organised, representing a diverse set of backgrounds, including pro-life, religious, and secular, and a range of concerns, including safety, societal value, and embryo politics. In contrast to those supporting legalisation, those opposing were often required to navigate and defend their position. This was the situation for the Church of England, which declared its support for legalisation after its initial declaration of opposition was questioned (Mason et al., 2015; Rayfield and McCarthy, 2015). The Church of England national adviser for medical ethics and health and social policy explained that while members of the Church would have liked to have seen more debate about the ethical differences between the two techniques and for further research to have been conducted before legalisation, they did not oppose legalisation in principle. This was also the case for parliamentarians, many of whom had to defend the allegation that they were opposed in principle to MRT and IVF more generally. The debates were remarkable in terms of which voices were absent. Although a few scientists expressed concern about various elements of MRT, by far the dominant scientific voice was in support of legalisation. Likewise, the UK mitochondrial debates did not feature any patient voices who were against legalisation, compared to the very strong narratives of those in support.

The issues for the against-cluster, in terms of being less organised and resourced, were compounded because they were operating against the grain of recent UK policy decisions on the topic of embryo research and use. The United Kingdom has a history of legalising novel practices in this area, including those prohibited in other nations. As such, the against-cluster's failure must be understood in relation to a sustained dominant way of thinking and acting in the United Kingdom, what we call a *sociotechnical imaginary*, that meant the UK context was always amenable to legalisation. Yet, while the against-cluster were not successful, it is important to note the role they played within the debates. Whether through institutional reports, expert groups, or public consultations, the presence of competing voices enabled the assessment of MRT to appear and thus become consultative. In this regard, the engagement of the against-cluster actually helped to legitimatise the process of review undertaken in the UK.

This given, it is not surprising that there were divergent views about the appropriateness of the review process and its outcome, which could be mapped on to broader beliefs about legalising MRT. Those supporting legalisation reflected on the success of a lengthy process of review based on transparency and respect for both the science and for the expression of alternative perspectives. Public support was explained in the context of clear communication strategies, of communicating complex information accurately, and a rightness in supporting the development of a reproductive technology that addressed patient need. Those against legalisation identified very different issues with a system that they considered problematic in many ways, pointing to a process of assessing safety that was rushed, collusion between key institutions, inappropriate representation of embryo research, detrimental impact of MRT on individuals and society, and inequality in resources that supported the dominant perspective.

4.6 LEGALISATION OF MRT IN THE UNITED KINGDOM

The UK reviews, consultations, and debates culminated in a final parliamentary debate and vote. In February 2015, the House of Commons and then the House of Lords confirmed overwhelming support in favour of supporting the legalisation of MRT. As a result of parliamentary approval, the Human Fertilisation and Embryology (MRT) Regulations 2015 came into force. While enabling MRT to be offered to patients, several restrictions are in place. Legalisation is limited to the two techniques developed at Newcastle. A third technique, *polar body transfer*, was considered in a separate review process published as an addendum to the 2014 scientific review, which concluded that it did not raise significantly different issues but was at a much earlier stage of development (HEFA, 2014a). MRT would only be available to those at risk of transmitting severe mitochondrial disease, and only through individual licences for clinics and patients. The complex nature of mitochondrial genetics including mtDNA heteroplasmy, the threshold effect, and mitochondrial genetic bottleneck, means that disease severity in offspring can be difficult to predict (Poulton et al., 2017; Chapter 1, this volume). Women seeking to utilize MRT will go through a process of assessment and support to ensure that MRT is an appropriate reproductive option and that they are aware of the risks and benefits (Gorman et al., 2018). The regulations specified that the mitochondrial donor would not be granted parental rights or responsibilities, and the child would not be able to access identifying information about the donor, although each could receive non-identifying information about the other. This stands in contrast to UK regulations about egg, sperm or gamete donation (Castro, 2016; Varvaštian, 2015). Finally, sex selection (i.e., selecting only male embryos), which would prevent the transmission of the donated genetic material to future generations (HFEA, 2013), would not be permitted on the basis that this would require additional intervention. The divergence between this UK policy and the position of other countries (see, e.g., the preference for sex selection noted by the National Academy of Medicine [2016; Chapter 6, this volume]) reflects UK prioritisation of protecting the embryo during the IVF process rather than addressing longer-term questions concerning future generations (Newson et al., 2016). In 2016, the final scientific report on efficacy and safety was published (HFEA, 2016) and the NHS confirmed that it would fund treatment for at least five years.

The legalisation of MRT was widely welcomed, with newspaper headlines highlighting not just the role that UK scientists played, but also the success of the UK-resourced system. One headline, for example, reported 'victory for the British researchers who have pioneered the technique and the medical establishment that has backed them' (Connor, 2015). Professor Doug Turnbull, the Newcastle-based scientist who led the development of MRT and played a prominent role in communicating its complexities within the debates, was awarded a knighthood in June 2016, in recognition of his research and support for patient care. In March 2017, almost a year and a half after the regulations came into force, the first UKi clinical licence was granted to the Wellcome Trust Centre for Mitochondrial Research at Newcastle.

While several licences for individual use of the techniques have been granted by the HFEA, at the time of writing it has not yet been made public whether these have led to any healthy births. It is possible that despite the United Kingdom being the first country to legalise MRT, the UK has not yet produced the first three-parent baby. In September 2016 (after UK legalisation but before the first use was licenced), an announcement was made that the first baby had been born using MRT through a clinical collaboration between a US-based team and a fertility clinic in Mexico (Hamzelou, 2016; González-Santos et al., 2018; Chapter 7, this volume), with several births subsequently announced elsewhere (Chapter 8, this volume). The announcements, and the scientist involved, were widely criticised for working outside of legal and ethical guidelines, spurring greater calls for more overt regulation and international collaboration (Mulvihill et al., 2017), including commentary from UK-based scientists (Lovell-Badge, 2019).

4.7 CONCLUSION

In this chapter we have highlighted the intensive work of individuals and institutions in persuading others of the benefits of a future world with, or without, MRT. The relationship between current practice and envisioned futures, central in making sense of emerging genetic technologies, is acknowledged in a body of sociological literature known as the 'sociology of expectations.' Notably, the way in which the future is constructed can help that particular future become a reality (Brown et al., 2000; Van Lente, 1993). Legalising MRT involved not just projecting a particular future for the technology, but also demonstrating how that future is knowable, ethical, desirable, and sanctionable (Dimond and Stephens, 2018). These four interrelated processes are evident in the topics we have discussed in this chapter. MRT was rendered knowable as much through the discussions about three-parent babies, mitochondria as battery, and the meanings of genetic modification as it was through scientific reports. Patient narratives were a key component of rendering MRT desirable, and ethicality was constructed primarily through the work of the Nuffield Council on Bioethics. Finally, sanctionability was constructed through parliamentary support in the context of a previously established and proved successful process of reviewing and assessing emerging technologies. Significantly, what counts as knowable, desirable, ethical, and sanctionable is enacted through these very processes.

Elsewhere we discuss in greater detail how the UK legalisation of MRT fits a broader pattern of consultations and legalisations around embryo use (Dimond and Stephens, 2018). We argue that the legalisation of MRT fits with the dominant sociotechnical imaginary within the United Kingdom—developed over many historical precedents—based on consultation practices leading to a legalisation process involving a permissive but highly scrutinised bureaucratic system. The legalisation of MRT in the United Kingdom is the latest iteration of this sociotechnical imaginary. Its legalisation contributes to this imaginary, confirming its success and the status of the United Kingdom as a gold standard of regulation. Previous iterations include IVF (Frith et al., 2011), preimplantation genetic diagnosis (Ehrich et al., 2008), human admixed embryos (Harvey and Salter, 2012; Williams and Gajevic, 2013), egg donation (O'Riordan and Haran, 2009), somatic cell nuclear transfer (therapeutic human cloning) (Haran et al., 2008), and human embryonic stem cells (Mikami and Stephens, 2016; Stephens et al., 2013). As we discuss next, it seems likely that the next iteration is already in process (Stephens and Dimond, 2016).

A key implication of the United Kingdom being the first to legalise MRT was that it was debated and resolved before questions arose about the development and usefulness of gene editing (CRISPR/Cas9). The familiar pattern of review was initiated, with the Nuffield Council on Bioethics (2016) for example, identifying, clarifying, and reporting on the ethical issues, and with the HFEA granting the world's first licence for CRISPR/Cas9 to be used on viable, normal human embryos. Research is exploring how CRISPR can be used to prevent the transmission of mitochondrial disease (Craven et al., 2017). CRISPR avoids the risk of 'carryover,' which was a key issue within the scientific reviews, and it does not involve the biological contribution of a third person (Gómez-Tatay et al., 2017). However, CRISPR brings with it new challenges (Chapter 10, this volume). MRT is a specialist IVF technique only relevant to and available through a small network of clinics and laboratories, where use can be closely regulated only for serious mitochondrial disease. There was clear responsibility for regulation of MRT in the United Kingdom through the HFEA, as well as a prefigured legal mechanism for legalisation through the 2008 HFE Act. CRISPR, in contrast, is a cheap, quick, and effective technique that can allow hundreds of genes to be targeted and 'edited' (Chan et al., 2015), and this means broad applicability beyond human health, including animal husbandry, environment, and warfare. Regulation will therefore be more challenging, compounded by the fact that it has already been taken up as part of the tool kit of biohackers who are developing and selling CRISPR kits for personal use (Pearlman, 2017; see also Knoepfler, 2015). Successful clinical outcomes (such as for childhood blindness and severe forms of spinal muscular atrophy) suggest a potential route for patient groups to become involved in championing the technology as a reproductive option.

While the United Kingdom's position as first to legalise MRT has been framed as 'openly challeng(ing) the fragile global policy with regard to germline gene modification' (Varvaštian, 2015: 424), it might also be seen as proof of a gold standard in regulation and a model for assessing future technologies. A recent collaborative report with the UK Royal Society and the US National Academies (2020) has noted that the UK pathway to MRT legalisation could usefully inform debates about gene editing. The review process has certainly contributed to a significant evidence base which can inform future national and international discussions (see Chapters 6 and 10, this volume; Cohen et al., 2020). Our work, alongside our colleagues, contributes by highlighting the role of the debates themselves in giving meaning to complex emerging technologies in order for their risks and benefits to be adequately assessed.

REFERENCES

Baylis, Francoise. 'The ethics of creating children with three genetic parents.' *Reproductive Biomedicine Online* 26 (2013): 531–534.

Baylis, Francoise. 'Human nuclear genome transfer (so-called mitochondrial replacement): Clearing the underbrush.' *Bioethics* 31, no. 1 (2017): 7–19.

Bredenoord, Annelien, Wybo Dondorp, Guido Pennings, and Guido De Wert. 'Ethics of modifying the mitochondrial genome.' *Journal of Medical Ethics* 37, no. 2 (2011): 97–100.

British Medical Association. 'For and against mitochondrial donation.' *The Times*, 2 February 2015. https://www.thetimes.co.uk/article/for-and-against-mitoch ondrial-donation-8vjnc7bs2kw.

Brown, Nik, Brian Rappert, and Andrew Webster (eds.). *Contested Futures: A Sociology of Prospective Science and Technology*. Aldershot, 2000.

Buchbinder, Mara, and Stefan Timmermans. 'Affective economies and the politics of saving babies' lives.' *Public Culture* 26, no. 172 (2014): 101–126.

Castro, Rosa J. 'Mitochondrial replacement therapy: The UK and US regulatory landscapes.' *Journal of Law and the Biosciences* 3, no. 3 (2016): 726–735.

Chan, Sarah, Peter J. Donovan, Thomas Douglas, Christopher Gyngell, et al. 'Genome editing technologies and human germline genetic modification: The Hinxton Group consensus statement.' *American Journal of Bioethics* 15, no. 12 (2015): 42–47.

Cohen, I. Glenn, Eli Y. Adashi, Sara Gerke, César Palacios-González, and Vardit Ravitsky. 'The regulation of mitochondrial replacement techniques around the world.' *Annual Review of Genomics and Human Genetics* 21 (2020): 565–586.

Cohen, Jacques, and Mina Alikani. 'The biological basis for defining bi-parental or tri-parental origin of offspring from cytoplasmic and spindle transfer.' *Reproductive Biomedicine Online* 26, no. 6 (2013): 535–537.

Connor, Steve. ''Three-parent babies': Britain votes in favour of law change.' *The Independent*, 3 February 2015. http://www.independent.co.uk/news/uk/polit ics/three-parent-babies-britain-votes-strongly-in-favour-of-lawchange-10021 265.html.

Craven, Lyndsey, Charlotte L. Alston, Robert W. Taylor, and Doug M. Turnbull. 'Recent advances in mitochondrial disease.' *Annual Review of Genomics and Human Genetics* 18 (2017): 257–275.

Craven, Lyndsey, Mary Herbert, Alison Murdoch, Julie Murphy, et al. 'Research into policy: A brief history of MRT.' *Stem Cells* 34, no. 2 (2016): 265–267.

Craven, Lyndsey, Mao-Xing Tang, Grainne S. Gorman, Petra De Sutter, et al. 'Novel reproductive technologies to prevent mitochondrial disease.' *Human Reproduction Update* 23, no. 5 (2017): 501–519.

Department of Health. 'Stem cell research: Medical progress with responsibility.' Department of Health, 2000. https://pubmed.ncbi.nlm.nih.gov/16218863/.

Department of Health. 'Mitochondrial donation: Government response to the consultation on draft regulations to permit the use of new treatment techniques to prevent the transmission of a serious mitochondrial disease from mother to child.' Department of Health, 2014. https://www.gov.uk/gov ernment/consultations/serious-mitochondrial-disease-new-techniques-to-prevent-transmission.

Dimond, Rebecca. 'Patient and family trajectories of mitochondrial disease: Diversity, uncertainty and genetic risk.' *Life Sciences, Society and Policy* 9, no. 1 (2013): 1–11.

Dimond, Rebecca, and Neil Stephens. 'Three persons, three genetic contributors, three parents: MRT, genetic parenting and the immutable grammar of the "three x x".' *Health: An Interdisciplinary Journal for the Social Study of Health, Illness and Medicine* 22, no. 3 (2017): 240–258.

Dimond, Rebecca, and Neil Stephens. *Legalising Mitochondrial Donation: Enacting Ethical Futures in UK Biomedical Politics*. Palgrave Pivot, 2018.

Ehrich, Kathryn, Clare Williams, and Bobbie Farsides. 'The embryo as moral work object: PGD/IVF staff views and experiences.' *Sociology of Health and Illness* 30, no. 3 (2008): 772–787.

Franklin, Sarah. *Biological Relatives: IVF, Stem Cells and the Future of Kinship*. Duke University Press, 2013.

Frith, Lucy, Ann Jacoby, and Mark Gabbay. 'Ethical boundary-work in the infertility clinic.' *Sociology of Health and Illness* 33, no. 4 (2011): 570–585.

Gamson, William A., and Andre Modigliani. 'Media discourse and public opinion on nuclear power: A constructionist approach.' *American Journal of Sociology* 95, no. 1 (1989): 1–37.

Gómez-Tatay, Lucia, Jose M. Hernández-Andreu, and Justo Aznar. 'Mitochondrial modification techniques and ethical issues.' *Journal of Clinical Medicine* 6, no. 3 (2017): 25.

Gonzalez-Santos, Sandra, Neil Stephens, and Rebecca Dimond. 'Narrating the first "three-parent baby": The initial press reactions from the United Kingdom, the United States, and Mexico.' *Science Communication* 40, no. 4 (2018): 419–441.

Gorman, Gráinne S., Robert McFarland, Jane Stewart, Catherine Feeney, and Doug M. Turnbull. 'Mitochondrial donation: From test tube to clinic.' *Lancet* 392, no. 10154 (2018): 1191–1192.

Greenfield, Andy. 'HFEA panel on mitochondrial replacement considered all submissions.' *The Guardian*, 24 July 2014. https://www.theguardian.com/scie nce/2014/jul/24/hfea-panel-mitochondrial-considered-all-submissions.

Haimes, Erica, and Ken Taylor. 'Sharpening the cutting edge: Additional considerations for the UK debates on embryonic interventions for mitochondrial diseases.' *Life Sciences, Society and Policy* 13, no. 1 (2017): 1.

Hamzelou, Jessica. 'Exclusive: World's first baby born with new "3 parent" technique.' *New Scientist*, 27 September 2016. https://www.newscientist.com/article/2107 219-exclusive-worlds-frst-baby-born-with-new-3-parent-technique.

Haran, Joan, Jenny Kitzinger, Maureen McNeil, and Kate O'Riordan. *Human Cloning in the Media: From Science Fiction to Science Practice*. Taylor and Francis, 2008.

Harvey, Alison, and Brian Salter. 'Anticipatory governance: Bioethical expertise for human/animal chimeras.' *Science as Culture* 21, no. 3 (2012): 291–313.

Herbrand, Cathy, and Rebecca Dimond. 'Mitochondrial donation, patient engagement and narratives of hope.' *Sociology of Health and Illness* 40, no. 4 (2017): 623–638.

Highfeld, Roger. 'Designer babies to wipe out diseases approved.' *The Telegraph*, 9 September 2005. https://www.telegraph.co.uk/news/uknews/1497972/Desig ner-babies-to-wipe-out-diseases-approved.html.

Houses of Commons. 2015, 3 February. http://www.publications.parliament.uk/pa/ cm201415/cmhansrd/cm150203/debtext/150203-0002.htm

House of Lords. 2015, 24 February. www.publications.parliament.uk/pa/ld201415/ ldhansrd/text/150224-0002.htm.

Human Fertilisation and Embryology Authority (HFEA). 'Scientific review of the safety and efficacy of methods to avoid mitochondrial disease through assisted conception.' 2011. http://hfeaarchive.uksouth.cloudapp.azure.com/www.hfea. gov.uk/docs/2011-04-18_Mitochondria_ review_-_fnal_report.pdf.

Human Fertilisation and Embryology Authority (HFEA). '*Mitochondria replacement consultation: Advice to government.*' 2013. http://hfeaarchive.uksouth.cloudapp. azure.com/www.hfea.gov.uk/docs/Mitochondria_replacement_consultation_-_ advice_for_Government.pdf.

Human Fertilisation and Embryology Authority (HFEAa). 'Review of the safety and efficacy of polar body transfer to avoid mitochondrial disease: Addendum to 'Third scientific review of the safety and efficacy of methods to avoid mitochondrial disease through assisted conception': Update 2014.' 2014. https://www.hfea.gov.uk/media/2610/2014-10-07_-_polar_body_transfer_revi ew_-_final.pdf.

Human Fertilisation and Embryology Authority (HFEAb). 'Third scientific review of the safety and efficacy of methods to avoid mitochondrial disease through assisted conception: Update 2014.' 2014. http://hfeaarchive.uksouth.cloudapp. azure.com/www.hfea.gov.uk/8807.html.

Human Fertilisation and Embryology Authority (HFEA). 'Scientific review of the safety and efficacy of methods to avoid mitochondrial disease through assisted conception: 2016 Update.' 2016. http://hfeaarchive.uksouth.cloud app.azure.com/www.hfea.gov.uk/docs/Fourth_scientifc_review_mitochondr ia_2016.pdf.

Hyslop, Louise A., Paul Blakeley, Lyndsey Craven, Jessica Richardson, Norah M. E. Fogarty, Elpida Fragouli, Mahdi Lamb, et al. 'Towards clinical application of pronuclear transfer to prevent mitochondrial DNA disease.' *Nature* 534, no. 7607 (2016): 383–386.

Jones, Caroline, and Ingrid Holme. 'Relatively (im)material: mtDNA and genetic relatedness in law and policy.' *Life Sciences, Society and Policy* 9, no. 4 (2013): 1–14.

Kelty, Christopher, and Aaron Panofsky. 'Disentangling public participation in science and biomedicine.' *Genome Medicine* 6, no. 1 (2014): 1–14.

Kerr, Anne, Sarah Cunningham-Burley, and Richard Tutton. 'Shifting subject positions: Experts and lay people in public dialogue.' *Social Studies of Science* 37, no. 3 (2007): 385–411.

Knoepfler, Paul. *GMO Sapiens: The Life-changing Science of Designer Babies*. World Scientific Publishing Company, 2015.

Lewens, Tim. 'The division of advisory labour: The case of "mitochondrial donation".' *European Journal for Philosophy of Science* 9 (2019): 1–19.

Lovell-Badge, Robin. 'CRISPR babies: A view from the centre of the storm.' *Development* 146, no. 3 (2019): dev175778.

Mason, Rowena, Ian Sample and Karen McVeigh. 'Church "irresponsible" for trying to sway MPs against mitochondrial donation law.' *The Guardian*, 2 February 2015. https://www.theguardian.com/science/2015/feb/02/church-groups-irresponsi ble-pushing-mps-against-ivf-law-change.

McNeil, Maureen, and Joan Haran. 'Publics of bioscience.' *Science as Culture* 22, no. 4 (2013): 433–451.

Mikami, Koichi, and Neil Stephens. 'Local biologicals and the politics of standardization: Making ethical pluripotent stem cells in the United Kingdom and Japan.' *BioSocieties* 11, no. 2 (2016): 220–239.

Mulkay, Michael. 'Rhetorics of hope and fear in the great embryo debate.' *Social Studies of Science* 23, no. 4 (1993): 721–742.

Mulvihill, John, Benjamin Capps, Yann Joly, Tamra Lysaght, Hub Zwart, Ruth Chadwick, et al. 'Ethical issues of CRISPR technology and gene editing through the lens of solidarity.' *British Medical Bulletin* 122, no. 1 (2017): 17–29.

National Academy of Medicine, National Academy of Sciences, and the Royal Society. *Mitochondrial Replacement Techniques: Ethical, Social, and Policy Considerations*. National Academies Press, 2016.

National Academy of Medicine, National Academy of Sciences, and the Royal Society. *Heritable Human Genome Editing*. The National Academies Press, 2020.

Newson, Ainsley, and Anthony Wrigley. 'Is MRT germ-line gene therapy? Classifications and ethical implications.' *Bioethics* 31, no. 1 (2017): 55–67.

Newson, Ainsley J., Stephen Wilkinson, and Anthony Wrigley. 'Ethical and legal issues in mitochondrial transfer.' *EMBO Molecular Medicine* 8, no. 6 (2016): 589–591.

Nuffield Council on Bioethics. *Novel Techniques for the Prevention of Mitochondrial DNA Disorders: An Ethical Review*. Nuffield Council on Bioethics, 2012.

Nuffield Council on Bioethics. *Genome Editing: An Ethical Review*. Nuffield Council on Bioethics, 2016.

O'Riordan, Kate, and Joan Haran. 'From reproduction to research: Sourcing eggs, IVF and cloning in the UK.' *Feminist Theory* 10, no. 2 (2009): 191–210.

Palacios-González, Cesar. 'Are there moral differences between maternal spindle transfer and pronuclear transfer?' *Medicine, Health Care and Philosophy* 20, no. 4 (2017): 1–9.

Pearlman, Alex. 'Biohackers are using CRISPR on their DNA and we can't stop it.' *New Scientist*, 15 November 2017. https://www.newscientist.com/article/mg23631 520-100-biohackers-are-using-crispr-on-their-dna-and-wecant-stop-it.

Poulton, Joanna, Josef Finsterer, and Patrick Yu-Wai-Man. 'Genetic counselling for maternally inherited mitochondrial disorders.' *Molecular Diagnosis & Therapy* 21, no. 4 (2017): 419–429.

Rayfield, Lee, and Brendan McCarthy. 'The Church of England and the three-parent controversy.' *The Guardian*, 1 February 2015. https://www.theguardian.com/commentisfree/2015/feb/01/church-of-england-three-parent-family.

Reubi, David. 'Re-moralising medicine: The bioethical thought collective and the regulation of the body in British medical research.' *Social Theory and Health* 11, no. 2 (2013): 215–235.

Scully, Jackie Leach. 'A mitochondrial story: Mitochondrial replacement, identity and narrative.' *Bioethics* 31, no. 1 (2017): 37–45.

Sparrow, Robert, Catherine Mills, and John Carroll. 'Gendering the seed: Mitochondrial replacement techniques and the erasure of the maternal.' *Bioethics* 35, no. 7 (2021): 608–614.

Stephens, Neil, Paul Atkinson, and Peter Glasner. 'Institutional imaginaries of publics in stem cell banking: The cases of the UK and Spain.' *Science as Culture* 22, no. 4 (2013): 497–515.

Stephens, Neil, and Rebecca Dimond. 'Debating CRISPR/cas9 and mitochondrial donation: Continuity and transition performances at scientific conferences.' *Engaging Science, Technology, and Society* 2 (2016): 312–321.

Strathern, Marilyn. *Reproducing the Future: Essays on Anthropology, Kinship and the New Reproductive Technologies*. Manchester University Press, 1992.

Subbaraman, Nidhi. 'Limit on lab-grown human embryos dropped by stem-cell body.' *Nature* 594, no. 7861 (2021): 18–19.

Turkmendag, Ilke. 'It is just a "battery": "Right" to know in mitochondrial replacement.' *Science, Technology, and Human Values* 43, no. 1 (2018): 56–85.

Van Lente, Harro. *Promising Technology: The Dynamics of Expectations in Technological Developments*. Proefschrift, 1993.

Varvaštian, Samuel. 'UK's legalisation of MRT in IVF treatment: A challenge to the international community or a promotion of life-saving medical innovation to be followed by others?' *European Journal of Health Law* 22, no. 5 (2015): 405–425.

Williams, Andy, and Slavko Gajevic. 'Selling science: Source struggles, public relations, and UK press coverage of animal–human hybrid embryos.' *Journalism Studies* 14, no. 4 (2013): 507–522.

Wilson, Duncan. 'Creating the "ethics industry": Mary Warnock, in vitro fertilization and the history of bioethics in Britain.' *BioSocieties* 6, no. 2 (2011): 121–141.

5

MRT in Australia

KARINNE LUDLOW

5.1 INTRODUCTION

Clinical mitochondrial replacement therapies (MRT) were prohibited in Australia and only limited research use allowed. But following the United Kingdom's response to MRT, discussed in Chapter 4, legalisation has recently been achieved by the federal government. Unlike the US approach to prohibition discussed in Chapter 6, clinical MRT were expressly prohibited by national legislation in 2002. Pursuant to that legislation, it was a criminal offence to create human embryos containing genetic material from more than two people or to make heritable changes to the human genome. These prohibitions are part of a national regulatory scheme which also previously prohibited the creation of any human embryos for research, including embryos created using mitochondrial-based techniques. Significant amendments in 2006 allowed limited creation and use of embryos for research provided that legislative and procedural rules are strictly followed.

However, legislation—the Mitochondrial Donation Law Reform (Maeve's Law) Act 2022 (Cth)—was passed by the federal parliament on 30 March 2022. Now in force, the legislation permits the clinical use of MRT and expands the permitted use of human embryos in MRT research. This chapter explores Australia's changing responses to MRT by first describing the regulatory framework before the 2022 reform. The pathway that led to that approach is then considered. The chapter then turns to reforms made to legalise MRT in Australia and the drivers for that change. The implications for genome editing and the influence of the development of

Karinne Ludlow, *MRT in Australia* In: *Reproduction Reborn.* Edited by: Diana M. Bowman, Karinne Ludlow, and Walter G. Johnson, Oxford University Press. © Oxford University Press 2023. DOI: 10.1093/oso/9780197616192.003.0006 genome editing on regulatory responses to MRT are addressed in the final parts of the chapter.

5.2 REGULATION OF MRT IN AUSTRALIA

MRT were illegal in Australia under two federal Acts: the Prohibition of Human Cloning for Reproduction Act 2002 (Cth) (POHCR Act) as it is now called and the Research Involving Human Embryos Act 2002 (Cth) (RIHE Act) (Figure 5.1).

Legislation that is similar—although not identical—to the national legislation (and to each other) is adopted in each Australian state and territory by complementary legislation in order to address constitutional limits on the Australian federal parliament and create a national regulatory scheme around human embryo research. However, while all states and territories also have their own legislation on the legal parentage of children and four have legislation relevant to assisted reproduction, there is no national scheme on these matters. The parliamentary committee that created the blueprint for the national scheme recommended that regulation of embryo research be kept separate from regulation of assisted reproductive technology (ART) because of the potential for products of embryo research (such as stem cells) to be applicable in areas beyond reproduction (Andrews Report, 2001). National consistency on ART practice is nevertheless achieved through

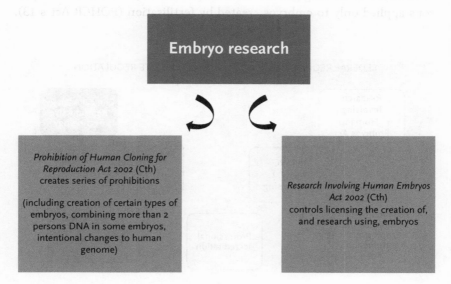

Figure 5.1 National legislation for embryo research.

professional accreditation by the Reproductive Technology Accreditation Committee (RTAC) of the Fertility Society of Australia (2014), which federal legislation requires of all Australian ART clinics. That accreditation obliges clinics to comply with RTAC's Code of Practice, and that Code in turn requires clinics to comply with guidelines written by the key federal regulatory stakeholder, the National Health and Medical Research Council (National Health and Medical Research Council, 2017; see National Health and Medical Research Council, 2018), although states and territories can override those guidelines. Regulatory change to enable clinical MRT had to accommodate this splintered governance (Figure 5.2).

While the Australian regulatory environment for human embryo research is more liberal than that of the United States (Chapter 6, this volume), Australian researchers are limited in the research they can undertake when compared with their UK counterparts (Chapter 4, this volume). The RIHE Act allows embryo research subject to a licensing process overseen by an NHMRC committee called the Embryo Research Licensing Committee (ERLC) and to the prohibitions in the POHCR Act. However, putting to one side the recent amendments to permit MRT, licenced embryo research is allowed only if the embryo is surplus from clinical ART or created by techniques *other than* fertilisation of an egg by sperm. Surplus ART embryos are too developed for most MRT research, making such research dependent on the creation of embryos by researchers. The prohibition on the intentional creation or development of embryos containing genetic material provided by more than two persons applied only to embryos created by fertilisation (POHCR Act s 13),

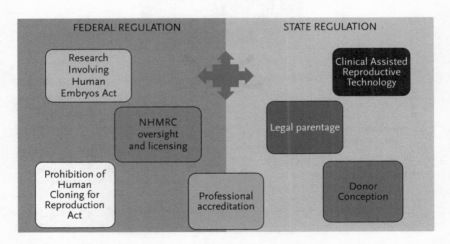

Figure 5.2 Division of regulation around MRT between federal and state governments.

although the prohibition on making heritable changes is not limited in that way (POHCR Act s 15). The governmental agreement between the federal, state, and territory governments establishing the embryo research regulatory scheme explains that the restriction on the maximum number of genetic contributors to human embryos was because of clinical safety and efficacy concerns (Morris, 2002; McLucas, 2002). Importantly, given clinical MRT require implantation into a woman, it is also a criminal offence to implant embryos created for research into a woman (POHCR Act ss 20(3) and (4)) or to develop them longer than 14 days (POHCR Act s 14). MRT also cannot be undertaken overseas with the intention of implantation in Australia because such embryos cannot be imported into Australia for clinical use (POHCR Act s 20(3) and (4)).

The distinction for licensable research based on how embryos are created meant Australian researchers could, until recent amendments, perform only limited forms of MRT. As the ERLC (the body responsible for licensing embryo research) explained in its submission to the 2018 Australian Senate Committee inquiry into MRT (discussed in Section 5.3), research into pronuclear transfer (PNT) was licensable in Australia because the transfer of the combined nuclear DNA (nDNA) of the intending parents from a fertilised egg of the intending mother to the enucleated fertilised egg of the donor occurs after the eggs have been fertilised. The development of the donor's egg, now containing the nDNA of the intending parents, is characterised as the creation of an embryo using techniques *other* than by fertilisation of an egg by sperm and is therefore allowed with a licence. Research into maternal spindle transfer (MST), on the other hand, is not licensable because it requires the creation of an embryo from *fertilisation* of a reconstructed egg, created by moving nDNA from the intending mother's egg to an unfertilised enucleated donor egg. Using the reasoning applied by the ERLC to the most understood and studied forms of MRT (namely, PNT and MST), research into second polar body transfer was also licensable but research into first polar body transfer or germinal vesicle transfer was not.

The practical implications for researchers of the second legislative provision relevant to MRT (POHCR Act s 15) are less clear. That provision prohibits the alteration of the genome of human cells in such a way that the alteration is heritable by the descendants of the human whose cell was altered, if that alteration is intended to be heritable. While the prohibition applies to eggs, fertilised eggs, or embryos involved in MRT, it is unclear what genome or heritable means in this context or whether it applies to research use (Taylor-Sands and Gyngell, 2018). As discussed by me elsewhere (Ludlow, 2020), the Australian provision does not expressly exclude mitochondrial DNA (mtDNA) but it is likely that the prohibition was not intended to prevent changes to mtDNA. However, the recent reforms discussed below now clarify that genome editing of both nDNA and mtDNA is prohibited while permitting licenced MRT.

5.3 THE PATHWAY TO CURRENT MRT REGULATION

In vitro fertilisation (IVF) has been used in Australian clinics since 1972 and the world's first reported IVF pregnancy (but not birth) occurred in 1973, in Melbourne (De Kretzer et al., 1973). However, Australian law did not intervene in the developing science until the 1980s, after the birth of the first baby in Australia from IVF (Demack Report, 1984).

In 1977, after recommendations by the Australian Law Reform Commission (1977: para 42.2), the Council of Australian Social Welfare Ministers referred the need for clarification on the legal position of the most controversial aspect of IVF at the time, artificial insemination by donor, to the Standing Committee of Attorney-Generals. The legal status of children born with the assistance of all IVF was later added to the Committee's tasks. Model legislation prepared for that Committee regarding the legal parentage of children was eventually adopted by all states and territories. Importantly for MRT because of its reliance on donated eggs, that legislation—as I have discussed elsewhere (Ludlow, 2015)—makes any genetic link between a child and donor irrelevant for legal parentage purposes. Nevertheless, a MRT egg donor will be a gamete donor or provider (or, to use the newer terminology, part of the child's genetic origins) under existing state law. This has important legal consequences. Most importantly, the child would have the right to know the identity of the donor. The mtDNA used to create all embryos implanted in one procedure into an intending mother must also be provided by one woman to avoid prohibitions on mixing reproductive material in a way that makes it difficult to know the genetic parents of a child without testing. Regulatory restrictions on the number of families to whom the one donor can donate would also apply. This is different to the UK's approach (Chapter 4, this volume), which does not treat the mtDNA donor as a gamete provider and has not limited the number of mtDNA donor siblings, deciding that mtDNA is insufficient to cause problems of consanguinity. The reforms address this issue of donor anonymity and are discussed below.

Much of Australia's early discussion and public interest in reproductive technology arose because of the birth of the first child by IVF in 1978 in the United Kingdom (Steptoe and Edwards, 1978), quickly followed by the first IVF birth in Australia in 1980, at Melbourne's Royal Women's

Hospital (Lopata et al., 1980). But what really attracted the public's attention and thereafter that of legislators was the tragic case of the Rioses. The Rioses, an American couple who had undertaken IVF in a Melbourne hospital, were killed in an air crash in 1983, leaving two frozen embryos behind (Blakeslee, 1984). As *The Washington Post* reported at the time, their death 'unleashed a storm of controversy' over what was to be done with the embryos (Costigan, 1984). Victoria, the state where the embryos were created and stored, had already begun an inquiry into the legal implications of IVF. Following the world's first birth from a previously frozen embryo in Melbourne (Trounson and Mohr, 1983), the fate of frozen embryos was added to the inquiry's remit only months before the Rioses death, and, during the year following the couple's death, five Australian states had (or commenced) inquiries on the regulation of IVF. Victoria's very influential reports, the Waller Committee Reports (Waller, 1983, 1984), led to the world's first IVF and associated embryo research legislation.

Two decades later, and in response to scientific advances in the creation of human life outside the body (such as cloning), the national scheme around human embryos discussed above was established. This included prohibiting the creation of embryos by fertilisation of a human egg by a human sperm containing genetic material provided by more than two persons or the placing of such embryos into a woman. The Committee that created the blueprint for that scheme was aware that the United Kingdom was intending to amend its legislation to permit researchers to explore 'the development of methods of therapy for mitochondrial disease' (Andrews Report, 2001: para 10.86). It was also aware that cytoplasmic transfer in embryos had resulted in live births in the United States (Andrews Report, 2001, [E8], [2.61] and [2.66]). But in contrast with the United States's perhaps unintended prevention of MRT (Chapter 6, this volume), it is clear that prohibition of MRT was intentional because parliamentary materials at the time explain that it was intended that this prohibition be broad enough 'to include other techniques, current or emerging, that may also involve the presence in a human embryo of a third party's DNA' (Commonwealth Senate, 2002: 9).

Unlike the United Kingdom, with its established history of reviewing the regulation of embryo research (Chapter 4, this volume), Australia's federal government has been reluctant to regularly review such regulation or to broaden the scope of permissible embryo research. The original 2002 legislation required review within three years of commencement, but that review was initiated very reluctantly, and the independent legislation review committee (Lockhart Review, 2005) was given only six months to do its work. A further review was undertaken in 2011, again because the legislation required it. However, recommendations following the 2011 review were largely concerned with the licensing process rather than addressing emerging technologies or expanding the scope of permitted research. Interestingly, while the Lockhart Committee had received 1,035 submissions, the 2011 review received only 262, perhaps demonstrating public acceptance of embryo research. A decade later and the government has not responded or acted on the 2011 review recommendations, and there has been no further review of Australian regulation of embryo research despite the scientific advancements in the field.

The six-member Lockhart Committee, made up of prominent lawyers, ethicists, and scientists, was tasked with assessing the scope and operation of the existing regulatory framework 'in light of changes in scientific or community understanding or standards since 2002, and any indications that the provisions are no longer appropriate and/or practical in their application.' The government took six months before responding to the committee's report, and even then, its response was to announce that it did not intend to take up any recommendations for change made by the committee (Murphy, 2006). However, following objections from the Victoria government and members of federal Cabinet, a bill proposing amendments was put forward in 2006. The subsequent debate on the bill was fought between supporters of broadening the scope of embryo research (including patient advocacy groups for motor neurone disease, spinal cord injuries, and diabetes and also medical and scientific researchers) and opponents seeking to further reduce that scope (such as the Anglican and Catholic Churches).

Amongst the Lockhart Committee's recommendations was one that the government consider permitting licensed research on the transfer of mtDNA in all embryos, but the 2006 amendments permit only the creation of embryos containing the genetic material of more than two persons *if* the embryos are made using techniques other than fertilisation (e.g., if they are created by cloning). This also produced the result described above, of permitting research into one form of MRT (namely, PNT) but not another (MST). The NHMRC raised the incongruity of allowing research into one form of MRT but not another when both have the same outcome during the 2011 review of the legislation (NHMRC Submission to Heerey Review, 2011, rec. 7). The NHMRC also submitted that mtDNA should be excluded from the meaning of genetic material for the purposes of the offence of creating embryos with more than two people's DNA. However, the 2011 review did not properly address these issues because it concluded that the techniques were not sufficiently advanced to be permitted (Heerey Review, 2011, rec. 7).

5.4 THE ROAD TO REFORM

With the rapid developments in MRT and the United Kingdom's legalisation of its clinical use, the Australian government began the process to permit clinical MRT whilst seeking to avoid the much needed overhaul of the broader regulatory framework for embryo research. Public calls for the legalisation of MRT in Australia (Dow and Cunningham, 2017) and advocacy by mitochondrial disease community groups, such the Mito Foundation, drove these steps to legalise MRT for research, training, and reproductive purposes. Mito Foundation, the peak support group for Australians with mitochondrial disease, was created in 2009 and describes itself as actively working to expand the reproductive options for such Australians.

In 2018, an Australian Senate Committee inquiry into MRT gave qualified support to clinical use but recommended that further consultation with the community, relevant experts, and the states and territories occur first (Australian Senate Community Affairs References Committee, 2018). The committee's view, based on 60 submissions and evidence given at a day of public hearings, was that Australians may not find MRT controversial (paras 5.90–5.92). The committee also recommended a form of state-sponsored medical tourism, proposing, as an interim measure until clinical MRT were available in Australia, that the Australian government begin discussions with UK authorities to facilitate access for Australian patients in the United Kingdom. This was not expressly taken up by the Australian government but the recently passed Maeve's Law has been accompanied by governmental ambition that Australia itself should become a destination for medical tourists seeking MRT (Commonwealth House of Representatives, 2021: 81).

The saving of healthcare costs for the community and for patients and their families was important in community and committee discussions. The committee referred to submissions on the issue after noting estimates by the UK Department of Health on the anticipated savings in healthcare. An Australian expert estimated that legalising MRT would bring between A\$33 million to A\$66 million per year in healthcare savings, based on a conservative estimate of 5 to 10 children born without mitochondrial disease per year (Australian Senate Community Affairs References Committee, 2018: para 2.47). Nevertheless, it was the strong potential of MRT to address the debilitating effects of inheriting mitochondrial disease that was given as the basis for the committee's conclusions (Australian Senate Community Affairs References Committee, 2018: Recommendation 1, para 5.99).

Following agreement by all Australian governments, the NHMRC—Australia's medical research regulator—undertook a series of community consultation activities in 2019, producing a final report in 2020 (Australian Government NHMRC, 2020). Those activities took a multimodal approach to obtaining community views on the social and ethical issues associated with MRT, including those parts of the community which may not otherwise engage with such debates. Following the United Kingdom's approach, this included a citizen's panel, webinars, public forums, and other forms of outreach. Mirroring the findings in the United Kingdom (Chapter 4, this volume), a number of submissions referred to 'three-parent baby' or 'three-parent IVF.' However, these references were made on both sides of the debate: namely, to justify opposition to MRT or to criticise such descriptions. Parliamentary debates on Maeve's Law also used those terms to oppose clinical MRT or to explain why such terms should not be used for MRT. Also relevantly here, the explanatory memorandum accompanying the reform bill asserts that resulting children will have only two biological parents, although also conceding that MRT impacts a child's characteristics and personality traits even though the majority of these are from the child's biological parents (Commonwealth House of Representatives, 2021: 77). The final statement by the citizens panel on MRT included reference to economic advantages through reduction in costs 'to the community of providing healthcare and disability support to people affected by mitochondrial disease and their families' as one justification for offering MRT to prospective parents (Australian Government NHMRC, 2020: Appendix E). However, this was only one of the four main reasons that the panel considered it important that the option of MRT be offered in Australia. The panel considered it important to help prevent children being born with mitochondrial disease and prevent suffering and untimely death, with the aim of improving quality of life. In addition, the panel noted that it could give people at risk of passing on mitochondrial disease an opportunity to have healthy children who are genetically related to both parents, and, finally, potentially it could help break the cycle of mitochondrial disease in families, reduce their emotional trauma, and improve their mental health and well-being.

Sex selection of embryos has been an important issue in public consultations and parliamentary discussions of the reforms. Whether prospective parents should be limited to using male embryos, as suggested by a high-level US committee (Chapter 6, this volume), or counselled with respect to the choice of using only female embryos (because of the possibility of carryover of mutated mtDNA from the prospective mother to the resulting embryo) was raised during a targeted roundtable of representatives from 23 academic and advisory bodies (that roundtable being one of the series of community consultation activities undertaken by the NHMRC). The roundtable concluded that 'while sex selection is currently used in IVF to prevent other significant diseases, restriction of mitochondrial donation to male embryos raises very different ethical issues. Participants were generally not in favour of restricting treatment availability in this way' (Australian Government NHMRC, 2020: 75). This issue was also raised in submissions to the earlier 2018 Senate Committee inquiry, with submissions suggesting that the presence of a degree of risk meant that 'the question whether to implant female embryos should be considered by the prospective parents after counselling' but that the use of female embryos should not be prohibited (Australian Senate Community Affairs References Committee, 2018: para. 3.66). The Senate Committee noted that the Australian Academy of Science had explained that the United Kingdom's rejection of using only male embryos in MRT was because 'this would require another intervention, in this case PGD, in an embryo that had already been subject to heavy manipulation, and would also halve the number of suitable embryos and reduce the chance of achieving a pregnancy' (Australian Senate Community Affairs References Committee, 2018, p. 90). The Senate Committee's final view was not to restrict clinical MRT to male embryos but to give detailed pretreatment counselling for those seeking MRT. Such counselling was described as important 'to ensure they are fully aware of the risks, efficacy and other options that may be available to them' (2018: 91). These conclusions were reflected in the original draft regulation of MRT discussed below and were particularly contentious during parliamentary debates.

A 13-member Expert Working Committee of the NHMRC was also commissioned to advise on the safety and efficacy of MRT, delivering its report in 2020 (Australian Government NHMRC, 2020b). The Expert Working Committee was instructed to focus on evidence that had emerged since the 2016 scientific review undertaken by United Kingdom's HFEA, and it concluded that there was no new significant evidence (Australian Government NHMRC, 2020b: 2). The Expert Committee was also instructed to consider whether MRT is distinct from germline genetic modification. The committee concluded that the term is inappropriate for MRT, although it observed that MRT does cause heritable changes to the genome.

Following completion of these activities, the Australian government released a public consultation paper proposing a two-stage model for the introduction of MRT to 'allow families to access the technique as quickly as possible', and explaining that MRT gives 'impacted families greater reproductive choices and reduce the burden of disease for future generations'

(Australian Government Department of Health, 2021b: 2, 5). The proposed model (albeit with little regulatory detail) was subject to public comment for five weeks in February–March 2021, and draft legislation and accompanying explanatory memorandum were introduced to the lower house of the federal parliament one week after close of the comment period. The government's summary of public comments on the proposed model (Australian Government Department of Health, 2021a: 2) asserts that there is support for MRT in Australia, stating that such support is based on

- the right of a child to the enjoyment of the highest attainable standard of health
- the prevention of disease and disability
- the promotion of choice and reproductive freedom, and
- reduced burden of disease for the community.

The summary report notes that ethical concerns about using the technique were raised by some comments, reflecting the feedback received as part of the 2018 Senate Inquiry and 2019–2020 NHMRC consultation process, as discussed above. That report summarises the key issues that were raised as being 'whether the use of this technology constitutes genetic modification, the creation and destruction of embryos, how to ensure privacy of individuals undertaking mitochondrial donation and whether there is a risk that financial incentives could be used to attract female donors' (Australian Government Department of Health, 2021a: 4). The NHMRC Community Consultation report (2020: 25) also notes that concerns were raised about 'exacerbating negative social perceptions and treatment of people with a disability' but that such concerns were not raised with the 2018 Senate inquiry (see also Chapter 2, this volume).

The speed at which the reform process has occurred perhaps reflects that the Australian Prime Minister was the patron of the Mito Foundation, the advocacy group behind moves to make MRT available in Australia. The Prime Minister made regular messages of support from the parliamentary floor in the years preceding the bill's introduction, including a tribute to a young woman who had lived in his electorate and whom he had met in 2012, and who died from mitochondrial disease in 2017 (Morrison, 2017). Consistently with the then Prime Minister's attitude, the Australian Minister for Health and Aged Care, when moving the proposed legislation in Parliament, explained that '[a]dvances in reproductive technology now mean that we can help by providing those families at risk of passing on the disease with a pathway to having a healthy child who can live a rich, full and long life' (Commonwealth Parliamentary Debates, 2021: 3279).

Whilst there were some submissions made during public consultation which opposed the legalisation of MRT, very little debate has taken place on the issue in the Australian media or broader public. Whether this is because of distraction caused by the pandemic or, as the first MRT inquiry in 2018 concluded, because MRT are not controversial to Australians or for some other reason is unclear. But the press conference held alongside of the introduction of the bill to Parliament attracted no questions, the focus being on other matters altogether (Australian Government Department of Health, 2021c). The government summary of the public's submissions on the proposed two-stage model for legalisation states that the key issues raised by opponents were 'due to the newness of the science, ethical concerns about using the technique and the appropriateness of publicly funding the technology' and that foremost of the ethical concerns was 'the creation and destruction of embryos.'

The legislation was the subject of a conscience vote in both houses of Parliament, meaning that Parliamentarians did not have to adopt their party's position on the issue when voting on the passage of the bill. The bill passed the lower house (the House of Representatives) in December 2021 after last-minute amendments (discussed below). It was then considered and passed by the upper house (the Senate) by a majority of 37 to 17 votes on 30 March 2022. The federal government has also committed US$4.4 million over four years to support implementation of MRT in Australia and has agreed to waive licence fees.

5.5 REFORMS

The model for implementation of MRT in Australia is closely based on the United Kingdom's approach and is described in this section. However, the legislative amendments needed to make that possible are not as straightforward in Australia as they were in the United Kingdom because of Australia's splintered governance of reproductive technology and because of the significantly less liberal regulation of embryo research. Importantly, legislative change was needed to permit the creation of human embryos by fertilisation for research purposes.

Maeve's Law amends the relevant federal legislation (namely, the POHCR Act and RIHE Act) to allow licences for laboratory-based and clinical trial research and training in MRT, including a clinical trial by a (still to be selected) single clinic. This first stage of the two-stage model is anticipated to continue for 10–12 years and is to determine the safety, efficacy, and feasibility of the technology and build Australian expertise. The clinical trial will also give a small number of affected families access to MRT in Australia (Commonwealth Parliamentary Debates, 2021). About 56 children are born in Australia each year with severe mitochondrial disease, and expert opinion is that MRT could be relevant to up to 60 pregnancies per annum in Australia (submission by David Thorburn and Kathryn North from Murdoch Children's Research Institute with Martin Delatycki from Victorian Clinical Genetics Services [2018] to 2018 Senate Committee inquiry). However, the number of trial participants will be far smaller. Licensing and monitoring of the clinical trial will be done by the ERLC, and it is proposed that detailed criteria will be created around who can deliver treatment, who can access treatment, and the monitoring and support of trial participants. The powers of the ERLC and its membership have been broadened to enable it to perform these roles (Australian Government Department of Health, 2021b: Appendix 1). Maeve's Law provides that transition to stage two will require approval of the federal Minister for Health, based on recommendations by experts, and will occur using regulations rather than amending legislation. The significance of this is that formal processes for the passage of legislation will not have to be followed, although such regulations can be disallowed by Parliament to make the process quicker. Other clinics can also be licensed to perform MRT during stage two. States and territories will, however, need to authorise the use of MRT in their own jurisdiction if they agree to ART clinics providing MRT in their jurisdiction (Australian Government Department of Health, 2021b: 7, 8; Commonwealth House of Representatives, 2021: 8) (Figure 5.3).

Five techniques of MRT are licensable, but importantly licences for clinical trials or clinical trial research and training can allow only two MRT forms: MST and/or PNT. Although there are ethical and legal differences between PNT and MST, particularly because PNT requires the destruction of an embryo, both will be licensable following the precedent set by the United Kingdom. Three other MRT techniques (germinal vesical transfer, first polar body transfer, and second polar body transfer) as well as MST and/or PNT can be permitted under preclinical research and training licences. In an attempt at 'future-proofing,' further techniques can be added as being licensable by the introduction of new regulations rather than amendment of the legislation itself.

The distinctions between the two groups of techniques—those that reconstruct an egg (MST, first polar body transfer, and germinal vesicle transfer) and those that reconstruct a zygote (PNT and second polar body

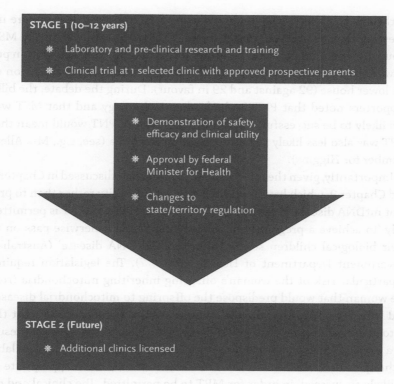

STAGE 1 (10–12 years)

- ❋ Laboratory and pre-clinical research and training
- ❋ Clinical trial at 1 selected clinic with approved prospective parents

- ❋ Demonstration of safety, efficacy and clinical utility
- ❋ Approval by federal Minister for Health
- ❋ Changes to state/territory regulation

STAGE 2 (Future)

- ❋ Additional clinics licensed

Figure 5.3 Two-staged model for introduction of MRT into Australia.

transfer)—are important in Australian law. As explained above, some research involving the reconstruction of zygotes as happens in PNT was already allowed in Australia but egg reconstruction research, such as in MST, was not. The ethical differences between the two groups of techniques were raised during the parliamentary debate on Maeve's Law in the lower house. Interestingly, and perhaps reflecting changing community attitudes to embryo research, despite research into MST being illegal (because of restrictions on researchers creating embryos for research using fertilisation), that form of MRT was preferred by some opponents. For example, one member of Parliament (Mrs Wicks, member for Robertson) explained that while she could support MST, she could not support PNT because she disagreed with intentionally creating an embryo to destroy it. Similarly, Mr Andrews (member for Menzies) sought the removal of the zygote reconstruction group (which includes PNT) from the bill because they involve the deliberate destruction of an embryo or zygote. Mr Andrews was instrumental in the introduction of the national framework that controls human embryo research in Australia, including the prohibition of the creation of research embryos using fertilisation. It is therefore interesting that he chose to object to the PNT group rather than the MST group. Amendments to exclude certain forms of MRT from legalisation put forward by Mr Andrews were overwhelmingly rejected after a division of the lower house (92 against and 29 in favour). During the debate, the bill's supporters noted that PNT is the leading technology and that MST was less likely to be successful. This meant exclusion of PNT would mean that MRT was also less likely to be successful in Australia (see, e.g., Mrs Allen, member for Higgins).

Importantly, given the international clinical trials discussed in Chapter 8 and Chapter 9, which have used MRT to treat infertility rather than to prevent mtDNA disease in resulting children, clinical use of MRT is permitted only 'to achieve a pregnancy in women who would otherwise pass on to their biological children severe mitochondrial DNA disease' (Australian Government Department of Health, 2021b: 7). The legislation requires 'a particular risk of the woman's offspring inheriting mitochondria from the woman that would predispose the offspring to mitochondrial disease', and with respect to that disease, that 'there is a significant risk that the mitochondrial disease that would develop in those offspring would result in a serious illness or other serious medical condition.' Other available techniques that could minimise these risks must also be 'inappropriate or unlikely to succeed' in order for MRT to be permitted. The clinical and diagnostic information needed by the ERLC to assess these matters is still to be developed. But to further ensure that MRT are restricted to addressing mitochondrial disease, clinical trial licences and clinical practice licences are to be subject to the condition that the woman being treated must also be approved by the ERLC.

Prospective parents will be required to attend pretreatment counselling, where the potential risks will be explained and the option to use mtDNA haplogroup matched donor eggs or to use other alternatives to MRT, such as donor eggs, adoption, fostering, or not having children will be discussed. The re-emergence of mtDNA disease in future generations is identified in the Explanatory Memorandum as a relevant risk which must also be discussed with prospective parents. Nevertheless, as the memorandum goes on to explain, it was not considered necessary to have mandatory sex selection of male embryos in order to manage that risk (para 130), and the United Kingdom's approach to the issue is relied on to justify this. Controversially though, the original draft legislation gave prospective parents the choice to reduce the risk of re-emergence by choosing to implant only male embryos. As briefly referred to above, sex selection in reproductive embryos is prohibited in Australia unless needed to reduce the risk of disease in the resulting child. A last-minute amendment, made during its passage through the lower house to ensure that the bill was passed, saw that choice taken away from parents. Instead, a new provision states that human embryos created using MRT are not to be selected on the basis of sex, and contravention of this will expose licence holders to a criminal penalty of up to five years of imprisonment.

Additional protections address the privacy of families and resulting children and ensure that invasive testing is not undertaken for routine monitoring after a child is born, although mandatory reporting of adverse events will be required. Rights and responsibilities for MRT egg donors are aligned with current ART regulation, meaning such donors will not be legal parents of resulting children, but children will have the right to apply for identifying information about their donor at an appropriate age. Donors, on the other hand, are not entitled to identifiable information about any child born of their donated egg unless contacted directly by that child. However, donors can apply for other information still to be prescribed by the regulations but which will presumably include the birth of a baby. They will not be paid for their eggs, but costs such as healthcare and travel are reimbursable under state and territory laws.

The amendments must be reviewed within seven years of enactment, but, reflecting the reluctance of the government to review the broader regulation of embryo research, this is only in relation to the MRT provisions.

5.6 CONCLUSION

The Australian Minister for Health and Aged Care concluded his parliamentary speech introducing the draft Maeve's Law by saying 'It is also essential that we remain at the forefront of advances in both medical science and reproductive technology' (Commonwealth Parliamentary Debates, 2021). Widening our focus beyond MRT, the Australian government has invested in the broader field of genomics. The Australian federal, state, and territory governments agreed to a National Health Genomics Policy Framework in 2017 to, amongst other things, embed genomics into the Australian health system and improve performance of mainstream genomic services. To support that goal, the 2018–2019 Australian Budget committed AUD$500 million to a Genomics Health Futures Mission focusing on clinical trials and research collaboration. In contrast with the timing of the United Kingdom's MRT legislation (Chapter 4, this volume), Australian reforms to permit clinical MRT are occurring at the same time as growing discussion about germline gene editing. In fact, both the Mito Foundation—the patient advocacy group responsible for much of the drive to legalise clinical MRT—and the federal government have been careful to differentiate between MRT and gene editing. Reflecting that, although the reforms provide some scope for future-proofing by permitting the addition of new, currently unknown, techniques to the list of licensable techniques (when such new techniques are proved safe and effective), these are restricted. The amendments prohibit 'techniques that use DNA from more than three people, that intentionally modify the nuclear or mitochondrial DNA (such as through gene editing), or that use synthetic materials to create a human zygote' (Commonwealth House of Representatives, 2021: para 36).

Complicating any discussion of gene editing in embryos is the debate over the distinction, if any, between MRT and other forms of modification to DNA. The definition of MST in Maeve's Law and accompanying Explanatory Memorandum make it clear that the removal or transfer of mtDNA or of maternal spindle material during MRT is not a modification of mtDNA or nDNA (Commonwealth House of Representatives, 2021: para 38 and Item 20 Bill). In its 2020 deliberations, the NHMRC Expert Working Committee could not agree on whether MRT are genetic modification, with some members pointing out that whole organelles are replaced rather than specific genes being edited or enabling the expression of artificial gene constructs, therefore concluding that MRT are not genetic modification. This approach is different from the conclusions of the US National Academies of Sciences, Engineering, and Medicine consensus paper on policy issues associated with MRT (National Academies, 2016). That paper concludes that MRT are genetic modification because genetic modification does not require direct editing of DNA (Chapter 6, this volume). In contrast and as noted by Dimond and Stephens (Chapter 4, this volume) the UK considers that genetic modification in this context is limited to modification of nDNA.

As I have discussed elsewhere (Ludlow, 2018), unlike in the United Kingdom, which has expressly excluded humans from the meaning of genetically modified organisms (GMOs) as used in relation to non-human organisms, Australia's GMO legislation includes humans within its scope if they have been genetically modified unless that modification is through somatic gene therapy. Maeve's Law excludes licensed MRT from the scope of the GMO legislation. Nevertheless, the division between germline and somatic modification remains an area of contestation when the possible gene editing of embryos is considered. The NHMRC Expert Working Committee concluded that MRT are germline modification because 'the key feature of mitochondrial donation is that it does result in potentially heritable changes to the genome. As such, the Committee concludes that mitochondrial donation can be a form of germline modification, since the modified mitochondrial genome can be inherited by future generations' (Australian Government NHMRC, 2020b: 20–21). However, the Committee also concluded that MRT 'for the purpose of preventing the transmission of mitochondrial DNA disease from a mother to her offspring is in contrast to some germline gene editing techniques that could potentially be used for the purpose of enhancement' (Australian Government NHMRC, 2020b: 19).

Nevertheless, to ensure that gene editing of mtDNA cannot occur in embryos intended for reproductive use, Maeve's Law permits researchers and clinicians to undertake MRT pursuant to specific exceptions to the relevant legislative prohibitions rather than by simply excluding mtDNA from the meaning of genetic material or genome for the purposes of the relevant prohibitions. For example, a new subsection was added to the provision that prohibits the creation of embryos by fertilisation which contains genetic material provided by more than two persons. That subsection exempts such creation if it is authorised under a MRT licence. The provision prohibiting heritable changes to the human genome has also been amended to include a similar exception. If the alternative approach of excluding mtDNA from the meaning of genetic material or genome had been taken, the result would have been the legalisation of gene editing of mtDNA. At this time, it is clear that this is a step too far for Australia.

ACKNOWLEDGEMENTS

This research is supported by the Australian government through the Australian Research Council's Discovery Projects funding scheme (project DP170100919) and the Department of Health's Medical Research Future Fund (project 76744). The views expressed in this work are the author's own.

REFERENCES

Andrews Report. 'Human cloning: Scientific, ethical and regulatory aspects of human cloning and stem cell research.' The Parliament of the Commonwealth of Australia, 2001. https://www.aph.gov.au/Parliamentary_Business/Committ ees/House_of_Representatives_Committees?url=laca/humancloning/conte nts.htm.
Australian Government Department of Health. 'Consultation summary report. Public consultation on the approach to introduce mitochondrial donation in Australia.' 2021a. https://www.health.gov.au/sites/default/files/documents/

2021/03/public-consultation-on-the-approach-to-introduce-mitochondrial-donation-in-australia-summary-report.pdf.

Australian Government Department of Health. 'Legalising mitochondrial donation in Australia. Public consultation paper.' February 2021b. https://consultati ons.health.gov.au/strategic-policy/mitochondrial-donation-in-australia/suppo rting_documents/Mitochondrial%20Donation%20%20Public%20Consultat ion%20Paper.pdf.

Australian Government Department of Health. 'Press conference in Canberra about Maeve's Law, COVID-19 vaccine rollout, and assistance to Papua, New Guinea.' 24 March 2021. https://www.health.gov.au/ministers/the-hon-greg-hunt-mp/ media/press-conference-in-canberra-about-maeves-law-covid-19-vaccine-roll out-and-assistance-to-papua-new-guinea.

Australian Government NHMRC. 'Mitochondrial donation community consultation report.' March 2020. https://www.nhmrc.gov.au/sites/default/files/docume nts/attachments/Consultation-report.pdf.

Australian Government NHMRC. 'Expert statement: Mitochondrial donation expert working committee.' March 2020b. https://www.nhmrc.gov.au/mitochondrial-donation/australian-government-department-health-consultation#download.

Australian Law Reform Commission. 'Human tissue transplants.' 1977. http://www. austlii.edu.au/au/other/lawreform/ALRC/1977/7.html.

Australian Senate Community Affairs Reference Committee. 'Science of mitochondrial donation and related matters.' Australian Parliament, 27 June 2018. https://apo.org.au/node/180206.

Blakeslee, Sandra. 'New issue in embryo case raised over use of donor.' *New York Times*, 21 June 1984. https://www.nytimes.com/1984/06/21/us/new-issue-in-embryo-case-raised-over-use-of-donor.html.

Commonwealth House of Representatives. 'Mitochondrial Donation Law Reform (Maeve's Law) Bill 2021, explanatory memorandum.' 2021. https://parlinfo. aph.gov.au/parlInfo/download/legislation/ems/r6697_ems_34f56965-6288-4da6-9a02-096f5b58d3c1/upload_pdf/JC001678.pdf;fileType=applicat ion%2Fpdfsearch=%22legislation/ems/r6697_ems_34f56965-6288-4da6-9a02-096f5b58d3c1%22.

Commonwealth Parliamentary Debates, House of Representatives, Bills. 'Mitochondrial Donation Law Reform (Maeve's Law) Bill 2021, second reading speech 24 March 2021 (Mr Greg Hunt).' 2021. https://www.aph.gov.au/Parliam entary_Business/Hansard/Hansard_Display?bid=chamber/hansardr/d64bb a7e-9b55-427c-aef1-2c98b347651d/&sid=0009.

Commonwealth Senate. 'Revised explanatory memorandum for Prohibition of Human Cloning Bill 2002.' 2002. https://www.legislation.gov.au/Details/C200 4B01312/Revised%20Explanatory%20Memorandum/Text.

Costigan, Peter. 'Scores seek to mother 2 embryos.' *Washington Post*, 20 June 1984, A1–A27. https://www.washingtonpost.com/archive/politics/1984/06/20/sco res-seek-to-mother-2-embryos/cc378859-77b0-4ee9-addb-2dc52d4db27d/.

De Kretzer, D., P. Dennis, B. Hudson, J. Leeton, A. Lopata, K. Outch, J. Talbot, and C. Wood. 'Transfer of a human zygote.' *Lancet* 302, no. 7831 (1973): 728–729.

Demack Report. 'Report of the special committee appointed by the Queensland government to enquire into the laws relating to artificial insemination, in vitro fertilisation and other related matters.' Queensland Government, 1984.

Dow, Alisha, and Melissa Cunningham. 'Call for change to human cloning law to prevent genetic disorder:' *The Age*, 21 September 2017. https://www.theage.

com.au/national/victoria/call-for-change-to-human-cloninglaw-to-prevent-genetic-disorder-20170920-gylgyo.html.

Fertility Society of Australia and New Zealand. 'Reproductive Technology Accreditation Committee Codes of Practice for ART units in Australia and New Zealand.' 2014. https://www.fertilitysociety.com.au/rtac-australia-new-zealand/.

Heerey Review, Legislation Review Committee. 'Legislation review: Prohibition of Human Cloning Act 2002 and Research Involving Human Embryos Act 2002.' Australian Government, 2011. https://www.nhmrc.gov.au/about-us/publications/2010-legislation-review-prohibition-human-cloning-reproduction-act-2002.

Lockhart Review. 'Legislation review: Prohibition of Human Cloning Act 2002 and the Research Involving Human Embryos Act 2002.' Australian Government, 2005. https://webarchive.nla.gov.au/awa/20060912052643/http://pandora.nla.gov.au/pan/63190/20060912-0000/www.lockhartreview.com.au/reports.html.

Lopata, Alexander, Ian W. H. Johnston, Ian J. Hoult, and Andrew I. Speirs. 'Pregnancy following intrauterine implantation of an embryo obtained by in vitro fertilization of a preovulatory egg.' *Fertility and Sterility* 33, no. 2 (1980): 117–120.

Ludlow, Karinne. 'Genes and gestation in Australian regulation of egg donation, surrogacy and mitochondrial donation.' *Journal of Law and Medicine* 23 (2015): 378–395.

Ludlow, Karinne. 'The policy and regulatory context of US, UK, and Australian responses to mitochondrial donation governance.' *Jurimetrics* 58 (2018): 247–265.

Ludlow, Karinne. 'Genetic identity concerns in the regulation of novel reproductive technologies.' *Journal of Law and the Biosciences* 7, no. 1 (2020): lsaa004.

McLucas, J. Commonwealth Senate. 'Prohibition of Human Cloning Bill 2002 second reading speech 11 November 2002 (Sen. Jan McLucas).' 2002. https://parlinfo.aph.gov.au/parlInfo/search/display/display.w3p;db=CHAMBER;id=chamber%2Fhansards%2F2002-11-11%2F0022;query=Id%3A%22chamber%2Fhansards%2F2002-11-11%2F0014%22.

Morris, Clive. Transcript 'Evidence to Senate Community Affairs Legislation Committee, reference: Research Involving Embryos and Prohibition of Human Cloning Bill 2002.' CA345. 26 September 2002. https://www.aph.gov.au/Parliamentary_Business/Committees/Senate/Community_Affairs/Completed_inquiries/2002-04/emb_cloning/hearings/index.

Morrison, Scott. 'Tribute to Kara Crawley.' 2017. https://youtu.be/vR3prMdgj_w.

Murphy, K. 'Coalition sticks to ban on stem cell research.' *The Age*. 22 June 2006. https://www.theage.com.au/national/coalition-sticks-to-ban-on-stem-cell-research-20060622-ge2kh2.html.

National Academies of Sciences, Engineering, and Medicine. *Mitochondrial Replacement Techniques: Ethical, Social, and Policy Considerations*. Washington, DC: National Academies Press, 2016.

National Health and Medical Research Council. 'Ethical guidelines on the use of assisted reproductive technology.' 2017. https://www.nhmrc.gov.au/about-us/publications/art.

National Health and Medical Research Council. 'Submission to Australian Senate Standing Committee on Community Affairs, inquiry into the science of mitochondrial donation and related matters.' 2018. Submission 4. https://www.aph.gov.au/Parliamentary_Business/Committees/Senate/Community_Affairs/MitochondrialDonation/Submissions.

Steptoe, Patrick C., and Robert G. Edwards. 'Birth after the reimplantation of a human embryo.' *Lancet* 312, no. 8085 (1978): 366.

Taylor-Sands, Michelle, and Christopher Gyngell. 'Legality of embryonic gene editing in Australia.' *Journal of Law and Medicine* 26, no. 2 (2018): 356–373.

Thorburn, David, Kathryn North, and Martin Delatycki. 'Submission to 2018 Senate committee inquiry.' Murdoch Children's Research Institute and Victoria Clinical Genetic Services, 2018. Submission 23. https://www.aph.gov.au/Parliamentary_Business/Committees/Senate/Community_Affairs/MitochondrialDonation/Submissions.

Trounson, Alan, and Linda Mohr. 'Human pregnancy following cryopreservation, thawing and transfer of an eight-cell embryo.' *Nature* 305, no. 5936 (1983): 707–709.

Waller, Louis. 'Waller Report: Committee to consider the social, ethical and legal issues arising from in vitro fertilisation: Report on donor gametes in IVF.' Victorian Government, 1983. ISBN 9780724155224.

Waller, Louis. 'Waller Report. Committee to consider the social, ethical and legal issues arising from in vitro fertilisation: Report on the disposition of embryos produced by in vitro fertilisation.' Victorian Government, 1984. https://www.parliament.vic.gov.au/papers/govpub/VPARL1982-85No168.pdf

6
MRT in the United States

I. GLENN COHEN, PRIYANKA MENON,
AND ELI Y. ADASHI

6.1 MRT'S PLACE IN THE LARGER UNITED STATES
REPRODUCTIVE TECHNOLOGY CONTEXT

The United States is often described as the "Wild West" of reproductive
technology use, either with envy or condemnation (Cohen et al., 2020: 2).
It is certainly true that when comparisons are drawn to many similarly
industrialised countries, such as Canada, Australia, the United Kingdom,
and Germany, the United States is generally more permissive in terms
of what reproductive technologies are available and how they may used.
Indeed, this difference has engendered some inbound medical travel (also
called medical tourism) to the United States. By contrast, part of what
makes the case of mitochondrial replacement therapy (MRT) so interesting, as we discuss in the next section, is that it is a regulatory context in
which the United States is *more* restrictive in its regulation of a reproductive technology than the United Kingdom and, arguably, than the direction in which Australia may be going (Chapter 4, this volume). With little
chance of this status quo shifting dramatically to alter this dynamic in the
foreseeable future, MRT will likely remain a unique case study within comparative health law.

Returning for now to the initial comparison suggested at the chapter's
outset, it is not so much that the United States has an overall *unregulated*

I. Glenn Cohen, Priyanka Menon, and Eli Y. Adashi, *MRT in the United States* In: *Reproduction Reborn*. Edited by:
Diana M. Bowman, Karinne Ludlow, and Walter G. Johnson, Oxford University Press. © Oxford University Press 2023.
DOI: 10.1093/oso/9780197616192.003.0007

sector of reproductive technology as that, in both the source of authority and the mode of regulation, it has a very *fragmented* regulatory structure. As a matter of American constitutional law, there is relatively little case law relevant to reproductive technologies (Cohen et al., 2020). The key United States Supreme Court precedents focus on access to abortion and contraception (a right to abortion, at least, now seriously undermined by the recent US Supreme Court decision in *Dobbs v. Jackson Women's Health Organization*), and the Court has assiduously avoided determining whether any prohibition on reproductive technology use can run afoul of the federal constitution (Cohen et al., 2020). Lower courts have also largely avoided declaring unconstitutional state restrictions on things such as surrogacy arrangements, though occasionally some will hold to the contrary (Cohen et al., 2020).[1] As discussed in this chapter's final section, whether there are bona fide constitutional claims pertaining to the use of a technology like MRT remains very uncertain.

At the federal level, there has also been precious little in the way of legislation that governs the *use* of reproductive technologies—we contrast this with legislation regarding the *funding* of relevant research below. Outside of an appropriations rider that pertains to gene editing (and arguably MRT, as discussed below), the main piece of legislation apart from funding is the Fertility Clinic Success Rate and Certification Act of 1992, which requires fertility clinics to report their success rates to the Centers for Disease Control on a standardised form.[2] This is in marked contrast to the UK Human Fertilisation and Embryology (HFE) Act[3] and its attendant Human Fertilisation and Embryology Authority (HFEA), which provides central legislative and administrative governance of many facets of the industry, as well as the Canadian Assisted Human Reproduction Act,[4] which similarly sets out in some detail how reproductive technologies may be used—including criminal penalties for prohibited acts.

Instead, much of the regulation of reproductive technologies in the United States is done through state-level law making: commercial surrogacy, for example, ranges from criminally prohibited to enforceable by contract depending on the specific state regulation involved. Where there is no legislation or governmental regulation, tort law partially fills the gap by limiting what kinds of technologies may be used and in what way. This is supplemented to some extent by professional self-regulation by fertility physicians (Cohen et al., 2020). For example, the American Society for Reproductive Medicine issues many ethics opinions and other documents meant to align practice. This "Swiss cheese" model of state legislation and regulation, tort law, and professional self-regulation still leaves a lot of discretion to individual providers of reproductive technologies. As a result, there is significant variance in the practice of reproductive medicine across the United States.

Within this context, the regulation of MRT stands out because the federal government has provided a single answer that creates a uniform rule that results in no provider variance: MRT is prohibited in this country. How did we get to this exceptional (given the history of United States reproductive technology) result? Section 6.2 discusses the answer.

6.2 THE ROAD TO THE UNITED STATES PROHIBITION ON MRT AND THE PROSPECTS FOR CHANGE

This section begins with some background on a regulatory technique that has been used to regulate other cutting-edge technologies in the reproductive and genetics space in the United States: the appropriations rider. It then discusses a proposal to create a regulatory pathway for MRT that was put forward by the National Academies of Sciences, Engineering, and Medicine (NASEM) but that ultimately never saw the light of day because of Congress's passage of an appropriations rider that prohibited MRT in the United States.

6.2.1 Appropriations Riders and Cutting Edge Reproductive and Genetic Technologies.

While (as discussed above) there has been relatively little by way of direct federal legislation in the reproductive context, there is a long history of using the 'power of the purse' to influence policy in adjacent areas. Perhaps most prominently, the Dickey-Wicker amendment was first introduced as a rider to the Balanced Budget Downpayment Act, the 1996 appropriations bill (H.R. 2880)[5], and has been approved every year since its initial introduction. The amendment prohibits the US Department of Health and Human Services from funding research for which human embryos have been created or in which human embryos have been destroyed (Dickey-Wicker Amend.). Four years after the Dickey-Wicker amendment's debut, in 2000, the National Institutes for Health (NIH) issued highly restrictive guidelines for scientists conducting research involving embryonic stem cells, requiring—among other restrictions—that such frozen embryos be obtained with private funds from fertility clinics (National Institutes of Health, 2000).

In 2001, the Bush administration issued an executive order that prohibited federal funding from use in research involving stem cells from human embryos and banned the creation of new stem cell lines (though the order left room for researchers working with existing cell lines to continue their work) (Spivak et al., 2017). Then, in 2005 and 2007, the House and the Senate passed versions of the Stem Cell Research Enhancement Act (H.R. 810 and S.5) that would have allowed for federal funding for stem cell research that involved stem cells originating from embryos originally created—but not ultimately used—for in vitro fertilisation (IVF) efforts. Both times, President Bush vetoed the legislation.

In 2009, the Obama administration reversed the Bush administration's policy, with President Obama's issuing of an executive order restoring federal funding for research involving embryonic stem cells (Obama, 2009; Executive Order No. 13,505). The NIH passed new guidelines shortly thereafter, following President Obama's lead (National Institutes of Health, 2009). By this time, however, the scientists who would have benefited from such funding had largely adapted to the federal funding landscape under the Bush administration. Researchers had turned to induced pluripotent (adult) stem cells (iPSCs) for their work (Murugan, 2009). Adding to the somewhat muted effect of these changes was President Obama's signing of H.R. 1105, the Omnibus Appropriations Act, which kept the Dickey-Wicker amendment intact and in force. Importantly, even in areas where the Dickey-Wicker amendment prohibits *federal* funds being used, it does not prohibit states or private parties from funding this research (Gugliotta, 2015). We shall see in a moment that this is in contrast to how Congress has handled MRT.

6.2.2 Food and Drug Administration's Authority and the National Academies' Proposal for a Regulatory Pathway for MRT in the United States

The Food and Drug Administration (FDA) has asserted that the regulation of MRT falls within its jurisdiction, similar to its assertions of jurisdiction over other reproductive technologies such as human cloning, cytoplasmic transfer, etc. (Cohen et al., 2020). As a result, the dominant regulatory paradigm used for regulating MRT in the United States is that of a therapeutic, such as a drug or biological product (Cohen et al., 2015). The statutory background for such jurisdiction comes from the Public Health Service Act[6] and the Federal Food, Drug, and Cosmetic Act,[7] which provides the FDA with the authority to regulate human cells, tissues, and cellular and tissue-based products (HCT/Ps). Among the HCT/Ps regulated by the FDA are bone, ligaments, amniotic membrane, oocytes, and embryos.

The FDA office charged with MRT regulation is the Center for Biologics Evaluation and Research (CBER). CBER maintains a wide spread of cellular, tissue, and gene therapeutics within its regulatory ambit (Cohen et al., 2015). CBER, working under its mandate to direct the use of 'human cells . . . in therapy involving the transfer of genetic material by means other than the union of gamete nuclei,' regulates HCT/Ps under 21 CFR §1270 and §1271. These regulations are aimed at preventing the spread of communicable diseases and maintaining records and, as such, require firms to follow three major requirements:

1. to register their HCT/Ps with the FDA;
2. to evaluate donors to reduce the risk that tissue transplantation spreads infectious disease; and
3. to follow the good tissue practices for HCT/Ps as outlined by the FDA.

As part of its regulatory efforts aimed at MRT, the FDA convened a meeting of its long-standing Cellular, Tissue, and Gene Therapies Advisory Committee with the aim of fostering a discussion concerning 'oocyte modification in assisted reproduction for the prevention of transmission of mitochondrial disease' (Cohen et al., 2020). The committee met to discuss the topic on 25 and 26 February 2014. Though the committee did not vote on any proposals charting a path forward as a result of its meeting, the committee's discussion ranged from the design of clinical trials to prevent the transmission of mitochondrial disease, to issues of informed consent, and to the potential harms and risks for both women and children involved in MRT (Food and Drug Administration, 2014a, 2014b). At the time of its meeting, the committee also received public comments detailing worry regarding the ethical, social, and political issues raised by MRT (National Academies of Sciences, Engineering, and Medicine, 2016).

The FDA, in hopes of addressing public concern surrounding MRT, then commissioned the Institute of Medicine (now the National Academy of Medicine [NAM]), to produce a report describing how the United States should regulate MRT. Carrying out its charge, NAM produced an extensive and considered report. The report ultimately concluded that MRT was not ethically forbidden and that the FDA should permit initial clinical research in MRT to go forward, thereby placing MRT on the standard path towards FDA review. However, the NAM report also detailed extensive conditions that should be required of such clinical research before it is allowed to progress, recommending that the FDA require

- The initial safety and minimisation of risk of MRT be established. Of highest priority was minimising risk to future children.
- Preclinical research should establish the likelihood of efficacy using in vitro modelling and animal and human embryo testing.
- All clinical investigations must only involve women who would otherwise have a chance of transmitting a serious mitochondrial DNA disease.
- A professional opinion, informed by the available evidence, must determine that if a woman with the risk of transmitting a serious mitochondrial DNA disease is also the woman who will carry the pregnancy, then neither the woman nor her foetus will suffer serious risks to their health if the pregnancy is carried to term.
- Only male embryos may be eligible for intrauterine transfer.
- Clinical investigations must be limited only to researchers with relevant expertise and skills.

Beyond these conditions, the report also offered further recommendations. One of its recommendations held that the FDA should use similar ethical standards in the regulation of MRT research as developed by the NAM, the NIH, and the International Society for Stem Cell Research (ISSCR) for the use of embryonic stem cells in research. Another recommendation concerned study design standards, advocating for the well-being for future-born children as highest priority, standardised study designs, and the collection of long-term information regarding the psychological and social effects on children born as a result of MRT. The report also concluded that research into the transfer of female embryos should take place only if there was clear evidence of safety and efficacy from male cohorts, animal testing demonstrated intergenerational safety, and the public and the FDA shared the same framework regarding the moral limits on heritable genetic modification. Last, the report provided that any action taken by the FDA concerning MRT should adhere to the principle of transparency, engage the public, involve collaboration with relevant stakeholders, maximise data quality, circumscribe the use of MRT, and require long-term follow-up.

Unfortunately, however, while the NAM Report was pending, Congress acted to essentially prevent the FDA from developing this proposed (or really any) regulatory pathway as to MRT. In 2016, as part of the budgeting process, Congress enacted a rider to the 2016 Appropriations Bill (Cohen and Adashi, 2016, citing Consolidated Appropriations Act, Sec. 749). This rider restricted the FDA from considering—or even 'acknowledging receipt' of an application seeking an exemption 'for investigational use of a drug or biological product . . . in research in which a human embryo is intentionally created or modified to include a heritable genetic modification' (Sec. 749). Instead, under this rider, the FDA is required to ignore such an application and deem it 'not received by the Secretary' (Sec. 749). Pursuing MRT without FDA approval would violate the Federal Food, Drug, and Cosmetic Act, and any attempt to get FDA approval is essentially dead on arrival because of the appropriations rider.

There was no debate on the rider upon its initial inclusion in the appropriations bill (Cohen et al., 2020). As a result, the congressional record regarding the rider offers few answers as to its motivation. One piece of evidence about congressional intent comes from a statement made by the Chairman of the House Committee on Science, Space, and Technology, Representative Lamar Smith, remarking on the 'alarming' nature of a 'recent report from China, where teams of researchers have begun to experiment with engineering DNA in human embryos' (Cohen, 2018, quoting 'The Science and Ethics of Genetically Engineered Human DNA': Hearing Before H. Comm. on Sci., Space, and Tech., 114th Cong. 9 [2015]: statement of Rep. Lamar Smith, Chairman, Comm. on Sci., Space and Tech.). Smith claims that, 'the scientific community members have been clear: the science and ethics of this new technology must be resolved in order to prevent dangerous abuses and unintended consequences.'

Whatever the congressional intent behind the rider, its effect has been to stifle completely attempts at clinical development of MRT in the United States despite some ambiguities about whether the amendment is rightfully understood as applying to the case of MRT. The FDA has taken an expansive approach to interpreting the reach of the rider and has included all varieties of MRT as falling within its prohibition. For instance, the FDA has issued at least one letter to a researcher on the grounds that he had '[used] MRT to form a genetically modified embryo' in the United States (Cohen et al., 2020; Malarkey, 2017). John Zhang, MD, in his capacity as CEO of the New Hope Fertility Center, was the recipient of the FDA's 2016 letter, was responsible for performing the maternal spindle transfer procedure for the first baby born as a result of MRT. What makes the FDA's letter to Dr Zhang even more exceptional as a marker of the FDA's regulatory ambit is that the relevant implantation took place in Mexico, not the United States (Cohen et al., 2020; Chapter 7, this volume).

As two of us (Cohen and Adashi) have argued, the rider seems to be aimed at prohibiting gene editing of nuclear DNA, but MRT has been something of an indirect casualty. In 2019, we convened a gathering at the Harvard Law School to explore the possibility of clarifying the scope of the rider and drawing distinctions between gene editing and MRT. As the *New York Times* described the issues we discussed at that event,

[p]roponents of MRT have long held that the procedure should be exempted from the current prohibition, in part because it does not involve altering any genetic code. Defective mitochondria are swapped out for healthy ones, but mitochondrial DNA governs only a handful of basic cellular functions. It is separate from nuclear DNA, which helps determine individual traits like physical appearance, intelligence and personality. That means MRT cannot be used to produce the genetically enhanced "designer babies" that so many people are concerned about.

That's not to say that the procedure is risk-free (Chapters 1 and 10, this volume). There's no way to know how safe or effective MRT is until doctors test it in humans. Clinical trials and the American regulatory apparatus were designed for exactly this purpose: to minimise risk without forgoing medical progress. But opponents of MRT say that, in this case, to proceed with such trials would be to subject future humans to an experiment that they are powerless to oppose (New York Times, 2019).

Perhaps resulting from those efforts or the coverage in the *New York Times*, shortly thereafter efforts were made to change the rider by members of the Agriculture Appropriations subcommittee within the Committee on Appropriations. Rather than draw a formal distinction between gene editing and MRT and limit the rider to the former—the course we recommended—these members made attempts to omit the rider from the appropriations bill altogether. This change would have then allowed the FDA to regulate MRT as it does other similar technologies—in its current form, the rider prohibits the FDA from even conducting review of clinical trial applications that involve such genetic modification. But it would also have had the effect of allowing the same process to unfold for gene editing since the same rider language applies to both. Removing the rider would equally remove the impediment for both.

The Agriculture Appropriations subcommittee approved a draft of the bill that left out the rider on 23 March 2019 (Ferguson, 2019). However, put to a voice vote by the entire House Appropriations Committee, these efforts to omit the rider failed (Ferguson, 2019). On the rider's importance, Aderholt—who once again introduced the amendment—remarked that, 'The ethics hadn't caught up with the science, and . . . the science has not caught up with the science.' (Joseph, 2019). Similarly, Sanford D. Bishop Jr., chairman of the Agriculture Appropriations subcommittee, supported reinstating the ban in the bill. Ultimately, the amendment was readopted by the House Appropriations Committee with only a single 'no' vote.

While the rider persists and is understood by FDA as preventing it from adopting any review of MRT, there are some reasons to believe that the story is not over, politically speaking. First, the rider's survival was not without dissent. Democratic Representative Debbie Wasserman-Schulz, the lone objector to the rider's renewal, remarked about the rider's importance for her own family. A carrier of the BRCA-2 mutation who was diagnosed with breast cancer in 2007, Wasserman-Schulz spoke of the research's importance for the well-being of her own children's children and generations after that:

> If we ever have an opportunity when they have children or when they decide to have a family, to have research advanced to a point where you could have their genetic material, when combined with their partner, altered so that that mutation could be cut off in our family tree and that risk of death and massive health care implications could be eliminated, that's incredibly important. (Joseph, 2019)

(To be fair, though, one might think she was referring more to gene editing than to MRT itself.)

Furthermore, although she was the only formal vote against it, Wasserman-Schulz was not alone in her dissatisfaction with the rider. Representative Nita M. Lowey, then-chairwoman of the House Appropriations Committee, 'reluctantly supported' reinserting the rider into the bill (Joseph, 2019). She remarked that she disapproved of the rider because it initially was introduced without debate and removed the FDA's ability to evaluate individual applications on their own merits (Ferguson, 2019). Representative Bishop's support of the rider was similarly equivocal: Bishop voiced support for Congress's consideration of the issue in the future, though he further remarked that he believed that 'today is not that time, and this appropriations committee markup is not that place' (Joseph, 2019).

As discussed above, there are many reasons to think the rider is motivated by a desire to limit gene editing and that MRT is more of an unintentional casualty of the way in which the language was drafted. MRT was named only cursorily in the House Committee's 2015 report and was not mentioned a single time in the House's hearing (Spivak et al., 2018). Moreover, the male-only MRT endorsed by the NASEM report might not fall within the amendment's scope at all: it is arguable that these MRTs do not consist of 'research in which a human embryo is intentionally created or modified to include a heritable genetic modification' (Cohen et al., 2020). Moreover, many of the ethical and social concerns underlying the rider seem to be absent in the case of male-only MRT as male embryos cannot (with a few exceptions) transmit the modified mitochondrial DNA to their offspring. This renders inert many of the potential rationales behind the amendment since there is little risk of inheritance of the modification.

We remain hopeful that Congress will consider a more targeted amendment to the rider the next time it is up for renewal, one that directly distinguishes MRT from gene editing and enables the FDA to review the former just as it would any other cutting-edge technology that is poised to help many families.

6.3 PROSPECTS FOR THE FUTURE ADDITIONAL LEGAL AND ETHICAL ISSUES: DISCUSSION AND CONCLUSIONS

How likely are we to see movement in the United States to liberalise its MRT process along the lines suggested by the NAM report?

There are some signs for optimism. First, the global landscape regarding the regulation of MRT is changing (Chapters 5, 8, and 9, this volume; Cohen et al., 2020). Given the United States's keen interest in the United Kingdom regulation of reproductive technology, including MRT, the advances made by the United Kingdom on this front, particularly the first MRT clinical trial in 2017, may bode well in terms of turning the political tides. Also encouraging were the statements (if not the votes) of the House members concerning the rider in 2019: these signs seem to indicate that consistent and focused political pressure may bring about congressional action (with the hopeful outcome of approval) regarding MRT. Moreover, there may be room for political advocacy groups to educate the public on MRTs and their unique ethical, social, and scientific status, opening an opportunity for such groups to press their cause by distinguishing MRT from germline gene editing. Indeed, some scholars have argued that there is only a small step between the passage of 2018's 'right to try' law—allowing for compassionate access to experimental drugs for patients with terminal illnesses who have exhausted all available options—and the FDA allowing families with mitochondrial disease and their physicians to bypass the MRT ban (Pompei and Pompei, 2019).

There are also, however, more systemic reasons to be pessimistic. The politics of abortion in the United States and the history of the Dickey-Wicker amendment discussed above suggest significant hurdles for federal funding of MRT-related *research*, given that it will involve human embryo destruction. Other countries, such as the United Kingdom, have no such barriers to research (Cohen et al., 2015). Similar sticky issues occur even within the *clinical* pathway set out by the NAM for possible adoption. For example, the NAM report left open the question of what to do with female embryos (and unused male embryos) should the initial clinical trials regarding MRT be unsuccessful. The two most obvious options, either destroying the embryos or keeping them frozen indefinitely, may be things that some in the United States Congress would adamantly oppose. Even prevailing national attitudes may be a reason for pause: viewing MRT as 'a beacon of national scientific prowess' has arguably helped further MRT's regulatory prospects within the United Kingdom (Chapter 4, this volume). By contrast, no such national pride exists for MRT within the United States despite equal scientific contributions to the development of MRT by American scientists (Cohen et al., 2015).

A different issue is presented by the other side of the same coin: the NAM proposal to allow male-only intrauterine transfer as a way of reducing concerns about heritability and intergenerational effects. In one sense, this amounts to a federal agency requiring as a condition of use of MRT that potential parents select their offspring on the basis of sex. Sex selection is, of course, a practice with a dark history both within the United States and in other parts of the globe. Setting aside potential legal worries for a moment, such a practice raises plausible ethical concerns given that the sex selection involved in MRT, at least as recommended by the NAM, is not directed at ensuring or protecting the health of the child. Instead, such sex selection seems to be aimed at preventing the transmission of germline modifications to future generations on the theory that MRT may cause unforeseen negative consequences in the future. As reason for limiting reproductive choices, however, the appeal to uncertain and hard-to-predict events that may take place far in the future may seem dubious. Indeed, at least one scholar argued that such grounds are insufficient to justify 'such an intrusive policy' and that 'a much more robust defence' of mandatory sex selection must be mounted by its proponents (Brandt, 2018: 442).

Turning now squarely to the legal questions, adoption of NAM's recommendation to approve male-only embryo transfer may leave the FDA open to constitutional challenge. Such a challenge could take two forms. First, potential challengers might allege a violation of their rights under the Due Process Clause of the Fourteenth Amendment, claiming that restricting their use of MRT in this way violates a constitutionally recognised right to procreative liberty. As noted above, the United States Supreme Court has thus far persistently avoided determining whether its existing precedents as to procreative rights—cases pertaining to abortion and contraception, primarily—apply at all to reproductive technologies, let alone one as path-breaking as MRT. As mentioned above, the Supreme Court's recent decision in *Dobbs v. Jackson Women's Health Organization* overruling *Roe v. Wade* and its progeny cast further doubt on this argument. Language from Justice

Alito's opinion for the Court suggests that the Court will be very unsympathetic to claims of constitutional protections for any reproductive technology that involves embryo destruction (Cohen et al., 2022).

Potential challengers might also argue that approval of male-only embryo transfer runs afoul of the Equal Protection Clause of the Fourteenth Amendment and thus amounts to the FDA unlawfully discriminating against women on the basis of sex. This raises the intriguing and thus-far unanswered question of whether the Equal Protection clause protects only already-born women or also extended to yet-to-be born women, thereby bringing programs aimed at preventing female embryos from being implanted (and thus being born) within its purview. If it is the latter, the Supreme Court has said such a program will only survive constitutional scrutiny if it is justified by an important state interest and carried out by a means that is substantially related to that interest. It is unclear whether the NAM report's provided justification—concern for the unforeseeable consequences of MRT for germline modifications for future generations—will pass muster. Given the Supreme Court's unwillingness to enter the fray and offer answers concerning the constitutionality of reproductive technologies more generally, it is unlikely the Supreme Court will provide an answer to these questions soon.

If the current United States ban stays in place while MRT remains available as it currently is or becomes more available in other countries, we may see more 'circumvention tourism'in which individuals travel abroad to undergo medical treatments or procedures that are otherwise banned, prohibited, or heavily regulated in their home countries (Cohen et al., 2022; Cohen 2011; Chapter 8, this volume). Such tourism, though, poses considerable safety and ethical risks. For instance, on the issue of MRT, patients may travel to countries where the technology is less well-regulated and understood, making it harder for patients and donors to understand the procedure itself as well as to provide informed consent. Such circumvention tourism is difficult to prevent. While Zhang ran afoul of the FDA because key parts of the MRT process were begun in the United States, it would not be hard for offshore clinics to design around that element of the FDA's jurisdiction and attract United States patients by maintaining few connections to the United States.

It is an odd result that in a country with one of the most permissive approaches to reproductive technologies in the world and some of the best scientists and clinicians aimed at providing reproductive assistance to patients that MRT remains the exception, effectively banned. While much of the world travels to the United States for surrogacy and other reproductive technologies, when it comes to MRT, it is United States patients who are forced to consider circumvention tourism. In this chapter, we have outlined how we have arrived at this situation, the potential for change, and some of the legal and ethical issues involved.

NOTES

1. See, for instance, *J. R. v. Utah*, 261 F. Supp. 2d 1268, 1296-1297 (D. Utah 2002) and *Lifchez v. Hartigan*, 735 F. Supp. 1361 (N.D. Ill. 1990).
2. Fertility Clinic Success Rate and Certification Act of 1992, Pub. L. No. 102-493, 106 Stat. 3146 (codified as amended in scattered sections of 42 U.S.C. (2012)).
3. Human Fertilisation and Embryology Act 2008. 2008. c. 22. https://www.legi slation.gov.uk/ukpga/2008/22/contents.
4. Assisted Human Reproduction Act. 2004. S.C. 2004, c.2. https://laws-lois.just ice.gc.ca/eng/acts/A13.4/FullText.html.
5. Balanced Budget Downpayment Act, Pub. L. No. 104-99, § 128, 110 Stat. 26, 34 (1996).
6. 42 U.S.C. ch. 6A § 201 et seq.
7. 21 U.S.C. 321(g).

REFERENCES

Brandt, Reuven. 'Mandatory sex selection and mitochondrial transfer.' *Bioethics* 32, no. 7 (2018): 437–444.

Cohen, I. Glenn. 'Circumvention tourism.' *Cornell Law Review* 97 (2011): 1309–1398.

Cohen, I. Glenn. 'The right(s) to procreate and assisted reproductive technologies in the United States.' In *The Oxford Handbook of Comparative Health Law*, Oxford University Press, 2020: 1009–1026.

Cohen, I. Glenn, Judith Daar, and Eli Y. Adashi. 'What overturning *Roe v Wade* may mean for assisted reproductive technologies in the U.S.' *JAMA* 328, no. 1 (2022): 15–16.

Cohen, I. Glenn, and Eli Y. Adashi. 'Mitochondrial replacement therapy: The IOM report and its aftermath.' *Nature Reviews Genetics* 17, no. 4 (2016): 189–190.

Cohen, I. Glenn, Eli Y. Adashi, Sara Gerke, César Palacios-González, and Vardit Ravitsky. 'The regulation of mitochondrial replacement techniques around the world.' *Annual Review of Genomics and Human Genetics* 21 (2020): 565–586.

Cohen, I. Glenn, Julian Savulescu, and Eli Y. Adashi. 'Transatlantic lessons in regulation of mitochondrial replacement therapy.' *Science* 348, no. 6231 (2015): 178–180.

Ferguson, Ellyn. 'Lawmakers put funding ban on human embryo gene editing research in Ag. bill.' *Roll Call*, 5 June 2019. https://www.rollcall.com/2019/06/05/lawmakers-put-funding-ban-on-human-embryo-gene-editing-research-in-ag-bill/.

Food and Drug Administration. 'Briefing document: Oocyte modification in assisted reproduction for the prevention of transmission of mitochondrial disease or treatment of infertility.' 2014a. https://wayback.archive-it.org/7993/2017011

3010712/http://www.fda.gov/downloads/AdvisoryCommittees/CommitteesM
eetingMaterials/BloodVaccinesandOtherBiologics/CellularTissueandGeneThe
rapiesAdvisoryCommittee/UCM385461.pdf.

Food and Drug Administration. 'Draft guidance for industry: Considerations for
the design of early phase clinical trials of cellular and gene therapy products.'
2014b. https://wayback.archive-it.org/7993/20170113010711/http://www.fda.
gov/downloads/AdvisoryCommittees/CommitteesMeetingMaterials/BloodVa
ccinesandOtherBiologics/CellularTissueandGeneTherapiesAdvisoryCommit
tee/UCM385457.pdf.

Gugliotta, Guy. 'The last decade's culture wars drove some states to fund stem cell
research.' *Kaiser Health News*, 6 November 2015. https://khn.org/news/the-
last-decades-culture-wars-drove-some-states-to-fund-stem-cell-research/.

Joseph, Andrew. 'Congress revives ban on altering the DNA of human embryos used
for pregnancies.' *Scientific American*, 5 June 2019. https://www.scientificameri
can.com/article/congress-revives-ban-on-altering-the-dna-of-human-embryos-
used-for-pregnancies/.

Malarkey, M. A. 'Letter to Dr John Zhang.' US Food & Drug Administration, 4 August
2017. https://www.fda.gov/media/106739/download.

Murugan, Varnee. 'Stem cell issue: Embryonic stem cell research: A decade of
debate from Bush to Obama.' *Yale Journal of Biology and Medicine* 82, no. 3
(2009): 101–103.

National Academies of Sciences, Engineering, and Medicine. 'Mitochondrial
replacement techniques: Ethical, social, and policy considerations.'
Washington, DC: National Academies Press, 2016.

National Institutes of Health. 'Guidelines for research using human pluripotent stem
cells.' 65 *Federal Register* 51,976 (2000).

National Institutes of Health. 'Guidelines for human stem cell research.' 74 *Federal
Register* 32,170 (2009).

New York Times Editorial Board. 'This editorial is not about designer babies.'
New York Times, sec. A, 12 April 2019. https://www.nytimes.com/2019/04/12/
opinion/three-parent-babies-mitochondria.html.

Obama, Barack. 'Removing barriers to responsible scientific research involving
human stem cells.' 2009. 74 *Federal Register* 10,667 (2009).

Pompei, Marybeth, and Francesco Pompei. 'Overcoming bioethical, legal, and
hereditary barriers to mitochondrial replacement therapy in the USA.' *Journal
of Assisted Reproduction and Genetics* 36, no. 3 (2019): 383–393.

Spivak, Russell A., I. Glenn Cohen, and Eli Y. Adashi. 'Germ-line gene editing
and congressional reaction in context: Learning from almost 50 years of
congressional reactions to biomedical breakthroughs.' *Journal of Law and
Health* 30 (2017): 20–54.

7

Contesting the 'No Rules' Label

ARTs in Mexico Before and After the First MRT Baby

SANDRA P. GONZÁLEZ-SANTOS AND
ABRIL SALDAÑA-TEJEDA

7.1   INTRODUCTION

In 2016, the British science communication magazine *The New Scientist*
published an article about the birth of the first baby conceived after a mitochondrial replacement therapy (MRT) was used to avoid the inheritance
of Leigh syndrome, a mitochondrial disease (Hamzelou, 2016). According
to the article, because mitochondrial replacement technologies had not
been approved in the United States, Zhang (the head of the US team) 'went
to Mexico instead, where he says "there are no rules"' (Hamzelou, 2016).
The idea that Mexico *has no rules* widely circulated in the US, British and
Mexican press (González-Santos et al., 2018). Is this depiction accurate?
What does 'not having rules' mean? What do 'rules' mean in this context?
What does not having rules, or having rules imply for the practice and use
of assisted reproductive services? This chapter focuses on the characteristics of Mexico's particular regulatory and legislative configuration and the
conditions that have made it possible to analyse what the 'no rules' label
means for the practice of MRT. We argue that 'no rules' does not mean 'anything goes,' just as having rules does not mean that they will be followed.

Sandra P. González-Santos and Abril Saldaña-Tejeda, *Contesting the 'No Rules' Label* In: *Reproduction Reborn*. Edited
by: Diana M. Bowman, Karinne Ludlow, and Walter G. Johnson, Oxford University Press. © Oxford University Press 2023.
DOI: 10.1093/oso/9780197616192.003.0008

'MRT' is the umbrella term under which two recently developed experimental procedures are gathered: maternal spindle transfer (MST), which manipulates oocytes, and pronuclear transfer (PNT), which manipulates embryos; in both cases, the aim is to aid in fertility problems and both require donated oocytes are needed (Chapter 1, this volume). These new procedures emerged into a technologically populated landscape where discussions about the philosophical, ethical, legal, social, and cultural implications of these biotechnologies have been taking place for more than 30 years (see also Chapter 2, this volume). These conversations could shape reflections concerning MRT. Hence, by looking at what is happening in the fields of assisted reproductive technologies (ART) and genetics in terms of their legislation and regulation, we try to discern if and how MRT fits into this landscape. It might be pertinent to clarify that this chapter is not a legal analysis, and, as such, it is a grounded speculative analysis (cf. Haraway, 2016) of the way that ART, genetics, and thus MRT are and could be regulated and legislated in Mexico.[1] Latour once wrote: 'Invisible things are invisible. Period. If they make other things move, and you can document these movements, then they are made visible' (2007: 150). We took Latour's words as a provocation to ask: What is (in)visible in the context of ART and MRT in Mexico? What moved when the 'first MRT baby' case emerged, what could have moved but didn't, and why was this so? These questions have taken us to many different places of inquiry; here we share many of them.

We begin with an overview of Mexico's situation in terms of infertility, mitochondrial diseases, and the ART market. This sets out the context in which ART and MRT could be offered. Then we look at how science, politics, and religion are perceived by Mexicans, which offers information that helps us speculate about whether these new procedures could be accepted or rejected within a wider public. We then describe the research environment of which ART is a part and the different policies that have shaped this research environment. Following this, we look at existing regulation since it is already setting out what should and should not be done; this will inform us regarding how MRT could be covered (or not) by these regulations. We then look at legislative proposals, focusing on how they describe who could be using ART, for which reasons, and how these services would affect the existing legislation on kinship to see if and how MRT could fit into these proposals. These proposals offer hints to what could be considered controversial or acceptable when (and if) MRT is brought to the table. We close the chapter with a speculative conclusion based on our analysis of the idea that Mexico has 'no rules' and the visibility of these technologies and of the rules that regulate them. We chose to focus on these areas because of the work done there to assemble ART and MRT as entities that, in the Mexican context, could or could not be practiced, regulated, and legislated (cf. Isasi et al., 2004; Morgan and Roberts, 2012).

7.2 ART MARKET, INFERTILITY, AND MITOCHONDRIAL DISEASES

In past decades, the number and distribution of ART services in Mexico has increased from two clinics located in two cities in 1985, to 116 services located in 22 states in 2019 (COFEPRIS, 2019). Most of these clinics are private; only a handful are part of the public healthcare or social security system. Insurance companies working in Mexico do not cover these services, thus the vast majority of ART users pay for these procedures themselves—most of the time 'out of pocket' or by taking out bank loans or asking for family loans. The cost of the procedures varies depending on the type of package or procedure selected. It has become common for clinics to offer packages: these include a set number of consultations and tests, a set number of cycles, and an insurance policy (which allegedly means that if a patient does not become pregnant, the fees are refunded). For example, in 2021, Mexican clinics were offering in vitro fertilisation (IVF) packages that ranged between US$1,762 (35,000 MXP) for one cycle of low ovarian stimulation IVF with no insurance, to US$13,418 (266,500 MXP) for the most inclusive package of IVF which includes four cycles of IVF, gamete donors, nutritionist and psychologist consultations, and insurance.

Like their patients, ART service providers have to find the economic resources to establish clinics (Ferber et al., 2020). They have done this either by aligning with hospitals, involving private investors, using their own resources, or through bank loans. When the number of clinics began to grow, practitioners had to fight for patients/clients, leading to an array of marketing strategies that has shaped the way these services are presented to the public: as procedures that are successful, safe, unproblematic, cutting-edge, and following Western standards.[2] All this has shaped the Mexican ART market as one oriented towards profit and subject to supply-and-demand market forces.

It is difficult to know how many people face infertility and use ART since there is no national compulsory registry of clinics, procedures, users, or births. Some turn to the approximations offered by the survey office (National Institute of Statistics and Geography/Instituto Nacional de Estadística y Geografía [INEGI]), which calculates that 15 percent of sexually active couples face fertility issues and that 1.5 million of these are in some type of ART treatment (Comisión Nacional de Bioética [CONBIOETICA], 2013). In Mexico, infertility is generally described as a problem faced by (mostly) women and couples, and it is associated with modern lifestyles that promote delaying pregnancy. It is not considered a public health issue but instead a problem mostly faced by the middle and upper echelons of society. We found this construction of infertility present in the clinics' social media, the press, the clinical context, and medical journals and conferences. Also present in the media and medical discourse, but to a lesser degree, was the association of infertility with obesity and diabetes, two public health issues that have been central to Mexico's health agenda for the past 30 years (González-Santos, 2021). What is seldom mentioned is an association between infertility and genetic conditions.

ART and genetics have followed different paths in Mexico. While reproductive medicine has mostly been practiced as a clinical service within the private sector and has usually been framed as a biomedical tool to aid individual reproductive aims, genomic medicine has been framed as a research area and a biomedical tool that will help further national projects.[3] As opposed to reproductive medicine, which is still a subspecialty of gynaecology, genomic medicine has been considered worthy of a public national institution—the National Institute of Genomic Medicine/Instituto Nacional de Medicina Genómica (INMEGEN), established in 2005—and of having a specific legislative framework: the Law on Biosafety and Genetically Modified Organisms, although this law largely focused on genetically modified non-human organisms (Chan and Medina Arellano, 2016). However, human genetics is practiced clinically at Mexican fertility clinics in the form of preimplantation genetic diagnosis (PGD). These are a set of procedures used to identify genetic disorders (Mendelian disorders, structural chromosome abnormalities, or mitochondrial disorders) prior to implanting the embryo (Geraedts and De Wert, 2009). Like PGD, one of the goals of MRT is to avoid the inheritance of genetic conditions known as mitochondrial diseases, a subset of what are known as *rare diseases*—rare due to both their low frequency and to the poor attention they receive. Not only are they not properly covered in Mexican medical schools' curricula, but they have only recently been contemplated within the healthcare system. Both the Rare Diseases National Registry and the Commission for the Analysis, Evaluation, Registry and Follow-up of Rare Disease were only recently created, the former in 2015 and the latter in 2017. Like the Ministry of Health, the registry only covers 20 diseases, none of which is a mitochondrial disease (Mejía Vázquez et al., 2020). Furthermore, these registries have not yet published any data[4] (Rivera-Silva et al., 2018). The Mexican Rare Diseases Federation (FEMEXR) estimates that 5 percent of Mexicans have a rare disease.[5] When the press takes up the issue of rare diseases, it mostly aims at raising awareness of their existence and the distress and hardship that these conditions imply for the family and the health system (see also, Chapter 3, this volume), not about biotechnologies to cure or prevent them. MRT would need to find its place within this stratified way that infertility is conceived and the limited attention given to mitochondrial diseases. The use of these procedure would need to be justified, considering the limited resources for healthcare (Baylis, 2018; Carbajal Rodriguez and Navarrete Martínez, 2015; Ramírez Coronel, 2019[6]).

7.3 SCIENCE: POLICY, PERFECTION, AND RESEARCH

Scholars in the area of science and technology studies (STS) have shown the importance of considering people's perception of religion, politics, science, and technology when studying the ways in which these activities are carried out, regulated, and legislated (Hackett et al., 2008; Palma et al., 2015). Drawing on these studies, in this section we look at the public's trust in science, technology, and medicine; the political and economic life of Mexico; and Mexico's research environments. This helps us articulate how the regulatory and legislative landscape of assisted reproduction (which encompasses MRT) is part of and shaped by these factors.

A common assumption is that, in Latin America, the power held by the Catholic Church and conservative groups, as well as the absence of a truly secular state, shapes legislation when it comes to biotechnological matters (Breña, 2015; World Health Organization, 2003). Fernando Zegers-Hochschild, a Chilean ART specialist, described Latin American societies as 'not scientifically driven', as societies whose 'decisions are triggered by emotional and religious influence rather than using the evidence provided by science and technology' (2011: 802). This explanation might hold some truth, but it needs heavy nuancing. Yes, religion is important in how worldviews are shaped; however, the way religion influences the acceptance or rejection of biotechnologies is not homogeneous throughout geographies or in all cases (Chapter 9, this volume). Attitudes towards IVF, abortion, and embryonic stem cell research, for example, are not equally affected by religion. Elizabeth Roberts found that ART was more readily accepted in Ecuador than in the United States because in Ecuador ART 'did not force the same kinds of reconsiderations of nature, life and kinship because such ideas were differently configured to begin with' (Roberts, 2012: xxiv). Moreover, she found an 'expanding IVF industry staffed and

supported by enthusiastic Catholics, who involved God in the process'
(Roberts, 2012: 23).

To further explore the influence of religion on the perception of and engagement with science in Mexico, we turn to the 2017 National Survey on
public perceptions of science and technology, which includes perceptions
on religion and politics (ENPECYT, 2017). The survey was carried out by
the Science and Technology National Council (CONACYT) and the INEGI
in 2017. It surveyed 3,200 households located in 43 urban areas (of
100,000 or more inhabitants) across all 32 states that make up the country.
We complement this information with the 2019 Gallup-Wellcome Global
Monitor and with the 2018 Latinobarómetro. The Gallup-Wellcome Global
Monitor survey focuses on geographical regions, something that can be
very problematic since geographical location does not equate to cultural,
economic, social, or political similarity or relations. In this chapter, we
only report on the result of the region that encompasses Costa Rica, the
Dominican Republic, El Salvador, Guatemala, Haiti, Honduras, Nicaragua,
and Panama as well as Mexico. The Latinobarómetro is produced by the
NGO Corporación Latinobarómetro; the data presented here are exclusive
to Mexico and gathers the views of 1,200 people. In Table 7.1 we extract
answers to the questions we found relevant for this chapter.

The results reported by the 2017 National Survey suggest that the public
perception of science is, overall, very positive. Scientists were seen as trustworthy; some respondents said even more trustworthy than religious
leaders and politicians. Respondents felt that the work done by scientists
is important for technological and economic development, that the government should support and invest in scientific research, and that more
people should work in scientific fields. The vast majority viewed scientific discoveries as fairly neutral; it was the uses of science and technology
that could be morally judged. Therefore, although people indicated that
governments should make scientists follow ethical guidelines (e.g., concerning animal experimentation), overall respondents felt that scientists
should be left to freely conduct research. In fact, less than half indicated
that scientists should be held responsible for the bad uses others make
of their discoveries. Moreover, many respondents felt the benefits of science outweigh its risks. Nevertheless, there was concern regarding the
speed at which science was progressing, making life more artificial and
dehumanised. Finally, when it came to the use of science (e.g., in healthcare), the majority trusted both methods that were not approved by the
scientific community (such as acupuncture, homeopathy, chiropractic, and
traditional health practices like *limpias*—a sort of cleansing) and those that
followed accepted scientific methods. In fact, many accepted cloning as a

Table 7.1 SURVEY RESULTS FOR PARTICIPANTS ASKED TO RATE TRUSTWORTHINESS

A. National Survey

Trust in Politicians and Religious Representatives

> 64.1% considered politicians not very trustworthy

> 72.3% considered people trusted religious faith too much and science not enough

Trust in Scientists

> 83.6% trusted scientists if they worked in public institutions

> 84.4% trusted scientists if they worked in a private university

Scientific Work

> 89.6% considered scientific research important for technological development

> 74% considered scientific research important for economic development

> 90.9% considered scientific discoveries were neither bad nor good; it was their use that could be morally judged

> 58.9% did not agree with holding scientists responsible for the bad uses others made of their discoveries

> 66.9% considered the benefits of scientific and technological development outweighs the dangers

> 45.8% viewed scientists as dangerous due to the power their knowledge gives them

> 48.2% did not see them as dangerous

> 74.8% felt the speed of scientific development was making life more artificial

> 53.6% felt the speed of scientific development was making life more dehumanised

> 89.5% agreed with having the government make scientists follow ethical guidelines

> 89% felt scientists should be left to research freely if they did their research ethically

> 60.7% disagreed with animal testing

Support Science

> 81.3% consider the government should support scientific research

> 92.% think that the government should invest more in research and development of science and technology

> 91.9% believe that more people should work in this field

> 74.3% rated sciences as the most interesting subject area, followed by humanities (62.2%) and social sciences (60.8%)

Trust in Medical Sciences

> 76.9% trusted methods not approved by science (such as acupuncture, homeopathy, chiropractic, and traditional health practices such as *limpias* [a sort of cleansing])

> 79.8% accepted cloning as a means to produce tissues and organs for transplantation

B. Gallup Welcome Survey

Trust in Politicians and Religious Representatives

> No Information

Trust in Scientists

> 27% of the surveyed trusted science

(continued)

Table 7.1 CONTINUED

58% of respondents have medium levels of trust in scientists, 11% high trust, and 27% low trust

Scientific Work

62% of the respondents considered that scientists' work benefited people like them

23% said that scientific research benefits most people

37% said that scientific research benefits some people

34% said that scientific research benefits only a few people

Support Science

No Information

Trust in Medical Sciences

81% of the respondents trusted doctors and nurses, and 76% trusted them when needing health advice

67% respondents have confidence in hospitals and health clinics

C. Latinobarómetro

Trust in Politicians and Religious Representatives

Out of 1,200 surveyed, 958 did not trust the police, 851 did not trust the parliament, 876 did not trust judicial power, 1,036 did not trust political parties, and 804 considered that Mexico's democracy was flawed.

---

mean of producing tissue and organs for transplantation (this survey did not include reproductive cloning). This coincides with what we previously found empirically: people viewed ART as an option to overcome fertility issues but also believed that other methods could help (González-Santos, 2016). Likewise, in the national TV and radio reporting on the first MRT procedure, one of the major concerns voiced was around the way the government could regulate these services, particularly if they adopted restrictive regulation.[7] Could this suggest that MRT could be found acceptable by the general public?

Although the data presented by the 2019 Gallup-Wellcome survey represent a region and not a specific country, it is worth considering. This survey found that about half of the respondents have medium levels of trust in scientists and that more than half felt that scientists' work benefited people like them. However, in a further question, the survey asked if people thought science benefits most, some, or a few people in their country—the responses were almost equally divided. When it came to healthcare matters, most people in the region trusted doctors and nurses.

Overall, these surveys show how science and religion can and do live side by side without conflict, that Mexicans trust science and scientists even more than politicians[8] and religious leaders. They depict Mexicans as interested in scientific information and supportive of investing public money in research and development since they believe that it will benefit the economy and well-being of their country. All this has been shaped by a shared view that the country is governed by a self-serving powerful elite (Latinobarómetro, 2018). They expressed that the government is not currently investing enough, nor does it establish the necessary conditions to promote scientific research per se nor research in collaboration with public and private institutions that would benefit all. This perception of low investment in science and technology is reinforced by decades of scientific and technological policies that do not incentivise research (Casas and Dettmer, 2007).

According to Article 25 of the General Law on Education, the state should invest 8 percent of gross domestic product (GDP) in education, of which 1 percent should go to promote research and development in science and technology. However, in the past decade, this goal has not been met and, in fact, during the current administration (2018–2024), state investment has decreased considerably (Organisation for Economic Co-operation and Development [OECD], 2021). Investment in science and technology in general comes from, first, universities, then the government and private business, and finally from nonprofit institutions (Foro Consultivo de Ciencia y Tecnología, 2018). One of the main governmental institutions in charge of promoting and supporting scientific research and technological development is the CONACYT. Among its responsibilities is financing projects through grants and supporting researchers who are part of the National Researchers System (Sistema Nacional de Investigadores) through a monthly economic stimulus (Palma et al., 2015).

Not only does Mexico invest very little in scientific research, but its infrastructure to conduct research as well as the infrastructure to translate health-related research into medical care also is being dismantled, particularly during the past three decades (Foro Consultivo de Ciencia y Tecnología, 2018; OECD, 2021).[9] Rosalba Casas and Jorge Dettmer (2007) analysed Mexico's scientific and technological policies of the past 70 years; they identify four periods. During the first period, comprising from 1930 to 1970, science was seen as capable of solving the country's economic problems, and thus science policies promoted industrialisation through a policy of substituting importation with nationally produced goods. The second period, from 1970 to 1980, was focused on catching up with the latest scientific and technological achievements. The academic and bureaucratic culture dominated scientific policy during that decade. The third period, from 1980 to 1990, had a pragmatic agenda, and the scientific activity was shaped by both the state and the academic community. During the latest period (from 1990 to 2000) scientific activity followed the emerging neoliberal project, hence was oriented towards and shaped by market demands.

ART was mostly developed and then disseminated during the past two periods (1980–2000). It was also when the National Bioethics Commission/ Comisión Nacional de Bioética (CONBIOETICA) was established in 1992, with the purpose of acting as the national advisory agency on bioethics, developing guidelines for public health policies and encouraging public participation in bioethical debates. Since its creation, CONBIOETICA has aimed at establishing a particularly secular research environment following a style of bioethics based on four principles—respect for autonomy, non-maleficence, beneficence, and justice—and informed mostly by medical and legal perspectives, although it has avoided taking a strong and active stand on bioethical issues (Ortiz-Millán and Kissling, 2020). The disciplinary composition of the Commission reflects this; it includes mainly physicians and lawyers, philosophers to a lesser degree, and lacks patients or social scientists. Take as an example the team put together in 2016, when the journal *Nature* consulted the CONBIOETICA on the bioethical implications of the MRT procedure conducted at the Mexican branch of the New Hope Clinic. This team was composed of a physician who was head of a private ART clinic and member of the Mexican Science Academy, a legal scholar who advises private ART clinics on legal issues, INMEGEN's director of the Department of Social, Ethical and Legal Studies, and a member of CONBIOETICA (Comisión Nacional de Bioética, 2017). We discuss this report in the following section.

In Mexico, as in most of Latin America, ART is practiced mostly in private clinics and within an overall research-unfriendly environment (Zegers-Hochschild, 2011). In addition to what has been described above, research into ART in Mexico is further shaped by the different demands of the clinical and research spheres. While medical schools do not encourage students to conduct and publish research, the Mexican College of Gynaecology and Obstetrics (COMEGO)—which is the medical association in charge of licensing practitioners—does require them to research, publish, and participate in conferences, all as a way of proving that they are staying up to date with the latest information. Furthermore, because most physicians work in private clinics, and some work in both private and public settings, their time and resources (human, technological, and economical) are primarily dedicated to caring for patients. Hence, the research they do manage to conduct is self-initiated, done after hours and during weekends, and must address issues relevant to the clinic, where patients have to agree to be both patients and research subjects. Furthermore, the

General Health Law states, in Article 68-IV, that family planning services include promoting research in areas of contraception and infertility, and, as mentioned before, the CONACYT funds scientific research. However, ART specialists working at infertility clinics do not seem to use CONACYT funding for their research projects. We infer this from looking at the papers and posters presented at medical conferences (such as the annual meetings of the Assisted Reproduction Medical Association or AMMR), which do not mention any financial support from CONACYT. This could be due to where and how research in ART is carried out.

7.4 CURRENT LEGISLATION, REGULATION, AND GUIDELINES

In this section we focus on the existing law and regulation that can and should be considered when thinking about MRT. In 2016, the specific procedure conducted was MST, hence all embryos produced were intended for implantation; however, not all were viable. Considering this, the laws that need to be analysed would pertain to ART in general and, more specifically, to gamete donation, genetic manipulation, and the use of gametes and embryos in experimental procedures. Legal rules address these issues, both in federal law and local legislation. In addition to analysing these laws, in this section we also look at guidelines suggested by the CONBIOETICA and professional associations (AMMR, COMEGO) as well as by the Latin-American professional association for ART (RedLara).

MRT is a new item in this list of procedures that have problematised the legal and the cultural establishment of kinship (Franklin, 2013; Freeman et al., 2014; Payne, 2016). Surrogacy, which has generated some degree of controversies, questions the Mexican cultural belief concerning maternity. This cultural belief states that the 'mother' is the person who gives birth ('*madre, la que te parió*').[10] Gamete donation has not been as controversial as surrogacy, perhaps because it does not necessarily interfere with the experience of carrying the pregnancy and giving birth and due to particular ways of understanding what genes and inheritance mean. For example, during information talks organised by clinics it is common to hear physicians comment on how mothers-in-law rarely check that their grandchildren are genetically related to their sons (in cases of sperm donation) and constantly repeat that children will end up looking like their parents (Becker et al., 2005). This resembles what happens in other contexts, particularly for those working for the public acceptance of MRT. It is common that they tend to downplay the biological relevance of the donors' genetic material while assigning motherhood to the woman who provides the embryo with the nucleus (Newman, 2014; Chapter 4, this volume). We need to further research how nuclear and mitochondrial genetics are understood in relation to kinship and identity within Mexican culture and thus to what extent birthing will continue to be privileged over genetics.

7.4.1 Existing Laws: Federal

Mexico's General Health Law (Ley General de Salud) contains a few articles pertinent to MRT. Article 68, for example, promotes research for aspects of family planning (and ARTs are a form of family planning), Article 46 sanctions artificial insemination without consent,[11] Articles 21 and 22 regulate research on human subjects, and Articles 43 and 56 regulate the use of embryos and fetuses and assisted fertilisation. Article 315 stipulates that healthcare establishments where cells and other body tissues are extracted, transplanted, and saved—as is the case with fertility clinics—need to undergo inspection by the Federal Commission for the Protection Against Sanitary Risks (COFEPRIS).[12] This inspection consists of evaluating the physical state of the clinic and the equipment used as well as the procedures followed for handling tissue and the correct disposal of biological material. If clinics pass the inspection, they are granted a license. In 2019, COFEPRIS issued 130 licenses (COFEPRIS, 2019). Article 316 states that these establishments must have a bioethics committee registered with CONBIOETICA (see also Articles 69 and 70 of the Health Law's guidelines). There are two types of bioethics committees: those for clinical practice and those for research (REC). In 2021, the list of hospital bioethics committees added up to 1,157; however, no more than a dozen were in ART clinics, and there were 394 research committees with even fewer ART clinics amongst them; New Hope Fertility Clinic, Jalisco, where the MRT procedure was conducted, was one of them.[13] The Centro Nacional de Transplantes (CENATRA) is in charge of overlooking transplants. They claim to keep track of gamete donations—who donates and who receives, the procedure used, and the outcome—but accessing this information is not easy since it is not included in their quarterly and annual reports.

The Law on Biosafety and Genetically Modified Organisms was written in 2005, to deal with issues concerning genetically modified organism (GMOs), but it does not consider the human genome.

Genetically modified organism: Any living organism, with the exception of human beings, that has acquired a novel genetic combination, generated through the specific use of techniques of modern biotechnology (Article 3, Section XXI).

7.4.2 Existing Laws: Local

There are state laws that regulate certain aspects of assisted reproduction. Here we look at the most relevant considering the number of clinics that operate in that particular state or due to the content of the regulation. It is worth highlighting that it is common to find in these codes that assisted reproduction and forced sterilisation are regulated within the same section, once more a view of reproduction and family planning as two sides of the same coin (González-Santos, 2020).

Approximately 22 million people live in the Greater Mexico City area, which is comprised of Mexico City and several municipalities of the Estado de México and Hidalgo. Not only is it one of the largest cities in the world, it is also a very dense area in terms of the number of ART clinics, with a total of 43 clinics: 35 registered in Mexico City and 8 in the Estado de Mexico (COFEPRIS, 2019). Both Mexico City and Estado de Mexico's Penal and Civil Codes forbid reproductive cloning and the creation of embryos for something other than reproduction, but they allow genetic manipulation for the purpose of avoiding genetic disorders.[14] This makes MST legal in these 43 clinics if used to avoid the inheritance of genetic conditions. Furthermore, Mexico's codes legislate in favour of giving every couple the right to use ART to form a family, which, in this case, includes same-sex couples given that, since 2009, same-sex marriage is allowed in this city. Since 2007, consanguinity is given to the intended parents even if donated gametes were used. Guerrero and Veracruz are two states with a similar system.

Puebla,[15] on the other hand, has very restrictive and conservative rules and sanctions pertaining to ART. In 2012, Puebla's Penal Code was amended to include, under Article 343,[16] prohibitions and sanctions if ART is carried out without the woman's consent; a limit to the number of embryos produced per cycle to three; and the prohibition of the creation of embryos for purposes other than reproduction; the creation of clones, chimeras, and hybrids (human genes with genes of other species); the manipulation of embryos, even if this is done as a diagnostic measure (hence PDG is prohibited as well); the selection of embryos for any and all eugenic motives (hence, selecting embryos based on their sex, race, morphological aspect, or the presence of diseases is prohibited);[17] the disposal of embryos for family planning matters; and embryo preservation. Given this, MRT would be illegal in Puebla.

7.4.3 CONBIOETICA Reports

The CONBIOETICA has published two reports on assisted reproduction. The first in 2013, which focused on ART in general (Comisión Nacional de Bioética, 2013), and the second in 2017 with special consideration on MRT (Comisión Nacional de Bioética, 2017). This second report draws heavily on the 2012 Nuffield Council report, the Oviedo Convention, and on a case taken to the Interamerican Human Rights Court (*Artavia Murillo v. Costa Rica*) but includes very little on national data or experiences. Overall, the report recommends establishing the regulation of ART following a secular perspective based on scientific concepts and following human rights guidelines. It also suggests considering these procedures experimental; thus, laws pertaining to experimental procedures should be followed— which means having the research protocol reviewed by a registered research ethics committee.[18] It also calls attention to Article 56 of the General Health Law because it states that ART is admissible only in cases of sterility (i.e., the incapacity to conceive after 12 months of frequent unprotected sexual intercourse), which is not always the case for women facing mitochondrial issues. In fact, the 2016 case, in which a Jordanian couple was treated with MRT by Dr Zhang and Dr Chávez Badiola at New Hope Mexico could be considered illegal since the woman's eggs were capable of being fertilised (hence, according the medical diagnosis, she was not infertile); instead, the problem was passing on a mitochondrial disease (Palacios-González and Medina-Arellano, 2017). This last point highlights the importance of how infertility is understood and how it is connected to the use of ART. Under some definitions of infertility, single people and same-sex couples are not considered infertile, thus they are not allowed to use ART: this could be considered discrimination through a scientific definition.

7.4.4 Medical Association Guidelines

Professional associations have also issued guidelines and standards. Nationally, there are two associations of ART professionals that have published both ethical and practical guidelines: one is the COMEGO (which licenses practitioners) and the other is the AMMR. Together they have published four documents stipulating best practices and ethical guidelines (Ambe et al., 2012; Caldiño et al., 2012; Ginecología y Obstetricia de México, 2011; Mansilla Olivares and Vital Reyes, 2019) and worked with policymakers to produce legislative proposals and standards of practice. However, none of these standards of practice or ethical guidelines has any legal power: they are recommendations and consensus decided on by the professional community and followed at their discretion—none contemplate MRT.[19]

The RedLara has also issued guidelines. RedLara was established in the early 1990s under the leadership of Fernando Zegers-Hochschild, a Chilean ART specialist, with the purpose of being a self-regulating community of professionals promoting collaboration and research. The association has accumulated enough reputation to be considered in the debates held at the parliament as a trustworthy organisation (see, e.g., Diaz Salazar, 2013). To become a member, clinics must undergo a certification process which involves examining the infrastructure of the clinic (physical conditions of the clinic and the equipment) and the procedures followed (particularly in the embryo and gamete labs).

The RedLara network embodies a particular perspective of how reproductive medicine should be practiced. Although this perspective might not be shared by all members of the networks nor by all members of the ART community, it does have an impact on the region's ART practice and on how it is or might be legislated. In 1998, RedLara published a consensus on the ethical and legal aspects of the use of ART (Zegers-Hochschild, 1998). Forty-two clinics from 11 countries participated. The document covered five areas: marital status required for eligibility, gamete donation, embryo cryopreservation, embryo research, and PGD. These issues were selected due to the relevance they had for legislative processes in the region; they were identified after the network conducted a study focusing on the attitudes among ART users in Chile, Colombia, and Brazil (Zegers-Hochschild, 1999). The consensus favoured the traditional heterosexual view of the family. Uses of ART that went beyond this purpose, uses that allowed for biologically impossible parentage, or that were considered subversive to the dominant cultural mode, were rejected. For example, single individuals or same-sex couples seeking parenthood were not considered eligible to use ART. In spite of the many changes in the field since 1998, the network has not published an updated version of its consensus.

Furthermore, RedLara systematically gathers, standardises, processes, and publishes data concerning the procedures and their outcomes since 1991. Through these annual reports it is possible to trace when certain procedures or practices were adopted by clinics in the region and when they were abandoned. For example, between 1993 and 1995, we see the decline of gamete intrafallopian transfer (GIFT) and the rise of intracytoplasmic sperm injection (ICSI), and, in 2012, the introduction of fertility preservation. This registry has also served as a way to call attention to important matters (e.g., in the 2002 report, multiple embryo transfer was declared an epidemic in Latin America). Thus far, MRTs have not been present in any of the reports or any of the publications.

7.5 NATIONAL LEGISLATIVE PROPOSALS

For Mexico, the turn of the century also meant an important change in government. For the first time in 60 years the institutional party lost the presidential seat to the conservative party (PAN). In this context of democratic renovation, the first proposal to legislate ART was presented in 1999 by the Green Party.[20] Every party registered in the electoral system in the past 20 years, with the exception of Morena (the newest political party), has presented or participated in the elaboration of these proposals. Likewise, during the first years of the new regime the Parliament organised talks to inform its members about the scientific and legal aspects of ART. The first was held in 2001, in Mexico City, and the second in 2004, in various cities across the country. The invited speakers—mostly physicians and legal academics—covered topics such as the causes of infertility, embryo development, human genetics, and the biological, technical, and legal aspects of ART. No users, social scientists, or philosophers were invited to give their perspectives.[21] However, a religious and conservative perspective was present throughout these presentations; for example, during the first talk, one speaker, a physician, twice declared that the origin of life started with Adam and Eve and later spoke of homosexuality as being against moral and legal principles and questioned whether legalising same-sex marriages, as in Sweden and Holland, was not in fact a step backwards rather than forwards (for more on this see, González-Santos, 2011).

More than 20 years later we find more than 20 proposals sitting on parliamentary desks collecting dust (see Box 7.1). These initiatives have followed a diversity of legislative strategies, with some suggesting the drafting of one single comprehensive law and others amending existing laws or establishing a set of standards of practice. The issues they cover are not always the same: some deal with legislating the offer and use of ART, others focus on including ART services as part of family planning schemes, some on prohibiting reproductive cloning and regulating stem cell research, a few suggest including the term 'embryo' in the existing health laws and

Box 7.1 INITIATIVES PRESENTED BY PARTIES TO THE PARLIAMENT

Gonzalez-Martinez (PVEM), 1999. Regulate ART, the disposal of genetic material and create a NOM. Gaceta Parlamentaria 252, 1999 Abril, pp. 12–23.

Lopez-Brito (PAN), 2002. Regulate research and the use of ART. Gaceta Parlamentaria 1097, 2002.09, pp. 53–57.

Leon Lerma, 2003.03 PRI, PRD, PT, PVEM Prohibit reproductive cloning. Gaceta Parlamentaria 1221, pp. 7–11.

Prieto Furken, 2003.04 PVEM Prohibit human cloning. Gaceta Parlamentaria 1240-1, pp. 55–58.

Rodriguez-Diaz, 2004.04 PRI Regulate ART. Gaceta Parlamentaria 148-1, pp. 79–94.

Garcia-Tinajero, 2004.12 PRD ART. Gaceta Parlamentaria 1639-1, pp. 28–37.

Gastelum-Bajo, 2005.02 PRI, PRD Reproductive health Gaceta Parlamentaria 1694-1, pp. 27–34.

Martinez-Alvarez, 2005.02 CON Include the term AR in the family planning laws Gaceta Parlamentaria 1699-1, pp. 4–6.

Martinez-Alvarez, 2005.04 CON Include the term AR in the family planning laws Gaceta Parlamentaria 1735-1, pp. 8–15.

Diaz-Salazar, 2005.04 PRI Attention to the infertile couple Gaceta Parlamentaria 1725-1, p. 70.

Diaz-Salazar, 2005.05 PRI Attention to the infertile couple Gaceta Parlamentaria 1749-1, pp. 90–96.

Ortiz-Dominguez, 2005.05 PAN Penalize genetic manipulation and cloning Gaceta Parlamentaria 1749-1, pp. 47–49.

Camarillo-Zavala, 2006.03 IND Stem cell research Gaceta Parlamentaria 1961-1, pp. 32–35.

Ortiz-Dominguez, 2006.08 PAN Include the term Embryo in the General Health Law Gaceta del Senado 14.

Morales-Sanchez, 2007.02 PRD Cloning Gaceta Parlamentaria 2189-11, pp. 35–38.

Esteva-Salinas, 2007.12 CON Law on AR n.a.

Castro-Trenti, Saro-Boardman, 2008.04 PRI, PAN Assisted Human Reproduction Law Gaceta del Senado 237.

Ortiz-Dominguez, Maki Esther, and Ángel Córdova Villalobos. 'Iniciativa con proyecto de decreto que adiciona el artículo 101 bis y deroga la fracción vii del articulo 314 de la Ley General de Salud.' 2016. http://sil.gobernacion.gob.mx/Archivos/Documentos/2006/08/asun_2263 207_20060809_1155231093.pdf.

regulations, and some touch on surrogacy. None of them, however, seeks to ban ART. They unanimously consider these procedures as a legitimate way to overcome fertility problems and avoid genetic diseases. They agree that infertility is a public health issue that should be covered in the public health system and that reproduction is a human right that should be protected. Overall, they agree that people older than 18, in a stable heterosexual relationship, and facing infertility or a heritable genetic problem are eligible for assisted reproduction. However, there are important differences between proposals when it comes to including or excluding non-heterosexual couples and single people, as well as when thinking about what procedures should be allowed (e.g., sex selection and surrogacy). The main rationale behind almost all efforts to regulate ART is to address the right of (mainly heterosexual) couples to form a family and avoid the use of procedures that threaten the accepted composition of a family (see, in Box 7.1, González-Martínez, 1999; Leon-Lerma, 2003; López-Brito, 2002).

Proposals justifying the need for legislation argue that, in the current state of affairs, the use of these services is creating many legal voids, leaving users, service providers, donors, and future offspring unprotected.[22] Some even argue that Mexico is in a vulnerable position since other countries already have such legislation (as we can see with the MRT case). According to some, the failure to pass these initiatives results from a combination of elements, which include the tensions that emerge from the ideological, moral, medical, and clinical debates that these issues spark; the strong influence of both the religious lobby and the LGBTQ+ lobby; and—above all—the different political gains implied in presenting a proposal versus passing one. Presenting proposals has been considered politically beneficial since it attracts media attention, generates debates, and helps put issues and names in the public agenda without having to fully assume a political and moral position. Passing laws, however, implies assuming a position, so it stirs up the interest and concern of stakeholders who see their interests threatened. Hence, the gain of presenting a proposal can turn into a political liability when voting to pass it. Although none of these proposals has passed, analysing what they suggest offers some insight into how a particular sector of society thinks about and is assimilating these issues. Likewise, this analysis can help us speculate if, where, and how MRT could fit into this assemblage.

A woman's age has been central to the discussions about infertility and ART in Mexico. One of the main explanations to the apparent increase in the use of ART has been that women are delaying pregnancy (which is commonly depicted in the fertility clinic websites). This would make sense since many ART users were subject to the family planning campaigns rolled out during the 1970s–1990s. These campaigns stressed the importance of studying and securing a job before becoming a parent. However, the numbers tell another story. According to the INEGI, women are not delaying their first pregnancy, they are in fact having babies sooner, they are having fewer children, and fewer of them are having children within a context of marriage (Instituto Nacional de Estadística y Geografía [INEGI], 2020). In other words, women are, on average, having children one year sooner than previously (from 22 to 21 years of age) and they are doing so mostly in the context of a civil partnership (*unión libre*). While these data do not specify the story of women who eventually seek help at ART clinics, it does reflect what González-Santos (2016) found in her research: women start visiting clinics when they are younger than the critical age of 35. The problem is that frequently they embark on a long pilgrimage through several clinics, which can take several years. Hence, many end the pilgrimage when they are well over 40 but few began the journey when they were older than 25. Regardless of the specific demographic and reproductive context in Mexico, proposals are suggesting age limits to women seeking ART services. This is important because one of the precursors of MRT was framed as aiding women whose infertility was related to egg problems associated with age (Barritt et al., 2001; Chen et al., 2016; Cohen and Scott, 1997; see also Chapter 1 and Chapter 9, this volume).

Legislating on MRT implies legislating on egg manipulation and donation. Gamete donation is contemplated and accepted in most proposals (in Box 7.1, see Diaz-Salazar, 2005; Esteva-Salinas, 2007; Garcia-Tinajero, 2004; Lopez-Brito, 2002; Martinez-Alvarez, 2005). Most proposals suggest that gamete donation should be confidential, anonymous, and not lucrative; undertaken with a written informed consent document or contract; and have a maximum of five or six live births per donor (no reason explaining this limit is given). Most consider protecting the identities of donor, recipient, and offspring, giving them access to identifying information when it is absolutely required for health issues (in Box 7.1, see Esteva-Salinas, 2007; Garcia-Tinajero, 2004; Martinez-Alvarez, 2005). To control the use of donated gametes, some proposals suggest creating a National Donor Registry (in Box 7.1, see Diaz-Salazar, 2005; Esteva-Salinas, 2007; Garcia-Tinajero, 2004; Martinez-Alvarez, 2005). One proposal suggests that a bioethics committee should evaluate each case before allowing access to these services (in Box 7.1, see Lopez-Brito, 2002). Concerning genetic manipulation of eggs, some proposals authorise manipulating pre-embryos but only for diagnostic purposes (in Box 7.1, see Gonzalez-Martinez, 1999; Ortiz-Dominguez, 2006). Of these, some say that diagnostic manipulation can only be done with the parents' consent and in cases in which the possible diagnosis implies an important health issue to the future development of the pre-embryo—and there must be a possibility of cure or solution to the problem (in Box 7.1, see Gonzalez-Martinez, 1999). Others state that the motive behind the procedure has to be to the benefit of the embryo, and that the nonpathogenic genetic content must be unaltered (in Box 7.1, see Ortiz-Dominguez, 2006). All this suggests that the use of MRT could be accepted as a method to prevent mitochondrial diseases but not to offer lesbian couples the opportunity to share a genetic link with the offspring.

Clinicians around the world originally framed MRT as offering the potential to prevent complex heritable mitochondrial diseases, which is considered an acceptable use of ART in all proposals. Recently, however, MRT has been seen as a way of offering genetic links to both intended parents in female same-sex couples (see the discussion between Palacios-González and Cavaliere [2019] and Baylis [2018]). Like other ARTs, these procedures allow more people to have genetically linked children. The inclusion of non-heterosexual couples as potential users of ART has been one of the disagreements between actors involved in drafting and voting for these proposals. Some proposals justify limiting the use of ART to heterosexual couples by highlighting the rights of the child-to-be. In 2000, a law protecting children's rights was passed.[23] Article 23 of this law states that children have the right to be part of a family. It states that the family, understood very traditionally as composed of one mother and one father, is fundamental for the social, economic, and cultural stability of Mexico. Furthermore, they argue that Mexico has signed international agreements that make bringing a child into a single-parent household illegal (the agreements are not specified). The fact that, in the first successful MRT case, the patients were a heterosexual couple could have contributed to the lack of controversy over this case in the Mexican media.

7.6 SPECULATION

Throughout this chapter we have tried to identify the actors who work to assemble (Latour, 2007) ART and MRT and their possibility (or not) of being regulated and legislated. We have identified as active factors in this process more than 20 legislative proposals, the existing regulations and the institutions that promote and overlook them, the public perception of science and technology, the public and private healthcare sectors, and the current science policy approach. The tensions and alliances between these actors have created a permissive and monitored ART practice. There is only one known case where MRT was used in Mexico; this exception has not mobilised the necessary actors to develop and pass a set of specific federal regulations, as has happened in other places like the United Kingdom (Chapter 4, this volume,).

Creating more specific legislation does not imply financial benefits for practitioners or the government. ART is mostly a clinical practice that takes place in the private sector, which means that the money that finances these services is private, coming mostly from users' pockets given that insurance companies do not cover these services. More specific legislation could limit who can access these services and what services can be offered. Legislating does not imply political benefits. As mentioned above, the political gain of delimiting who and what is allowed is less than the costs of potential political conflicts in prohibiting or allowing controversial procedures. This is particularly important if we consider what the national survey quoted above registered: that 56.7 percent of respondents felt the issues being researched were not closely connected with the nation's reality (its problems and potentials). Other issues were considered in more pressing need of research, clinical and political attention, and regulation (e.g., issues related to obesity and diabetes).

Furthermore, as suggested by the national survey, there is little trust in governmental institutions and politicians (Latinobarometro, 2018). Mexicans believe that scientific research, if practiced ethically, should be left to self-regulate, which is the case with ART (ENPECYT, 2017). The lack of a single cohesive federal law allows clinics and clinicians to navigate freely through ethical decisions according to their own moral and social stances. Nevertheless, there are governmental institutions and professional organisations certifying, licensing, and overseeing the practice of ART (COFEPRIS, CONBIOETICA, RedLara, AMMR, COMEGO). However, this does not mean that all clinics and clinicians offering these services are certified and licensed.

For some, the absence of regulation might fuel genetic and reproductive cross-border care across the region (Chapter 8, this volume), but effective regulation might also have the effect of favouring foreign patents for the use of such technologies. For instance, Colombia's criminal code allowed for 'the fertilisation of human ova for research and diagnostic purposes if they have a therapeutic goal.' Soon after such regulation was passed, in 2014, the country received the first request from Jennifer Doudna and Emmanuelle Charpentier to patent CRISPR/Cas 9 in the country (Bermúdez and Lizarazo-Cortés, 2016). Overall, what this case and others have shown is that passing specific federal legislation does not mean that the state has the means of implementing it. Laws need infrastructure to be applied. Hence, just as not having specific federal or local laws does not mean that anything goes, having them does not mean that services will not be offered. This is particularly important because many current international debates on the future of new reproductive technologies (i.e., human genome editing) tend to focus on the importance of rigorous national norms and regulations and compliance with international conventions (Adashi and Cohen, 2020; Coller, 2019; Chapter 10, this volume).

7.7 CONCLUSION

Most proposals understand ART as a set of therapeutic procedures and tend to see them as acceptable when used by heterosexual couples to address infertility issues. Hence, considering the existing laws and the many proposals that have been presented, we speculate that MRT could be accepted to overcome infertility or avoid a genetic condition when used by heterosexual couples diagnosed with infertility or with a genetic disorder that can be passed down to their children. However, this would require public acceptance of genetic manipulation (and our study of ART and MRT still falls short of speculating if this could happen). Furthermore, given the conservative position most proposals have, other uses of MRT—for example, by same-sex female couples—might be prohibited. This conservative position matters since it excludes same-sex couples and signals a very fixed notion of relationships involving one woman and one man.

This chapter is located in a section of this edited volume interested in understanding the evolution of regulatory frameworks for MRT—how legislation went from 'there to here.' In the Mexican case, 'there' could be when the first medical association concerned with infertility was established (in 1949), when the first clinics appeared (in the mid-1980s), when those clinics produced their first successful babies (in the late 1980s), when a local law was amended to consider ART (e.g., the 1997 Tabasco code), when the first national legislative proposal was presented (in 1999), when certain state laws established specific prohibitions concerning ART (in 2012, for the case of Puebla), or when the national governmental institutions that oversee the practice of ART were established (COFEPRIS, CENATRA, and CONBIOETICA). In all these moments, guidelines, rules and regulations were produced. All of these 'theres' led to today's 'here': a country with a productive and active ART industry, with a national professional network (AMMR) connected to international associations (RedLara, American Society for Reproductive Medicine [ASRM], European Society of Human Reproduction and Embryology [ESHRE]); that caters to a local and international clientele (of patients and clinicians); that is coherent with its economic, political, and social context (a highly stratified service); and that has been described by some as having 'no rules' but that, in reality, has many rules and regulations that simply do not resemble or work in the same way as in other contexts. The road that took us from 'there' to 'here' has been paved with pragmatic decisions taken by politicians, policymakers, and clinicians. Studying the case of Colombia, Shaw (2019) suggests that, due to the lack of regulation, investors and clinicians might consider investing in reproductive technologies risky (establishing clinics or training people) given that they can easily be made illegal. This has not been the case in Mexico: the lack of a single cohesive federal law specific for ART has not dissuaded investors, practitioners, nor the majority of consumers—only, perhaps, international consumers seeking surrogacy. Proof of this is the growing industry. Nonetheless, the current state of affairs needs rethinking and new voices in the conversation—for example, the perspectives of social scientists, patients, and those conceived through these procedures.

NOTES

1. For a legal analysis of MRT in Mexico, see Palacios-González and Medina-Arellano (2017). Here we follow Haraway's idea of speculative narrative as a way of articulating existing conditions into a possible future (Haraway, 2016). We view it as grounded because our speculations are strongly based on empirical data mostly generated by us.
2. Although the General Health Law has rules and regulations concerning publicity (Reglamento en Materia de Publicidad) and there are a few articles that could pertain to the marketing strategies used in these campaigns (see Articles 5, 11, 14), no action that we know of has taken place regarding the sort of publicity used by fertility clinics, a situation that could be argued is offering false expectations.
3. See the project of mapping the Mexican genome (López Beltrán, 2011).
4. Author's email communication with Mexican Rare Diseases Federation.
5. According to Dr Alejandro Chávez Badiola, the medical director of the New Hope Fertility clinic, where the first case of MRT took place, there are between 6,000 and 17,000 cases of rare diseases in Mexico.
6. 'I want to live in a world where there is genuine concern for matters of social justice and careful attention to the judicious use of limited resources (time, talent and treasure [in this case human eggs and money]) for the benefit of us all. Too often, as is the case with the argument advanced by Palacios-Gonzalez and Cavaliere, the ethical acceptability of a technology is examined with no (or little) attention the fact that there are many social priorities and limited resources' (Baylis, 2018: 2).

7. See *Despierta*, morning news show (Loret de Mola, C., 2016); *Que Tal Fernanda*, a midday magazine radio show, and *Nunez*, a weekend radio programme.

8. The 2018 Latinobarómetro found that Mexicans do not trust the government nor its institutions. Out of 1,200 surveyed, 958 did not trust the police, 851 did not trust the Parliament, 876 did not trust judicial power, 1,036 did not trust political parties, and 804 felt that Mexico's democracy was flawed.

9. Some authors, like Hebe Vessuri (1987), argue that this research-unfriendly environment encourages scientists and researchers to migrate to the United States and Europe. See also the National Survey on Public Perception of Science and Technology (INEGI, 2017).

10. See Article 227 of the Federal Penal Code, which states that motherhood is determined by birthing and considers it a crime if a woman tries to register a child she did not birth as her own. Tabasco's Civil Code was amended in 1997 to make surrogacy contracts valid, thus children born through these procedures could be registered as the intended mother's child (see Articles 92 and 380 Bis2 Fractions I and II). However, in 2015–2016, this code was reamended with the intention of restricting surrogacy for non-Mexicans and requiring a diagnosis that places same-sex couples at risk of not being able to use these procedures (Domínguez, 2019). Since 2013, Sinaloa also has a law that allows for surrogacy under certain conditions, while Coahuila and Querétaro specifically prohibit it. For more on this, see GIRE's report on surrogacy at https://gestacion-subrogada. gire.org.mx/#/.

11. In some states nonconsensual artificial insemination is a cause for the legal interruption of pregnancy.

12. COFEPRIS was established in 2001, with the purpose of overseeing a wide variety of issues, from the control of clinical trials for new drugs to the operation of ART clinics (Palma et al., 2015).

13. Information found at https://www.gob.mx/salud/conbioetica/articulos/comites-de-bioetica, accessed on 26 November 2021.

14. Mexico City's Penal Code (2021), Chapter I, On Assisted Procreation, Artificial Insemination and Forced Sterilization, Art. 149–153; and Chapter II, On Genetic Manipulation, Art. 154–155. Mexico City's Civil Code (2021), Art. 58, Art. 63, Chapter 1 Art. 293; Chapter III Art. 162.

15. Puebla is a religious and conservative state with 10 clinics registered in COFEPRIS.

16. This is section 9, 'Delitos en Materia de Esterilización y Reproducción Asistida / Crimes Concerning Sterilisation and Assisted Reproduction.'

17. However, abortion for grave eugenic reasons is not penalised (Article 343 section IV).

18. *General Health Law* Article 100.

19. For an analysis of these four documents, see González-Santos (2021).

20. Unless specified otherwise, all proposals analysed are proposals to legislate at the national level.

21. As an example, take the group working to pass a set of standards of practice (Norma Oficial Mexicana or NOM). This group included ART practitioners who were heads of fertility clinics and members of medical associations (such as AMMR, RedLara, and COMEGO), members of women's health and rights organisations (GIRE and IPAs, which are not the same as patient groups), representatives of the public health system and two social security systems

(IMSS and ISSTE), one member of a pro-life association (Provida), and one from a Bioethics association (Colegio de Bioética).

22. What worries many policymakers and activists is how to establish legal kinship in cases of gamete or embryo donation and in cases of surrogacy, particularly since 2016, when the law changed in the state of Tabasco affecting non-Mexican intended parents and their children.

23. Ley para la protección de los derechos de niñas, niños y adolescents.

REFERENCES

Adashi, Eli Y., and I. Glenn Cohen. 'Heritable human genome editing: The International Commission report.' *JAMA* 324, no. 19 (2020): 1941–1942.

Ambe, Alberto Kably, Carlos Salazar López Ortiz, Claudio Serviere Zaragoza, Gerardo Velázquez Cornejo, Efraín Pérez Peña, Roberto Santos Haliscack, Martha Luna Rojas, et al. 'Consenso nacional Mexicano de reproducción asistida.' *Revista Mexicana de Medicina de la Reproducción* 4, no. 2 (2012): 68–113.

Barritt, Jason A., Steen Willadsen, Carol Brenner, and Jacques Cohen. 'Cytoplasmic transfer in assisted reproduction.' *Human Reproduction Update* 7, no. 4 (2001): 428–435.

Baylis, Françoise. '"No" to lesbian motherhood using human nuclear genome transfer.' *Journal of Medical Ethics* 44, no. 12 (2018): 865–867.

Becker, Gay, Anneliese Butler, and Robert D Nachtigall. 'Resemblance talk: A challenge for parents whose children were conceived with donor gametes in the US.' *Social Science & Medicine* 61, no. 6 (2005): 1300–1309.

Bermúdez, Natalia Lamprea, and Óscar Lizarazo-Cortés. 'Técnica de edición de genes CRISPR/Cas9. Retos Jurídicos para su regulación y uso en Colombia.' *Rev. Prop. Inmaterial* 21 (2016): 79.

Breña, Roberto. 'Emancipation process in New Spain and the Cádiz constitution.' In *The Rise of Constitutional Government in the Iberian World: The Impact of the Cádiz Constitution of 1812*, edited by Scott Eastman and Natalia Sobrevilla Perea, pp. 42–62. University of Alabama Press, 2015.

Caldiño, F., J. García, G. Ortega, J. Salcido, and J. Ramírez. 'Diagnóstico de la pareja infértil y tratamiento con técnicas de baja complejidad.' *Guía de Practica Clínica*, Instituto Mexicano del Seguro Social, Evidencias y Recomendaciones, 2012. Catálogo de guías de práctica clínica: IMSS-621-13.

Carbajal Rodríguez, Luis, and Juana Inés Navarrete Martínez. 'Enfermedades raras.' *Acta Pediátrica de México* 36, no. 5 (2015): 369–373.

Casas, Rosalba, and J. Dettmer. 'Construyendo un paradigma de política científico tecnológica para México.' In *Educación, ciencia, tecnología y competitividad*, edited by Calva Jose Luis, pp. 137–155. México DF: Miguel Angel Porrúa, 2007.

Chan, Sarah, and M. Medina Arellano. 'Genome editing and international regulatory challenges: Lessons from Mexico.' *Ethics, Medicine and Public Health* 2, no. 3 (2016): 426–434.

Chen, Serena H., Claudia Pascale, Maria Jackson, Mary Ann Szvetecz, and Jacques Cohen. 'A limited survey-based uncontrolled follow-up study of children born after ooplasmic transplantation in a single centre.' *Reproductive Biomedicine Online* 33, no. 6 (2016): 737–744.

COFEPRIS. Listado de Establecimientos Autorizados para Reproducción Asistida, 2019. Accessed 13 November, 2022. https://www.gob.mx/cms/uploads/att achment/file/439319/SEASS_RA.pdf.

Cohen, Jacques, and Richard Scott. 'Birth of infant after transfer of anucleate donor oocyte cytoplasm into recipient eggs.' *Lancet* 350, no. 9072 (1997): 186–187.

Coller, Barry S. 'Ethics of human genome editing.' *Annual Review of Medicine* 70 (2019): 289–305.

Comisión Nacional de Bioética (CONBIOETICA). 'Hacia una ley de reproducción humana asistida.' Secretaría de Salud, April 2013. https://www.gob.mx/cms/ uploads/attachment/file/470859/14._Hacia_una_ley_RHA_2013.pdf.

Comisión Nacional de Bioética (CONBIOETICA). 'Consideraciones bioéticas en torno a la reproducción humana asistida, con referencia específica a las técnicas de reemplazo mitocondrial.' Secretaría de Salud, March 2017. https://www.gob.mx/cms/uploads/ attachment/file/470839/9._RHA_reemplazo_mitocondrial_2017.pdf.

Diaz Salazar, María Cristina. 'Iniciativa con proyecto de decreto por el que se reforman los artículos 13, apartado a, fracción ii; 17 bis; la denominación del título décimo cuarto; 313 fracciones ii y iii; 314 fracción viii; 315 fracciones iii y iv; 319; así mismo se adicionan la fracción v bis al 3°; la fracción iv al 313; las fracciones viii bis y xii bis al 314; la fracción v al 315 de la Ley General de Salud, relativo a la reproducción humana médicamente asistida.' 2013. http://sil.gobe rnacion.gob.mx/Archivos/Documentos/2013/05/asun_2981653_20130508_ 1368029460.pdf.

Domínguez, Karla Cantoral. 'Gestación subrogada en México: Su proyección en las relaciones privadas internacionales.' *Barataria: revista castellano-manchega de ciencias sociales* 25 (2019): 163–177.

Encuesta sobre la Percepción. Pública de la Ciencia y la Tecnología en México (ENPECYT). 2017. Accessed 7 November 2022. https://www.inegi.org.mx/ programas/enpecyt/2017/.

Franklin, Sarah. *Biological Relatives: IVF, Stem Cells and the Future of Kinship*. Duke University Press, 2013.

Freeman, Tabitha, Susanna Graham, Fatemeh Ebtehaj, and Martin Richards, eds. *Relatedness in Assisted Reproduction*. Cambridge University Press, 2014.

Foro Consultivo de Ciencia y Tecnología. 'Inversión para ciencia, tecnología e innovación en México' (No. 011; p. 6). Oficina de Información Científica y Tecnológica para el Congreso de la Unión, 2018. https://www.foroconsultivo. org.mx/INCyTU/documentos/Completa/INCYTU_18-011.pdf.

Gallup-Wellcome. 'Global Monitor: How does the world feel about science and health? First wave findings.' *Wellcome*, 2019. https://wellcome.org/sites/default/files/ wellcome-global-monitor-2018.pdf.

Geraedts, J. P. M., and De Wert, G. M. W. R. 'Preimplantation genetic diagnosis.' *Clinical Genetics* 76, no. 4 (2009): 315–325.

Ginecología y Obstetricia de México. 'Lineamientos en infertilidad.' *Ginecología y Obstetricia de México* 79, no. 11 (2011): 659–673.

González-Santos, Sandra P. *The Sociocultural Aspects of Assisted Reproduction in Mexico* [Doctoral Thesis, University of Sussex]. 2011. http://sro.sussex.ac.uk/7081/.

González-Santos, Sandra P. 'Peregrinar: El ritual de la reproducción asistida.' *Reprodução assistida e relações de gênero na América Latina* (2016): 265–288.

González-Santos, Sandra P. *A Portrait of Assisted Reproduction in Mexico: Scientific, Political, and Cultural Interactions*. Palgrave Macmillan, 2020.

Gonzalez-Santos, Sandra P. 'La pregunta por el riesgo y la medicalización en la reproducción asistida.' In *Enfrentar la Adversidad. Riesgo y Medicalización en México*, edited by A. Murguía Lores, pp. 89–116. Universidad Nacional Autónoma de Mexico, 2021.

González Santos, Sandra P., Neil Stephens, and Rebecca Dimond. 'Narrating the first 'three-parent baby': The initial press reactions from the United Kingdom, the United States, and Mexico.' *Science Communication* 40, no. 4 (2018): 419–441.

Hackett, Olga. In *The Handbook of Science and Technology Studies*, edited by Edward J. Hackett, Michael Lynch, and Judy Wajcman. MIT Press, 2008.

Hamzelou, Jessica. 'Exclusive: World's first baby born with new "3 parent" technique.' *New Scientist*, 27 September 2016. https://www.newscientist.com/article/2107 219-exclusive-worlds-first-baby-born-with-new-3-parent-technique/.

Haraway, Donna J. *Staying with the trouble: Making kin in the Chthulucene*. Duke University Press, 2016.

Instituto Nacional de Estadística y Geografía. *Encuesta sobre la Percepción Pública de la Ciencia y la Tecnología en México*. CONACYT-INEGI, 2017.

Instituto Nacional de Estadística y Geografía (México). *Mujeres y hombres en México 2020/Instituto Nacional de Estadística y Geografía—México*: INEGI, c2021. ix, p. 294. http://cedoc.inmujeres.gob.mx/.

Isasi, Rosario M., Bartha M. Knoppers, Peter A. Singer, and Abdallah S. Daar. 'Legal and ethical approaches to stem cell and cloning research: A comparative analysis of policies in Latin America, Asia, and Africa.' *Journal of Law, Medicine and Ethics* 32, no. 4 (2004): 626–640.

Latinobarometro. 'Informe latinobarómetro 2018.' *Coorporación Latinobarómetro*, 2018. https://www.latinobarometro.org/lat.jsp.

Latour, Bruno. *Reassembling the Social: An Introduction to Actor-Network-Theory*. Oxford University Press, 2007.

López Beltrán, Carlos (Ed.). *Genes y Mestizos: Genómica y Raza en la Biomedicina Mexicana*. Mexico City: Ficticia Editorial, 2011.

Loret de Mola, C. *Despierta. Televisa* (TV Program). 2016.

Mansilla Olivares, Armando, and Víctor Vital Reyes. 'Documento de postura: Prevención, diagnóstico y tratamiento de la infertilidad.' Academia Nacional de Medicina de México A.C., 2019. http://anmm.org.mx/publicacio nes/ultimas_publicaciones/Infertilidad-ISBN.pdf.

Mejía Vázquez, Rocío, Héctor Salgado Schoelly, and Francisco Delgado Cruz. 'Medicamentos huérfanos y efermedades raras.' Secretaría de Salud de la Ciudad de México, 2020. https://salud.cdmx.gob.mx/storage/app/media/2018-2024/medicamentos/boletines2020/Boletin1feb2020.pdf.

Morgan, Lynn M., and Elizabeth F. S. Roberts. 'Reproductive governance in Latin America.' *Anthropology and Medicine* 19, no. 2 (2012): 241–254.

Newman, Stuart A. 'Deceptive labeling of a radical embryo construction technique.' *Huffington Post*, 31 January 2014. https://www.huffpost.com/entry/deceptive-labeling-of-a-r_b_6213320.

Ortiz-Millán, Gustavo, and Frances Kissling. 'Bioethics training in reproductive health in Mexico.' *International Journal of Gynecology and Obstetrics* 151, no. 2 (2020): 308–313.

Organisation for Economic Cooperation and Development (OECD). 'Main science and technology indicators.' OECD, 2021. https://www.oecd.org/mexico/.

Palacios-González, César, and Giulia Cavaliere. ' "Yes" to mitochondrial replacement techniques and lesbian motherhood: A reply to Françoise Baylis.' *Journal of Medical Ethics* 45, no. 4 (2019): 280–281.

Palacios-González, César, and María de Jesús Medina-Arellano. 'Mitochondrial replacement techniques and Mexico's rule of law: On the legality of the first maternal spindle transfer case.' *Journal of Law and the Biosciences* 4, no. 1 (2017): 50–69.

Palma, Verónica, Fernando J. Pitossi, Stevens K. Rehen, Cristina Touriño, and Iván Velasco. 'Stem cell research in Latin America: Update, challenges and opportunities in a priority research area.' *Regenerative Medicine* 10, no. 06 (2015): 785–798.

Payne, Jenny G. 'Grammars of kinship: Biological motherhood and assisted reproduction in the age of epigenetics.' *Signs: Journal of Women in Culture and Society*, 41, no. 3 (2016): 483–506.

Ramírez Coronel, Maribel. '¿Habrá cabida para los tratamientos huérfanos?' *El Economista*, 27 February 2019. https://www.eleconomista.com.mx/opinion/ Habra-cabida-para-los-tratamientos-huerfanos-20190227-0026.html.

Rivera-Silva Gerardo, Fernando Treviño-de la Fuente, and Ma Guadalupe Treviño-Alanísa. 'Rare diseases in Mexico.' *Revista medica del Instituto Mexicano del Seguro Social* 56, no. 3 (2018): 214.

Roberts, Elizabeth. *God's Laboratory Assisted Reproduction in the Andes*. University of California Press, 2012.

Shaw, Malissa Kay. 'Doctors as moral pioneers: Negotiated boundaries of assisted conception in Colombia.' *Sociology of Health and Illness* 41, no. 7 (2019): 1323–1337.

Vessuri, Hebe M. 'The social study of science in Latin America.' *Social Studies of Science* 17, no. 3 (1987): 519–554.

World Health Organization. 'Assisted reproduction in developing countries facing up to the issues (Progress in Reproductive Health Research No. 63).' World Health Organization, 2003. https://www.who.int/reproductivehealth/publications/ infertility/progress63.pdf?ua=1.

Zegers-Hochschild, Fernando. 'Consenso Latinoamericano en aspectos ético-legales relativos a las técnicas de reproducción asistida.' *Cuadernos de Saúde Pública* 14, no. sp.1 (1998): s140–s146.

Zegers-Hochschild, Fernando. 'Attitudes towards reproduction in Latin America. Teachings from the use of modern reproductive technologies.' *Human Reproduction Update* 5, no. 1 (1999): 21–25.

Zegers-Hochschild, Fernando. 'Barriers to conducting clinical research in reproductive medicine: Latin America.' *Fertility and Sterility* 96, no. 4 (2011): 802–804.

8

Medical Tourism and Multilevel Regulation for MRT in the European Union

WALTER G. JOHNSON AND DIANA M. BOWMAN

8.1 INTRODUCTION

The European Union and closely related states remain an active site of innovation in and clinical testing of mitochondrial replacement therapies (MRT) and other mitochondria-based forms of advanced assisted reproductive technologies (ARTs). Considerable basic and translational science has occurred in laboratories in Europe to develop MRT techniques, which all generally aim to produce a human embryo containing the nuclear DNA of two biological parents and the mitochondria (and mitochondrial DNA, mtDNA) of a donor woman. While still an EU member state, the United Kingdom became the first jurisdiction to adopt legislation authorising MRT solely to prevent heritable mitochondrial disease in 2015 (Chapter 4, this volume), although no children were known to be born from the technique prior to Brexit. In 2016, Greek regulators applied existing legislation to approve a clinical trial of an MRT technique for the purpose of treating infertility, resulting in the births of at least six children by 2021. At least one clinic in Ukraine has offered MRT services since 2017, and journalistic reports suggest that a handful of EU citizens have travelled to Ukraine

Walter G. Johnson and Diana M. Bowman, *Medical Tourism and Multilevel Regulation for MRT in the European Union*
In: *Reproduction Reborn*. Edited by: Diana M. Bowman, Karinne Ludlow, and Walter G. Johnson, Oxford University Press.
© Oxford University Press 2023. DOI: 10.1093/oso/9780197616192.003.0009

to undergo treatment for infertility (e.g., Stein, 2018). Yet, despite these developments, supranational regulators and EU institutions have largely refrained from commenting or taking action on the use of MRT in Europe and by Europeans elsewhere (MacKellar, 2018; van Beers, 2020).

This chapter reviews and examines the authorisation, use, and governance of MRT in the EU context to date, with a specific focus on jurisdictions that have been particularly active in making ARTs, including MRT, accessible to individuals seeking such services. We begin by providing an overview of healthcare systems in the EU, which are driven at the national level rather than supranationally, and resulting issues of reproductive tourism that already occur with existing ARTs. Within this context, the chapter then examines the UK and Greek authorisations of MRT, real or potential medical tourism to Ukraine, and the lack of a clear response from EU institutions. Notably, supranational regulators have refrained from taking action on MRT regardless of their intended use—whether to avoid heritable mitochondrial disease or to treat complex infertility (cf., Chapter 2, this volume). The chapter then reflects on the potential clinical, social, and regulatory futures of MRT and other advanced ARTs in the European setting, raising questions for national and supranational policymakers to consider in the coming years.

8.2   HEALTH LAW, PUBLIC HEALTH POLICIES, AND CROSS-BORDER MEDICAL FLOWS IN THE EU

The European Union is, today, arguably the world's most successful free market, with a myriad of regulatory instruments having been passed over the decades to break down national borders within the block and promote the free movement of people, investment, goods, and services (Meunier and Nicolaïdis, 2006; Ogbor and Eromafuru, 2018; see also the Single Market Act). Despite the push for a single market, one area in which national governments have continued to exhibit significant—although not exclusive—control has been health (Brooks and Guy, 2021). This tiered governance approach is arguably best illustrated by reference to pharmaceutical products: the European Medicines Agency (EMA), for example, was established at the supranational level to ensure the safety and efficacy of pharmaceutical products for humans and animals within the EU. It is, however, bodies such as Germany's Bundesinstitut für Arzneimittel und Medizinprodukte (BfArM) or Croatia's Agency for Drugs and Medical Devices (HALMED) that act as independent regulatory bodies over such products at the national level (Mrazek, 2002; Permanand, 2006). It is not surprising, therefore, that there is little harmonisation across the European Union when it comes to health and public health policies (Abraham and Lewis, 2014).

While the European Union has therefore limited influence on decision-making within the health sphere, Article 168 of the Treaty on the Functioning of the European Union States seeks to create some general obligations on Member States related to public health, including the establishment of a high level of human health protection (Article 168(1)) and fostering cooperation across jurisdictions (Article 168(2)). The commitment to quality is reflected in healthcare performance, with many EU countries being ranked highly in terms of key quality measures such as access to care, equity, and healthcare outcomes (see, e.g., Schneider et al., 2021). This commitment is evident in terms of their investment in the healthcare sector, with Germany, for example, spending in 2019 the equivalent of 11.7 percent of its gross domestic product on health (European Commission, 2021). Germany was not alone, with France (11.1 percent) and Sweden (10.9 percent) similarly making large financial investments in health (European Commission, 2021).

The high level of healthcare available in many EU countries has ensured that many of its Member States have been the beneficiaries of medical tourism (Carrera and Lunt, 2010; Horowitz et al., 2007). "Medical tourism" refers to the practice and business of patients crossing jurisdictional borders to obtain medical care that is inaccessible in their home jurisdiction for fiscal, legal, or other reasons (Cohen, 2014). This has been especially true for countries such as Poland, which is able to offer quality treatment at costs significantly lower than many of their neighbours (Carrera and Bridges, 2006; Lubowiecki-Vikuk and Dryglas, 2019).

Directive 2011/24/EU of the European Parliament and Council of 9 March 2011 on the application of patients' rights in cross-border healthcare (the European Directive on patient rights in cross-border healthcare) reinforces this right to seek healthcare outside one's own country (Bieńkowska et al., 2020). Directive 2011/24/EU sets out

[the] rules for facilitating the access to safe and high-quality cross-border healthcare and promotes cooperation on healthcare between member states, in full respect of national competencies in organising and delivering healthcare (Article 1),

including the framework for reimbursement (Footman et al., 2014). In doing so, the European Union has endorsed medical tourism across the block for its citizens (Androutsou and Metaxas, 2019).

While estimates vary, Market Data Forecasts (2021) have suggested, for example, that the value of medical tourism in the European Union is likely to be around US$7.26 billion in 2021, with their forecasts suggesting growth to US$17.26 billion by 2026. At the same time, data presented by Statistica (Stewart, 2018) suggest that 5 percent of EU citizens seek treatment outside their home country and that 33 percent are willing to travel to another country for care; this number increases to 53 percent when framed around being able to access a higher level of care. For the purposes of this chapter, the 'possibility to have access to specific treatments that are not available in their homelands' was identified as a key reason for seeking treatment outside one's home country (Stewart, 2018).

With reproductive treatment being regulated at the national level, it is not surprising that a patchwork of regulatory approaches exists across the European Union (Flatscher-Thoni and Voithofer, 2015) and contribute to the valuable EU medical tourism market. A 2018 online survey conducted by Calhaz-Jorge et al. (2020) on ARTs and intrauterine insemination (IUI) for the European IVF Monitoring (EIM) Consortium reported that of the 43 (of 44) European countries that responded to the survey, 39 countries had specific legislative schemes in place for ARTs. These frameworks varied significantly in terms of, for example, access, allowable techniques, minimum and maximum age, and anonymity, as well as level of public funding—if at all—provided by the country (Calhaz-Jorge et al., 2020), with marital status, sexual orientation, and age being substantial barriers to access in many jurisdictions. While Denmark had, for example, taken a very liberal approach to providing access to sperm for so-called socially infertile single woman and lesbian couples (Calhaz-Jorge et al., 2020; see also Adrian and Kroløkke, 2018), France only recently (mid-2021) passed legislation giving such individuals this right to access IVF treatments (Calhaz-Jorge et al., 2020; Cobert, 2021). France was not alone in limiting access, with Calhaz-Jorge et al. (2020) noting that at the time of the survey, only 18 (of 43) allowed treatment for lesbian couples. Surrogacy was permitted, or just not expressly regulated, in just 16 countries including, for example, Greece and Ukraine (Calhaz-Jorge et al., 2020). While the majority of countries provided some level of public funding for ARTs, all but one had rules around maximum age for women wishing to access treatment (Calhaz-Jorge et al., 2020).

The findings reported by Calhaz-Jorge et al. (2020) shine a bright light on the diversity of approaches, ranging from very strict to more liberal, and highlight why 'procreative tourism' as coined by Knoppers and Le-Bris (1991) or 'fertility tourism,' as framed by Bergmann (2011), is an economically valuable market. For Pennings (2002: 341), reproductive travelling is a pragmatic solution to the problem of how to combine the democratic system which proceeds according to the majority rule, with a degree of individual freedom for the members of the minority.

In contrast, experts such as Flatscher-Thoni and Voithofer (2015) have sought to question whether harmonisation across the EU offers a superior approach and provide a sketch of what this might look like and what the benefits to those seeking access to ARTs may include. The complexities of doing so formally are, however, eloquently articulated by van Beers (2015: 134) who suggests that 'we should not be surprised to find in a nearby future that a European harmonisation of ART laws has *de facto* already taken place: a free market approach to reproductive questions.' As illustrated by the following sections, this is, we would argue, exactly the situation the European Union finds itself in today in relation to MRT.

8.3 MULTILEVEL REGULATION OF MRT IN EUROPE

The EU structure gives rise to multilevel governance (Hooghe and Marks, 2001) in the provision of health services as well as in the regulation of medical products and procedures. Accordingly, while the governance of reproductive medicine occurs largely at the national level, regulatory structures and decisions at higher and lower levels of government may also influence policy outcomes. Legal and ethical norms at the international, supranational, national, and local levels may trigger in various combinations during the regulation of MRT empowering actors ranging from the European Commission (EC) to national regulatory bodies to institutional thical review boards. The activity of transnational non-state bodies, such as medical professional organisations, further complicates this picture and decentralises authority over reproductive medicine and technologies in the European setting. This framework currently privileges national-level decision-making on MRT and, as illustrated in Section 8.2, offers little coordination around policy issues such as medical tourism, medical follow-up with children born, parental status of the donor woman, or whether techniques can or should be used solely to prevent disease or may also be offered to attempt to treat complex infertility.

While most policy around and regulation of reproductive medicine and ARTs occur at the national level, international or supranational law could arguably still cover MRT techniques or other advanced reproductive technologies. The Oviedo Convention, a Council of Europe treaty, entered into force in 1999 to establish and clarify human rights norms that should apply to biomedical practice. In particular, Article 13 of the Convention provides

> [a]n intervention seeking to modify the human genome may only be undertaken for preventive, diagnostic or therapeutic purposes and only if its aim is not to introduce any modification in the genome of any descendants,

against the backdrop of Article 1, appealing to protecting human 'identity' and 'integrity.' Participation in the Convention is voluntary and, not surprisingly, incomplete. Germany and Belgium, for example, are not parties to the Convention, while Italy and the Netherlands signed but never ratified the treaty.

Even for those parties to the Convention, whether Article 13 triggers for MRT will depend tightly on whether decision-makers determine that the term 'human genome' includes or excludes mtDNA (Ishii and Hibino, 2018). No international consensus exists on this definitional point, with Australian, UK, and US officials or experts all making different determinations on whether MRT constitute germline editing or genetic modification (Ludlow 2018; see also Chapters 4 and 5, this volume). Notably, a protocol to the Oviedo Convention to prohibit human reproductive cloning focuses on the 'nuclear gene set,' which appears to exclude mitochondrial genomics (entering into force in 2001). Whether or how this language in the protocol could influence the interpretation of Article 13 remains unclear. At this time, EU institutions have not made a clear determination on their view of how Article 13 should or may apply to MRT.[1]

At the supranational level, EU legislation also offers potential sources of legal norms to guide behaviour on the authorisation and use of MRT, yet these norms appear to require further interpretation to specifically cover MRT. Highest in the hierarchy of norms, Article 3(2)(b) of the EU Charter of Fundamental Rights issues a 'prohibition of eugenic practices.' Although this provision could potentially be read broadly enough to capture MRT, this would stretch the text and rationale of the provision considerably (van Beers, 2020). Similarly, Article 3(2)(d) prohibits 'the reproductive cloning of human beings' without referencing underlying techniques of nuclear transfer, thereby likely not applying to MRT techniques either. The Clinical Trial Regulations (Regulation (EU) No 536/2014) provide rules on trials for medical products, and Article 90 reads '[n]o gene therapy clinical trials may be carried out which result in modifications to the subject's germ line genetic identity.' The Regulations replaced Directive 2001/20/EC, which contained the same language, but neither document defines the term 'germ line genetic identity,' leaving ambiguity about its applicability to MRT. The EU Tissue and Cell Directives, including Directive 2004/23/EC and subsequent implementing legislation, generally set standards on safety and performance which can apply to ARTs. Yet these rules do not appear to address elements of MRT techniques either directly or indirectly, such as on oocyte donation (Ishii and Hibino, 2018). Furthermore, no EU-level legislation currently addresses human reproductive cloning (Langlois, 2017) or techniques of nuclear transfer, which might otherwise capture MRT techniques.

Nor does patent law offer a convenient regulatory avenue, as *ordre public* norms in EU patent law may render MRT unpatentable on moral grounds (Varvaštian, 2015; see Sherkow et al., 2021). Notably, the European Union has not publicly enforced supranational law on prior uses of other types of mitochondrial manipulation in advanced ARTs, including the use of cytoplasmic transfer in Italy in 2001, leading to the birth of twins (Dale et al., 2001); autologous mitochondrial transfer in Spain in the mid-2010s, resulting in at least seven children from the technique (Labarta et al., 2019); or cytoplasmic transfer occurring in the Czech Republic from at least 2002 to 2018, reporting nearly 30 births (Sobek et al., 2021).

In the absence of supranational regulation, international litigation under European legal instruments could present another route to more co-ordinated governance of MRT. However, while commentators have noted since 2015 that a case could be brought under EU law before the European Court of Justice (ECJ) against the United Kingdom (while it was a member state) or Greece (Varvaštian, 2015; see van Beers, 2015), no appropriate case appears to have been brought before the ECJ at the time of writing. Furthermore, individuals cannot bring legal questions stemming from the Oviedo Convention before the European Court of Human Rights (ECHR) and must instead rely on the norms from the European Convention of Human Rights, which are not specific to biomedicine (Varvaštian, 2015). Similarly, while the ECHR has considered cases regarding ARTs, the Court has generally refrained from questioning national decision-making (van Beers, 2015).

8.4 NATIONAL AND TRANSNATIONAL MRT SCHEMES IN THE EU

The applicability of EU law to MRT was first tested against the UK legislation authorising particular MRT techniques under a strict regulatory regime involving clinic licensing and approval for individual treatments. The UK move came after substantial yet contested public engagement and a favourable report from the Nuffield Council on Bioethics, with restrictions on MRT treatment to only be used for the purpose of preventing heritable mitochondrial diseases (Chapter 4, this volume). The United Kingdom was still an EU Member State at the time this legislation came into effect; however, neither the EC nor the European Medicines Agency appeared to take any public action in response to the UK legislation despite the potential applicability of supranational or international legal norms discussed above.

Following a formal complaint submitted to the EC by a civil society organisation, MacKellar (2018) reports that the EC instead determined that the techniques authorised by the United Kingdom did not fall under the Clinical Trial Regulations, finding that the techniques did not qualify as 'medicinal products' within the scope of the regulations. The EC also determined that the UK regime, through its licensing component, complied with applicable standards from the Tissue and Cell Directives requiring Member States to license entities working with human tissues and cells. Furthermore, the EC concluded that the EU Charter of Fundamental Rights would not apply because the United Kingdom was enacting its own national-level policy rather than implementing EU law (MacKellar, 2018). Notably, these opinions were obtained through a civil society organisation—European Bioethical Research—submitting a formal complaint to the EC, and the EC's interpretations of EU law do not appear to be published elsewhere at this time. The opinions also left unclear whether this same rationale would apply to MRT intended for treating infertility, instead of the UK goal of preventing heritable mitochondrial disease.

In September 2016, the Greek National Authority of Assisted Reproduction provided approval for a clinic in Athens, the Institute of Life, and the Spanish firm Embryotools to begin a human clinical trial of one MRT technique—maternal spindle transfer (Kostaras, 2018). As opposed to the UK framework, the Greek trial has specifically tested the effectiveness of MRT in treating complex infertility in prospective parents. The National Authority, which regulates ARTs and licenses ART clinics in Greece, exercised its existing authority under national Law 3305/2005 to review and approve proposals to conduct research with the intent of initiating a human pregnancy. This is notable because Greece did not enact novel legislation to authorise MRT but instead relied on its existing statutes to enable trials to proceed and monitor their progress (Johnson and Bowman, 2022). However, in 2017, the Hellenic National Bioethics Commission (2017: 5) issued a report recommending against proceeding with 'all clinical applications' of MRT, given the contemporary 'lack of sufficient evidence at an international level . . . in order to substantiate the efficacy and the safety of MRT.' It is unclear whether or how this report impacted the Greek National Authority's authorisation. The clinical trial concluded in May 2020, ultimately reporting six live births by May 2021 after beginning with 25 patients with complex infertility (Costa-Borges et al., 2020).[2] Press releases by the clinical team indicate that at least five of the six mothers are Greek, although it is difficult based on publicly available documentation to confirm whether participants travelled to Greece to undergo treatment.

It is unclear whether and to what extent the EC's interpretation of EU law reported by MacKellar (2018) applies to the Greek case, especially as the EC responded to the civil society complaint on the UK regime prior to the Greek National Authority's authorisation. Of course, no public enforcement action took place during the course of the Greek clinical trial, suggesting that the EC viewed this case of regulatory approval in the same or similar way to the UK legislation. Moreover, no other EU institutions have made public statements or taken regulatory actions against the Greek clinical trial or its approval. The clinical team may seek approval of their MRT technique in Spain—where Embryotools is based—despite the rigorous approval process (Cohen et al., 2020), which could provide another opportunity for supranational regulation as more individual national-level determinations on MRT proceed.

Beyond Greece, current EU Member States may take a variety of different approaches to regulating MRT within their own jurisdiction in the continued absence of supranational regulation. As illustrated in Section 8.2, notable differences exist among Europeans and between EU Member States on the values and norms guiding reproductive medicine and advanced ART development (see Pennings, 2002). While Greek law elevates the value of reproductive autonomy, for instance, German policy remains highly averse to technologies which alter the human germline, likely including MRT (Νόμος 3305/2005, art. 1; Jasanoff and Metzler, 2020). Furthermore, some national law targeting human reproductive cloning might apply to MRT depending on interpretive decisions, such as Spanish legislation prohibiting 'nuclear transfer' techniques for human reproduction (Ley 14/2006, art. 26). Some jurisdictions also have existing national law prohibiting human germline editing that may capture MRT, although states including the Netherlands appear likely to interpret such law as prohibiting only nuclear DNA modifications while still permitting MRT (Netherlands Commission on Genetic Modification and Health Council of the Netherlands, 2017). Attempts to bridge these gaps in values and law at the supranational level could expose EU institutions or policymakers to legal challenges or political backlash from various constituencies, which likely contributes to the dominance of national-level decision-making for ART policy in Europe already (van Beers, 2015).

In this setting, and given the significance of Directive 2011/24/EU, reproductive tourism for MRT within the European Union appears possible and perhaps likely once a national government approves one or more techniques for clinical use—whether to prevent mitochondrial diseases and/or to treat complex infertility. Approval of MRT techniques in only some EU Member States—or approval of different techniques in different states or for different intended uses—may exacerbate the challenges of reproductive tourism should European patients in a state without approval simply travel to an EU state permitting the service they wish to receive. This potential for MRT tourism evokes the ongoing normative tensions raised by other forms of reproductive tourism in the European Union, as discussed above (Pennings, 2002; van Beers, 2015).

Issues of medical tourism for MRT services may not only present an internal issue for the European Union, but may also raise challenges from EU citizens or residents travelling elsewhere to undergo MRT. For example, the Nadiya Clinic in Kiev has marketed pronuclear transfer services to both Ukrainian residents and international patients through an ostensible clinical trial since at least 2018, although patients are charged to receive these treatments (Stein, 2018; see Mazur et al., 2019). Ukraine shares borders with four EU Member States—Hungary, Poland, Romania, and Slovakia—and may offer a convenient place for European patients (as well as non-European patients) with sufficient means to travel for advanced ART treatment.[3] Journalists have reported that patients have indeed travelled across borders to receive MRT services at the Nadiya Clinic, including from EU Member State Sweden and the United Kingdom while still a Member State (Stein, 2018), though reports of subsequent births are difficult to find. These potential incidents of EU citizens engaging in medical tourism for MRT treatment outside the block may only increase over time should treatments for disease prevention or infertility alike remain unavailable in many EU states. The incidents also raise questions about whether MRT services are being conducted consistent with standards and values that EU law and policymakers would impose on domestic treatments, particularly if those MRT services are offered for treating infertility in addition to avoiding disease.

Moreover, no expert review or public consultation processes have occurred at the EU level to guide MRT policymaking, in sharp contrast to the comprehensive approaches of Australia (Chapter 5, this volume) and the United Kingdom (Chapter 4, this volume) or the expert reviews conducted in Singapore (Chapter 9, this volume) and the United States

(Chapter 6, this volume). To date, no expert review or public engagement process on MRT has been announced by an EU institution, nor have reports been published by EU policymakers on the issues these techniques raise. Very limited public discussion at the EU level appears to have been published in English, beyond the public discussion sparked by the UK legislation (Chapters 3 and 4, this volume; see Herbrand, 2021), though a more thorough multilingual review may be a valuable future empirical contribution. For the foreseeable future, it appears that regulatory policy for MRT will remain firmly at the national level, and national governments should consider public consultation with their residents prior to making decisions around the techniques.

Instead of supranational regulators, transnational actors may have a greater role in harmonisation or orchestration of MRT standards and services across Europe. For example, the European Society of Human Reproduction and Embryology (ESHRE), a medical professional organisation, issued a statement condemning MRT intended to treat infertility rather than prevent mitochondrial disease shortly after the news of the first birth in Athens (ESHRE, 2019). While the statement did not take an explicit position on the permissibility of MRT to avoid disease, the ESHRE statement did appear to praise the United Kingdom's stringent regulatory criteria for offering the techniques for this purpose. Notably, the ESHRE is open to membership for practitioners outside the European Union, although preliminary data suggest at least some European clinicians are aware of and implement ESHRE guidance to some extent (Gameiro et al., 2019). The effectiveness of transnational actors in guiding MRT national policy and cross-jurisdictional clinical practice or standards merits further empirical study in the EU context and beyond.

8.5 CONCLUSION

The governance of MRT in the European Union, like regulation for many ARTs, occurs predominantly at the national level and lacks strong supranational policy or coordinating efforts. This fragmentation within the EU system enables Member States to set policies responsive to their own set of cultural, religious, and moral values (see also Chapters 5, 7, and 9, this volume). A number of regimes, as highlighted by Calhaz-Jorge et al. (2020), continue to be highly restrictive and present significant barriers to individuals seeking treatment within their own country. While this fragmentation currently exists in a relatively stable form for controversial services such as surrogacy, reform is occurring, opening up access to individuals who may have been previously excluded from accessing ARTs at home. The passage of Directive 2011/24/EU created what has become a highly successful medical marketplace within the European Union. Its passage has provided the framework for reproductive tourism generally and will, going forward, likely pave the way for EU citizens to readily access the small number of clinics offering MRT within the region.

While it appears unlikely at this time that clinics offering such advanced forms of ARTs will be overwhelmed with individuals seeking MRT for therapeutic purposes, the potential application of the techniques to treat individuals suffering from complex fertility problems does open up a much larger potential market for clinics. The Institute of Life appears, at least at this time, to be one of the few clinics in the world actively—or at least openly—exploring the technique for intended uses beyond preventing heritable diseases, with their research still being in its infancy. Based on published data, it would appear that their clinical trial, approved in 2016, has resulted in what would appear to be six live births to date from a pool of 25 participants. We suspect that, for MRT to become an acceptable, widespread solution for infertility within the medical community, significantly more basic research and reporting will have to take place.

Without supranational state organisations engaging in MRT regulation across EU Member States, transnational professional organisations, private entities, clinical facilities, and members of the scientific and medical communities may become more prominent actors in the governance of these techniques across European jurisdictions. The ESHRE condemnation of the Greek clinical trials, specifically of the use of MRT to treat infertility, could already signal a potential role for this non-state actor or other professional societies to play a coordinating role at the level of practicing physicians rather than national health systems. Formal or informal clinical standards for when, why, and how to best offer MRT services to potential patients, in combination with other tools such as medical malpractice litigation, may still promote positive clinical outcomes—albeit in a less coordinated or transparent manner than state regulation. Such transnational regulation of MRT by non-state actors would see governance extending out 'sideways' instead of vertically within the European Union's multilevelled governance structure (Hooghe and Marks, 2001; Vogel, 2010). While non-state oversight has its own limitations from perceived accountability and democratic legitimacy deficits, this mode may offer an alternative route to supranational coordination for still pursuing good clinical standards and harmonisation in an EU market enabling medical tourism. Future empirical study will be required to explore the extent of transnational MRT regulation possible in the EU context and evaluate its potential effectiveness.

While regulating MRT in the European Union poses ongoing policy and orchestration challenges, some of the supranational inaction may also be partially attributable to the relatively low level of political and public scrutiny these techniques have received at the EU level despite their clinical use. However, this general ambivalence could change if other advanced ARTs such as human heritable genome editing (HHGE) enter clinics or policy conversations (Chapter 10, this volume). Since the use of HHGE in China sparked intense global scrutiny (Greely, 2021), the first proposed or actual use of HHGE in Europe could ignite regulatory debates in the European Union that could potentially extend to MRT as well. While the EC's interpretation of EU law as applied to MRT may exclude HHGE as well (MacKellar, 2018; van Beers, 2020), political scrutiny of how EU law applies to HHGE—in areas ranging from clinical trials and medical products to human rights—could result in shifts that intentionally or indirectly capture MRT. Notably, a recent joint statement on HHGE from the national bioethics councils of France, Germany, and the United Kingdom called for 'broad societal debate' and the implementation of national legislation prior to any clinical application of these technologies (Comité Consultatif National d'Éthique et al., 2020), which could potentially prompt societal and legal debate in Europe over MRT in the process. Arguably, it may be advances within the field of HHGE, rather than MRT, that place the additional pressures on EU institutions to harmonise or otherwise coordinate this contested area of reproductive health policy.

NOTES

1. In 2013, 34 members (of 324) of the Parliamentary Assembly of the Council of Europe signed a written declaration which appears to intimate that Article 13 should preclude MRT and concludes that 'the creation of children with genetic material from more than two progenitor persons . . . is incompatible with human dignity and international law.' However, the declaration is nonbinding and reflects a minority (~10.5 percent) of the Assembly: 'Parliamentary Assembly Written Declaration on the Creation of Embryos with Genetic Material from More than Two Progenitor Persons.' Council of Europe Written Declaration Doc. 13325, 3 October 2013. https://pace.coe.int/en/files/20204.
2. The sixth birth following maternal spindle transfer was reported by the Institute of Life on 26 May 2020: https://www.iolife.eu/en/sixth-baby-born-using-the-maternal-spindle-transfer-method/.

3. However, the recent invasion of Ukraine by the Russian Federation in February 2022 may significantly impact the potential to travel to and receive MRT treatment in Ukraine, at least in the near term.

REFERENCES

Abraham, John, and Graham Lewis. *Regulating Medicines in Europe: Competition, Expertise and Public Health*. Routledge, 2014.

Adrian, Stine Willum, and Charlotte Kr\u00f8l\u00f8kke. 'Passport to parenthood: Reproductive pathways in and out of Denmark.' *NORA-Nordic Journal of Feminist and Gender Research* 26, no. 2 (2018): 112–128.

Androutsou, Lorena, and Theodore Metaxas. 'Measuring the efficiency of medical tourism industry in EU member states.' *Journal of Tourism Analysis: Revista de Análisis Turístico* 26, no. 2 (2019): 115–130.

Bergmann, Sven. 'Fertility tourism: Circumventive routes that enable access to reproductive technologies and substances.' *Signs: Journal of Women in Culture and Society* 36, no. 2 (2011): 280–289.

Bieńkowska, Daria, Agnieszka Lipska-Sondecka, and Ryszard Kozłowski. 'Cross-border access to health care in the European Union as a sustainable development policy.' *European Research Studies* 23, no. 3 (2020): 85–92.

Brooks, Eleanor, and Mary Guy. 'EU health law and policy: Shaping a future research agenda.' *Health Economics, Policy and Law* 16, no. 1 (2021): 1–7.

Calhaz-Jorge, Carlos, C. H. De Geyter, Markus S. Kupka, Christine Wyns, Edgar Mocanu, Tatiana Motrenko, Giulia Scaravelli, et al. 'Survey on ART and IUI: Legislation, regulation, funding and registries in European countries: The European IVF-monitoring Consortium (EIM) for the European Society of Human Reproduction and Embryology (ESHRE).' *Human Reproduction Open* 2020, no. 1 (2020): hoz044.

Carrera, Percivil, and Neil Lunt. 'A European perspective on medical tourism: The need for a knowledge base.' *International Journal of Health Services* 40, no. 3 (2010): 469–484.

Carrera, Percivil M., and John F. P. Bridges. 'Globalization and healthcare: Understanding health and medical tourism.' *Expert Review of Pharmacoeconomics & Outcomes Research* 6, no. 4 (2006): 447–454.

Cobert, Sylvie. 'France legalizes IVF for lesbians and single women.' *AP News*, 29 June 2021. https://apnews.com/article/europe-france-health-government-and-politics-ced76e5bcd3ee22870ae128f59e5e437.

Cohen, I. Glenn. *Patients with Passports: Medical Tourism, Law, and Ethics*. Oxford University Press, 2014.

Cohen, I. Glenn, Eli Y. Adashi, Sara Gerke, César Palacios-González, and Vardit Ravitsky. 'The regulation of mitochondrial replacement techniques around the world.' *Annual Review of Genomics and Human Genetics* 21 (2020): 565–586.

Comité Consultatif National d'Éthique pour les sciences de la vie et de la santé (France), Deutscher Ethikrat (Germany), & Nuffield Council on Bioethics (UK). 'Joint statement on the ethics of heritable human genome editing.' 3 March 2020. https://www.nuffieldbioethics.org/assets/pdfs/Joint-statement.pdf.

Costa-Borges, Nuno, Eros Nikitos, Katharina Spath, Klaus Rink, Konstantinos Kostaras, Ioannis Zervomanolakis, George Kontopoulos, et al. 'First registered pilot trial to validate the safety and effectiveness of maternal spindle transfer to overcome infertility associated with poor oocyte quality.' *Fertility and Sterility* 114, no. 3 (2020): e71–e72.

Dale, Brian, Martin Wilding, Giuseppe Botta, Marianna Rasile, Marcella Marino, Loredana Di Matteo, Giuseppe De Placido, and Alfredo Izzo. 'Pregnancy after cytoplasmic transfer in a couple suffering from idiopathic infertility: Case report.' *Human Reproduction* 16, no. 7 (2001): 1469–1472.

European Commission. 'Current healthcare expenditure relative to GDP, 2019.' *Healthcare Expenditure Statistics*, December 2021. https://ec.europa.eu/euros tat/statistics-explained/index.php?title=Healthcare_expenditure_statistics.

European Society of Human Reproduction and Embryology (ESHRE). 'Spindle transfer in the treatment of infertility: An ESHRE position statement.' 9 July 2019. https://www.eshre.eu/Europe/Position-statements/Spindle-transfer.

Flatscher-Thöni, Magdalena, and Caroline Voithofer. 'Should reproductive medicine be harmonized within Europe?' *European Journal of Health Law* 22, no. 1 (2015): 61–74.

Footman, K., C. Knai, R. Baeten, K. Glonti, and M. McKee. 'Cross-border health care in Europe, Policy Summary 14.' World Health Organization, 2014. https://www.euro.who.int/__data/assets/pdf_file/0009/263538/Cross-border-health-care-in-Europe-Eng.pdf.

Gameiro, S., M. Sousa-Leite, and N. Vermeulen. 'Dissemination, implementation and impact of the ESHRE evidence-based guidelines.' *Human Reproduction Open* 2019, no. 3 (2019): hoz011.

Greely, Henry T. *CRISPR People: The Science and Ethics of Editing Humans*. MIT Press, 2021.

Hellenic National Bioethics Commission. 'Recommendation: Mitochondrial replacement for the prevention of mitochondrial diseases.' 4 April 2017. https://archive.bioethics.gr/images/pdf/gnomes/recommendation_mitochond rial_replacement_final__eng.pdf.

Herbrand, Cathy. 'Silences, omissions and oversimplification? The UK debate on mitochondrial donation.' *Reproductive Biomedicine & Society Online* 14 (2021): 53–62.

Hooghe, Liesbet, and Gary Marks. *Multi-level Governance and European Integration*. Rowman & Littlefield, 2001.

Horowitz, Michael D., Jeffrey A. Rosensweig, and Christopher A. Jones. 'Medical tourism: Globalization of the healthcare marketplace.' *Medscape General Medicine* 9, no. 4 (2007): 33.

Ishii, Tetsuya, and Yuri Hibino. 'Mitochondrial manipulation in fertility clinics: Regulation and responsibility.' *Reproductive Biomedicine & Society Online* 5 (2018): 93–109.

Jasanoff, Sheila, and Ingrid Metzler. 'Borderlands of life: IVF embryos and the law in the United States, United Kingdom, and Germany.' *Science, Technology, & Human Values* 45, no. 6 (2020): 1001–1037.

Johnson, Walter G., and Diana M. Bowman. 'Inherited regulation for advanced ARTs: Comparing jurisdictions' applications of existing governance regimes to emerging reproductive technologies.' *Journal of Law and the Biosciences* 9, no. 1 (2022): lsab034.

Knoppers, Bartha M., and Sonia LeBris. 'Recent advances in medically assisted conception: Legal, ethical and social issues.' *American Journal of Law & Medicine* 17, no. 4 (1991): 329–361.

Kostaras, K., N. Costa-Borges, P. Psathas, G. Calderón, and E. Nikitos. 'Spindle transfer for the treatment of infertility problems associated to poor egg quality: A pilot trial.' *ISRCTN* (2018): 11455145.

Labarta, Elena, Maria José de Los Santos, Sonia Herraiz, Maria José Escribá, Alicia Marzal, Anna Buigues, and Antonio Pellicer. 'Autologous mitochondrial transfer as a complementary technique to intracytoplasmic sperm injection to improve embryo quality in patients undergoing in vitro fertilization—a randomized pilot study.' *Fertility and Sterility* 111, no. 1 (2019): 86–96.

Langlois, Adèle. 'The global governance of human cloning: The case of UNESCO.' *Palgrave Communications* 3, no. 1 (2017): 1–8.

Lubowiecki-Vikuk, Adrian, and Diana Dryglas. 'Central and Eastern Europe as a medical tourism destination: A case study of Poland.' *Almatourism-Journal of Tourism, Culture and Territorial Development* 10, no. 19 (2019): 25–43.

Ludlow, Karinne. 'The policy and regulatory context of US, UK, and Australian responses to mitochondrial donation governance.' *Jurimetrics* 58, no. 3 (2018): 247–265.

MacKellar, Calum. 'Can maternal spindle transfer and pronuclear transfer be prohibited under EU legislation?' *European Journal of Health Law* 25, no. 1 (2018): 57–74.

Market Data Forecasts. 'European medical tourism market size (2021–2026).' April 2021. https://www.marketdataforecast.com/market-reports/europe-medical-tourism-market.

Mazur, Pavlo, Lada Dyachenko, Viktor Veselovskyy, Yuliya Masliy, Maksym Borysov, Dmytro O. Mykytenko, and Valery Zukin. 'Mitochondrial replacement therapy give no benefits to patients of advanced maternal age.' *Fertility and Sterility* 112, no. 3 (2019): e193.

Meunier, Sophie, and Kalypso Nicolaïdis. 'The European Union as a conflicted trade power.' *Journal of European Public Policy* 13, no. 6 (2006): 906–925.

Mrazek, Monique F. 'Comparative approaches to pharmaceutical price regulation in the European Union.' *Croatian Medical Journal* 43, no. 4 (2002): 453–461.

Netherlands Commission on Genetic Modification & Health Council of the Netherlands. 'Editing human DNA: Moral and social implications of germline genetic modification.' March 2017. https://cogem.net/app/uploads/2019/07/Germline-Modification1.pdf.

Ogbor, John Oghenechuko, and Edward G. Eromafuru. 'Regional trade blocs, location advantage and enterprise competitiveness in the global economy.' *Archives of Business Research* 6, no. 6 (2018): 11–27.

Pennings, Guido. 'Reproductive tourism as moral pluralism in motion.' *Journal of Medical Ethics* 28, no. 6 (2002): 337–341.

Permanand, Govin. *EU Pharmaceutical Regulation: The Politics of Policy-making.* Manchester University Press, 2006.

Schneider, E. C., A. Shah, M. M. Doty, R. Tikkanen, K. Fields, and R. D. Williams. 'Mirror, mirror 2021—reflecting poorly: Health care in the US compared to other high-income countries.' Commonwealth Fund, 2021.

Sherkow, Jacob S., Eli Y. Adashi, and I. Glenn Cohen. 'Governing human germline editing through patent law.' *JAMA* 326, no. 12 (2021): 1149–1150.

Sobek, Ales, Emil Tkadlec, Eva Klaskova, and Martin Prochazka. 'Cytoplasmic transfer improves human egg fertilization and embryo quality: An evaluation of sibling oocytes in women with low oocyte quality.' *Reproductive Sciences* 28, no. 5 (2021): 1362–1369.

Stein, Rob. 'Clinic claims success in making babies with 3 parents' DNA.' *NPR*, 6 June 2018. https://www.npr.org/sections/health-shots/2018/06/06/615909572/ins ide-the-ukrainian-clinic-making-3-parent-babies-for-women-who-are-infertile.

Stewart, Conor. 'Medical tourism in Europe: Statistics & facts.' *Statista*, 28 September 2018. https://www.statista.com/topics/3292/medical-tourism-in-europe/.

van Beers, Britta C. 'Is Europe "giving in to baby markets?" Reproductive tourism in Europe and the gradual erosion of existing legal limits to reproductive markets.' *Medical Law Review* 23, no. 1 (2015): 103–134.

van Beers, Britta C. 'Rewriting the human genome, rewriting human rights law? Human rights, human dignity, and human germline modification in the CRISPR era.' *Journal of Law and the Biosciences* 7, no. 1 (2020): lsaa006.

Varvaštian, Samvel. 'UK's legalisation of mitochondrial donation in IVF treatment: A challenge to the international community or a promotion of life-saving medical innovation to be followed by others?' *European Journal of Health Law* 22, no. 5 (2015): 405–425.

Vogel, David. 'The private regulation of global corporate conduct: Achievements and limitations.' *Business & Society* 49, no. 1 (2010): 68–87.

LAWS CITED

Charter of Fundamental Rights of the European Union, OJ C 326/02, 26.10.2012.

Communication from the [European] Commission: Single Market Act: Twelve levers to boost growth and strengthen confidence: Working together to create new growth, COM(2011)206, 13.4.2011.

Consolidated version of the Treaty on the Functioning of the European Union, OJ C 326/01, 26.10.2012.

Council of Europe Treaty No.164. [Oviedo Convention] Convention for the Protection of Human Rights and Dignity of the Human Being with regard to the Application of Biology and Medicine: Convention on Human Rights and Biomedicine. 1997. https://www.coe.int/en/web/conventions/full-list/-/conv entions/treaty/164.

Council of Europe Treaty No. 168. [Oviedo Convention Protocol] Additional Protocol to the Convention for the Protection of Human Rights and Dignity of the Human Being with regard to the Application of Biology and Medicine, on the Prohibition of Cloning Human Beings. 1998. https://www.coe.int/en/web/conv entions/full-list/-/conventions/treaty/168.

Directive 2001/20/EC of the European Parliament and of the Council of 4 April 2001 on the Approximation of the Laws, Regulations and Administrative Provisions of the Member States Relating to the Implementation of Good Clinical Practice in the Conduct of Clinical Trials on Medicinal Products for Human Use, OJ L 121, 1.5.2001.

Directive 2004/23/EC of the European Parliament and of the Council of Mar. 31, 2004 on Setting Standards of Quality and Safety for the Donation, Procurement, Testing, Processing, Preservation, Storage and Distribution of Human Tissues and Cells, OJ L 102, 7.4.2004.

Directive 2011/24/EU of the European Parliament and Council of 9 March 2011 on the Application of Patients' Rights in Cross-border Healthcare, OJ L 88, 4.4.2011.

Ley 14/2006, de 26 de mayo, sobre técnicas de reproducción humana asistida, Boletín Oficial del Estado n. 126, May 27, 2006, BOE-A-2006-9292 [On Assisted Human Reproduction Techniques] (Spain).

Νόμος 3305/2005, Εφαρμογή της ιατρικώς υποβοηθούμενης αναπαραγωγής, ΦΕΚ Α 17/Α/27.01.2005 [Law 3305/2005, Application of Medically Assisted Reproduction] (Greece).

Regulation (EU) No 536/2014 of the European Parliament and of the Council of Apr. 16, 2014 on Clinical Trials on Medical Products for Human Use, and Repealing Directive 2001/20/EC, OJ L 158, 27.5.2014.

9

Asia

TETSUYA ISHII

9.1 INTRODUCTION

Mitochondria are cellular organelles with their own genome (mitochondrial DNA; mtDNA). Human eggs have many mitochondria: 200,000–300,000 copies of mtDNA per cell (Schatten et al., 2014). Because paternal mitochondria are specifically digested in fertilised eggs, mtDNA is passed from mother to offspring, forming approximately 30 mtDNA haplogroups in humans (van Oven and Kayser, 2009). It is well understood that specific mtDNA mutations in eggs can cause the onset of mitochondrial diseases in the resultant offspring (Koopman et al., 2012). It has also been suggested that some gene mutations that affect mitochondrial functions could be associated with infertility (Harper et al., 2017). Thus, several mitochondrial manipulation techniques have been developed in laboratories and performed at fertility clinics (Ishii, 2018).

In 1997, a clinic in the United States reported the world's first birth via mitochondrial manipulation (Cohen and Scott, 1997). The clinic considered whether infertility due to insufficient embryonic development was associated with characteristics of the cytoplasm of the patient's eggs. Cytoplasm containing mitochondria taken from a donor egg was, together with a sperm cell from the husband, injected into the wife's eggs. The transfer of such manipulated embryos into the wife's womb led to the birth of a girl. The clinic performed more such cytoplasmic transfer

Tetsuya Ishii, *Asia* In: *Reproduction Reborn*. Edited by: Diana M. Bowman, Karinne Ludlow, and Walter G. Johnson, Oxford University Press. © Oxford University Press 2023. DOI: 10.1093/oso/9780197616192.003.0010 interventions, leading to 17 childbirths in total. However, two foetuses in two different pregnancies turned out to have Turner syndrome, resulting in one miscarriage and one elective abortion. Another child born through cytoplasmic transfer was diagnosed with a pervasive developmental disorder (Barritt, 2001). On the other hand, the UK first permitted two types of mitochondrial replacement techniques in 2015, to prevent the onset of serious mitochondrial diseases in offspring, but not to treat infertility (UK Department of Health, 2015). Such permitted techniques can replace most (but not all) aberrant mitochondria (mitochondria containing mutated mtDNA) with viable mitochondria via nuclear transfer between eggs or embryos (Hyslop et al., 2016; Kang et al., 2016; Yamada et al., 2016).

Mitochondrial manipulation usually involves egg donation. Of course, the direct use of donor eggs can overcome infertility and prevent the onset of mitochondrial disease in offspring; however, the resultant offspring are not genetically related to the mother in terms of the nuclear genome (nDNA), potentially leading to 'resemblance talk' in the family. Although mitochondrial manipulation can help prospective parents have genetically related offspring, it undoubtedly remains experimental as a form of human reproduction and has been subjected to regulatory interventions. In 2001, the US Food and Drug Administration (FDA) decided to review protocols for mitochondrial manipulation under Investigational New Drug exemptions in response to concerns of de facto germline genetic modification, but the review by the FDA was in itself later prohibited by a budget law (Castro, 2016; Cohen and Adashi, 2016; Chapter 6, this volume). It is of particular note that, prior to the UK legalisation, a form of mitochondrial replacement had already been performed in China as an infertility treatment and not for disease prevention (Zhang et al., 2016). Although this attempt led to a triplet pregnancy, it ultimately resulted in no live births: two foetuses died after one was selectively terminated. Subsequently, in 2003, the Chinese Ministry of Health (CMOH) established the Standards for Human Assisted Reproductive Technology Specifications and the Ethical Principles for Human Assisted Reproductive Technology and Human Sperm Bank and prohibited cytoplasmic transfer and nuclear transfer (Ishii and Hibino, 2018). However, the clinical cases of mitochondrial manipulation and regulations governing them in other Asian countries are less known compared with those in the Western world (Ishii and Hibino, 2018; Schandera and Mackey, 2016). This chapter examines the implFunications of experimental reproduction involving mitochondrial manipulation in China, Japan, Singapore, and Taiwan while considering their religions and beliefs.

9.2 CONCEPT AND IMPLICATIONS OF GERMLINE MITOCHONDRIAL MANIPULATION

The mitochondrion is an organelle present in the cytoplasm of cells. It is characterised by containing its own genome (mtDNA). Mitochondrial functions are carried out through coordinated gene expression from the mtDNA as well as the nDNA (Schatten et al., 2014; Chapter 1, this volume). The most important function is carried out by the respiratory chain that produces energy for living activities while precisely controlling the production of deleterious free radicals.

Mitochondrial manipulation in the reproductive cells or embryos supplements or restores mitochondrial functions in order to enhance the viability of eggs in the treatment of unexplained infertility (mitochondrial or cytoplasmic transfer) or to reduce the mutated mtDNA load of the eggs or zygotes primarily to prevent the inheritance of mitochondrial disease by the offspring from the mother (mitochondrial replacement) (Ishii and Hibino, 2018). The use of mitochondrial replacement to prevent the inheritance of mitochondrial disease by offspring can be regarded as a form of infertility treatment because women who have offspring affected by mitochondrial disease often experience miscarriages, probably due to dysfunctional mitochondria in their eggs (White et al., 1999). Indeed, a Chinese group performed mitochondrial replacement in the zygotes in 2003 for an infertile woman who failed two in vitro fertilization (IVF) cycles, as illustrated in Table 9.1.

To achieve either of the two goals of mitochondrial manipulation, a supply of functional mitochondria or cytoplasm containing such mitochondria is required. Mitochondrial replacement uses enucleated donor eggs or enucleated donor zygotes and fuses them to the nuclei of the prospective parents (Hyslop et al., 2016; Kang et al., 2016; Yamada et al., 2016). In mitochondrial or cytoplasmic transfer, mitochondria or cytoplasm taken from donor eggs (or zygotes) is often injected into the patient's infertile eggs (Cohen and Scott, 1997; Huang et al., 1999). However, egg donation requires medication, hormonal stimulation, and surgical egg retrieval. The process of egg retrieval can impose a certain level of burden and risk on the egg donor, making donor eggs difficult to obtain compared with donor sperm (Palacios-González, 2016). For this reason, mitochondrial or cytoplasmic transfer occasionally uses mitochondria derived from the cytoplasm of the patient's own cells, such as granulosa cells (Kong et al., 2003a and 2003b; Oktay et al., 2015; Tzeng et al., 2001).

Importantly, mitochondrial manipulation assumes that the mitochondria used to supplement or replace dysfunctional material are functional and

Table 9.1 CLINICAL IMPLEMENTATIONS OF GERMLINE MITOCHONDRIAL MANIPULATION IN ASIA

Case no.	Report	Place of practice	Manipulation	Origin of mitochondria for transfer	Subjects	Results	Remarks
1[a]	Huang et al. (1999)	Taiwan	Cytoplasmic transfer	Donor tripronucleate zygotes	Nine women with more than 5 IVF or ICSI failures (32–42 year old)	Five healthy infants were born from four recipients. No pregnancies in the remaining five recipients.	<30 year-old women who underwent IVF donated tripronucleate zygotes.
2[a]	Tzeng et al. (2001)	Taiwan	Autologous mitochondrial transfer	Autologous granular cells	Patients older than 38, recurrent implantation failure, prolonged.	Three clinical pregnancies. One of the cases: A twin pregnancy in a 36-year-old patient with infertility of 9 years, showed normal 46XX and 46XY, respectively.	Conference paper, not peer-reviewed article. 500–5000 mitochondria were injected in each oocyte.
3	Kong et al. (2003a)	China	Autologous mitochondrial transfer	Autologous granular cells	A 37-year-old woman with two miscarriages after IVF.	Three clinical pregnancies. One of the cases: A twin pregnancy in a 36-year-old patient with infertility of 9 years, showed normal 46XX and 46XY, respectively.	First live births via autologous mitochondrial transfer in Chinese mainland.
4	Kong et al. (2003b)	China	Autologous mitochondrial transfer	Autologous granular cells	A 46-year-old infertile woman.	A triplet pregnancy. At 5th week of pregnancy, one fetus ceased to develop. At 30th week, two normal infants (boy and girl) were born via caesarean section.	About 3000 mitochondria were transferred into each oocyte.

#	Reference	Country	Technique	Material	Subjects	Outcome	Notes
5	Zhang et al. (2003)	China	Mitochondrial replacement (nuclear transfer between eggs)	Zygotes created using donor oocytes and spermatozoa of patient's partner	A 30-year-old nulligravida woman who failed two IVF cycles.	A singleton pregnancy ended in a miscarriage at 9th week.	First reported at a conference in 2003. Peer-reviewed article published in 2016. Electrofusion of nuclei and enucleated zygote was performed.
6[a]	Morimoto et al. (2016)	Japan	Autologous germline mitochondrial energy transfer	Autologous 'oogonial precursor cells'	Thirty women with more than one IVF failures (20–50 years old).	A triplet pregnancy. After selective reduction of a fetus, the other foetuses prematurely delivered and died.	Information left is from protocol registry (ID: UMIN000021387) and report on such as TV. No peer-reviewed papers published.

IVF, in vitro fertilisation; ICSI, intracytoplasmic sperm injection.
[a]Single arm, nonrandomized, open-labelled, uncontrolled studies.

that the number of mitochondria is sufficient for reproductive purposes; however, information regarding these assumptions has generally remained unclear in previous reports (Table 9.1) (Fakih et al., 2015; Heindryckx et al., 2015; Huang et al., 1999; Kong et al., 2003a, 2003b). In addition, there is a genealogical tree made up of genetic groups (haplogroups) with a specific mtDNA variant; however, the potential for mixing different mtDNA haplogroups in the germline has not been considered in cytoplasmic transfer treatments (Huang et al., 1999; Kong et al., 2003a, 2003b; Tzeng et al., 2001). Furthermore, the mechanical and chemical stresses of mitochondrial manipulation on the patient's eggs or zygotes might have reproductive consequences (Ishii, 2018; Chapter 1, this volume). Notably, in mitochondrial replacement, the micropipette used to transfer the nucleus is of much larger calibre than that used for intracytoplasmic sperm injection (ICSI) in the cytoplasmic or mitochondrial transfer procedure. Fusion of the nucleus (or nuclei) with enucleated eggs (or zygotes) uses the Sendai virus or electrical stimulus, the safety of which for human reproduction is not fully confirmed. To date, only several dozen clinical mitochondrial manipulation studies have been reported worldwide; these are all small, open-labelled studies (Ishii, 2018). The safety and effectiveness of germline mitochondrial manipulation are still uncertain.

Therefore, germline mitochondrial manipulation remains experimental as a method of human reproduction, and its use as an infertility treatment or for disease prevention in offspring is not assured.

9.3 MITOCHONDRIAL MANIPULATION IN ASIA

The reports of mitochondrial manipulation in Asia are reviewed here. Various germline manipulation techniques have been developed in Taiwan, China, and Japan. To treat intractable infertility cases, some physicians inject mitochondria or cytoplasm containing mitochondria into the patient's egg. Others use the more radical procedure of nuclear transfer to replace the patient's egg-cytoplasm with the donor's egg-cytoplasm. To date, no reports of mitochondrial manipulation have been published from Singapore.

9.3.1 Cytoplasmic Transfer in Taiwan

Soon after a birth via cytoplasmic transfer occurred in the US, a Taiwanese clinic reported another cytoplasmic transfer in 1999 (see Table 9.1) (Huang et al., 1999). Instead of donor eggs, the clinic used tripronucleate zygotes (eggs abnormally fertilised with two sperm cells), which are by-products of IVF. The internal review board of that clinic approved this cytoplasmic transfer study. Informed consent was obtained from both cytoplasm donors and recipients. The clinic recruited nine infertile women who had experienced repeated implantation failure after 5 to 20 IVF or ICSI cycles; the participants included two women younger than 35. The cytoplasm (including mitochondria) of donated tripronucleate zygotes was injected into the wife's eggs, together with the husband's sperm cells. As a result, five infants without chromosomal abnormalities were born from four women, but no pregnancies occurred in the remaining five women. Although these results may seem promising, it should be noted that the former four women might not have conceived because of the cytoplasmic transfer but because eggs of a better quality had just been retrieved. Moreover, it was unclear whether such implantation failures were associated with cytoplasmic factors including the mitochondria. The results of such an open-labelled uncontrolled study involving only nine participants could be considered unconvincing. The transfer of cytoplasm from tripronucleate zygotes is asynchronous compared with the transfer of cytoplasm from eggs, and this may pose risks for the resultant children (Barritt et al., 2001). Notably, the resultant children have genomes from three individuals: nDNA derived from the wife and husband and mtDNA from the wife and a female donor. This genomic state might affect the child's health due to the uncontrolled production of deleterious free radicals. The Taiwanese clinic asserts that the offspring born of cytoplasmic transfer remain healthy (Lee Women's Hospital, 2017). However, no peer-reviewed papers have been published regarding the follow-up of such offspring. The only peer-reviewed paper on follow-up after cytoplasmic transfer was published in the US; however, it was a limited survey that primarily depended on statements of parents of offspring born of the mitochondrial manipulation, although this is generally the case with reproductive medicine (Ishii, 2018). In Taiwan, the cytoplasmic transfer using tripronucleate zygotes in 1999 attracted the attention of the regulatory authority, thus triggering a regulatory discussion of cytoplasmic transfer. The current regulations are examined in Section 9.4.1.

9.3.2 Autologous Mitochondrial Transfer in China, Japan, and Taiwan

Autologous mitochondrial transfer does not depend on egg donation, as such. In 2001 and 2003, three studies of autologous mitochondrial transfer were reported, one from Taiwan and two from China (see Table 9.1) (Kong et al., 2003a, 2003b; Tzeng et al., 2001). In these three studies, hundreds to thousands of mitochondria taken from the patient's own cumulus granular cells that surround the eggs in the ovaries were injected into the eggs of patients who had experienced implantation failures or miscarriages. Autologous granular cell mitochondrial transfer (AGCMT) adds the patient's mitochondria to her own eggs; however, the mtDNA of cumulus cells is not necessarily identical to that of the eggs due to the mutations in different cells and/or the process of extracting cytoplasm and enriching mitochondria. In addition, these three studies did not determine the genotypes of the injected mtDNA and the egg's mtDNA. For this reason, AGCMT can induce the co-existence of more than one type of mitochondrial genome within an egg (heteroplasmy) by mixing mitochondria from granular cells and eggs. Those AGCMT studies led to a number of pregnancies and live births; however, a foetal death and a miscarriage occurred in two of the Chinese studies (Kong et al., 2003a, 2003b).

From 2016 to 2017, a clinic in Japan, in collaboration with a US biotechnology company, OvaScience, carried out the Autologous Germline Mitochondrial Energy Transfer (AUGMENT) study for infertility treatment (Table 9.1).[1] AUGMENT also uses autologous mitochondria, not from cumulus cells but from 'oogonial precursor cells' (Fakih et al., 2015). However, the presence of oogonial precursor cells in adult women has been scientifically controversial (Heindryckx et al., 2015). The AUGMENT study in Japan resulted in some live births, which were widely reported in the media (HORAC Grand Front Osaka Clinic, 2017). However, the clinic recruited young women in their 20s who may still have maintained fertility. In addition, they included among the participants women who underwent IVF only once (Table 9.1). Several safety concerns were raised over AUGMENT studies performed in other countries. Namely, the European Society of Human Reproduction and Embryology and the British Fertility Society raised doubts about the safety as well as efficacy of AUGMENT due to undisclosed technical details, including the mtDNA status, in the preparation and transfer of mitochondria (Heindryckx et al., 2015). These doubts suggest that the effect of AUGMENT on fertility is uncertain. More importantly, mitochondrial manipulation can affect the resultant offspring, and these effects could appear later in their lives. Notably, OvaScience, which started the AUGMENT fertility program in 2011, ended the program through a reverse merger in 2018 (Meiling, 2018). Thus, this program to globally commercialise a reproductive technique has ended.

9.3.3 Mitochondrial Replacement Study in China

A more radical mitochondrial manipulation was carried out in Asia. In 2003, a Chinese clinic performed embryonic mitochondrial replacement for a 30-year-old woman who had embryonic arrest at the two-cell stage in previous IVF cycles (Table 9.1) (Zhang et al., 2016). The physicians used a larger micropipette (30–40 μm, 5–6 times the size of that used in ICSI) to transfer the nuclei of the couple's zygote to enucleated zygotes that were made using donor eggs and the husband's sperm cells. In the zygotes that were reconstituted through nuclear transfer and electrofusion, most of the cytoplasm (including mitochondria) was replaced with that of the donor zygotes. Likewise, in cytoplasmic transfer performed in Taiwan, the embryos made through mitochondrial replacement had genomes from three different individuals: a wife, a husband, and a female donor. The mitochondrial replacement led to a triplet pregnancy. To facilitate live births, one of the three foetuses was selectively terminated. However, the other two foetuses died of respiratory distress and cord prolapse, respectively. The clinic asserted that the karyotypes of the foetuses were normal without presenting detailed data. Moreover, the clinic claimed without sufficient data that the nDNA of the foetuses and the patient matched, that the mtDNA profiles of the foetuses and donor were identical, and that the patient's mtDNA was not detected in the foetuses. Notably, the risk to human reproduction caused by electrofusion remains unclear. This case increased excitement but also serious concern over the health of the resultant children if the reproductive technique based on nuclear transfer becomes widely used. Namely, the critics stated that mitochondrial replacement involving nuclear transfer is perilously close to human cloning. Those who oppose nuclear transfer have also pointed out that there exist unknown hazards to the resultant children, and as evidence they cite the deaths of the foetuses in China (Cohen and Malter, 2016; Grady, 2003; Pearson, 2003).

9.4 REGULATORY IMPLICATIONS

As shown in the preceding section, several reproduction studies of mitochondrial manipulation have been performed in China, Japan, and Taiwan. Such clinical studies aimed to treat intractable infertility cases; however, the consequences of the procedure raised scientific and ethical concerns (Cohen and Malter, 2016; Hawes et al., 2002). The next section examines the past and present regulations placed on mitochondrial manipulation in those three countries and Singapore, where the legalisation of mitochondrial replacement is currently under discussion. In addition to the regulation of germline genetic modification, the regulation of egg donation is analysed because some mitochondrial manipulations, such as cytoplasmic transfer and mitochondrial replacement, require donor eggs as the source of functional mitochondria.

9.4.1 Taiwan

In Taiwan, studies of the use of cytoplasmic transfer and AGCMT to treat intractable infertility cases were published in 1999 and 2001, respectively (Table 9.1). As mentioned in Section 9.3.1, the cytoplasmic transfer performed in 1999 prompted a regulatory discussion in the government. The report on AGCMT in 2001 also attracted some international attention (Pearson, 2004). To understand the current regulation of mitochondrial manipulation in Taiwan, let us carefully examine the Artificial Reproduction Act that was promulgated in 2007 (hereafter referred to 'the Act').

The 2007 Act, for which the competent authority is the Ministry of Health and Welfare (MOHW), intends to improve the development of artificial reproduction while protecting the rights and interests of infertile couples, the resultant children, and gamete donors, and observing ethics and safeguarding the health of people (Article 1). The Act requires the MOHW to organise an advisory committee to regularly discuss the enforcement of the 2007 Act (Article 4).

First, it should be noted that no articles relevant to germline genetic modification were stipulated in the 2007 Act, as shown by Table 9.2. The 2007 Act allows the clinical study of 'artificial reproduction' (conception and birth not involving sexual intercourse, with assistance from reproductive techniques), which constitutes human subject research in compliance with the regulations of the Medical Care Act. On the other hand, the Act prohibits 'artificial reproduction' using 'reproductive cells or embryos provided exclusively for research purposes.' Seemingly, the Act does not prohibit AGCMT, in which granular cells (not 'reproductive cells') are used for infertility treatment. Notably, Article 8 of the 2007 Act permits anonymous egg donation for which the donor is compensated to cover her expenses for necessary examinations, medical treatment, transportation, and nutritional products and to compensate for the loss of working hours (nutrition expenses). It seems unclear whether or not the prohibition of 'artificial reproduction' using 'reproductive cells or embryos provided *exclusively* for research purposes' (emphasis added) is applied to cytoplasmic

Table 9.2 THE REGULATIONS REGARDING CLINICAL USE OF MITOCHONDRIAL MANIPULATION IN FOUR ASIAN COUNTRIES

Jurisdiction	Relevant domestic legislation	Relevant provisions for interpretation	Legality of mitochondrial manipulation procedures	Competent authorities
China[a]	Civil Code 2020 Biosafety Act 2020 Ministry of Health Standards for Human Assisted Reproductive Technology and the Ethical Principles for Human Assisted Reproductive Technology and Human Sperm Bank 2003	Article 1009 of Civil Code 2020. Article 40 and 41 of Act 2020. Article 7 and Article 9 of Chapter 3, Specifications 2003. 7, Article 3 of Chapter 1, Ethical Principles 2003.	Generally, mitochondrial manipulation procedures are all regulated based on Civil Code and Biosafety Act 2020. Specifications and Principle 2003 explicitly prohibited cytoplasmic transfer and mitochondrial replacement.	Chinese Ministry of Health (CMOH) and relevant departments of the people's government at the county level or higher.
Japan	Act on Regulation of Human Cloning Techniques 2000 Guidelines on Specified Embryos 2000 under the Act 2000 Ministry of Health, Labour and Welfare Guidelines for Clinical Research such as Gene Therapy 2019	Article 4 of Act 2000 Article 2 of Guidelines 2000 under Act 2000. Article 7 of Guidelines 2019.	Act and Guidelines 2000 prohibit embryonic mitochondrial replacement. While, egg mitochondrial replacement and other mitochondrial manipulation procedures are not addressed in the regulations.	Ministry of Education, Culture, Sports, Science and Technology (MEXT) for Act 2000. Ministry of Health, Labour and Welfare.
Singapore	Human Cloning and Other Prohibited Practices Act 2004	Article 7 of Act 2004	No mitochondrial manipulation procedures allowed.	Ministry of Health (MOH).
Taiwan	Artificial Reproduction Act 2007	Item 1, Article 16 Article 17 of Act 2007	Generally, it is unclear whether Act 2007 regulates mitochondrial manipulation procedures.	Ministry of Health and Welfare (MOHW).

[a]Article 336-1 of *Chinese Criminal* Code can be applied to the reproductive uses of genome (gene) editing and cloning, not mitochondrial manipulation.

transfer, AUGMENT, or mitochondrial replacement, which use donor eggs ('oogonial precursor cells' in AUGMENT) to enhance the possibility of fertility (Table 9.2).

Those legal analyses suggest that Taiwan assumes a neutral attitude or indifference to mitochondrial manipulation. This may be partly because Taiwan promotes fertility tourism for foreign couples who seek donor eggs and infertility treatment (Peng, 2019). However, the MOHW has not approved any clinical studies using the mitochondrial manipulation technique since 2007. Other than the two reports published in 1999 and 2001, no studies of mitochondrial manipulation have recently been published from Taiwan.

9.4.2 China

In 2001, the CMOH enacted four guidelines, two for methods including the Managerial Method for Human Assisted Reproductive Technology and the Managerial Method for Human Sperm Bank, and two sets of technical standard including the Technical Standard for Human Assisted Reproductive Technology and the Technical Standard for Human Sperm Bank (Qiao and Feng, 2014). As mentioned above, the 2003 report of foetal deaths after embryonic mitochondrial replacement raised several ethical concerns. Such concerns over the consequences of mitochondrial replacement prompted the CMOH to immediately undertake a regulatory response to experimental reproductive techniques. In 2003, the CMOH amended the four guidelines and enacted the Standards for Human Assisted Reproductive Technology and the Ethical Principles for Human Assisted Reproductive Technology and Human Sperm Bank. Importantly, the Standards and Ethical Principles 2003 largely prohibit experimental mitochondrial manipulation as well as human cloning (as illustrated by Table 9.2). Namely, the 2003 Guidelines clearly mention 'egg-cytoplasmic transplantation and nuclear transfer techniques' in the Standards section and 'egg-cytoplasmic transplantation and nuclear transplantation' in the Ethical Principles section, which are respectively considered cytoplasmic transfer and mitochondrial replacement. With regard to other mitochondrial manipulation techniques, the 2003 Guidelines also prohibit the clinical use of AUGMENT. The mitochondria to be transferred are derived from the cytoplasm of *oogonial (egg) precursor cells*, suggesting that AUGMENT can be considered 'egg-cytoplasmic transplantation.' Other than the 2003 report on mitochondrial replacement, two AGCMT cases were also reported from China in 2003. Nonetheless, AGCMT might fall outside the scope of the 2003 Guidelines. The relevant articles in the 2003 Guidelines that prohibit egg-cytoplasmic transplantation and nuclear transfer are not applicable to AGCMT because mitochondria that are transferred to the patient's eggs are derived from cumulus granular cells (not eggs) and also because AGCMT does not involve nuclear transfer.

Thus, the 2003 Standards for Human Assisted Reproductive Technology and the Ethical Principles for Human Assisted Reproductive Technology and Human Sperm Bank explicitly prohibit cytoplasmic transfer, AUGMENT, and mitochondrial replacement; however, the 2003 Guidelines are rules for medical professionals without any penal provisions, which may limit their enforcement with respect to people other than medical professionals. Indeed, university researchers violated the prohibition on 'genetically manipulating human gametes, zygotes, and embryos for the purpose of reproduction' that is part of the 2003 Guidelines. They performed human reproduction involving CRISPR-Cas9 genome-editing (a genetic engineering tool awarded the Nobel Prize in Medicine in 2020; see Chapter 10, this volume) to create human beings with resistance to HIV infection, and one of them (a researcher, but not a physician) announced the births of genetically manipulated twins in 2018. However, the announcement immediately raised ethical concerns worldwide. Of particular note were strongly worded criticisms posted online by more than 100 Chinese researchers, such as '[d]irectly jumping into human experiments can only be described as crazy' (Cyranoski and Ledford, 2018). In December 2019, three researchers were found guilty of 'conducting illegal medical practices' in China by forging ethical review documents and misleading practitioners into unknowingly implanting edited embryos into two women. The principal investigator was sentenced to three years in prison and fined 3 million Chinese yuan (US$429,000) and other two researchers were also fined (Normile, 2019).

In response to the ineffective relevant regulation, the Chinse government enacted two laws which enable stricter oversight of human reproduction involving experimental techniques as shown in Table 9.2.[2] In the China-first Civil Code enacted in 2020, Article 1009 stipulates that,

Engaging in medical and scientific research activities related to human genes, human embryos, etc., shall abide by laws, administrative regulations and relevant national regulations, shall not endanger human health, violate ethics and morals, and shall not harm public interests.

One of the 'laws' is Article 40 of the 2020 Biosafety Act stipulating that,

Clinical research on new biomedical technologies shall pass ethical review and be carried out in medical institutions with corresponding conditions; for human clinical research operations, it shall be carried out by health professionals who meet the corresponding conditions.[3]

Article 41 of the Biosafety Act stresses that the CMOH and relevant departments of the people's government shall follow-up and evaluate biotechnology applications in accordance with the legislation and take effective remedial and control measures in a timely manner if they find biosafety risks in the activities. Some commentators expressed a relatively optimistic view that the new laws will undoubtedly constitute a comprehensive regulatory framework for overseeing activities related to human genome editing (Cao and Jia, 2021). Others pointed out that the regulatory reform could put in place stricter administrative procedures for Chinese institutions and their foreign partners to follow, and this may impede scientific progress (Song and Joly, 2021). More recently, the Chinese Criminal Code was amended in 2021, including the addition of Article 336-1 stipulating that

> [i]mplanting gene-edited or cloned human embryos into humans or animals, or implanting gene-edited or cloned animal embryos into humans, where the circumstances are serious, shall be sentenced to fixed-term imprisonment or criminal detention of not more than three years, and shall be fined; where the circumstances are particularly serious, sentenced to fixed-term imprisonment of not less than three years but not more than seven years, and fined.

This amendment of the Criminal Code shows a Chinese blanket ban on such experimental reproductions by enforceable means. However, this clause can be applied to only reproduction involving genome editing and cloning because mitochondrial manipulation alters the content of mitochondria in the germline but does not modify the genome and genes in themselves and does not result in cloning even if it involves nuclear transfer.

As observed above, ethical and legal issues have been raised in China by clinical studies on germline genetic modifications, including mitochondrial replacement and genome editing. We should continue to monitor the relevant progression and effectiveness of current regulations in China. Moreover, can the human rights of offspring who were already born via germline genome editing be fundamentally protected (Ishii, 2021)?

9.4.3 Japan

In 2000, Japan passed the Act on Regulation of Human Cloning Techniques to regulate human cloning and other experimental reproduction methods

(Table 9.2) (Ishii, 2020). The Guidelines on Specified Embryos adopted in 2000 under the Act prohibit reproduction using 'Human Embryonic Nuclear Transfer Embryos,' which can be interpreted to refer to embryonic mitochondrial replacement; however, the 2000 guidelines do not cover egg manipulations, including mitochondrial replacement and other mitochondrial manipulation techniques such as cytoplasmic transfer, AGCMT, and AUGMENT. On the other hand, Ministry of Health, Labour and Welfare (MHLW) Guidelines for Clinical Research such as Gene Therapy from 2015 prohibit clinical research involving the genetic modification of human germ cells and embryos (Article 7). Based on the 2015 Guidelines, one might suppose that clinical research involving mitochondrial manipulation is prohibited in Japan. However, the prohibitive article is applied to clinical research involving 'gene therapy,' which refers to 'administering gene or gene-transferred cells to the human body' (1 Definition of Article 2). Notably, all mitochondrial manipulations transfer the organelles that contain mtDNA including genes; however, those techniques do not directly transfer naked genes or DNA. For this reason, some germline manipulations, including mitochondrial manipulation, were allowed when the AUGMENT study was performed from 2016 to 2017. However, the news report of births that occurred after AUGMENT led to discussions regarding whether AUGMENT was prohibited under the Guidelines 2015 and whether there was a need to reconsider the regulation governing experimental reproductive techniques in the Minister of Health, Labour and Welfare's press conference and in the committees of the Science Council of Japan (Ishii, 2019). However, the MHLW remained silent regarding the permissibility of AUGMENT and other mitochondrial manipulations. In 2019, to respond to regulatory issues raised by the scandal regarding genome-edited babies in China, the MHLW Guidelines for Clinical Research such as Gene Therapy were amended. The definition of 'gene therapy' was expanded, including 'modifying a targeted, specific base sequence of gene in humans' and 'administering genetically-modified cells to the human body' in addition to 'administering gene or gene-transferred cells to the human body.' Again, it appears that the amendment of the definition of gene therapy failed to include mitochondrial manipulation because mitochondrial manipulation does not involve any genetic modification in the mtDNA.

With regard to experimental techniques used for human reproduction, such regulatory responses in Japan can be regarded as occurring on an ad hoc basis or as noncomprehensive. Japan is now one of the world's most active countries in the field of reproductive medicine; however, infertile couples repeatedly undergo IVF and ICSI using their own gametes because gamete donation is not common in Japan (Banker et al., 2021). In Japan, the declining birth rate and aging population are significant problems. It is unlikely that more regulations will be placed on reproductive medicine, particularly reproductive techniques that can maintain genetic relatedness between parents and children.

9.4.4 Singapore

It is worth discussing a recent movement related to the legalisation of mitochondrial manipulation in Singapore. In 2015, the UK legalised mitochondrial replacement to allow women who have eggs with an mtDNA mutation that is responsible for mitochondrial disease to have offspring free from that disease (Chapter 4, this volume). Singapore, which has historically had a close relationship with the UK, then started to consider legalising this controversial reproductive technique. In 2005, the Bioethics Advisory Committee (BAC) that was established by the Singapore Cabinet in 2000 issued a moratorium stating that human reproduction involving germline genetic modification should not be allowed (Ho, 2019). In April 2018, the BAC issued a consultation paper "Ethical, Legal and Social Issues Arising from Mitochondrial Genome Replacement Technology" (Ong, 2018). The BAC received feedback from the public and from religious groups in June 2018; however, it has not yet made a formal recommendation to the government regarding whether to legalise this reproductive technique.

The current regulation relevant to mitochondrial manipulation in Singapore, aside from the BAC's forthcoming recommendation, is discussed below, focusing on clinical research and clinical use. The most relevant legislation is the Human Cloning and Other Prohibited Practices Act 2004, illustrated in Table 9.2. Article 7 of this law prohibits developing a human embryo created other than by the fertilisation of a human egg by human sperm. Namely, no person shall develop any human embryo that is created by a process other than the fertilisation of a human egg by human sperm for a period of more than 14 days, excluding any period when the development of the embryo is suspended. This implies that no embryo created using any mitochondrial manipulation can be used for human reproduction. Simultaneously, this also implies that human embryo research involving mitochondrial manipulation can proceed for 14 days of development after fertilisation. The 2004 Act has no specific articles regarding mitochondrial manipulation or germline genetic modification. Article 7 could be considered unclear regarding whether the prohibition is applicable to clinical research involving such experimental reproductive techniques. However, the 2004 Act is understood to mean that the clinical use of such experimental reproductive techniques is not allowed in Singapore, a position underpinned by a moratorium issued by the BAC in 2005.[4] Indeed, no reports of mitochondrial manipulation have been published from Singapore thus far.

Taking into consideration the fact that no births following mitochondrial replacement have been reported from the UK, the BAC or the Singaporean government appear to be pausing in order to confirm any progress in the clinical use of mitochondrial replacement in the UK. According to the UK Human Fertilisation and Embryology Authority's Code of Practice, non–UK-residents can undergo mitochondrial replacement and can participate in the follow-up of children born as a result of this technique (Human Fertilisation and Embyology Authority [HFEA], 2019). If Singapore also legalises mitochondrial replacement, that country and the UK can take a global leadership role in advanced reproductive medicine, which could also enable couples in each country to visit the other to undergo mitochondrial replacement. From the standpoint of reproductive globalisation, we should pay close attention to the policy regarding mitochondrial replacement in Singapore, in addition to the clinical consequences in the UK.

9.5 DISCUSSION

9.5.1 Clinical, Ethical, and Regulatory Distinctions Between Infertility Treatment and Disease Prevention

Based on past reports of mitochondrial manipulations, such as cytoplasmic transfer, autologous mitochondrial transfer, and mitochondrial replacement, the clinical applications in Taiwan, China, and Japan were reviewed. One of the salient points that emerged from this review is that all mitochondrial manipulations were implemented for the purpose of having genetically related offspring without directly using donor eggs. On the other hand, the UK permits mitochondrial replacement only to prevent maternal transmission of mtDNA mutations responsible for mitochondrial disease to offspring. Notably, the prevention of mitochondrial disease in future offspring using mitochondrial replacement also results in having a genetically related child without that disease. Because the use of mitochondrial manipulations in human reproduction remains experimental, it is worth considering the clinical and ethical distinctions between the use of mitochondrial manipulation to treat infertility and that to prevent mitochondrial disease in the offspring.

The beneficiary of mitochondrial manipulation as an infertility treatment is seemingly the prospective mother, whereas the beneficiary in its use for disease prevention is the future offspring (Chapter 2, this volume). It is a clinical fact that mothers who have children with mitochondrial disease often experience miscarriages (White et al., 1999), which can be regarded as a form of infertility. In addition, the use of this technique can be seen as beneficial for women who are consequently able to have children free from mitochondrial disease because such women and their families more generally are relieved of emotional stress, care burden, the economic burdens associated with healthcare, and grieving the death of a child (Chapter 3, this volume). These considerations suggest that the use of mitochondrial manipulation for disease prevention clinically and ethically overlaps with that for infertility treatment.

Nonetheless, it is worth reconsidering the UK's decision to grant permission for mitochondrial replacement only for disease prevention in the offspring. It should be noted that the number of infertile patients is larger than the number of women who wish to have children free from mitochondrial disease. From a social standpoint, the world's first legal regulation of germline genetic modification might aim to introduce the reproductive technique on a limited basis (Dimond and Stephens, 2018). Later, the UK could consider widening the use of mitochondrial replacement, including for infertility treatment. While the UK's approach is rational, the uncontrolled uses of mitochondrial manipulation in several Asian countries, particularly Taiwan and Japan, could be problematic socially.

9.5.2 Impact of Religion and Teaching in Asia

Religious beliefs play a large role in how human reproduction and family-building practices are carried out in different countries (Sallam and Sallam, 2016; but see Chapter 7, this volume). As mentioned above, several couples in Asia consented to an experimental mitochondrial manipulation method that can affect the resultant embryos, foetuses, and offspring. Other than the scientific literacy of the population of any given country, their religion and teachings might impact their decisions regarding whether to participate in mitochondrial manipulation. Although it is not possible to know the religious beliefs and teaching of a particular individual, it is possible to consider the impact of these factors to some extent based on the religion and teachings dominant in China, Japan, and Taiwan; this is not possible in Singapore, which is a multiracial and multireligious society.

With regard to the moral status of the human embryo and foetus, we can describe three different sets of beliefs: the 'all,' 'none,' and 'gradualist' positions (Tsai, 2005). Those adopting the 'all' position hold that human embryos already possess full human status, a position close to that of Catholicism. For them, experimental genetic intervention in human embryos ('humans'), including mitochondrial manipulation, are at present unethical since a relevant addendum to their position is that there be no risk of adverse events, no use of reproductive techniques, and few or no wasted 'humans.' By contrast, the 'none' position, which is observed in Confucianism, believes that human embryos or foetuses have no moral status and therefore deserve no special moral consideration before birth. Those holding the 'none' position would accept mitochondrial manipulation that can help them have genetically related offspring (i.e., the nDNA is shared between parent and child). The 'gradualist' position considers human embryos as potential human beings but not actual humans until birth. In this position, human embryos possess a special status that deserves a certain degree of respect, which increases along with their development. Therefore, those holding the 'gradualist' position, as well as those holding the 'none' position, may accept mitochondrial manipulation that is experimental but can help them have genetically related children.

It is said that Confucian values of filial piety and familial obligation are still an influence in the Chinese population. It is also said that approximately 60 percent of Japanese people in the modern age have no religion; however, approximately 40 percent follow Buddhism (Pew Templeton, 2010), which has fewer teachings about human reproduction than Christianity and currently accepts reproductive medicine. The major religions and cultural influences in Taiwan are Buddhism and Taoism. Importantly, Confucianism still dictates reproductive decisions for some Taiwanese people (Ko and Muecke, 2005). It should also be noted that Confucianism was introduced to Japan earlier than Buddhism. Confucian values, which are different from those of Christianity in the Western world, may underpin infertile couples' willingness to consent to mitochondrial manipulation that could help them have genetically related offspring. However, the regulations governing germline genetic modification have been enacted in line with politico-religious separation; that is, they are primarily based on considerations related to domestic politics and reproductive globalisation.

9.6 CONCLUSION: AN ASIAN PERSPECTIVE

As observed above, four countries—Taiwan, China, Japan, and Singapore—have taken different regulatory approaches to germline genetic modification, which is most often carried out to treat cases of intractable infertility. In Taiwan, cytoplasmic transfer and AGCMT were performed two decades ago, and the regulation of such experimental reproductive techniques in Taiwan is ambiguous. More recently in Japan, AUGMENT was implemented in 2016–2017, and the results of this procedure attracted some attention. Japan then amended the relevant ministerial guidelines; however, it appears that the resultant guidelines are not comprehensive in their regulation of mitochondrial manipulation. In China, two different scandals not related to AGCMT have occurred: foetal deaths took place after the use of mitochondrial replacement as an infertility treatment in 2003, and the birth of children who were the product of genome-editing performed to create human beings with resistance to HIV infection in 2018. The first scandal immediately resulted in the prohibition of most germline genetic modifications in the ministerial guidelines. However, some university researchers have violated the ministerial rules and performed germline genome-editing. The second scandal led to the conviction of three researchers and the enactment of more enforceable laws against the use of such experimental reproductive techniques. Conversely, Singapore is now discussing the legalisation of mitochondrial replacement, which was inspired by the UK's legalisation of mitochondrial replacement to prevent the passing on of mitochondrial disease from the mother to her offspring.

The regulation of experimental mitochondrial manipulation has varied in the four countries discussed here. In some of them, Confucian teachings still influence people's approach to raising a family, perhaps enabling couples to consent to mitochondrial manipulation that could allow them to have genetically related children. However, those countries adopted different regulatory responses to the controversial reproductive technique. The present discussion suggests that the regulations regarding mitochondrial manipulation have been developed in response to domestic politics and/or the impact of reproductive globalisation, rather than the influence of religious and cultural beliefs.

ACKNOWLEDGEMENTS

This work was supported by a JSPS Grant-in-Aid for Scientific Research (B) (19H01188) and by a JSPS Grant-in-Aid for Challenging Exploratory Research (20K20745).

NOTES

1. Protocol ID: UMIN000021387. Autologous germline mitochondrial energy transfer (AUGMENT). 2016/04/01-2017/08/04. Morimoto et al. from Sunkaky Medical Corporation, HORAC Grand Front Osaka Clinic. https://upload.umin. ac.jp/cgi-open-bin/ctr/ctr_view.cgi?recptno=R000024309.
2. Civil Code 2020. http://www.npc.gov.cn/npc/c30834/202006/75ba6483b8344 591abd07917e1d25cc8.shtml.
3. Biosafety Act 2020. http://www.npc.gov.cn/npc/c30834/202010/bb3bee512 2854893a69acf4005a66059.shtml. Those two laws strengthen the enforcement of the Standards for Human Assisted Reproductive Technology and the Ethical Principles for the Human Assisted Reproductive Technology and Human Sperm Bank 2003 and oversee the rise of experimental reproductive techniques.
4. The Bioethics Advisory Committee (BAC) Genetic Testing and Genetic Research (2005) paras 4.51 and 4.52, Recommendation 11, paras 4.53–4.58, Recommendation 12.

REFERENCES

Banker, Manish, Silke Dyer, Georgina M. Chambers, Osamu Ishihara, Markus Kupka, Jacques de Mouzon, Fernando Zegers-Hochschild, and G. David Adamson. 'International Committee for Monitoring Assisted Reproductive Technologies (ICMART): World report on assisted reproductive technologies, 2013.' *Fertility and Sterility* 116, no. 3 (2021): 741–756.

Barritt, Jason A. 'Rebuttal: Interooplasmic transfers in humans.' *Reproductive Biomed Online* 3 (2001): 47–48.

Barritt, Jason A., Steen Willadsen, Carol Brenner, and Jacques Cohen. 'Cytoplasmic transfer in assisted reproduction.' *Human Reproduction Update* 7, no. 4 (2001): 428–435.

Cao, Yanlin, and Fei Jia. 'Legal response to the gene-edited babies event.' *Medicine, Science and the Law* 61, no. 2 (2021): 159–160.

Castro, Rosa J. 'Mitochondrial replacement therapy: The UK and US regulatory landscapes.' *Journal of Law and the Biosciences* 3, no. 3 (2016): 726–735.

Cohen, I. Glenn, and Eli Y. Adashi. 'Science and regulation: The FDA is prohibited from going germline.' *Science* 353, no. 6299 (2016): 545–546.

Cohen, Jacques, and Henry Malter. 'The first clinical nuclear transplantation in China: New information about a case reported to ASRM in 2003.' *Reproductive BioMedicine Online* 33, no. 4 (2016): 433–435.

Cohen, Jacques, and Richard Scott. 'Birth of infant after transfer of anucleate donor oocyte cytoplasm into recipient eggs.' *Lancet* 350, no. 9072 (1997): 186–187.

Cyranoski, David, and Heidi Ledford. 'Genome-edited baby claim provokes international outcry.' *Nature* 563, no. 7731 (2018): 607–609.

Dimond, Rebecca, and Neil Stephens. *Legalising Mitochondrial Donation: Enacting Ethical Futures in UK Biomedical Politics.* Springer, 2018.

Fakih, Michael H., Mohamad El Shmoury, Julia Szeptycki, Dennis B. dela Cruz, Caroline Lux, Suleman Verjee, Colleen M. Burgess, et al. 'The AUGMENTSM treatment: Physician reported outcomes of the initial global patient experience.' *Journal of Fertilization: In Vitro, IVF-Worldwide, Reproductive Medicine, Genetics & Stem Cell Biology* 3, no. 3 (2015): 1000154.

Grady, Denise. 'Pregnancy created using egg nucleus of infertile woman.' *New York Times*, 14 October 2003. https://www.nytimes.com/2003/10/14/us/pregna ncy-created-using-egg-nucleus-of-infertile-woman.html.

Harper, J. C., Kristiina Aittomäki, Pascal Borry, Martina C. Cornel, G. De Wert, W. Dondorp, Joep Geraedts, et al. 'Recent developments in genetics and medically-assisted reproduction: From research to clinical applications.' *Human Reproduction Open* 2017, no. 3 (2017): hox015.

Hawes, Susan M., Carmen Sapienza, and Keith E. Latham. 'Ooplasmic donation in humans: The potential for epigenic modifications.' *Human Reproduction* 17, no. 4 (2002): 850–852.

Heindryckx, B., C. Eguizabal, S. Chuva de Sousa Lopes, M. Geens, and R. Vassena. 'ESHRE SIG stem cells, opinion statement: The use of mitochondrial transfer to improve ART outcome. 2015. https://www.eshre.eu/Specialty-groups/Special-Interest-Groups/Stem-Cells.aspx.

Ho, Calvin W. L. 'The regulation of human germline genome modification in Singapore.' In *Human Germline Genome Modification and the Right to Science: A Comparative Study of National Laws and Policies*, edited by Andrea Boggio, Cesare PR Romano, and Jessica Almqvist, pp. 516–540. Cambridge University Press, 2019.

HORAC Grand Front Osaka Clinic. 'Reports of AUGMENT treatment on TV.' 2017. https://www.ivfhorac.com/ivfjapan/date/2017?cat=5.

Huang, Chun-Chia, Tzu-Chun Cheng, Han-Hsin Chang, Ching-Chien Chang, Chung-I. Chen, Jiaen Liu, and Maw-Sheng Lee. 'Birth after the injection of sperm and the cytoplasm of tripronucleate zygotes into metaphase II oocytes in patients with repeated implantation failure after assisted fertilization procedures.' *Fertility and Sterility* 72, no. 4 (1999): 702–706.

Human Fertilisation and Embryology Authority (HFEA). *Human Fertilisation and Embryology Authority. 33.33. Mitochondrial Donation, Code of Practice*. UK Government, 2019.

Hyslop, Louise A., Paul Blakeley, Lyndsey Craven, Jessica Richardson, Norah M. E. Fogarty, Elpida Fragouli, Mahdi Lamb, et al. 'Towards clinical application of pronuclear transfer to prevent mitochondrial DNA disease.' *Nature* 534, no. 7607 (2016): 383–386.

Ishii, Tetsuya. 'Reproductive medicine involving mitochondrial DNA modification: Evolution, legality, and ethics.' *Reproductive Health* 4, no.1 (2018): 88–99.

Ishii, Tetsuya. 'The regulation of human germline genome modification in Japan.' In *Human Germline Genome Modification and the Right to Science: A Comparative Study of National Laws and Policies*, edited by Andrea Boggio, Cesare PR Romano, and Jessica Almqvist, pp. 441–468. Cambridge University Press, 2019.

Ishii, Tetsuya. 'Assignment of responsibility for creating persons using germline genome-editing.' *Gene and Genome Editing* 1 (2021): 100006.

Ishii, Tetsuya, and Yuri Hibino. 'Mitochondrial manipulation in fertility clinics: Regulation and responsibility.' *Reproductive Biomedicine & Society Online* 5 (2018): 93–109.

Kang, Eunju, Jun Wu, Nuria Marti Gutierrez, Amy Koski, Rebecca Tippner-Hedges, Karen Agaronyan, Aida Platero-Luengo, et al. 'Mitochondrial replacement in human oocytes carrying pathogenic mitochondrial DNA mutations.' *Nature* 540, no. 7632 (2016): 270–275.

Ko, Nai-Ying, and Marjorie Muecke. 'Reproductive decision-making among HIV-positive couples in Taiwan.' *Journal of Nursing Scholarship* 37, no. 1 (2005): 41–47.

Kong, L. H., Zhong Liu, Hong Li, Liang Zhu, S. L. Chen, and F. Q. Xing. 'First twins born in Mainland China by autologous granular cell mitochondria transfer.' *Di 1 jun yi da xue xue bao/Academic Journal of the First Medical College of PLA* 23, no. 9 (2003a): 990–991.

Kong, L. H., Zhong Liu, Hong Li, Liang Zhu, and F. Q. Xing. 'Pregnancy in a 46-year-old woman after autologous granular cell mitochondria transfer.' *Di 1 jun yi da xue xue bao/Academic Journal of the First Medical College of PLA* 23, no. 7 (2003b): 743–747.

Koopman, Werner J. H., Peter H. G. M. Willems, and Jan A. M. Smeitink. 'Monogenic mitochondrial disorders.' *New England Journal of Medicine* 366, no. 12 (2012): 1132–1141.

Lee Women's Hospital. 'Through egg harvesting to have a daughter Taiwan's first 'three-parent baby' shows up.' 28 March 2017. https://ivf.ivftaiwan.com/news-detail/141/.

Meiling, Brittany. 'Once a multibillion-dollar company, OvaScience ends a pennystock vehicle for Millendo's reverse merger.' *Endpoints News*, 9 August 2018. https://endpts.com/once-a-multibillion-dollar-company-ovascience-ends-a-pennystock-vehicle-for-millendos-reverse-merger/.

Normile, Dennis. 'Chinese scientist who produced genetically altered babies sentenced to 3 years in jail.' *Science*, 30 December 2019. https://www.science.org/content/article/chinese-scientist-who-produced-genetically-altered-babies-sentenced-3-years-jail.

Oktay, Kutluk, Volkan Baltaci, Murat Sonmezer, Volkan Turan, Evrim Unsal, Aysun Baltaci, Suleyman Aktuna, and Fred Moy. 'Oogonial precursor cell-derived autologous mitochondria injection to improve outcomes in women with multiple IVF failures due to low oocyte quality: A clinical translation.' *Reproductive Sciences* 22, no. 12 (2015): 1612–1617.

Ong, Sandy. 'Singapore could become the second country to legalize mitochondrial replacement therapy.' *Science*, 6 June 2018. https://www.science.org/content/article/singapore-could-become-second-country-legalize-mitochondrial-replacement-therapy/.

Palacios-González, César. 'Mitochondrial replacement techniques: Egg donation, genealogy and eugenics.' *Monash Bioethics Review* 34, no. 1 (2016): 37–51.

Pearson, Helen. 'Human fertility experiment prompts wrath.' *Nature News*, 14 October 2003. https://www.nature.com/articles/news031013-4.

Pearson, Helen. 'Egg injection boosts fertility.' *Nature News*, 20 October 2004. https://www.nature.com/articles/news041018-10.

Peng, Sydney. 'Why are Japanese and Filipinos coming to "make babies" in Taiwan?' *CommonWealth Magazine*, 16 March 2019. https://english.cw.com.tw/article/article.action?id=2324.

Pew Templeton. 'Global religious futures project: Japan.' 2010. http://www.globalreligiousfutures.org/countries/japan.

Qiao, Jie, and Huai L. Feng. 'Assisted reproductive technology in China: Compliance and non-compliance.' *Translational Pediatrics* 3, no. 2 (2014): 91–97.

Sallam, H. N., and N. H. Sallam. 'Religious aspects of assisted reproduction.' *Facts, Views & Vision in ObGyn* 8, no. 1 (2016): 33.

Schandera, Johanna, and Tim K. Mackey. 'Mitochondrial replacement techniques: Divergence in global policy.' *Trends in Genetics* 32, no. 7 (2016): 385–390.

Schatten, Heide, Qing-Yuan Sun, and Randall Prather. 'The impact of mitochondrial function/dysfunction on IVF and new treatment possibilities for infertility.' *Reproductive Biology and Endocrinology* 12, no. 1 (2014): 1–11.

Song, Lingqiao, and Yann Joly. 'After He Jianku: China's biotechnology regulation reforms.' *Medical Law International* 21, no. 2 (2021): 174–192.

Tsai, D. F. C. 'Human embryonic stem cell research debates: A Confucian argument.' *Journal of Medical Ethics* 31, no. 11 (2005): 635–640.

Tzeng, C., R. Hsieh, S. Chang, N. Tsai, Y. Cheng, and Y. Wei. 'Pregnancy derived from mitochondria transfer (MIT) into oocyte from patient's own cumulus granulosa cells (cGCs).' *Fertility and Sterility* 76, no. 3 (2001): S67–S68.

UK Department of Health. The Human Fertilisation and Embryology (Mitochondrial Donation) Regulations, 2015. https://www.legislation.gov.uk/uksi/2015/572/made.

van Oven, Mannis, and Manfred Kayser. 'Updated comprehensive phylogenetic tree of global human mitochondrial DNA variation.' *Human Mutation* 30, no. 2 (2009): E386–E394.

White, Sarah L., Veronica R. Collins, Rory Wolfe, Maureen A. Cleary, Sara Shanske, Salvatore DiMauro, Hans-Henrik M. Dahl, and David R. Thorburn. 'Genetic counseling and prenatal diagnosis for the mitochondrial DNA mutations at nucleotide 8993.' *American Journal of Human Genetics* 65, no. 2 (1999): 474–482.

Yamada, Mitsutoshi, Valentina Emmanuele, Maria J. Sanchez-Quintero, Bruce Sun, Gregory Lallos, Daniel Paull, Matthew Zimmer, et al. 'Genetic drift can compromise mitochondrial replacement by nuclear transfer in human oocytes.' *Cell Stem Cell* 18, no. 6 (2016): 749–754.

Zhang, John, Guanglun Zhuang, Yong Zeng, Jamie Grifo, Carlo Acosta, Yimin Shu, and Hui Liu. 'Pregnancy derived from human zygote pronuclear transfer in a patient who had arrested embryos after IVF.' *Reproductive Biomedicine Online* 33, no. 4 (2016): 529–533.

PART III

Looking Forward

10

Future Technological Advancements

KEVIN DOXZEN

10.1 INTRODUCTION

The list of motivations and rationales behind developing and using assisted reproductive technologies (ARTs) is constantly growing. For many, ARTs offer an opportunity to overcome infertility or prevent the transmission of heritable diseases. The mother of Louise Brown, the first child conceived via in vitro fertilisation (IVF) in 1978, suffered from blocked fallopian tubes and ovarian adhesions (Steptoe and Edwards, 1978). After nine years of infertility, she opted for an experimental procedure that would pave the way for conceiving 8 million children globally over the next 40 years (Fauser, 2019). In 1990, another ART was introduced into society's reproductive repertoire. Following IVF, prospective parents could test embryos for genetic defects before implantation (Handyside et al., 1990). Countries now offer preimplantation genetic testing for hundreds of genetic mutations (Johnson, 2019). The trajectory and eventual global impact of emerging ARTs are unpredictable but history has shown that a desire for genetically related children can instigate remarkable technological innovation.

The drive to overcome reproductive barriers continues to spur technology development, most recently leading to the invention of mitochondrial replacement therapy (MRT). This ART, as described in other chapters, would benefit thousands of families globally every year suffering from mitochondrial genetic diseases, yet its future remains questionable

Kevin Doxzen, *Future Technological Advancements* In: *Reproduction Reborn*. Edited by: Diana M. Bowman, Karinne Ludlow, and Walter G. Johnson, Oxford University Press. © Oxford University Press 2023. DOI: 10.1093/oso/9780197616192.003.0011 as governments wrestle with the ethical, legal, and social implications of this technology (Cohen et al., 2020). While countries evaluate the value and risk of MRT, other biotechnologies are rapidly advancing in the background, technologies that this chapter sets out to examine. Specifically, this chapter covers the development, applications, and repercussions of genome engineering, in vitro gametogenesis (IVG), and artificial wombs.

10.2 GENOME ENGINEERING

Preimplantation genetic screening operates within the confines of inherited DNA, selecting amongst embryos that all contain parental genes. The genetic makeup of IVF embryos is constrained by mendelian genetics, a limitation for couples looking beyond their own gene pool for solutions to reproductive problems. Although the therapeutic necessity for introducing novel genes or targeted alterations to an embryo's genome is rare, as argued later in this section, these scenarios still exist. As the safety and efficacy of genetic engineering technology progresses in sectors outside of human reproduction, pressure to apply these tools to germline genome engineering (GGE) continues to grow. This section discusses advancements in genetic engineering and covers initial experimentation on human germ cells. These case studies expose difficulties in performing GGE to both nuclear and mitochondrial DNA. This section concludes with advancements in genome engineering technology that may one day move GGE from the lab to the clinic and the ethical considerations society must confront along the way.

10.2.1 Nuclear DNA Engineering

In the early 2000s, researchers at the University of Utah engineered an enzyme capable of precisely locating and cutting specific sequences of DNA (Urnov, 2018). Tangential research revealed that DNA, once cut, is repaired using natural cellular repair mechanisms, categorised into two main pathways:

1. Cut strands are rejoined in an error-prone process called *nonhomologous end joining* (NHEJ). NHEJ can result in the insertion or deletion of nucleotides (indels), leading to codon frameshifts and the inactivation of a gene (knockout).
2. Template DNA, which can be provided by the researcher, is inserted (knock-in) at the site of the break in a process called *homology-directed*

repair (HDR). This orchestrated process of DNA cutting and repair via HDR or NHEJ was called 'genome editing.'[1]

Multiple iterations of programmable DNA-cutting enzymes have improved the speed and efficacy of genome editing. These tools include zinc finger nucleases (ZFNs), transcription activator-like effector nucleases (TALENs), and, most recently, *clustered regularly interspaced short palindromic repeats* (CRISPR) (Carroll, 2021). Unlike ZFNs and TALENs, which locate DNA sequences using engineered proteins, CRISPR enzymes use small guide RNAs that identify DNA sequences through complementary base pairing (Jinek et al., 2012). This RNA-guided mechanism reduced the cost and time required for genetic engineering experiments, leading to wide adoption and broad application of CRISPR technology (LaManna and Barrangou, 2018). Immediate interest gravitated towards therapeutic uses; in particular, treating rare monogenetic diseases (Konishi and Long, 2021). Examples of targeting disease-specific cell and tissue types across the body include hematopoietic stem cells for sickle cell disease, retinal tissue for Leber congenital amaurosis, and lung cells for cystic fibrosis (Da Silva Sanchez et al., 2020; Frangoul et al., 2021; Rasoulinejad and Maroufi, 2021).

Therapeutic somatic cell genome editing has displayed promising results during preliminary clinical trials. These early indications have led some scientists, including George Daley, Dean of Harvard Medical School, to argue that the future of this technology, if proved safe, should consider extending benefits beyond a single patient, offering intergenerational therapeutic value through GGE (Daley et al., 2019). This position is countered by questions of utility and the role that GGE would serve where preimplantation genetic diagnosis (PGD) may fall short. The widespread desire for couples to have a healthy, biologically related child suggests that demand would exist for GGE if proved safe and effective (Hendriks et al., 2017).

The most straightforward cases where PGD is insufficient are scenarios in which prospective parents are homozygous for an autosomal-dominant disease (e.g., Huntington´s disease or Marfan syndrome) or where both parents are homozygous for an autosomal-recessive disease (e.g., cystic fibrosis) (Ranisch, 2020). In these cases, no IVF embryos would lack the disease-causing allele. These situations are rare because such diseases are usually lethal before reproductive age or are extremely debilitating (Mertes and Pennings, 2015). Some ethicists argue that rarity should not justify a full stop on the use of GGE if it is the most reasonable option for healthy children (Ranisch, 2020).

Other than instances in which there are no embryos without deleterious mutations, parents may have too few unaffected embryos to go through the necessary number of IVF rounds for a successful birth. For example, three out of four embryos will carry a mutation if both parents are heterozygous for autosomal-dominant conditions. Additionally, disease-free embryos are often discarded for other reasons including morphological abnormalities; therefore, GGE could be used purely as a means to increase the number of viable embryos and would decrease the risk to biological mothers who might otherwise need to go through additional cycles of ovarian stimulation (De Wert et al., 2018). Early arguments for or against the use of GGE for therapeutic purposes were based on the premise that CRISPR could be safe and effective in germ cells, an assumption that had yet to be tested until 2015.

In 2015, Junjiu Huang and his colleagues from Sun Yat-sen University in Guangzhou, China, received approval from the university hospital's Medical Ethical Committee to conduct genome editing experiments on embryos. The research team attempted to correct a mutated *HBB* gene responsible for β-thalassaemia, an inherited blood disorder, in nonviable embryos obtained from a local fertility clinic (Liang et al., 2015). Weeks before Huang's publication, prominent scientists essentially called for a global moratorium on GGE, elevating the subsequent controversy and criticism of the experiments (Baltimore et al., 2015). Over the next two years, other research teams carried out three similar attempts to correct genetic variants for clinical applications in affected embryos (Kang et al., 2016; Ma et al., 2017; Tang et al., 2017). Subtle differences between these studies revealed three key observations about the safety and efficacy of GGE (Hershlag and Bristow, 2018).

As Hershlag and Bristow summarise, the first observation was that at least a subset of all embryos resulted in the intended genetic modification. Second, the timing of the genome-editing procedure impacted the frequency of 'mosaicism.' Mosaic embryos are composed of two or more different cell types. When the genome-editing machinery was introduced into zygotes (fertilised eggs), the developing embryos were mosaic, having both edited and unedited cells. Alternatively, mosaicism was avoided if CRISPR molecules were injected into an oocyte (an immature egg cell) simultaneously with sperm fertilisation. Third, timing also impacted the number of 'off-target' mutations, genetic changes at sites other than the intended location. Identical or similar DNA sequences may appear throughout a single genome, raising the probability that CRISPR molecules may bind and cut the wrong DNA target. Off-target cutting can generate mutations as the cell attempts to repair the DNA breaks using the NEHJ DNA repair pathway. Since a vast majority of the human genome does not code for protein or serve a clearly defined function, most of these off-target mutations pose little risk, but a single mutation in an essential gene, such as the p53 tumour suppressor gene, could lead to cancer or other health problems. In the context of GGE, genome editing at the zygote stage increased the chances of off-targets, while introducing CRISPR into a mature oocyte along with sperm minimised off-targets. These early studies demonstrated that both mosaicism and off-target mutations were minimised when CRISPR was injected along with sperm into an oocyte, revealing the most effective experimental protocol.

These findings introduce a twist in the clinical prospects of GGE. Screening for a genetic mutation in an embryo is commonly performed on Day 3 of fertilisation at the six- to eight-cell stage. At this point, attempts to correct a disease-causing mutation through genome editing may lead to high mosaicism and off-target mutations. Alternatively, performing GGE on a mature oocyte or sperm presupposes that the genetic mutation is identified (e.g., when both parents are homozygous for an autosomal-dominant condition). Regardless of how GGE would be used, further experimentation would be necessary to improve the burgeoning technology. Determining what experiments to conduct and how to ethically regulate GGE became a central concern for international scientific and political communities.

10.2.2 Germline Genome Engineering Ethics and Politics

In December 2015, the US National Academies of Sciences (NAS) and National Academy of Medicine, the United Kingdom's Royal Society of the United Kingdom, and the Chinese Academy of Sciences cosponsored The International Summit on Human Gene Editing. This high-profile meeting aimed to articulate under what conditions GGE would be ethically permissible. In February 2017, more than a year following the Summit, the NAS and NAM released a consensus report containing the official positions of the Academies (Committee on Human Gene Editing: Scientific, Medical, and Ethical Considerations et al., 2017). The report's authors outlined a 10-point checklist under which GGE would be permissible for clinical use, including criteria such as restricting uses to 'preventing a serious disease or condition,' a distinction, which they and others acknowledge has no clear boundaries (Doxzen and Halpern, 2020). They state that the most acceptable use of preventing serious diseases would entail 'converting causative genetic variants to nondeleterious variants.' Overall, the report had a permissive rather than precautionary tone, captured in their statement, 'heritable germline genome-editing trials must be approached with caution, but caution does not mean they must be prohibited.' In the end, the authors created a strict yet tentative roadmap towards ethically accept-able uses of GGE, a 'yellow light' that some, including Edward Lanphier of DNA editing company Sangamo Therapeutics, said changes the tone to an 'affirmative position' (Kaiser, 2017). In the years between the Summit and the report, authoritative bodies had already given their approval for GGE for basic research.

In 2016, UK scientists at the Francis Crick Institute received approval from the UK Human Fertilisation and Embryology Authority (HFEA), marking the first time a national regulatory authority endorsed embryo ed-iting (Callaway, 2016a). Under this proposal, researchers would use viable embryos, and all cells would be discarded within a week after fertilisation. Unlike the 2015 Chinese experiment, this research sought to understand molecular mechanisms behind embryo development, with implications for elucidating causes of infertility. Not long after the UK approval, GGE for basic research was authorised by a university ethics board in Sweden (Callaway, 2016b).

The global conversation behind GGE continued to evolve as countries began seriously considering embryo-editing research proposals. Survey data from a representative sample of 1,600 US adults indicated that 65 per-cent of respondents viewed germline therapy as acceptable (Scheufele et al., 2017). Alternatively, 26 percent of those polled were opposed to germline enhancement applications. This warming attitude towards GGE for ther-apeutic purposes was the backdrop on which the Second International Summit Human Genome Editing was held in Hong Kong, in November 2018. The chosen location of this event was a concerted effort to bring voices from Asian countries to the forefront of the conversation. A day before the start of the Summit, news broke of a Chinese scientist, Dr. He Jiankui, who had allegedly implanted CRISPR-edited embryos resulting in the birth of twin girls (Regalado, 2018). This announcement set off a cascade of con-demnation and global backlash (Greely, 2019; Chapter 9, this volume). He attempted to recreate a naturally occurring gene variant that provides HIV immunity. The CCRΔ32 allele, found in people of northern European an-cestry, is a 32-base pair deletion in the CCR5 gene that prevents the proper functioning of a protein involved in HIV infection. He stated that he was motivated by a stigma in China associated with contracting HIV (Lovell-Badge, 2019).

Although no formal peer-reviewed paper was published, He presented experimental results during the Summit, data which confirmed the error-prone outcomes from earlier GGE studies (Greely, 2019). One of the implanted embryos was a heterozygote, meaning that one chromosome was unedited, while both embryos showed signs of mosaicism, raising the possibility that the twins are not immune to HIV. In neither embryo was He able to recreate the naturally occurring Δ32 allele, but instead disrupted the gene in ways never previously studied.

Organisers of the Summit released a statement condemning He's experiments as 'disturbing' and 'irresponsible,' which reflected the general reaction from the global scientific community (Baltimore et al., 2018). Conversely, an initial response from China's chief official newspaper *People's Daily* praised He's work, calling it 'a milestone accomplishment China has achieved in the area of gene-editing technologies' (Nie, 2018). This public acclaim was quickly offset by a group of 122 Chinese scientists and ethicists who published a joint statement on Weibo, a social media site, denouncing the work as 'crazy' and calling for stricter rules (Rathi and Huang, 2018: 100). The Chinese government immediately suspended He's work and began an investigation. In January, authorities announced that He 'intentionally dodged supervision, raised funds and organized researchers on his own to carry out the human embryo gene-editing intended for reproduction, which is explicitly banned by relevant regulations' (Greely, 2019). In December 2019, He and his colleagues were convicted of 'illegal medical practice' for their editing of human embryos for reproductive purposes, resulting in three years in prison and a fine of approximately US$450,000 (Song and Joly, 2021). Since He's announcement, China's highest legislative body, the National People's Congress, and two departments overseeing biotechnology have initiated expansive regulatory reform in genetic and human embryo research (Song and Joly, 2021). He's deceptive and misleading participant consent forms, which experts suggest underwent fraudulent ethical review, exemplified the need for Chinese regulatory and ethical reform from the local to national level (Shaw, 2020). Ethicists have stated that recent changes to China's ethical rules now position the country in line with other developed countries (Greely, 2019; Chapter 9, this volume).

The fallout from He's announcement has motivated a reassessment of international regulatory frameworks, an evaluation of soft law and code of conduct practices, and a reinforcement of the imperative for public engagement (Adashi et al., 2020; Jasanoff et al., 2019; Marchant, 2021; Townsend, 2020). Experts point towards the United Kingdom's Human Fertilisation and Embryonic Authority as a model for approving research or clinical GGE proposals (Nature Editorial, 2019). This independent entity would serve as an international regulator to whom researchers could present GGE project proposals and provide justifications for genetically altering human gametes and embryos. Groups have also called for a whistleblowing mechanism to shed light on activities that diverge from rules or standards, exposing such practices to authorities and the public (International Commission on the Clinical Use of Human Germline Genome Editing et al., 2020). In July 2021, an expert advisory committee commissioned by the World Health Organisation (WHO) released a governance framework and set of recommendations to provide guidance on strengthening oversight of genome editing activities across institutional, national, regional, and international levels (WHO Expert Advisory Committee on Developing Global Standards for Governance and Oversight of Human Genome Editing, 2021).

10.2.3 Mitochondrial DNA Engineering

Although a majority of genetic diseases stem from mutations within nuclear DNA, a subset of devastating conditions results from faulty genes within the small, circular genomes of mitochondria. A single cell contains between 1,000–2,000 mitochondria, and each mitochondrion contain dozens of genomes. The mutation rate of mitochondrial DNA (mtDNA) is approximately 100-fold higher than nuclear DNA, resulting in sequence variability amongst genomes within a single cell or mitochondrion. Cells containing a mixture of mitochondrial genome sequences are referred to as having *heteroplasmy*, while cells with only one type of mitochondrial genome are characterized by *homoplasmy*.

The 37 genes within the mitochondrial genome control cellular energy production. More than 270 genetic variants are attributed to mitochondrial diseases. Once thought rare, about 1 in 4,300 people suffer from diseases caused by mtDNA mutations, many of which affect the nervous system (Gorman et al., 2015). Homoplasmic mitochondrial mutations can lead to debilitating diseases often affecting single organs or tissues (e.g., Leber hereditary optic neuropathy, which leads to a loss of vision in both eyes; Stewart and Chinnery, 2015). Diseases from heteroplasmic mitochondrial variants manifest once enough mitochondrial genomes are mutated, passing a disease threshold. The severity of heteroplasmic diseases can depend on the number (load) of mutated genomes and often affect multiple organs.

While arguments persist surrounding the efficacy of PGD to protect against the transmission of disease-causing mtDNA mutations, it is clear that heteroplasmy makes it difficult to ensure the birth of healthy children through embryo screening (Mitalipov et al., 2014; Steffann et al., 2014). In an effort to offer couples a more reliable clinical alternative to PGD, researchers have developed mitochondrial replacement therapy (MRT).

While multiple methods of MRT exist (covered in preceding chapters of this volume), they all rely on the contribution of healthy mitochondria from a donor woman.

Despite ethical and legal challenges, parents have successfully undergone MRT in a handful of countries, including Mexico and Greece (Gallagher, 2019; Zhang et al., 2017; Chapters 7 and 8, this volume). Although MRT gives parents the chance to have a biologically related child, the procedure uses genetic material from a donor, which is why MRT children are often referred to as 'three-parent babies.' One form of MRT, called *spindle transfer*, involves extracting nuclear DNA from a mother's unfertilised egg and introducing that DNA into a donor egg containing healthy mitochondria, which is then used for fertilisation. A second form of MRT, *pronuclear transfer*, begins with fertilising eggs from the mother and a donor with sperm from the father. The pronuclei are removed before fusing and the pronuclei from the mother's fertilised egg is inserted into the fertilised egg of the donor. Deploying genome-engineering approaches would prove less invasive than swapping intracellular DNA and cytoplasmic molecules between eggs. Targeted mtDNA modifications would also bypass the use of donor material by directly correcting pathogenic variants.

Initial attempts to target mtDNA used restriction endonucleases (REs) attached to short amino acid chains (peptides) that facilitate the transport of REs into the mitochondria. Once inside, these mitochondrial REs (mtREs) specifically recognise and cleave sequences found in pathogenic genomes, ideally shifting the mtDNA heteroplasmic load. Mitochondria do not have double-stranded break (DSB) repair mechanisms, thus cleaved pathogenic genomes are naturally degraded and replaced by healthy DNA in order to maintain the same copy number of genomes within the organelle (Srivastava and Moraes, 2001). Difficulty in engineering mtREs for targeting new pathogenic DNA sequences limited the utility of this approach. The emergence of programmable nucleases like TALENs and ZFNs allowed researchers to target a broader range of mtDNA variants, thus overcoming the limitations of mtREs and demonstrating effective physiological rescue (Gammage et al., 2016; Hashimoto, 2015). Both mitoTALENs and mtREs have been used in mouse embryos to prevent germline transmission of mitochondrial diseases by inducing a heteroplasmic shift via selective elimination of mutated mtDNA (Reddy, 2015). These early results show promise to treat inheritable mitochondrial diseases, yet ongoing studies are necessary to address long-term effects of the procedures. For example, reducing mtDNA copy number below a certain threshold has been shown to create pregnancy problems in mice (Wai et al., 2010).

Recent advancements in CRISPR technology have spurred interest into whether an RNA-guided platform could provide wider flexibility and simplify the overall mtDNA targeting process. Unfortunately, the feature that makes CRISPR so versatile is the same property that undermines its mitochondrial efficacy. Contrary to nuclear import, RNA cannot effectively transport across mitochondrial membranes. While some researchers have tested novel RNA structures to facilitate importation, others suggest that the CRISPR guide RNAs will prove problematic for mtDNA targeting (Gammage et al., 2018; Chapter 1, this volume). Given the limitations of CRISPR, finding an alternative mechanism capable of altering mtDNA sequences rather than initiating the degradation of pathogenic mitochondrial genomes is necessary to address homopathic diseases. To this end, researchers discovered a toxic bacterial deaminase enzyme that converts base pairs from C•G to T•A (Mok et al., 2020). By splitting the protein in half, researchers inhibited the enzyme's toxicity. They then attached one half of the enzyme to DNA-binding proteins, and, by targeting two adjacent regions within the mitochondrial genome, they were able to correct pathogenic mutations. Although editing efficiency remains low (5–50 percent) and available targeting sequences are limited, this RNA-free approach directly corrects disease-causing mutations and may offer an alternative to PGD, MRT, or other mtDNA-targeting nucleases.

10.2.4 Next-Generation Genome Engineering

Initial efforts to make targeted genetic changes in living cells were a result of inducing a DSB in the DNA and co-opting cellular repair machinery to insert, delete, or alter base pairs. Engineering via DSB has led to significant advancements in clinical therapeutic applications, yet further investigation has revealed harmful drawbacks of this process.

While considerable attention has been given to 'off-target' mutations, the potential for DSB-induced 'on-target' effects may pose an even greater health risk. On-target effects are unintended consequences of cleaving the DNA at the intended location. Studies have shown that DSB cleavage can result in large deletions, chromosomal rearrangements, and loss of chromosomes in multiple human cell types including embryos (Kosicki et al., 2018; Leibowitz et al., 2021; Zuccaro et al., 2020). One major concern of these on-target effects is the onset of cancer due to increased expression of oncogenes.

Although optimising guide RNA sequence design and target location can minimise the impact of on-target effects, the best way to avoid unwanted outcomes is to circumvent DNA cleavage altogether (Thomas et al., 2019). Researchers have developed alternative approaches to genome engineering that do not require DSBs but instead use the DNA targeting capability of CRISPR proteins without their cleavage activity. Mutating one or both catalytic sites of Cas9 prevents double-stranded DNA cleavage without inhibiting binding. Using this platform, researchers are able to alter the genome without DSBs. By tethering a deaminase enzyme to Cas9, researchers can convert single bases through a process called *base editing* (Komor et al., 2016). Alternatively, attaching methylation enzymes to deactivated Cas9 proteins can introduce heritable targeted and reversible changes to the epigenome (Nuñez et al., 2021).

In addition to unwanted on-target effects, early CRISPR engineering approaches were inefficient at knocking-in new sequences of DNA (Banan, 2020). To overcome this limitation, researchers developed *prime editing*, which does not require a DSB and uses reverse transcription to introduce new DNA (Anzalone et al., 2019). Not long after, researchers discovered CRISPR proteins that interact with transposons, long genome sequences capable of changing locations within a genome (Klompe et al., 2019). Preliminary studies have demonstrated that these transposons can help insert long DNA sequences at specific genomic sites, offering the possibility of introducing whole genes into human genomes. As more naturally occurring and engineered CRISPR tools are added to a growing arsenal of available genetic engineering technologies, researchers will continue to improve the accuracy, precision, and breadth of targeted heritable changes.

10.3   IN VITRO GAMETOGENESIS

The absence of viable gametes is a common cause of infertility for many couples. Polycystic ovary syndromes (PCOS), ovarian cancer, premature ovarian insufficiency, and other ovarian diseases can all prevent the development of healthy eggs (Zhang et al., 2020). For men, nonobstructive azoospermia (NOA) and chemoradiotherapy targeting cancer can reduce sperm count. Before undergoing cancer treatments, prospective parents may cryopreserve gametes, but this approach is not available for prepubertal patients. The prospect of IVG, generating artificial gametes from stem cells, would offer gamete-compromised parents a chance to have genetically related children. Adoption of this technology would also allow same-sex couples the opportunity to have a child genetically related to both parents. This section begins with the technological development of IVG, transitioning into potential use cases. This section concludes with scientific, ethical, and regulatory concerns unique to IVG that may prevent or limit the use of this technology.

10.3.1 IVG Technology Development

The development of mature gametes begins with primordial germ cells (PGCs). PGCs develop into germ cells that enter into either spermatogenesis or oogenesis to generate either sperm or eggs. The method of reproducing this process in a culture dish is called *in vitro gametogenesis*. Induction of gamete formation can begin with two types of stem cells: adult stem cells from testis or ovaries, or pluripotent stem cells, which include embryonic stem cells (ESCs). In lieu of ESCs, somatic cells can be genetically reprogrammed into induced pluripotent stem cells (iPSCs), providing another alternative starting point for IVG.

Scientists have demonstrated the feasibility of IVG using mouse models. Starting with both ESCs and iPSCs, the entire cycle of the mouse female germline was recreated in vitro (Hikabe et al., 2016). Scientists also used ESCs to generate sperm-like cells, which they used to fertilise oocytes and produce fertile offspring (Zhou et al., 2016). The proof-of-concept mouse studies showed that production of PCGs in vitro can lead to viable germ cells. Replicating these results from mice to nonhuman primate or human cells has proved difficult. Despite a current inability to produce mature germ cells, researchers have still been able to generate human PGC-like cells from iPSCs, leading to the formation of oogonia, precursors to mature oocytes (Yamashiro et al., 2018).

10.3.2 IVG Future Applications

Proponents of IVG suggest a range of potential use cases, both independent of and in combination with other ART methods (Cohen et al., 2017; Greely, 2016). Upstream of generating viable embryos for pregnancy, the production of artificial gametes (AG) would allow for in vitro disease modelling and the advancement of infertility research (Hayashi et al., 2012). Creating mature gametes from immortal cell lines of infertile individuals would remove a bottleneck created by limited source material. Generating iPSC-derived gametes from patient cells could also be used to identify germline diseases and diagnose causes of infertility.

Stimulating ovaries to retrieve eggs poses the most significant medical risk during IVF. This step can result in hyperstimulation syndrome, in which the ovaries increase in size with side effects ranging from nausea and abdominal pain to heart and kidney problems. IVG could circumvent the egg retrieval process and prevent the pain associated with the procedure. For people who have undergone chemotherapy or other treatments that disrupt gamete viability, and for whom ovary stimulation is not an option, IVG could provide a new source of germ cells for IVF.

After diagnosing a genetic disease or molecular cause of infertility, IVG could be paired with genome engineering technology to correct problematic mutations at any point in the IVG process. For mitochondrial diseases stemming from high mutational loads, IVG could generate gametes starting with stem cells identified to have mutational loads below a pathogenic threshold. The ability for IVG to produce significantly more gametes than through normal IVF methods means that coupling IVG with PGD would allow parents to screen many more embryos, thus increasing the probability of identifying desirable cells.

The potential of IVG to produce both sperm and egg means that same-sex partners would have the opportunity to have a child who is genetically related to both parents. Conceivably, this method would also allow a single woman to have a child without genetic material from another individual (Suter, 2016). Irrespective of the application, continued research into the genetic and epigenetic changes resulting from induced pluripotency and subsequent IVG must be further explored (Ma et al., 2014). Establishing a set of standards by which to measure the reproducibility of creating gametes outside of the body will be necessary to lay the groundwork towards human testing (Handel et al., 2014).

10.3.3 IVG Ethics and Regulation

The prospect of IVG raises ethical concerns shared with GGE, preimplantation genetic diagnosis (PGD), and other ARTs. In particular, IVG would require the creation and destruction of human embryos during preclinical and clinical testing, an act that raises both religious and secular concerns. The uniqueness of IVG, in this regard, does not pertain to the disposal of embryos, which applies to other ARTs, but instead is characterised by the sheer number of discarded cells. IVG could create conditions in which gametes, primarily eggs, are no longer rate-limiting materials. When paired with IVF, IVG could produce hundreds or thousands of viable embryos available for screening (Bourne et al., 2012). The potential to create near unlimited embryos leads into a second ethical concern: *germline genetic enhancement*.

In the United States, the majority of PGD cycles primarily focus on aneuploidy testing and identifying single-gene disorders, thus limiting sequencing to specific genomic loci (Stern, 2014). Recent improvements in single-cell whole-genome sequencing of IVF embryos would allow for broader analysis of an embryo's genomic landscape (Murphy et al., 2020). In parallel, advancements in other high-throughput omics (i.e., transcriptomic, epigenomics, and proteomics) would provide further insight into subcellular conditions impacting embryos' health and developmental outcomes (Bai et al., 2021). Currently, creating sophisticated bioinformatic pipelines capable of mapping this biological information onto traits is limited by our scientific understanding. As this bottleneck improves, IVG would contribute to concerns of germline genetic enhancement by exposing parents to a long list of potential children with a wide variety of desirable traits.

In addition to embryo disposal and germline genetic enhancement, two ethical concerns shared with other ARTs, IVG presents two novel areas of ethical quandaries. First, IVG could introduce new family structures. Through IVG, same-sex couples could have children as closely genetically related to them as parents who created a child through sexual reproduction. Starting with iPSCs from either a male or female, IVG could potentially lead to functional gametes of both sexes. Scientists have successfully generated both sperm and egg from male mouse ESCs (Kerkis et al., 2007), suggesting that same-sex male couples could have a child that is genetically related to both of them through IVG, IVF, and surrogacy. As for same-sex female couples, only oocytes have been generated from female ESCs, yet a mouse was created with the DNA of two females, suggesting that a child from a same-sex couple could have the same parental ratios as generated from normal sexual reproduction (Kono et al., 2004; Palacios-González et al., 2014). Ethical and cultural critiques of same-sex adoption and surrogacy receive varying degrees and types of pushback across different cultural contexts (Beyrer, 2014). These stances can also fluctuate over time (Balluck, 2021). The use of IVG for same-sex couples to have genetically related children could be met with equal or even more ardent criticism, as it suggests 'playing God' and other connotations of unnaturalness. For instance, the reprogramming of somatic cells into stem cells in order to generate germ cells follows different developmental paths than the formation of naturally occurring eggs and sperm. Similarly, contributing both halves of a child's genetic makeup from the same sex does not adhere to reproductive norms. Alternatively, advocates make the case of reproductive justice and beneficence in using IVG for same-sex reproduction (Notini et al., 2020).

A more ethically problematic use of IVG is *multiplex genetic parenting* (Palacios-González et al., 2014). This application would allow a child to have four genetically related parents through the following scenario: first, two couples would generate two embryos using normal IVF or IVG. Second, ESCs would be removed from each embryo and differentiated using IVG to be used for IVF. Similar to ethical arguments against MRT and the idea of 'three-parent babies,' multiplexed genetic parenting presents ethical concerns around disrupting the child's sense of self (Nuffield Council on Bioethics, 2012; Chapter 2, this volume). Others support the idea of ART's role in social experimentation, arguing that multiple parents would offer reproductive autonomy and allow multiple individuals to engage in genetic parenting together (Palacios-González et al., 2014).

In addition to impacting family structures, IVG raises the possibility of generating AG for reproductive purposes without a person's knowledge or consent (Smajdor and Cutas, 2014). The ease of obtaining someone's skin cells or other starting material, with the intention of generating iPSCs for IVG, creates feasible scenarios in which unwitting parents could be held responsible for their unintended child's quality of life. Similar concerns were raised for human reproductive cloning via somatic cell nuclear transfer (SCNT) (Orentlicher, 1999). These concerns are not without precedent. In England, a woman stole sperm from an ex-husband and tricked an IVF clinic into initiating two pregnancies (Satkunarajah, 2011). The husband was eventually forced to pay child support. Instances of sperm theft and the potential of AG suggest that legal precedent for genetic relatedness to dictate parental responsibility requires re-examination and updating. Changes to these rules will also impact same-sex marriages and other instances of non-genetically related parenthood.

10.4 ARTIFICIAL WOMBS

Extreme prematurity (22–28 weeks) is the leading cause of infant morbidity and mortality, even in developed countries (Mathews et al., 2015; Patel et al., 2015). Although improvements in prenatal care have lowered viable gestation time to slightly less than 22 weeks, improved survival is associated with increased frequency of severe health issues like respiratory failure stemming from underdeveloped lungs and other organ immaturity (Althabe et al., 2012; Cable, 2018). This chapter's final section shifts the focus away from fertilising and screening single cells and considers the larger vessel responsible for bringing a child to term. Artificial wombs and artificial placentas would ideally serve as an incubator to prolong the development of extremely premature infants (EPIs), allowing organ maturation. This section tracks the history of artificial womb development and its most recent progress towards human clinical testing. The chapter concludes by discussing future applications of this technology and ways in which these uses may force updates to current legal systems.

10.4.1 Early Technological Development

For nearly a century, society has been enamoured by the idea of *ectogenesis*, the implantation and full development of foetuses in vitro (James, 1987). Advancing beyond speculative science fiction, researchers aspire to realise ectogenesis by creating artificial uteri, also known as 'artificial wombs.' These devices would operate by connecting to a source of maternal blood or replacement fluids, supplying nutrients and oxygen to an incubating foetus while disposing of waste material (Bulletti et al., 2011).

Early studies to engineer an artificial womb began in 1958, prolonging the lives of previable human foetuses for several hours by supplying oxygen to a warmed perfusion chamber (Westin et al., 1958). Over the next decade, researchers optimised oxygen delivery and fluid containers, slowly improving survival times. After roughly 20 years of abated research due to improvements in neonatal care, interest in artificial wombs resurfaced in the 1990s (De Bie et al., 2021). During this time, focus on artificial womb research shifted to improving organ maturation and overall foetal wellbeing, in preparation for clinical translation.

In addition to engineering artificial environments capable of supporting foetal development, early ectogenesis research aimed to understand and recreate embryo implantation. In 1988, scientists in Italy first reported experimental embryo implantation in an ex vivo extracorporeally perfused uterus—existing outside of the body (Bulletti et al., 1988). Although this research program was eventually stopped due to strong political opposition, early ex vivo perfusion studies exposed researchers to the utero biological mechanisms behind implantation, a step towards engineering a viable artificial environment (Bulletti et al., 2011). Much of the ongoing work surrounding embryo implantation has centred around elucidating the underlying biology of the epithelial endometrial interface, a critical region of the uterus that undergoes changes during implantation.

10.4.2 The Future of Artificial Wombs

In the mid 1990s, Yoshinori Kuwabara from Juntendo University in Tokyo developed a technique called *extrauterine foetal incubation* (EUFI), which he used to support foetal goats for up to three weeks (Klass, 1996). His method involved threading catheters through vessels in the goats' umbilical cords, supplying the foetuses with oxygenated blood, while the premature bodies were suspended in artificial amniotic fluid heated to body temperature.

In the 2010s, three groups published reports showcasing updated artificial placenta and artificial womb technologies, more closely mimicking utero physiology. A research team at the University of Michigan engineered an artificial placenta capable of supporting a foetal lamb for 17 days (Gray et al., 2013; McLeod et al., 2019). Artificial placentas differ from wombs in that they provide nutrition and gas exchange without submerging the foetus in warm fluid. Although this system promoted lung development, various cardiac problems arose (Bryner et al., 2015; Coughlin et al., 2019). Not long after, research groups from Perth, Australia and Sendai, Japan developed artificial wombs that successfully supported foetal lambs that equated to extremely premature human infants (22–24 weeks old) (Usuda et al., 2019). Surviving for almost 1 week, the lambs demonstrated healthy brain, lung, and cardiac function. Around the same time, a team from the Children's Hospital of Philadelphia Research Institute created an artificial womb nicknamed the 'biobag,' which sustained preterm lamb foetuses for 4 weeks, followed by a safe delivery (Partridge et al., 2017). These recent reports have led some experts to suggest that human testing may only be several years away (Couzin-Frankel, 2017).

Complete ectogenesis not only requires the gestation of a preterm foetus, but also the initial embryo implantation. A research team out of Israel are pushing the limits of ex utero embryogenesis using a rotating culture platform (Aguilera-Castrejon et al., 2021). The team removed embryos from mice after 5 days of gestation and grew them for 6 more days in their ex utero environment. The 10-day mark equates to about halfway through the mice's full gestation. The team later announced that they repeated the experiment using fertilised eggs retrieved from mouse oviducts (Day 0) and grew them for an additional 11 days ex utero (Kolata, 2021).

Combining the rotating cultural platform with other artificial womb technologies could bring researchers closer to fulfilling complete ectogenesis, yet some researchers say that motors, tubes, and other mechanical parts may not be necessary in the future. Advancements in 3D printing, tissue regeneration, and uterine stem cell differentiation could one day help create model uteri made of living cells (Laronda et al., 2017; Magalhaes et al., 2020; Miyazaki et al., 2018).

10.4.3 Applications and Ethical Questions

EPIs undergo prolonged intensive care after birth. Their lives depend on mechanical ventilators, radiant warmers, and gastrostomy tubes. Determining whether artificial wombs are an extension of EPI intensive care or whether ex utero gestation is an innately different form of assistance raises profound ethical and legal questions (Romanis, 2018). In multiple countries, *viability* is the point at which a foetus is provided some legal protections (*Roe v. Wade*, 410 U.S. 113, 1973; De Proost et al., 2021). If artificial wombs support the gestation of previable foetuses, then legal protections must reconsider the concept of viability (Romanis, 2020). Additionally, the use of artificial wombs forces legal systems to re-evaluate rights given to children before and after birth. For example, England and Wales offer a foetus no legal personality, whereas after birth it is given all the rights and protections of a child (Alghrani and Brazier, 2011). Does transferring a pre- or just-viable foetus from a uterus to an artificial womb constitute a form of birth?

Complications in pregnancy not only pose risks to developing foetuses but can also jeopardise the health of mothers. Dangerous pregnancies can force mothers to choose between their own well-being or the life of their prospective child. In cases where a mother needs surgery, radiation, or other harmful procedure, delivery may be delayed until the foetus crosses the viability threshold (Walker, 2015). Access to an artificial womb would allow mothers to ensure the safe development of their future child as well as increase the odds of their own survival by not delaying their medical procedure.

Achieving complete ectogenesis by starting with IVF embryos could address infertility caused by health and social factors. For prospective mothers, artificial wombs capable of supporting early embryogenesis could offer a gestational option other than surrogacy in instances where uteri are damaged due to trauma. Alternatives to surrogacy would be popular in countries where surrogacy is currently banned, including much of Europe, or highly restricted (Bromfield and Rotabi, 2014). Artificial wombs could also help address human rights concerns associated with global surrogacy arrangements, which involve a commercial transaction for surrogacy across international borders and often with lower-income countries.

Complete ectogenesis could also offer an alternative to surrogacy for other types of prospective parents, including gay men and transgender women. When combined with IVG, socially infertile couples could produce a child without the assistance of a third person, thus creating the opportunity for alternative family structures.

10.5 CONCLUSION

The aforementioned technologies are not an exhaustive list of current and future innovation poised to impact human reproduction. Advancements across other technologies, including noninvasive preimplantation genetic testing and embryo screening using artificial intelligence, will shape the future landscape of human reproduction by improving diagnoses, protecting prospective parents and preventing the inheritance of debilitating genetic diseases (Burks et al., 2021; Johnson and Bowman, 2020). Apart from these powerful technologies, this chapter sought to identify areas of scientific exploration that could fundamentally alter our conception of reproduction. The areas of genetic engineering, IVG, and artificial wombs are not purely hypothetical. Decades of research in each domain have led to proof-of-concept experiments, incrementally moving the needle from science fiction to clinical relevancy.

These technologies share two primary areas of benefit: health outcomes and alternative family structures. Genetic engineering and IVG could be used to either correct or avoid harmful genetic or other biological sources of disease. Artificial wombs could play a crucial role in facilitating the healthy development of previable foetuses. Additionally, these ARTs would create new opportunities for prospective parents to have genetically related children without the use of a third party. Parental desires for genetic-relatedness are a driver of ART innovation and will continue to provide a demand signal to improve the safety and efficacy of these technologies (Chateauneuf and Ouellette, 2017).

Despite their potential to alleviate disease and foster parenthood, the previously described ARTs are not without reason for concern. Access barriers to these technologies could further exacerbate reproductive health inequalities within and across countries. In the United States, 40 percent of women have limited or no access to nearby reproductive clinics, while only one third of sub-Saharan African countries have an IVF clinic (Grose, 2020). Future transformative ARTs will be expensive and require sophisticated facilities, meaning that wealthy individuals will most likely benefit from these technologies (Doxzen and Halpern, 2020). Local, regional, and national jurisdictions have different private and public ART coverage policies, further complicating equitable access to these technologies (Mladovsky and Sorenson, 2010). Restricted or minimal coverage would limit access to those who can pay out-of-pocket, while a ban or barred services of select ARTs due to policy could result in medical or circumvention tourism (Cohen, 2018). Monitoring the societal repercussions and unanticipated externalities of both offering and restricting future ARTs, as well as communicating and coordinating with other countries to prevent disparate policies, will be essential in the ethical deployment of these technologies.

Maximising the benefits and minimising the harms of future ARTs requires a recognition of the 'pacing problem' and the use of soft law and agile governance (Marchant, 2011; Marchant Allenby, 2017; World Economic Forum, 2018). Current regulatory systems are insufficient to provide effective oversight of emerging ARTs due to technological novelty and the speed of innovation and scientific discovery. Governments are setting up horizon scanning committees (e.g. UK's Human Fertilisation and Embryology Authority) to anticipate the societal impact of ART applications and apply such foresight to guide policy decisions. In the private sector, companies can establish codes of conduct and set standards to promote self-regulation. Active dialogue between ART innovators and regulators, and the establishment of reflexive public–private partnerships will be vital in the future success of emerging reproductive technologies.

NOTE

1. For the purposes of this chapter, we include genome editing within the broader category of genetic engineering, which includes alterations beyond inserting, deleting, or swapping nucleotides, such as targeted chemical modifications of the epigenome.

REFERENCES

Adashi, Eli Y., Michael M. Burgess, Simon Burall, I. Glenn Cohen, Leonard M. Fleck, John Harris, Soren Holm, et al. 'Heritable human genome editing: The public engagement imperative.' *The CRISPR Journal* 3, no. 6 (2020): 434–439.

Aguilera-Castrejon, Alejandro, Bernardo Oldak, Tom Shani, Nadir Ghanem, Chen Itzkovich, Sharon Slomovich, Shadi Tarazi, et al. 'Ex utero mouse embryogenesis from pre-gastrulation to late organogenesis.' *Nature* 593, no. 7857 (2021): 119–124.

Alghrani, Amel, and Margaret Brazier. 'What is it? Whose it? Re-positioning the fetus in the context of research?' *The Cambridge Law Journal* 70, no. 1 (2011): 51–82.

Althabe, Fernando, Christopher Paul Howson, Mary Kinney, Joy Lawn, and World Health Organization. 'Born too soon: The global action report on preterm birth.' 2012. https://apps.who.int/iris/bitstream/handle/10665/44864/9789241503433_eng.pdf?sequence=1.

Anzalone, Andrew V., Peyton B. Randolph, Jessie R. Davis, Alexander A. Sousa, Luke W. Koblan, Jonathan M. Levy, Peter J. Chen, et al. 'Search-and-replace genome editing without double-strand breaks or donor DNA.' *Nature* 576, no. 7785 (2019): 149–157.

Bai, Dongsheng, Jinying Peng, and Chengqi Yi. 'Advances in single-cell multi-omics profiling.' *RSC Chemical Biology* 2 no. 2 (2021): 441–449.

Balluck, Kyle. 'Supreme Court unanimously sides with Catholic adoption agency that turned away same-sex couples.' *The Hill*. 17 June 2021. https://thehill.com/reg ulation/court-battles/558925-supreme-court-sides-with-catholic-adoption-age ncy-that-turned-away.

Baltimore, David, Paul Berg, Michael Botchan, Dana Carroll, R. Alta Charo, George Church, Jacob E. Corn, et al. 'A prudent path forward for genomic engineering and germline gene modification.' *Science* 348, no. 6230 (2015): 36–38.

Baltimore, David, R. Alta Charo, George Q. Daley, Jennifer A. Doudna, Kazuto Kato, Jin-Soo Kim, Robin Lovell-Badge, et al. 'Statement by the organizing committee of the Second International Summit on Human Genome Editing.' *The National Academies of Sciences, Engineering, and Medicine*, 2018. https:// www.nationalacademies.org/news/2018/11/statement-by-the-organizing-committee-of-the-second-international-summit-on-human-genome-editing.

Banan, Mehdi. 'Recent advances in CRISPR/Cas9-mediated knock-ins in mammalian cells.' *Journal of Biotechnology* 308 (2020): 1–9.

Beyrer, Chris. 'Pushback: The current wave of anti-homosexuality laws and impacts on health.' *PLOS Medicine* 11, no. 6 (2014): e1001658.

Bourne, Hannah, Thomas Douglas, and Julian Savulescu. 'Procreative beneficence and in vitro gametogenesis.' *Monash Bioethics Review* 30, no. 2 (2012): 29-48.

Bromfield, Nicole F., and Karen Smith Rotabi. 'Global surrogacy, exploitation, human rights and international private law: A pragmatic stance and policy recommendations.' *Global Social Welfare* 1, no. 3 (2014): 123–135.

Bryner, Benjamin, Brian Gray, Elena Perkins, Ryan Davis, Hayley Hoffman, John Barks, Gabe Owens, et al. 'An extracorporeal artificial placenta supports extremely premature lambs for 1 week.' *Journal of Pediatric Surgery* 50, no. 1 (2015): 44–49.

Bulletti, Carlo, Valerio Maria Jasonni, Stefania Tabanelli, Luca Gianaroli, Patrizia Maria Ciotti, Anna Pia Ferraretti, and Carlo Flamigni. 'Early human pregnancy in vitro utilizing an artificially perfused uterus.' *Fertility and Sterility* 49, no. 6 (1988): 991–996.

Bulletti, Carlo, Antonio Palagiano, Caterina Pace, Angelica Cerni, Andrea Borini, and Dominique de Ziegler. 'The artificial womb: Ectogenesis.' *Annals of the New York Academy of Sciences* 1221, no. 1 (2011): 124–128.

Burks, Channing, Kristin Van Heertum, and Rachel Weinerman. 'The technological advances in embryo selection and genetic testing: A look back at the evolution of aneuploidy screening and the prospects of non-invasive PGT.' *Reproductive Medicine* 2, no. 1 (2021): 26–34.

Cable, Amanda. '"Miracle" baby born two weeks before legal abortion limit.' *Daily Mail*, 16 February 2018. https://www.dailymail.co.uk/femail/article-1021034/ The-tiniest-survivor-How-miracle-baby-born-weeks-legal-abortion-limit-clung-life-odds.html.

Callaway, Ewen. 'UK scientists gain licence to edit genes in human embryos.' *Nature News* 530, no. 7588 (2016a): 18.

Callaway, Ewen. 'Gene-editing research in human embryos gains momentum.' *Nature News* 532, no. 7599 (2016b): 289.

Carroll, Dana. 'A short, idiosyncratic history of genome editing.' *Gene and Genome Editing* 1 (2021): 100002.

Chateauneuf, Doris, and Françoise Romaine Ouellette. 'Kinship within the context of new genetics: The experience of infertility from medical assistance to adoption.' *Journal of Family Issues* 38, no. 2 (2017): 177–203.

Cohen, Glenn. 'Circumvention medical tourism and cutting edge medicine: The case of mitochondrial replacement therapy.' *Indiana Journal of Global Legal Studies* 25, no. 1 (2018): 439–462.

Cohen, I. Glenn, Eli Y. Adashi, Sara Gerke, César Palacios-González, and Vardit Ravitsky. 'The regulation of mitochondrial replacement techniques around the world.' *Annual Review of Genomics and Human Genetics* 21, no. 1 (2020): 565–586.

Cohen, I. Glenn, George Q. Daley, and Eli Y. Adashi. 'Disruptive reproductive technologies.' *Science Translational Medicine* 9, no. 372 (2017): eaag2959.

Committee on Human Gene Editing: Scientific, Medical, and Ethical Considerations, National Academy of Sciences, National Academy of Medicine, and National Academies of Sciences, Engineering, and Medicine. *Human Genome Editing: Science, Ethics, and Governance*. Washington, DC: National Academies Press, 2017.

Coughlin, Megan A., Nicole L. Werner, Joseph T. Church, Elena M. Perkins, Benjamin S. Bryner, John D. Barks, John K. Bentley, et al. 'An artificial placenta protects against lung injury and promotes continued lung development in extremely premature lambs.' *ASAIO Journal* 65, no. 7 (2019): 690–697.

Couzin-Frankel, Jennifer. 'Fluid-filled "biobag" allows premature lambs to develop outside the womb.' *Science*, 25 April 2017. http://www.sciencemag.org/news/2017/04/fluid-filled-biobag-allows-premature-lambs-develop-outside-womb.

Da Silva Sanchez, Alejandro, Kalina Paunovska, Ana Cristian, and James E. Dahlman. 'Treating cystic fibrosis with MRNA and CRISPR.' *Human Gene Therapy* 31, no. 17–18 (2020): 940–955.

Daley, George Q., Robin Lovell-Badge, and Julie Steffann. 'After the storm—A responsible path for genome editing.' *New England Journal of Medicine* 380, no. 10 (2019): 897–899.

De Bie, Felix R., Marcus G. Davey, Abby C. Larson, Jan Deprest, and Alan W. Flake. 'Artificial placenta and womb technology: Past, current, and future challenges towards clinical translation.' *Prenatal Diagnosis* 41, no. 1 (2021): 145–158.

De Proost, L., E. J. T. Verweij, H. Ismaili M'hamdi, I. K. M. Reiss, E. A. P. Steegers, R. Geurtzen, and A. A. E. Verhagen. 'The edge of perinatal viability: Understanding the Dutch position.' *Frontiers in Pediatrics* 9 (2021): 634290.

De Wert, Guido, Björn Heindryckx, Guido Pennings, Angus Clarke, Ursula Eichenlaub-Ritter, Carla G. van El, Francesca Forzano, et al. 'Responsible innovation in human germline gene editing: Background document to the recommendations of ESHG and ESHRE.' *European Journal of Human Genetics: EJHG* 26, no. 4 (2018): 450–470.

Doxzen, Kevin, and Jodi Halpern. 'Focusing on human rights: A framework for CRISPR germline genome editing ethics and regulation.' *Perspectives in Biology and Medicine* 63, no. 1 (2020): 44–53.

Fauser, Bart C. J. M. 'Towards the global coverage of a unified registry of IVF outcomes.' *Reproductive BioMedicine Online* 38, no. 2 (2019): 133–137.

Frangoul, Haydar, David Altshuler, M. Domenica Cappellini, Yi-Shan Chen, Jennifer Domm, Brenda K. Eustace, Juergen Foell, et al. 'CRISPR-Cas9 gene editing for sickle cell disease and β-thalassemia.' *New England Journal of Medicine* 384, no. 3 (2021): 252–260.

Gallagher, James. '"Three-person" baby boy born in Greece.' *BBC News*, Health, 11 April 2019. https://www.bbc.com/news/health-47889387.

Gammage, Payam A, Edoardo Gaude, Christopher B. Jackson, Joanna Rorbach, Marcin L. Pekalski, Alan J. Robinson, Marine Charpentier, et al. 'Near-complete elimination of mutant MtDNA by iterative or dynamic dose-controlled treatment with MtZFNs.' *Nucleic Acids Research*, 44, no. 16 (2016): 7804–7816.

Gammage, Payam A., Carlos T. Moraes, and Michal Minczuk. 'Mitochondrial genome engineering: The revolution may not be CRISPR-ized.' *Trends in Genetics* 34, no. 2 (2018): 101–110.

Gorman, Gráinne S., Andrew M. Schaefer, Yi Ng, Nicholas Gomez, Emma L. Blakely, Charlotte L. Alston, Catherine Feeney, et al. 'Prevalence of nuclear and mitochondrial DNA mutations related to adult mitochondrial disease.' *Annals of Neurology* 77, no. 5 (2015): 753–759.

Gray, Brian W., Ahmed El-Sabbagh, Sara J. Zakem, Kelly L. Koch, Alvaro Rojas-Pena, Gabe E. Owens, Martin L. Bocks, et al. 'Development of an artificial placenta V: 70h veno-venous extracorporeal life support after ventilatory failure in premature lambs.' *Journal of Pediatric Surgery* 48, no. 1 (2013): 145–153.

Greely, Henry T. *The End of Sex and the Future of Human Reproduction*. Harvard University Press, 2016.

Greely, Henry T. 'CRISPR'd babies: Human germline genome editing in the "He Jiankui Affair."' *Journal of Law and the Biosciences* 6, no. 1 (2019): 111–183.

Grose, Jessica. 'When it comes to fertility, access is everything.' *The New York Times*, Parenting, 17 April 2020. https://www.nytimes.com/2020/04/17/parenting/fertility/fertility-treatment-cost-access.html.

Handel, Mary Ann, John J. Eppig, and John C. Schimenti. 'Applying "gold standards" to in-vitro-derived germ cells.' *Cell* 157, no. 6 (2014): 1257–1261.

Handyside, A. H., E. H. Kontogianni, K. Hardy, and R. M. Winston. 'Pregnancies from biopsied human preimplantation embryos sexed by y-specific DNA amplification.' *Nature* 344, no. 6268 (1990): 768–770.

Hashimoto, Masami. 'MitoTALEN: A general approach to reduce mutant MtDNA loads and restore oxidative phosphorylation function in mitochondrial diseases.' *Cell Therapy* 23, no. 10 (2015): 1592–1599.

Hayashi, Yohei, Mitinori Saitou, and Shinya Yamanaka. 'Germline development from human pluripotent stem cells toward disease modeling of infertility.' *Fertility and Sterility* 97, no. 6 (2012): 1250–1259.

Hendriks, S., K. Peeraer, H. Bos, S. Repping, and E. A. F. Dancet. 'The importance of genetic parenthood for infertile men and women.' *Human Reproduction* 32, no. 10 (2017): 2076–2087.

Hershlag, Avner, and Sara L. Bristow. 'Editing the human genome: Where ART and science intersect.' *Journal of Assisted Reproduction and Genetics* 35, no. 8 (2018): 1367–1370.

Hikabe, Orie, Nobuhiko Hamazaki, Go Nagamatsu, Yayoi Obata, Yuji Hirao, Norio Hamada, So Shimamoto, et al. 'Reconstitution in vitro of the entire cycle of the mouse female germ line.' *Nature* 539, no. 7628 (2016): 299–303.

Human Fertilisation and Embryology Authority (HFEA). 'Our authority, committees and panels.' Accessed 22 February 2022. https://www.hfea.gov.uk/about-us/our-authority-committees-and-panels/.

International Commission on the Clinical Use of Human Germline Genome Editing, National Academy of Medicine, National Academy of Sciences, and The Royal Society. *Heritable Human Genome Editing*. Washington, DC: National Academies Press, 2020.

James, David N. 'Ectogenesis: A reply to Singer and Wells.' *Bioethics* 1, no. 1 (1987): 80–99.

Jasanoff, Sheila, J. Benjamin Hurlbut, and Krishanu Saha. 'Democratic governance of human germline genome editing.' *The CRISPR Journal* 2, no. 5 (2019): 266–271.

Jinek, Martin, Krzysztof Chylinski, Ines Fonfara, Michael Hauer, Jennifer A. Doudna, and Emmanuelle Charpentier. 'A programmable dual-RNA–guided DNA endonuclease in adaptive bacterial immunity.' *Science* 337, no. 6096 (2012): 816–821.

Johnson, Martin. 'Human in vitro fertilisation and developmental biology: A mutually influential history.' *Development* 146, no. 17 (2019): dev183145.

Johnson, Walter G., and Diana M. Bowman. 'Emerging technologies and the future of assisted reproductive technology.' *Jurimetrics* 60, no. 3 (2020): 247–252.

Kaiser, Jocelyn. 'U.S. panel gives yellow light to human embryo editing.' *Science*, 14 February 2017. http://www.sciencemag.org/news/2017/02/us-panel-gives-yellow-light-human-embryo-editing.

Kang, Xiangjin, Wenyin He, Yuling Huang, Qian Yu, Yaoyong Chen, Xingcheng Gao, Xiaofang Sun, and Yong Fan. 'Introducing precise genetic modifications into human 3PN embryos by CRISPR/Cas-mediated genome editing.' *Journal of Assisted Reproduction and Genetics* 33, no. 5 (2016): 581–588.

Kerkis, Alexandre, Simone A. S. Fonseca, Rui C. Serafim, Thais M. C. Lavagnolli, Soraya Abdelmassih, Roger Abdelmassih, and Irina Kerkis. 'In vitro differentiation of male mouse embryonic stem cells into both presumptive sperm cells and oocytes.' *Cloning and Stem Cells* 9, no. 4 (2007): 535–548.

Klass, Perri. 'The artificial womb is born.' *New York Times*, Magazine, 29 September 1996. https://www.nytimes.com/1996/09/29/magazine/the-artificial-womb-is-born.html.

Klompe, Sanne E., Phuc L. H. Vo, Tyler S. Halpin-Healy, and Samuel H. Sternberg. 'Transposon-encoded CRISPR–cas systems direct RNA-guided DNA integration.' *Nature* 571, no. 7764 (2019): 219–225.

Kolata, Gina. 'Scientists grow mouse embryos in a mechanical womb.' *New York Times*, Health, 17 March 2021. https://www.nytimes.com/2021/03/17/health/mice-artificial-uterus.html.

Komor, Alexis C., Yongjoo B. Kim, Michael S. Packer, John A. Zuris, and David R. Liu. 'Programmable editing of a target base in genomic DNA without double-stranded DNA cleavage.' *Nature* 533, no. 7603 (2016): 420–424.

Konishi, Colin T., and Chengzu Long. 'Progress and challenges in CRISPR-mediated therapeutic genome editing for monogenic diseases.' *Journal of Biomedical Research* 35, no. 2 (2021): 148–162.

Kono, Tomohiro, Yayoi Obata, Quiong Wu, Katsutoshi Niwa, Yukiko Ono, Yuji Yamamoto, Eun Sung Park, et al. 'Birth of parthenogenetic mice that can develop to adulthood.' *Nature* 428, no. 6985 (2004): 860–864.

Kosicki, Michael, Kärt Tomberg, and Allan Bradley. 'Repair of double-strand breaks induced by CRISPR–Cas9 leads to large deletions and complex rearrangements.' *Nature Biotechnology* 36, 8 (2018): 765–771.

LaManna, Caroline M., and Rodolphe Barrangou. 'Enabling the rise of a CRISPR world.' *CRISPR Journal* 1, no. 3 (2018): 205–208.

Laronda, Monica M., Alexandra L. Rutz, Shuo Xiao, Kelly A. Whelan, Francesca E. Duncan, Eric W. Roth, Teresa K. Woodruff, and Ramille N. Shah. 'A bioprosthetic ovary created using 3D printed microporous scaffolds restores ovarian function in sterilized mice.' *Nature Communications* 8, no. 1 (2017): 15261.

Leibowitz, Mitchell L., Stamatis Papathanasiou, Phillip A. Doerfler, Logan J. Blaine, Lili Sun, Yu Yao, Cheng-Zhong Zhang, et al. 'Chromothripsis as an on-target consequence of CRISPR–Cas9 genome editing.' *Nature Genetics* 53, no. 6 (2021): 895–905.

Liang, Puping, Yanwen Xu, Xiya Zhang, Chenhui Ding, Rui Huang, Zhen Zhang, Jie Lv, et al. 'CRISPR/Cas9-mediated gene editing in human tripronuclear zygotes.' *Protein & Cell* 6, no. 5 (2015): 363–372.

Lovell-Badge, Robin. 'CRISPR babies: A view from the centre of the storm.' *Development* 146, no. 3 (2019): dev175778.

Ma, Hong, Nuria Marti-Gutierrez, Sang-Wook Park, Jun Wu, Yeonmi Lee, Keiichiro Suzuki, Amy Koski, et al. 'Correction of a pathogenic gene mutation in human embryos.' *Nature* 548, no. 7668 (2017): 413–419.

Ma, Hong, Robert Morey, Ryan C. O'Neil, Yupeng He, Brittany Daughtry, Matthew D. Schultz, Manoj Hariharan, et al. 'Abnormalities in human pluripotent cells due to reprogramming mechanisms.' *Nature* 511, no. 7508 (2014): 177–183.

Magalhaes, Renata S., J. Koudy Williams, Kyung W. Yoo, James J. Yoo, and Anthony Atala. 'A tissue-engineered uterus supports live births in rabbits.' *Nature Biotechnology* 38, no. 11 (2020): 1280–1287.

Marchant, Gary E. 'Addressing the pacing problem.' In *The Growing Gap Between Emerging Technologies and Legal-Ethical Oversight*, edited by Gary Marchant, Braden R. Allenby, and Joseph R. Herkert, pp. 199–205. Springer, 2011.

Marchant, Gary E. 'Global governance of human genome editing: What are the rules?' *Annual Review of Genomics and Human Genetics* 22 (2021): 385–405.

Marchant, Gary E., and Brad Allenby. 'Soft law: New tools for governing emerging technologies.' *Bulletin of the Atomic Scientists* 73, no. 2 (2017): 108–114.

Mathews, T. J., Marian F. MacDorman, and Fay Menacker. 'Infant mortality statistics from the 2013 period linked birth/infant death data set. National vital statistics reports.' Hyattsville, MD: National Center for Health Statistics, 2015.

McLeod, Jennifer S., Joseph T. Church, Megan A. Coughlin, Benjamin Carr, Clinton Poling, Ellery Sarosi, Elena M. Perkins, et al. 'Splenic development and injury in premature lambs supported by the artificial placenta.' *Journal of Pediatric Surgery* 54, no. 6 (2019): 1147–1152.

Mertes, Heidi, and Guido Pennings. 'Modification of the embryo's genome: More useful in research than in the clinic.' *American Journal of Bioethics* 15, no. 12 (2015): 52–53.

Mitalipov, Shoukhrat, Paula Amato, Samuel Parry, and Marni J. Falk. 'Limitations of preimplantation genetic diagnosis for mitochondrial DNA diseases.' *Cell Reports* 7, no. 4 (2014): 935–937.

Miyazaki, Kaoru, Matthew T. Dyson, John S. Coon V, Yuichi Furukawa, Bahar D. Yilmaz, Tetsuo Maruyama, and Serdar E. Bulun. 'Generation of progesterone-responsive endometrial stromal fibroblasts from human induced pluripotent stem cells: Role of the WNT/CTNNB1 pathway.' *Stem Cell Reports* 11, no. 5 (2018): 1136–1155.

Mladovsky, Philipa, and Corinna Sorenson. 'Public financing of IVF: A review of policy rationales.' *Health Care Analysis* 18, no. 2 (2010): 113–128.

Mok, Beverly Y., Marcos H. de Moraes, Jun Zeng, Dustin E. Bosch, Anna V. Kotrys, Aditya Raguram, FoSheng Hsu, et al. 'A bacterial cytidine deaminase toxin enables CRISPR-free mitochondrial base editing.' *Nature* 583, no. 7817 (2020): 631–637.

Murphy, Nicholas M., Tanya S. Samarasekera, Lisa Macaskill, Jayne Mullen, and Luk J. F. Rombauts. 'Genome sequencing of human in vitro fertilisation embryos for pathogenic variation screening.' *Scientific Reports* 10, no. 1 (2020): 3795.

Nature Editorial. 'Germline gene-editing research needs rules.' *Nature* 567, no. 7747 (2019): 145.

Nie, Jing-Bao. 'He Jiankui's genetic misadventure: Why him? Why China?' *Hastings Center*, Blog, 5 December 2018. https://www.thehastingscenter.org/jiankuis-genetic-misadventure-china/.

Notini, Lauren, Christopher Gyngell, and Julian Savulescu. 'Drawing the line on in vitro gametogenesis.' *Bioethics* 34, no. 1 (2020): 123–134.

Nuffield Council on Bioethics. *Novel Techniques for the Prevention of Mitochondrial DNA Disorders: An Ethical View*. Nuffield Council on Bioethics, 2012.

Nuñez, James K., Jin Chen, Greg C. Pommier, J. Zachery Cogan, Joseph M. Replogle, Carmen Adriaens, Gokul N. Ramadoss, et al. 'Genome-wide programmable transcriptional memory by CRISPR-based epigenome editing.' *Cell* 184, no. 9 (2021): 2503–2519.

Orentlicher, David. 'Cloning and the preservation of family integrity.' *Louisiana Law Review* 59, no. 4 (1999): 1019–1040.

Palacios-González, César, John Harris, and Giuseppe Testa. 'Multiplex parenting: IVG and the generations to come.' *Journal of Medical Ethics* 40, no. 11 (2014): 752–758.

Partridge, Emily A., Marcus G. Davey, Matthew A. Hornick, Patrick E. McGovern, Ali Y. Mejaddam, Jesse D. Vrecenak, Carmen Mesas-Burgos, et al. 'An extra-uterine system to physiologically support the extreme premature lamb.' *Nature Communications* 8, no. 1 (2017): 15112.

Patel, Ravi M., Sarah Kandefer, Michele C. Walsh, Edward F. Bell, Waldemar A. Carlo, Abbot R. Laptook, Pablo J. Sánchez, et al. 'Causes and timing of death in extremely premature infants from 2000 through 2011.' *New England Journal of Medicine* 372, no. 4 (2015): 331–340.

Ranisch, Robert. 'germline genome editing versus preimplantation genetic diagnosis: Is there a case in favour of germline interventions?' *Bioethics* 34, no. 1 (2020): 60–69.

Rasoulinejad, Seyed Ahmad, and Faezeh Maroufi. 'CRISPR-based genome editing as a new therapeutic tool in retinal diseases.' *Molecular Biotechnology* 63, no. 9 (2021): 768–779.

Rathi, Akshat, and Echo Huang. 'More than 100 Chinese scientists have condemned the CRISPR baby experiment as "crazy."' *Quartz*, 26 November 2018. https://qz.com/1474530/chinese-scientists-condemn-crispr-baby-experiment-as-crazy/.

Reddy, Pradeep, Alejandro Ocampo, Keiichiro Suzuki, Jinping Luo, Sandra R Bacman, Sion L Williams, Atsushi Sugawara, et al. 'Selective elimination of mitochondrial mutations in the germline by genome editing.' *Cell* 161, no. 3 (2015): 459–469.

Regalado, Antonio. 'Exclusive: Chinese scientists are creating CRISPR babies.' *MIT Technology Review*, 25 November 2018. https://www.technologyreview.com/2018/11/25/138962/exclusive-chinese-scientists-are-creating-crispr-babies/.

Romanis, Elizabeth Chloe. 'Artificial womb technology and the frontiers of human reproduction: Conceptual differences and potential implications.' *Journal of Medical Ethics* 44, no. 11 (2018): 751–755.

Romanis, Elizabeth Chloe. 'Is "viability" viable? Abortion, conceptual confusion and the law in England and Wales and the United States.' *Journal of Law and the Biosciences* 7, no. 1 (2020): lsaa059.

Satkunarajah, Nisha. 'Woman 'stole' husband's sperm to have children.' *BioNews*, 6 June 2011. https://www.bionews.org.uk/page_93006.

Scheufele, Dietram A., Michael A. Xenos, Emily L. Howell, Kathleen M. Rose, Dominique Brossard, and Bruce W. Hardy. 'U.S. attitudes on human genome editing.' *Science* 357, no. 6351 (2017): 553–554.

Shaw, David. 'The consent form in the Chinese CRISPR study: In search of ethical gene editing.' *Journal of Bioethical Inquiry* 17, no. 1 (2020): 5–10.

Smajdor, A., and D. Cutas. 'Artificial gametes and the ethics of unwitting parenthood.' *Journal of Medical Ethics* 40, no. 11 (2014): 748–751.

Song, Lingqiao, and Yann Joly. 'After He Jiankui: China's biotechnology regulation reforms.' *Medical Law International* 21, no. 2 (2021): 174–192.

Srivastava, Sarika, and Carlos T. Moraes. 'Manipulating mitochondrial DNA heteroplasmy by a mitochondrially targeted restriction endonuclease.' *Human Molecular Genetics* 10, no. 26 (2001): 3093–3099.

Steffann, Julie, Nadine Gigarel, David C. Samuels, Sophie Monnot, Roxana Borghese, Laetitia Hesters, Nelly Frydman, et al. 'Data from artificial models of mitochondrial DNA disorders are not always applicable to humans.' *Cell Reports* 7, no. 4 (2014): 933–934.

Steptoe, Patrick C., and Robert G. Edwards. 'Birth after the reimplantation of a human embryo.' *The Lancet* 312, no. 8085 (1978): 366.

Stern, Harvey. 'Preimplantation genetic diagnosis: Prenatal testing for embryos finally achieving its potential.' *Journal of Clinical Medicine* 3, no. 1 (2014): 280–309.

Stewart, James B., and Patrick F. Chinnery. 'The dynamics of mitochondrial DNA heteroplasmy: Implications for human health and disease.' *Nature Reviews Genetics* 16, no. 9 (2015): 530–542.

Suter, Sonia M. '*In Vitro* gametogenesis: Just another way to have a baby?' *Journal of Law and the Biosciences* 3, no. 1 (2016): 87–119.

Tang, Lichun, Yanting Zeng, Hongzi Du, Mengmeng Gong, Jin Peng, Buxi Zhang, Ming Lei, et al. 'CRISPR/Cas9-mediated gene editing in human zygotes using Cas9 protein.' *Molecular Genetics and Genomics* 292, no. 3 (2017): 525–533.

Thomas, Mark, Gaetan Burgio, David J. Adams, and Vivek Iyer. 'Collateral damage and CRISPR genome editing.' *PLoS Genetics* 15, no. 3 (2019): e1007994.

Townsend, Beverley A. 'Human genome editing: How to prevent rogue actors.' *BMC Medical Ethics* 21, no. 1 (2020): 95.

Urnov, Fyodor D. 'Genome editing B.C. (Before CRISPR): Lasting lessons from the "Old Testament."' *The CRISPR Journal* 1, no. 1 (2018): 34–46.

Usuda, Haruo, Shimpei Watanabe, Masatoshi Saito, Shinichi Sato, Gabrielle C. Musk, Ms Erin Fee, Sean Carter, et al. 'Successful use of an artificial placenta to support extremely preterm ovine fetuses at the border of viability.' *American Journal of Obstetrics and Gynecology* 221, no. 1 (2019): 69.e1–69.e17.

Wai, Timothy, Asangla Ao, Xiaoyun Zhang, Daniel Cyr, Daniel Dufort, and Eric A. Shoubridge. 'The role of mitochondrial DNA copy number in mammalian fertility1.' *Biology of Reproduction* 83, no. 1 (2010): 52–62.

Walker, Peter. 'Baby delivered early to allow mother's cancer treatment dies.' *The Guardian*, 20 December 2015. http://www.theguardian.com/uk-news/2015/dec/20/baby-delivered-early-to-allow-mothers-cancer-treatment-dies.

Westin, Björn, Rune Nyberg, and Göran Enhörning. 'A technique for perfusion of the previable human fetus.' *Acta Paediatrica* 47, no. 4 (1958): 339–349.

World Economic Forum. *Agile Governance: Reimagining Policy-Making in the Fourth Industrial Revolution*. Geneva, 2018.

WHO Expert Advisory Committee on Developing Global Standards for Governance and Oversight of Human Genome Editing. *Human genome editing: A framework for governance*. Geneva: World Health Organization, 2021.

Yamashiro, Chika, Kotaro Sasaki, Yukihiro Yabuta, Yoji Kojima, Tomonori Nakamura, Ikuhiro Okamoto, Shihori Yokobayashi, et al. 'Generation of human oogonia from induced pluripotent stem cells in vitro,' *Science* 362, no. 6412 (2018): 356–360.

Zhang, John, Hui Liu, Shiyu Luo, Zhuo Lu, Alejandro Chávez-Badiola, Zitao Liu, Mingxue Yang, et al. 'Live birth derived from oocyte spindle transfer to prevent mitochondrial disease.' *Reproductive BioMedicine Online* 34, no. 4 (2017): 361–368.

Zhang, Pu-Yao, Yong Fan, Tao Tan, and Yang Yu. 'Generation of artificial gamete and embryo from stem cells in reproductive medicine.' *Frontiers in Bioengineering and Biotechnology* 8 (2020): 781.

Zhou, Quan, Mei Wang, Yan Yuan, Xuepeng Wang, Rui Fu, Haifeng Wan, Mingming Xie, et al. 'Complete meiosis from embryonic stem cell-derived germ cells in vitro.' *Cell Stem Cell* 18, no. 3 (2016): 330–340.

Zuccaro, Michael V., Jia Xu, Carl Mitchell, Diego Marin, Raymond Zimmerman, Bhavini Rana, Everett Weinstein, et al. 'Allele-specific chromosome removal after Cas9 cleavage in human embryos.' *Cell* 183, no. 6 (2020): 1650–1664.e15.

11

Placing MRT in the Evolution of Reproduction

KARINNE LUDLOW, WALTER G. JOHNSON,
AND DIANA M. BOWMAN

11.1 INTRODUCTION

Naming this volume *Reproduction Reborn* invites important debate about the significance of mitochondrial replacement therapies (MRT) to human reproduction. As Mann et al. (Chapter 1) observe, MRT are on the cusp of offering at least some families the only realistic hope for preventing the propagation of debilitating genetic diseases caused by mutations in the mitochondrial DNA (mtDNA) while having a biologically related child. But as a number of contributors to this edited volume explain, the number of women for whom clinical MRT could actually make a difference is very small.

Placing MRT as another step in the ongoing evolution of assisted reproductive technologies (ART) arguably assists in MRT's legitimisation, given the widespread global acceptance of ART today. Ludlow (Chapter 5), Cohen et al. (Chapter 6), González-Santos and Saldaña-Tejeda (Chapter 7), Johnson and Bowman (Chapter 8), and Doxzen (Chapter 10) place the emergence of MRT in this context. Ishii (Chapter 9), in his consideration of responses in Taiwan, China, Japan, and Singapore, suggests that the use of MRT to treat infertility and to prevent maternal transmission of mtDNA

Karinne Ludlow, Walter G. Johnson, and Diana M. Bowman, *Placing MRT in the Evolution of Reproduction*
In: *Reproduction Reborn*. Edited by: Diana M. Bowman, Karinne Ludlow, and Walter G. Johnson, Oxford University Press.
© Oxford University Press 2023. DOI: 10.1093/oso/9780197616192.003.0012

mutations can both be regarded as forms of infertility treatment because they result in a child. Nevertheless, describing MRT simply as 'infertility' treatment, even while acknowledging the various understandings of that term, does not portray the whole picture (see Sparrow et al., Chapter 2), particularly given the exclusion of the use of MRT to treat intractable infertility in those countries that expressly regulate MRT or are in the process of doing so.

MRT could be placed as part of advances in the creation of life outside the body and use of human embryos in research into early human development. Mann et al. (Chapter 1) lay useful foundations for such a framing by placing the origins of MRT science in the embryo micromanipulation techniques of the 1980s, investigating embryonic development. However, as they observe, MRT differs from earlier embryo micromanipulation techniques in the unprecedented level of egg manipulation needed and the involvement of gametes from three rather than two people. Such advances, particularly those in the 1990s and early 2000s around cloning (more correctly known as *somatic cell nuclear transfer*) and pluripotent stem cells, triggered global responses as well as the introduction of numerous domestic and professional regulatory frameworks. Despite a general consensus at that time among the international scientific community that reproductive human cloning should not be allowed, attempts by countries such as France and Germany to pass a United Nations treaty banning the practice failed in 2003 (Perry, 2004). While negotiations ultimately resulted in the adoption of a nonbinding declaration in 2005 (the United Nations Declaration on Human Cloning), only 83 members voted in favour, with countries such as China and the United Kingdom voting against the measure, and others, such as Greece and the Russian Federation, abstaining from the vote (United Nations, 2005). More recently, while the announcement by Chinese scientist He Jiankui in 2018 that he had used CRISPR to create gene-edited babies (the so-called *CRISPR babies*) resulted in a global controversy (Normile, 2018), concern among countries was not so great as to result in an international ban or framework to govern the technology (Greely, 2019). Some of these earlier responses to embryo research are important hurdles (or roadblocks) to MRT now (see Cohen et al., Chapter 6), although, as Dimond and Stephens (Chapter 4) explain, they can also facilitate the introduction of MRT. The response by the international community to cloning and the CRISPR babies also suggests that there is unlikely to be any appetite for a binding agreement on MRT.

But it is the final thread in weaving MRT's story that provides the strongest claim to the title *Reproduction Reborn*. MRT are a genetic technology. This does not of itself make MRT significant enough to justify the claim of rebirth, even when the technology is applied to reproduction. After all, there is growing use of gene therapies to treat human health challenges, and genetic technologies such as preimplantation genetic testing are already regularly used in ART, with the science and consequences for patients of that testing being thoroughly explored by Mann et al. (Chapter 1), Herbrand (Chapter 3), and Doxzen (Chapter 10). What makes MRT revolutionary, we think, is that intentional change is made at the earliest stage of human development. That change is the subject of some of the most complex and interesting debates around reproduction of our times.

As for all 'rebirths,' there are broader repercussions from MRT that must also be addressed. How will debates about MRT inform responses to other innovative technologies, such as in vitro gametogenesis, artificial wombs, and—particularly—genome editing? Like MRT, these bring repercussions for future generations and may offer the only real solution to intractable infertility, other genetic diseases, or the creation of alternative family structures with biological links. But, unlike MRT, germline gene editing may not require the degree of egg manipulation, may not need contributions from three human sources, and may not be motivated to overcome infertility. What will these and other differences mean?

How social values relevant to MRT clinical practice are and should be implemented by legal and policy apparatuses is the subject of this volume. This chapter takes us on the pathway that led to the position we are in today by first tracing the growing use of ART and earlier forms of cytoplasmic and mitochondrial transfer around the world in Section 11.2. It then considers, in Section 11.3, the influence of the important actors in the MRT debate in shaping the evolution of MRT and their regulation. These actors include those with mitochondrial disease and their families, the public, the media, and religious and governmental bodies. Transnational actors and events also influence MRT's trajectory and this is considered in

Section 11.4 and Section 11.5 consider the unique questions raised by MRT that could be addressed by regulation and the difficulties for that regulation if a jurisdiction decides to respond through regulation. Sections 11.6 and 11.7 turn to the impact of the development of human heritable genome editing (HHGE) for MRT and, turning our analysis 180 degrees, then considers what responses to MRT tell us about the use of other technological advancements, such as in vitro gametogenesis, artificial wombs, and HHGE. Concluding thoughts around MRT are brought together in the final section.

11.2 THE UNFOLDING PATHWAY

Whether seen as a step in the evolution of ART, another advance in embryo research, or important because of its use as a genetic reproductive technology, foundations for the regulatory pathway for MRT introduction were laid decades before the 2016 birth of a boy whose mother had undergone intrauterine transfer in Mexico following MRT in a New York clinic (Kolata, 2016). ART had been the subject of debate since the 1940s, even though successful use was still decades away (Demack Report, 1984). Initially, much of that very earliest debate concerned the use of artificial insemination with, for example, the United Kingdom's Feversham Committee recommending in 1960 that although the practice should be strongly discouraged, it did not require regulation by law. But the development of in vitro fertilisation (IVF) from the 1960s (Edwards et al., 1969), culminating in the successful births of children (the first, in the United Kingdom in 1978, followed by births in 1980 in Australia and 1981 in the United States) triggered inquiries in a number of jurisdictions and resulted in the world's first legislative control of assisted human reproduction and associated embryo research in Victoria, Australia, in 1984 (Ludlow, Chapter 5). This was the beginning of a trend to use regulation to respond to novel reproductive technologies, including IVF, surrogacy, and the use of donated gametes or embryos, and to the social and ethical issues raised by them such as the parentage of resulting children and access to the technology. The decision to regulate reproductive technologies is itself controversial and does not occur in every jurisdiction. Nevertheless, as Herbrand (Chapter 3) so movingly explains, the introduction of limited and conditional access to reproductive techniques continues as an important element that makes reproductive decisions especially complicated for prospective patients at risk of mitochondrial disorders.

As described by Mann et al. (Chapter 1), MRT has developed over many years, and their eventual arrival into clinical practice was not unexpected. The late 1990s saw the use of cytoplasmic transfer to treat infertility, in 1997 in the United States, 1998 in Taiwan, and 2001 in Italy. Live births resulting in seemingly healthy children occurred in all of these countries, with further births from cytoplasmic transfer reported in the Czech Republic in the decades since then (Sobek et al., 2021). Further live births resulted from autologous mitochondrial transfer in Taiwan (2001) and China (2003), where the technique was again applied to treat infertility (Ishii, Chapter 9). Then, 2016 saw Greek regulators approve a small clinical trial of MRT to treat infertility, with that trial concluding in 2020, also having achieved live births (Johnson and Bowman, 2022). Autologous transfer procedures also became available in a Japanese clinic in 2016 (operating until 2017), Spain (2015–2017), and clinics in Canada and the United Arab Emirates (unclear dates, circa 2014–2015) to treat infertility; again, live births were reported at each site (Chapters 8 and 9, this volume; Fakih et al., 2015; Labarta et al., 2019). 2017 saw the birth of a child following MRT to treat infertility in the Ukraine, where MRT continues to be available for domestic and foreign patients (although that availability has inevitably been impacted by the 2022 Russian invasion of that country). Nevertheless, the success of MRT in treating infertility rather than to address the transmission of mitochondrial DNA disorders is not proved, as explained by Ishii (Chapter 9), and it is MRT's use to address maternal transmission of mitochondrial disease that has spurred express legislative change.

A report by the UK Department of Health at the turn of this century recognised that transmission of mitochondrial disease caused by mtDNA mutations could be prevented through ART (UK Department of Health, 2000). But while the United Kingdom then moved to permit licensed research in the area, Australia responded to developments in cytoplasmic transfer by expressly prohibiting most MRT research and clinical use in its 2002 legislation around embryo research (Ludlow, Chapter 5). The United Kingdom, consistently with its approach to embryo research more generally, later acted to enable the introduction of MRT into clinical practice once experts were satisfied that the technology was sufficiently developed, with the pathway to that outcome being carefully traced by Dimond and Stephens in Chapter 4. This included the 2008 amendment of UK legislation to enable consideration of reform to legalise clinical MRT and the 2012 Nuffield Council on Bioethics Report on the use of MRT to prevent mitochondrial DNA disorders.

An expert committee of the US Food and Drug Administration (FDA) considered the use of oocyte modification in ART to prevent the transmission of mitochondrial disease in 2014, shortly before the United Kingdom became the first country to expressly legalise clinical MRT. The first baby born following MRT to prevent mitochondrial disease was delivered in the United States in 2016, the same year that the US National Academies of Science, Engineering, and Medicine reported on the ethical, social, and policy considerations around MRT and just after the US Congress enacted a rider to the 2016 Appropriations Bill restricting the FDA from considering applications regarding human embryo research where such embryos are intentionally created or modified to include a heritable genetic modification (Chapter 5). Other countries followed with inquiries and reports around MRT, including Mexico's Comisión Nacional de Bioética

(CONBIOETICA) in 2017 (Chapter 7), and 2018 reports from an Australian Senate committee inquiry (Chapter 5) and Singapore's Bioethics Advisory Committee (Chapter 9). These and subsequent developments are explored in the relevant contributions in this volume. The governments of other countries are also pushing the conversation around genetic advances, including Qatar, Russia, and Israel, although not all prefer MRT over other possible solutions. For example, experts have suggested that, from an Islamic perspective, CRISPR/Cas9-mediated germline gene editing is a less scientifically and ethically complex procedure than MRT to treat mitochondrial disease because it does not require cell donation (Isa et al., 2020).

However, while not all countries have been considered in this volume, those that are demonstrate a range of national environments for MRT with, for example, UK legislation expressly permitting clinical MRT (subject to a licensing procedure) at one end of the spectrum and the United States's (perhaps unintended, as explained by Cohen et al. in Chapter 6) prohibition of MRT at the other end. Dimond and Stephens (Chapter 4) assert that the United Kingdom's response to MRT reflects its long-standing and liberal attitude to supporting licensed embryo research to enable scientific development and its history of legalising novel practices in such research and use; this resulted in the first licence for embryonic research on mitochondrial disease being granted by the relevant UK agency in 2005 and the first licence to perform pronuclear transfer (PNT) research in 2006, and culminated in the world's first express legalisation of clinical MRT in 2015. Contributions to this volume also demonstrate the difficulties caused by fragmented regulation which delay or complicate the introduction of technologies such as MRT. The United States, for example, has a fragmented regulatory structure in regards to both the source of authority and mode of regulation, using administrative governance rather than direct legislation to prohibit MRT (Chapter 6). Similarly, Australia has a fragmented structure although it has taken steps to overcome that in its federal legislation allowing MRT (Chapter 5). The United Kingdom, on the other hand, is described as having 'central legislative and administrative governance of many facets of ART' (Cohen et al., Chapter 6: p. 130), and, as noted above, has already legalised MRT.

Ishii (Chapter 9) explains how clinical MRT were unsuccessfully performed in China in 2003, and are now expressly prohibited in that country. Clinical MRT were also expressly prohibited in Australia, although recent parliamentary action has changed that (Ludlow, Chapter 5). Nevertheless, as with responses to embryo research generally, many countries have not taken explicit regulatory action in response to MRT. This means that their regulatory stance is not clear, even if there is pre-existing

ART regulation. Johnson and Bowman (Chapter 8) describe, for example, how pre-existing Greek ART regulation meant the MRT clinical trials referred to above could go ahead in that country. González-Santos and Saldaña-Tejeda (Chapter 7) reach similar conclusions in regard to Mexico. On the other hand, the pre-existing ART regulations of some jurisdictions seem to prohibit MRT, such as in Singapore, or to prohibit particular forms of MRT, such as Japan (Ishii, Chapter 9). This range of environments provides very useful material from which important conclusions can be drawn. But those environments are also shaped by social values expressed alongside the evolving use of MRT, and it is to those values and the voices of important stakeholders that we turn now.

11.3 IDENTIFICATION AND MOBILISATION OF SOCIAL VALUES

Some of the most important voices in the MRT debate are those of potential patients. But, as observed by Herbrand (Chapter 3), little has been said about how women at risk of transmitting mitochondrial disorders view and experience their situation and make their reproductive decisions. Herbrand addresses this deficit in this volume by thoughtfully examining the fundamental perspectives of UK women. She identifies five elements related to mitochondrial disorders that make reproductive decision-making particularly difficult for at-risk prospective parents. Herbrand concludes that, despite these difficulties, many of the women who participated in her studies never considered giving up on having a biological child and deployed much effort to have what she called a double imperative of a healthy and biologically related child.

Consistently with Herbrand's observation of a double imperative driving most women's reproductive decisions, Sparrow et al. (Chapter 2; p. 33) conclude that MRT is,

> most appropriately understood as a technology to facilitate the securing of a relationship of 'genetic relatedness' where a mother would otherwise only be able to give birth to a child unaffected by mitochondrial disease by the use of donor oocytes.

Dimond and Stephens (Chapter 4: p. 88) also address the representation of MRT as 'the only option for some women to have healthy, genetically related children' as being a powerful part of what they call the 'interpretive package' used to give MRT meaning. Ishii (Chapter 9) considers that it is the maintenance of genetic relatedness that can be pursued using MRT that makes it unlikely that further restrictions will be placed on MRT in Japan, after making the astute observation that all mitochondrial manipulation in Taiwan, China, and Japan have been for the purposes of having genetically related offspring *without* using donor eggs. Similarly, Australia's public consultation process has shown that the opportunity to have healthy, genetically related children is a leading justification for permitting clinical MRT (Ludlow, Chapter 5). Singapore, which like Australia is historically close to the United Kingdom, has also had a public consultation process but the results are not publicly available (Ishii, Chapter 9).

However, there is diversity in the scenarios of people affected by mitochondrial disorders, and these are also explored by Herbrand (Chapter 3). Herbrand describes how these heterogeneous experiences cause social isolation, amongst other things. This diversity makes even more extraordinary the willingness of mitochondrial disorder patient support groups and the families themselves to work for legalisation of MRT to assist the small number of people who could take advantage of it. Having recognised that goodwill though, some participants, as Herbrand notes, hope that debates around MRT legalisation will increase public awareness of mitochondrial disease more generally. Indeed, the way the technology is discussed in the public arena has itself been the subject of study and is explored by Dimond and Stephens (Chapter 4) and Sparrow et al. (Chapter 2) in this volume.

But whether MRT is valued as a public health measure is less clear. González-Santos and Saldaña-Tejeda (Chapter 7) observe that, in Mexico, where the intrauterine transfer for the first MRT birth to avoid passing on mitochondrial disease occurred, infertility is described as a problem faced mostly by women and couples associated with their modern lifestyle, including the delay of pregnancy. It is, they note, also seen as a problem of the middle and upper echelons of society. But this attitude is changing even in Mexico, where many of the legislative proposals to change ART regulation described by González-Santos and Saldaña-Tejeda now agree that infertility is a public health issue. Nevertheless, caution is needed in bringing public health arguments to support MRT as a response to infertility or to the inherited conditions to be addressed by it. As Sparrow et al. (Chapter 2) warn, it is not the case that public health considerations should play no role in deciding whether it is appropriate to use MRT, but caution is needed in the value judgements in state support for MRT and to avoid the risk of coercion as the technology becomes widely available. They add that disability perspectives are understudied and raise this as an area for future research.

Religion is another important actor in some countries, as in Mexico and in the Asian countries discussed in Chapter 9 by Ishii. González-Santos and Saldaña-Tejeda (Chapter 7) observe that religious influence on a society does not mean that ART (and presumably MRT) is unacceptable, pointing to research that demonstrates that ART is better accepted in Ecuador than in the United States. Ishii contrasts the moral status of human embryos in Catholicism with that in Confucian values to conclude that if and when Confucian values impact decisions around reproductive technology, infertile couples are more likely to be willing to consent to MRT that assist in having a genetically related child. In contrast, Ishii observes that the regulatory responses to germline genome editing in those countries considered by him are based on reproductive globalisation rather than religious values. He argues, in Chapter 9, that the different regulatory responses in countries where populations hold Confucian beliefs indicate that MRT regulation is developed in response to values other than religious and cultural beliefs. This is consistent with actions in countries such as the United Kingdom, Australia, and Singapore, where deliberate steps have been taken to create public participation in bioethical debates using a secular style of bioethics informed by medical and legal perspectives.

Governmental and expert bodies, which often encourage public participation, play a fundamental role in mobilising social values. Not only do reports written by such bodies provide insight into the attitudes of the government and citizens of the relevant jurisdiction, but they also demonstrate contrasting possible responses to MRT. Cohen et al. (Chapter 6: 138-139) suggest that the UK government sees MRT as a 'beacon of national scientific prowess' in its consideration of clinical MRT but that there is no such national pride in the US MRT debates. Cohen et al. also point out that legalisation was described in the UK press as putting it ahead of other countries on the scientific and commercial front. On this issue, González-Santos and Saldaña-Tejeda (Chapter 7) observe that the first birth in which MRT was used to address a mitochondrial disorder was framed in one Mexican program as a national breakthrough that could offer hope to patients (national and international) and that Mexico's regulatory framework was itself framed as enabling. They also observe that there is a need for patient voices in the conversation in Mexico. Similarly, Dimond and Stephens (Chapter 4) describe media reports of MRT's legalisation in the United Kingdom as a victory for British researchers and note that a knighthood was awarded to the scientist who led MRT development and was prominent in debates to have it legalised.

Economic considerations though, such as the financial costs and benefits of using MRT to address mitochondrial disease, have not been strong drivers of the technology's adoption, at least in the United Kingdom according to Dimond and Stephens (Chapter 4). They explain that the economic impact of MRT may not be significant in the long term because of the small number of patients and where use is government-funded. This conclusion that economic impact is not a significant motivator in MRT debates is consistent with the observation by Sparrow et al. (Chapter 2) that while MRT could potentially reduce the overall incidence of mito-chondrial disease in the community (assuming that MRT is used by at-risk parents), descriptions of the technology typically emphasise its positive aspects of creating 'healthy' embryos rather than determining what sort of people are brought into existence. Nevertheless, Herbrand (Chapter 3) demonstrates that reproductive technologies, at the individual level, raise numerous challenges in terms of costs, risks, invasiveness, availability, and suitability and warns that these should not be underestimated for those seeking MRT. She also notes that her research with participants within the United Kingdom showed, that unlike for other inherited conditions, such as inherited deafness, the sense for mitochondrial disease was that it 'had to be avoided by all means *and if possible eradicated*. It was never considered as a disability that could be an important element of one's identity' (em-phasis added) (p. 77). This difference between Herbrand's results and the observations of Sparrow et al. could be because Herbrand's research was confined to people at risk of transmitting mitochondrial disorders or be-cause of the timing of the research, with Herbrand's work having been carried out earlier than that considered by Sparrow et al. Differences be-tween UK and Australian social values could be an alternative explanation, particularly as economic considerations were raised in the Australian public and government discussions albeit as only one of a number of justifications for legalisation (Chapter 5). Further research is needed to disclose the true cause.

As to national priority setting and allocation of resources, which are described by Sparrow et al. (Chapter 2) as a frequently raised argument against MRT, these were largely excluded from the UK debate by the scope of the Nuffield Council Report which, according to Dimond and Stephens (Chapter 4), essentially set the boundaries for the MRT debate in the UK. Australia's approach (Chapter 5) will include government financial sup-port to patients to ensure equitable access to MRT, at least during the multiyear clinical trial, and is particularly important given the physical size of Australia and that only one clinic will be permitted to offer the tech-nology. But, as Sparrow et al. (Chapter 2) observe, while it may be wrong to single out MRT as immoral because the money spent on it could be used elsewhere, the impact of the allocation of donor eggs to MRT on the avail-ability of other ART warrants serious consideration.

What is also clear, as Cohen et al. (Chapter 6) observe, is that any country that prohibits or restricts access to MRT can be expected to prompt medical tourism (or, as Cohen et al. call it, 'circumvention tourism' (p. 140) or, as discussed by Johnson and Bowman (Chapter 8), reproductive, procreative, or fertility tourism). Taiwan promotes fertility tourism for foreign couples, which is accommodated within its existing ART regulatory framework. Ishii (Chapter 9) suggests that Taiwan has a neutral attitude or indifference to MRT, which may mean that MRT would also be available to foreigners. Johnson and Bowman record the enormous economic value of medical tourism in the European Union in their discussion of the authorisation, use, and governance of MRT in that jurisdiction. Significant variation in the legislative schemes for ART between EU countries, which inevitably impact the regulation of MRT, means MRT tourism is inevitable. Indeed, as Johnson and Bowman explain in Chapter 8, a clinic in Kyiv is already taking advantage of this and offering MRT for EU and non-EU citizens (although this is likely impacted by the Russian invasion of Ukraine). Ishii notes that the United Kingdom's Code of Practice means non-UK citizens can access MRT within its borders, although, because of privacy considerations protecting the identity of applicants who undergo MRT, it is not clear that this has occurred. Ludlow (Chapter 5) records that the Australian government had said that it would consider supporting Australians to gain access to MRT in the United Kingdom but it has not (publicly at least) done so. The Australian government has also expressed an ambition to become a destination for MRT for people who are not Australian citizens (Chapter 5).

The public's voice is an important part of the MRT debate although it is arguable whether public consultation or opinion has driven any changes different from what would otherwise have occurred or whether it is instead used to justify the conclusions that government and/or expert bodies have already reached. Several of the chapters in this volume seem to make this point. For example, Cohen et al. (Chapter 6) observe as a sign for optimism in liberalising the United Sstates MRT process that 'there may be room for political advocacy groups to educate the public on MRTs' (p. 138). Herbrand (Chapter 3) places the emergence of the UK public's attention to mitochondrial disorders as beginning when parliamentary debates and public consultation around MRT legalisation occurred, mostly between 2012 and 2015. The control and assessment of the extensive public consultation process in the United Kingdom is thoroughly dissected by Dimond and Stephens in Chapter 4. Public consultation processes, many of them based on those of the United Kingdom, have also been used in Singapore (Ishii, Chapter 9) and Australia (Ludlow, Chapter 5). This contrasts with the situation in the European Union, where no expert review or public consultation processes have occurred at the EU level to guide MRT policymaking (Johnson and Bowman, Chapter 8). There has also been some public consultation and discussion in the United States (Cohen et al., Chapter 6) and Mexico, although González-Santos and Saldaña-Tejeda (Chapter 7) call for greater public participation in Mexico.

11.4 IMPACT OF INTERNATIONAL FRAMEWORKS AND BODIES

As this edited volume illustrates, a patchwork of legislative frameworks and tools have been employed by jurisdictions to allow for or prohibit MRT. In some countries, MRT has been quietly taking place within pre-existing legislative regimes, adding to the heterogenous governance landscape. While public consultation and dialogue have occurred in countries such as the United Kingdom and Australia as part of the legislative reform process (see Herbrand, Chapter 3; Dimond and Stephens, Chapter 4; Ludlow, Chapter 5), MRT has not—for the most part—generated the intense public scrutiny and/or global scientific backlash seen in response to, for example, human germline editing (Greely, 2019). Nor have we witnessed a push for a more global approach to governing the technology. In the absence of harm, the patchwork of regulatory approaches appears likely to persist.

That is not to say, however, that there will not be some diffusion of approaches, tools, and instruments across jurisdictional borders. As highlighted by Cohen et al. (Chapter 6), the first baby born as a result of MRT used to address a mitochondrial disorder involved clinical expertise and facilities shared across two countries, with the family flying in from a third. Dr John Zhang, the team lead and founder of New Hope Fertility Center in New York, has indicated his desire to work 'with partners around the world' in order to 'reach out to more families that might need help' (Reardon, 2016). Some of Zhang's work has focused on using mitochondrial techniques to treat infertility rather than prevent mitochondrial disease. For example, as Ishii (Chapter 9) discusses, in 2003 Zhang performed mitochondrial replacement to treat infertility in a 30-year-old woman at a Chinese clinic before Chinese regulations were changed to prohibit such procedures. New Hope Fertility has scaled its operations to create an international network that now spans Mexico, Russia, and China (New Hope Fertility, 2022), allowing for Zhang and others to shape MRT policy within these jurisdictions. A second example of a (now ended) international partnership working to globally commercialise a related reproductive technology, namely the autologous germline mitochondrial energy transfer (AUGMENT), is also discussed by Ishii in Chapter 9. In that case the technology was used for infertility treatment at a clinic in Japan in collaboration with a US biotechnology company, OvaScience.

Other actors and instruments are similarly guiding MRT policy across multiple jurisdictions. As discussed by Johnson and Bowman (Chapter 8), the European Society of Human Reproduction and Embryology (ESHRE), a medical professional organisation based in Europe but with membership open to professionals in non-EU countries, has been explicit in its condemnation of MRT being used as an infertility treatment. And while the Latin American Assisted Reproduction Network (RedLara), the Latin American professional association for ART, appears to have been silent on MRT to date, in their chapter González-Santos and Saldaña-Tejeda (Chapter 7) highlight how influential the professional body has been in shaping ART policy across the region. Issuance of guidance by RedLara on MRT—should they choose to do so—would, based on precedent, carry significant weight with clinicians across the region. Analogous bodies to ESHRE and RedLara exist across other regions, with a myriad of informal and formal communication mechanisms existing between them, thus opening up the possibility of the diffusion of guidance, best practice, and standards between the different organisations and regions.

Conferences also provide powerful forums for the international diffusion of attitudes and norms as illustrated by the Asilomer Conference and the first and second International Summit of Human Gene Editing (in 2015 and 2018) (Berg et al., 1975; Olson and National Academies of Sciences, Engineering, and Medicine, 2016; National Academies of Sciences, Engineering, and Medicine, 2019). While such meetings do not produce binding regulatory tools, Marchant (2021: 394) has argued that they are important for global norm development because they 'contribute to technology governance both by providing a forum for discussion and debate and by providing a sense of emerging consensus on appropriate applications and safeguards for an emerging technology.' The first meeting of the International Society for Reproductive Nuclear Transfer (ISRNT) was scheduled to take place in Kyiv, Ukraine, on 11–14 May 2020. While the conference was ultimately cancelled due to COVID-19, it signals a demand within the global scientific community and other relevant stakeholders for tailored discussions on advanced reproductive technologies including MRT. The resumption of in-person events, and the acceleration of MRT into the clinical space, is likely to see a myriad of such conferences emerge in the coming years.

In contrast with domestic regulation, the application of existing supranational and/or global legal instruments to shape the MRT landscape is limited, with little appetite among stakeholders to push in this direction. Johnson and Bowman's (Chapter 8) analysis of the application of the Council of Europe's Convention of Human Rights and Biomedicine (the

Ovideo Convention) suggests that while the Convention prohibits HHGE, MRT likely falls outside of its scope. Moreover, with the Convention having been ratified by only 29 member states of the Council of Europe (as of December 2021), and zero non-member states of the Council of Europe (Council of Europe, 2021), its reach is limited. In its 2021 report on human genome editing, the World Health Organisation (WHO) did not call out MRT, suggesting that—at least at this time—the technique does not warrant the same level of attention as genome editing nor the same level of governance and oversight (World Health Organisation [WHO], 2021a, 2021b, 2021c).

11.5 MATTERS FOR REGULATORY RESPONSE

The years of scientific advances and research discussed by Mann et al. (Chapter 1), together with the voices discussed above, have driven the introduction of clinical MRT. Whether that introduction (and the introduction of other reproductive technologies) should be regulated is a question that countries have responded to in different ways. But if MRT is to be regulated, close consideration of MRT debates and regulatory responses considered by the contributors to this volume demonstrate the matters that could be addressed. Useful information can be drawn not only from those countries that have created specific MRT regulation (United Kingdom and Australia) but also from countries where MRT is prohibited (United States and China) or existing regulation is ambivalent (European Union, Taiwan, Mexico).

The most fundamental issue to be addressed is access to the technology. Those countries which have expressly legalised MRT have limited access to those women seeking to avoid transmission of mitochondrial DNA disorders, to have a healthy and genetically related child. Dimond and Stephens (Chapter 4) observe that the Nuffield Council on Bioethics report, in establishing the parameters for ethical debate in that country, excluded alternative uses such as potential uses for older women seeking infertility treatment and non-heteronormative families seeking to create genetic links with their children. Australian legislation also limits MRT to the avoidance of mitochondrial DNA disorders (Ludlow, Chapter 5). The creation of a genetically related child is, as discussed above (see also Chapters 2, 3, 5 and 9), a central justification and motivation for clinical MRT whether it is described as being used to avoid transmission of mitochondrial disorders or to treat infertility. It is unsurprising therefore that the use of MRT to create a genetic link in non-heteronormative families is suggested by some to be a further legitimate use of MRT. Given that access to ART by non-heteronormative people remains problematic in some jurisdictions, the legitimacy of such use is contentious. MRT for such purpose has, so far as known, not occurred, but as the real and longer-term risks to the child become better known, the push for expansion for this use (and the use of other emerging reproductive technologies discussed later in this chapter) may become stronger. In regards to the use of MRT for other infertility reasons, such as rejuvenation of eggs, Ishii (Chapter 9) explains that scientific evidence of success is unclear. Until this use is properly established, it is unlikely MRT will be permitted for that purpose in those jurisdictions with specific MRT regulation but may continue (or begin) in jurisdictions where no explicit regulatory action has been taken on the matter, such as Greece, Ukraine, Taiwan, Japan (for meiotic spindle transplantation [MST] at least), or Mexico (see Chapters 7–9).

Even where the general purpose of MRT's use is settled, the criteria to be met before access is granted may also be addressed. The two regulatory models specifically created for MRT (in the United Kingdom and Australia) both include a number of criteria to be satisfied before access is given. However, these models demonstrate some slight variation at the granular level. Both, for example, require the clinic *and* the patient (and partner, if any) to be licensed before access is granted. In licensing the patient, the UK regulations require that there be a particular risk that the eggs or embryos of the woman seeking treatment may have mitochondrial abnormalities caused by mtDNA. Furthermore, there must be a significant risk that a person with those abnormalities will develop a serious mitochondrial disease (Human Fertilisation and Embryology [Mitochondrial Donation] Regulations 2015 [UK], regulations 5 and 8). Australian regulations are similar but require 'a particular risk of the woman's offspring inheriting mitochondria from the woman that would predispose the offspring to mitochondrial disease' and that, in regards to such disease, 'there is a significant risk that the mitochondrial disease that would develop in those offspring would result in a serious illness or other serious medical condition.'

These criteria show that both countries have been careful to confine MRT to disorders caused by mtDNA and exclude those caused by nDNA mutations. Nevertheless, there are two interesting differences in the precise language used. Australia's legislation avoids reference to embryos, referring instead to offspring. This may be to avoid reopening debates around embryo research in Australia, given that the changes to allow MRT will, for the first time, permit Australian researchers to create embryos for research purposes using traditional fertilisation. Indeed, this issue was a flashpoint in parliamentary debates, with many opponents to the legislation justifying their position by reference to objecting to the creation of zygotes for deliberate destruction (Ludlow, Chapter 5).

The second difference is around the risk to a person with the abnormalities carried by the egg or embryos of the woman seeking treatment (UK) or offspring of the woman seeking treatment (Australia). The UK regulations require assessment of the risk that mitochondrial abnormalities will cause the person with them to *develop serious mitochondrial disease*. The Australian legislation requires assessment of the risk that the *mitochondrial disease would result in serious illness or other serious medical condition*. The difference here is that while the UK regulations arguably treat the inheritance of mtDNA mutations as mitochondrial abnormalities (which may develop into disease), the Australian legislation refers to the inheritance of the mutations as the disease, which may or may not develop into an illness or condition. The significance, if any, of those differences is still to be seen but it may perhaps be an outcome of the underexploration of disability perspectives that was noted above because, as one scholar (Seng, 2003: 128, citing Brown, 1985) has suggested, defining disease 'requires implicit value judgements between physical states that are desirable and those that are disvalued.'

Herbrand (Chapter 3) sensitively explores the meaning of regulatory hurdles to access from the patients' perspective, identifying the problems caused for patients by scientific and practical difficulties in determining and assessing the risk of transmission as well as uncertainty about the illness trajectory when a mutation is passed on. This makes assessing which patients meet criteria to access MRT very complex, and it is not surprising that both the United Kingdom and Australia have given the task to expert bodies. An expert committee of the United Kingdom's HFEA is tasked with determining on a case-by-case basis whether there is sufficient scientific evidence that access criteria are met (Chapter 4), and Australia has largely adopted that approach, including expanding the membership of an existing expert embryo research committee of the national health regulator to facilitate its consideration of MRT licence applications (Chapter 5).

But even where a potential patient satisfies access criteria, she may also need funding to actually receive such treatment. Ensuring equitable access to MRT and ART more broadly is a fundamental consideration for regulators. For example, as Doxzen (Chapter 10) points out, 40 percent of women in the United States have limited or no access to fertility clinics, and the situation is worse in other jurisdictions, such as sub-Saharan African countries. The UK and Australian governments both fund clinical MRT although there may be criteria additional to those discussed above to gain access to that funding or to publicly funded healthcare.

A second fundamental issue for regulation of clinical MRT concerns the specific forms or techniques of MRT that will be allowed. The two most developed MRT are PNT and MST although, as explained by Mann et al. (Chapter 1) and Ishii (Chapter 9), scientists are exploring other techniques. The only clinic expressly licensed to provide MRT in the United Kingdom has so far used PNT. From a scientific perspective, the success of MRT is impacted by the specific procedure used, although it is not known whether the consequences for any resulting child are also impacted. Mann et al. (Chapter 1), for example, observe that the frequency of development to blastocyst stage for PNT in human zygotes is nearly the same as for unmanipulated controls. In contrast, for MST, data from animal models are varied and limited. Returning our focus to regulation impacting the specific forms of permitted MRT, some jurisdictions such as Mexico, for example, have no specific national regulation of either ART or MRT (Chapter 7). Therefore, subject to subnational laws or professional self-regulation, any form of MRT can be undertaken. The embryo transferred to the mother in Mexico, that went on to become the first live birth following modern MRT to address a mitochondrial disorder, was the result of MST. In those jurisdictions with pre-existing regulation of embryo research and/or ART, clinical use of all or some forms of MRT may also already be possible, even without further legislative change. Japan's current regulations, for example, discussed by Ishii (Chapter 9), have not been amended to expressly respond to the latest developments in MRT but nevertheless seem to allow MST while prohibiting PNT. The Greek and Ukraine clinics discussed by Johnson and Bowman (Chapter 8) have used MST and PNT, respectively.

The specific forms of permitted MRT are important because they raise different ethical concerns, as noted by Dimond and Stephens (Chapter 4), Ludlow (Chapter 5), and González-Santos and Saldaña-Tejeda (Chapter 7). Ludlow discusses how these differences were raised during the 2021 and 2022 Australian Parliamentary debates, but no changes were made in response to them and both PNT and MST are permitted. Dimond and Stephens note that the Church of England, which ultimately supported legalisation in the United Kingdom, would have liked more debate on the ethical differences between PNT and MST. UK regulations allow only PNT and MST, but the legislative amendments to the 2008 HFE Act mean further techniques can be added through changes to the regulations, which, although subject to Parliamentary rejection, do not need Parliamentary approval. Australia's legislation similarly attempts to 'future-proof' by naming three further techniques, in addition to PNT and MST, which can be licensed for preclinical use and, if proved to be safe and effective to the satisfaction of an expert committee, can be added as licensable for clinical use, subject to disallowance by Parliament, without the need for Parliament to amend relevant legislation.

Parentage of children conceived with the assistance of MRT is a further contentious issue that regulators will need to address. Dimond and Stephens (Chapter 4) explore the parentage aspects of the MRT debates as well as the use of language around parentage in their contribution to this volume. Parentage has traditionally relied on giving birth (see González-Santos and Saldaña-Tejeda, Chapter 7), provision of a gamete, or intention, and not on the kind of genetic material contributed. Sparrow et al. (Chapter 2) conclude that whether mtDNA donors should be considered a parent of the child conceived as a result of MRT is a matter of social choice. Nevertheless, the governments of the UK and Australia have drawn a line to prevent mtDNA donors claiming legal parentage based on the (lack of) impact on the 'personal characteristics' of future generations. In expert and public discussions considered by Dimond and Stephens and Sparrow et al. it was noted that many expert reports and public discussions have downplayed that impact, particularly in the United Kingdom, where legislation has been used to not only deny claims by mtDNA donors to legal parenthood but also to genetic parenthood. As discussed in the next section of this chapter though, that response inevitably shapes the regulatory landscape for other technologies.

In addition to parentage, whether the resulting child should have the right to identifying information about the mtDNA donor also needs to be addressed. The history of divisiveness over what and how information about donor identity is shared in ART, even where MRT is not used, makes it inevitable that this issue will be divisive. In Taiwan and many European nations and US states, for example, ART egg donors are anonymous; in the United Kingdom and Australia, egg donors' identity is recorded and available to resulting children. But while Australia intends to make the identity of mtDNA donors available to resulting children, the United Kingdom has not done so. Sparrow et al. (Chapter 2) argue that if there is a 'right to know' gamete donors in ART, then it should also extend to gamete donors in MRT. Not providing identifying information about the mtDNA donor, Dimond and Stephens (Chapter 4) argue, renders the donor (and her physical and emotional labour) invisible in debates. They explain that scholars have suggested that this approach was taken in the United Kingdom to ease the legalisation of MRT and because it was feared that to do otherwise could have a detrimental impact on egg donor recruitment. Further subsidiary details follow from a country's approach to mtDNA donor status, including whether to limit the number of families a mtDNA donor can donate to, whether to limit the number of mtDNA donor siblings, and whether the egg donation pathway should be the same regardless of whether an egg is to be used for ART or MRT.

Finally, the potential health impacts for the child that have been the centre of much of the MRT debate (the well-being of the future-born child being identified as the highest priority in, for example, the report by the National Academies of Sciences, Engineering, and Medicine (NASEM) discussed in Cohen et al. [Chapter 6]) must be addressed. Balancing on-going monitoring of children against the invasion of privacy and risk of medicalisation will be needed. In this context, it is striking that the parents of the first child born from modern MRT to avoid a mitochondrial disorder have denied any further follow-up to the clinical team that performed the assisted reproductive treatment (Liu et al., 2017). Reportedly this was due to privacy concerns given the attention their case had received. It was also reported as being due to immigration issues, providing an example of the difficulties created by transnational care and follow-up raised above. It is likely that these as well as issues around the appropriate consent process will, as Johnson and Bowman (Chapter 8) discuss, be dealt with by trans-national professional organisations, private entities, clinical facilities, and members of the scientific and medical communities rather than legislative bodies. Responses to HHGE, such as the establishment of an international registry for human genome editing clinical trials (mostly somatic at this point) by the WHO (2021a, 2021b, 2021c) could provide useful models here. And, as Doxzen (Chapter 10) concludes with respect to emerging technologies beyond MRT, monitoring societal repercussions and unantic-ipated externalities of offering and restricting future ART and action to prevent disparate policies will be essential in ethical deployment. However, while possibly useful, examples such as the WHO registry are likely to have the same limitations faced by domestic regulation in regards to deferment to children's privacy and autonomy. Despite this, responses to HHGE have been important in shaping responses to MRT, and it is to that which we now turn.

11.6 HERITAGE OF HUMANITY: WHAT THE DEVELOPMENT OF HUMAN HERITABLE GENOME EDITING MEANS FOR MRT

The human genome has been described as the heritage of humanity (UNESCO Universal Declaration on the Human Genome and Human Rights Article 1). Multilateral agreements reflecting that attitude dis-courage changes to that heritage: the UNESCO Universal Declaration, for example, suggests germline interventions may be contrary to human dignity (Articles 11 and 24); the Oviedo Convention (Convention on Human Rights and Biomedicine) rejects permanent modifications in the human genome by genetic modification unless for preventive, diagnostic, or therapeutic purposes (Article 13). Similarly, the domestic regulatory frameworks of some countries expressly prohibit changes to the human genome. The US appropriations bill rider, for example, which the US FDA views as restricting it from considering MRT, applies to 'research in which a human embryo is intentionally created or modified to include a heritable genetic modification' (Cohen et al., Chapter 6; p. 134). Japan also expressly prohibits gene therapy, defined as including modification to specific base sequences in genes (Ishii, Chapter 9).

This framing, together with the emergence of HHGE (the historical development and current areas of active research of which are addressed in Doxzen's contribution to this volume), plays an important role in shaping responses to MRT. Although different technologies, both MRT and HHGE make intentional changes. Newly emerging strategies for improving MRT are also beginning to use HHGE tools to eliminate mitochondrial carry-over by selectively degrading mutant mtDNA through the targeting of nucleases to mtDNA based on sequence specificity, further entwining the technologies (Mann et al., Chapter 1; Doxzen, Chapter 10).

Given the framing described above, it matters whether there is a distinction between MRT and other emerging technologies. As Cohen et al. (Chapter 6) note, advocacy groups may use these distinctions to justify the regulatory approach taken to MRT. Certainly in Australia, care was taken by the patient group advocating for MRT legalisation and by the politicians that supported it to distinguish MRT from HHGE in discussions, reports, and the legislation (Ludlow, Chapter 5). But the distinctions drawn may also be used to justify moves towards legalisation of other technologies and provide instruction and guidance in addressing future reproductive technologies. As highlighted in a number of chapters in this volume, patient groups could, for example, begin to champion HHGE in particular as a reproductive option. In comparison with MRT, HHGE using CRISPR is cheaper, and it is relevant and available to those beyond ART patients and clinics (Dimond and Stephens, Chapter 4) and, as Doxzen (Chapter 10) points out, HHGE could also be less invasive than swapping intracellular DNA and cytoplasmic molecules between eggs or zygotes, as occurs in MRT.

The MRT debates show that distinctions are commonly drawn between changes to the human genome by MRT and other changes, such as those by HHGE, on basis that

- mtDNA is not considered part of the genome for these purposes
- heritable (or germline) change must be passed on to descendants to be genetic modification that maybe contrary to human dignity
- replacement of mtDNA is not a 'change' for the purposes of genetic modification.

Each of these distinctions is discussed below.

11.6.1 Distinction Based on a Difference Between Mitochondrial DNA and Nuclear DNA

Many contributions to this volume note the impact (or not) of mtDNA on a person's identity. There is an ongoing narrative that mtDNA has no or little role to play in personal characteristics or identity. Much of this narrative is driven by a desire to distance MRT from claims that it enables 'designer babies,' whereby parents select the traits of their children. For example, a 2019 gathering at Harvard Law School, referred to in the contribution by Cohen et al. (Chapter 6; pp. 135–136), is reported as distinguishing between MRT and heritable genetic modification on that basis, the report saying that mtDNA,

> is separate from nuclear DNA, which helps determine individual traits like physical appearance, intelligence and personality. That means MRT cannot be used to produce the genetically enhanced "designer babies" that so many people are concerned about.

MtDNA's lack of impact on the resulting child's personal characteristics was also used in the United Kingdom to distinguish between a person's contribution of mtDNA compared with nDNA to justify anonymous mtDNA donation and the donor not being given parental status (Dimond and Stephens, Chapter 4).

Closely related to this distinction on the basis of impact on personal characteristics of the resulting child are distinctions on the basis of the relative amount of mtDNA compared with nDNA or on the basis of whether it is nDNA or mtDNA that is changed. For example, the United Kingdom Department of Health's report discussed by Dimond and Stephens (Chapter 4: p. 93) concluded that MRT is not genetic modification for the purposes of the UNESCO Declaration because, according to the report, such genetic modification is limited to changes to 'nuclear DNA (in the chromosomes) that can be passed on to future generations.'

However, such distinctions are not universally accepted, as demonstrated by the FDA's expansive approach to the appropriations rider discussed by Cohen et al. (Chapter 6), which results in the FDA's attitude that MRT is heritable genetic modification. Furthermore, this narrative that mtDNA does not impact the resulting child's identity and is therefore different from nDNA is contested. Herbrand, for example, concludes that diagnosis of mitochondrial mutations for her adult participants 'usually constituted a profound biographical disruption in participants' life,' including in terms of their personal identity (Chapter 3; p. 66). Sparrow et al. (Chapter 2) also contest this distinction, pointing out a number of problems with it, including that it is precisely because the mitochondria can be so significant for a child's phenotype and life prospects that MRT is done at all.

11.6.2 Distinction Based on Whether Change Is 'Passed On': What Does Heritable Mean?

A second frequently suggested distinction drawn between MRT and other emerging reproductive technologies is that MRT is not heritable if confined to male embryos. The driver for suggestions to limit clinical MRT to male embryos by bodies such as NASEM and originally suggested as an option for Australian parents in draft MRT legislation is that inheritance of mitochondria is only from the maternal line. Because male gametes do not pass on mitochondria, Cohen et al. (Chapter 6) note that it is arguable that male-only MRT is not heritable genetic modification and is therefore not prohibited by the US appropriations bill rider relied on by the FDA to prohibit MRT. They also discuss that many of the ethical and social concerns underlying the rider are absent in male-only MRT. In contrast, Dimond and Stephens's examination (Chapter 4) of the approach of the UK Department of Health discloses that the Department accepted that MRT is germline modification because the result (avoiding disease) is passed on through generations whether male or female embryos are used, even though the 'new' mitochondria themselves may not be.

It is arguable that the US NASEM's position discussed by Cohen et al. shows that 'heritable' means something different in the US when compared to its meaning in other countries. It seems, for NASEM at least, that a change is not heritable if that change in the DNA is not passed on to descendants, as when males born using MRT do not contribute mitochondria to their children. Given that it is the use of MRT to eradicate mtDNA mutations that makes it an attractive technology for some, this difference in understanding is important. Herbrand's contribution (Chapter 3) for example, discusses her finding that it is because her participants want the human gene pool changed to eradicate mtDNA mutations causing disease that they support MRT.

11.6.3 Distinction Based on the Meaning of Change

The Harvard Law School gathering of eminent experts referred to above and discussed in the contribution by Cohen et al. (Chapter 6: p. 135) is reported as concluding that MRT does not involve altering any genetic code; instead mtDNA is 'swapped out.' This language reflects a further distinction sometimes drawn between MRT and other technologies, that distinction being on the basis that replacement of entire organelles such as mitochondria is not genetic modification of the human genome. Sparrow et al. (Chapter 2) discuss a number of other significant disanalogies between MRT and other technologies similar to this distinction, including whether homologous recombination is used. It could also be argued that the important matter here is that the mtDNA used in the creation of the resulting child in MRT will be an already existing haplotype rather than a unique sequence. Therefore, there is continuity in the human genome. However, this argument seems weak: using HHGE, for example, to cause an embryo to have a common, unmutated form of a particular DNA sequence is not permitted (although moves to allow that may happen).

It may be that distinctions in this third group are really around the possibility of unknown impacts, such as off-target mutations or other changes, caused by a reproductive technology. There is, as Sparrow et al. discuss, more data and scientific advances around risks to the resulting child of MRT than for other emerging technologies which may address these concerns. In any case, we (the editors) consider that the most significant concern underlying each of the distinctions identified above is 'selection.' MRT involves replacing the mitochondria of the intending mother with 'healthy' mitochondria of a donor, without other targeted or chosen changes to the resulting embryo. Other than some discussion around matching haplotypes (Mann et al., Chapter 1), there has been no suggestion of choosing 'the best' mitochondria for use in MRT (if such a thing exists). Claims that there is no or little difference in the person who would have resulted if there had not been MRT, that future generations will not be impacted, or that change is made so the resulting child can be healthy all seek to distance the technology from association with selection of resulting children or enhancing their characteristics.

Ultimately, whether a distinction between MRT and other reproductive technologies is justified depends on, as Sparrow et al. (Chapter 2) elegantly conclude, the grounds on which the other technologies are morally problematic. Nevertheless, even before clinical use of new technology is permitted, its development and public discussion gives hope to those who may be assisted by it and, as Sparrow et al. also observe, the legalisation of MRT is likely to have implications for social attitudes towards other technologies of germline modification. The responses to MRT provide useful instruction on these, and it is to those that we now turn.

11.7 WHAT RESPONSES TO MRT TELL US ABOUT THE USE OF GENOME EDITING AND OTHER FUTURE ADVANCEMENTS

The MRT debates demonstrate the importance of distinguishing between creating a (healthy, genetically related) child compared with selecting a (healthy, genetically related) child. This distinction may explain why the recommendation by the US NASEM to confine clinical MRT to male embryos was so awkwardly received in other countries. The Oviedo Convention supports sex selection in ART only where it is to avoid serious hereditary sex-related disease, and sex selection for nonmedical reasons is expressly prohibited in many countries including the United Kingdom, Australia, and Taiwan. The United Kingdom rejected the idea of limiting clinical MRT to male embryos on the basis (according to Cohen et al., 2020: 568) that it would require additional intervention (to perform sex selection), reduce the number of available embryos for transfer, and exclude female embryos. Dimond and Stephens (Chapter 4) suggest that the United Kingdom's rejection of using male-only embryos in MRT reflects its prioritisation of the protection of the embryo during IVF over longer-term questions concerning future generations. The Australian government initially suggested participants in the proposed MRT clinical trial be given the opportunity to confine intrauterine transfer to male embryos, but this was removed during Parliamentary debates on the legislation after criticism that it may enable sex selection (Ludlow, Chapter 5). Three justifications were given by the government for the removal of this option: sex selection creates a risk to the viability of the embryo and is unnecessary; it is unreasonable to expect families to make this decision given the differences of opinion internationally and among experts; and it would equate to 'selective erasure of female embryos, hence future girls and women' (Australia House of Representatives, Supplementary Explanatory Memorandum, 2021: 2).

Even in the United States, where sex selection in ART is allowed for nonmedical reasons, Cohen et al. (2020) have observed, in work outside this volume, that MRT discussions have been careful to refer to the use of male embryos rather than to the destruction of female embryos. Cohen et al. (Chapter 6) identify that some members of Congress may find the inevitable destruction or indefinite freezing of female embryos problematic if the male-only approach is adopted. The use of the PNT form of MRT could similarly be expected to be controversial if or when MRT is debated in the US Congress. Debate in the Australian Parliament illustrates the problematic nature of PNT, where a second fertilised egg is created (and destroyed) in order to provide the nDNA of the resulting child.

As for MRT, in vitro gametogenesis (IVG) also offers prospective parents the opportunity to create genetically related children. But this technology, rather than being intended to produce a benefit for the resulting child and their descendants, offers a solution for those who are gamete-compromised. Doxzen (Chapter 10) explains the range of scenarios for which proponents may seek to use IVG and traces the technological development of this emerging technology. He points out that this technology could be paired with HHGE to correct problematic mutations or could be used (together with PGT) as an alternative to MRT. But it is the potential to create near unlimited embryos and allow selection amongst them that raises one of the most significant concerns around IVG. As Doxzen explains, 'IVG would contribute to concerns of germline genetic enhancement by exposing parents to a long list of potential children with a wide variety of desirable traits. Combining IVG with GGE in order to introduce, remove, or alter genomic sequences, increases concerns of enhancement' (Chapter 10: p. 230). Like MRT, IVG may enable new family structures while, as Doxzen suggests, challenging our understanding of reproductive norms and parental status.

HHGE is another emerging genetic technology that may be used in reproduction. As Herbrand reminds us, mitochondrial disorders can be transmitted by both parents when the mutation is in the nDNA, and nuclear defects cause about 80 percent of the mitochondrial disorders that severely affect babies and children (Herbrand, 2017). HHGE offers a potential solution when mutation on the nDNA rather than mtDNA is responsible for mitochondrial disease. It also may offer an alternative to MRT where a mtDNA mutation is the cause of the disorder (Mann et al., Chapter 1). But as Doxzen (Chapter 10) so usefully identifies, in addition to the expected further experimentation and regulatory, social, and ethical issues that would need to be overcome, there are practical difficulties that must be overcome before HHGE can be performed. These will be particularly problematic for countries such as Australia, the United States, China,

Japan, some EU countries, and possibly Singapore, which do not permit or restrict the creation of embryos for research purposes. As Doxzen points out, screening for disease-causing genetic mutations in an embryo is commonly performed on Day 3 of fertilisation, but, at this point, it is too late to attempt to correct the mutation through HHGE. Doing so may lead to high mosaicism and off-target mutations. There are similar practical scientific difficulties with performing HHGE on mature oocytes or sperm. The genetic mutation must have been identified for this to be useful as, for example, when both parents are homozygous for an autosomal-dominant condition.

Echoing the MRT debate, public and government responses to HHGE have been mixed; Doxzen records how the Chinese press, for example, initially acclaimed as a milestone accomplishment for China the HHGE experiments by scientist He which resulted in the 2018 birth of the CRISPR babies but that this was quickly offset by denunciation by scientific and other experts as well as the government and saw the eventual imprisonment of the scientist. Also reminiscent of what has happened with MRT, almost in parallel with the US decision not to allow the FDA to review proposals around HHGE (discussed in Cohen et al., Chapter 5), the UK regulator was granting a licence for HHGE research to the Francis Crick Institute to use CRISPR on human embryos (see Doxzen, Chapter 10), babies were born following the use of such technology in China (Ishii, Chapter 9), and the international community is considering permitting such use.

Responses to MRT will be important in responding to calls for access to other emerging reproductive technologies. In particular, the United Kingdom's approach to legalisation of MRT and the resulting regulatory framework is seen by some, such as the US NASEM and the UK Royal Society, as a potential model for CRISPR (Dimond and Stephens, Chapter 4). As Johnson and Bowman (Chapter 8) note, in 1997, the Oviedo Convention rejected genetic modification to introduce permanent modifications into the human genome in most cases but makes an exception where modification is for preventative, diagnostic, or therapeutic purposes. Whether HHGE to enable the birth of a healthy genetically related child is a therapeutic purpose is unclear. In any case, as explained by Sparrow et al. (Chapter 2), the therapeutic case for MRT is weak and, we (the editors) suggest that this is likely to be the same for HHGE. And, as Dimond and Stephens (Chapter 4) add, it is the relevance of HHGE to areas beyond reproduction and its accessibility that makes the imposition of boundaries on HHGE more difficult than for MRT. Any steps to permit HHGE will need boundaries, particularly around the purpose of its use. In an effort to prevent any such use, Australia's reforms to permit MRT include provisions that make it clear that intentionally modifying the nuclear or mitochondrial DNA such as through HHGE remains prohibited (Ludlow, Chapter 5).

Distinctions and justifications drawn around MRT provide a useful lens for considering the future pathways of HHGE and other reproductive technologies, assuming that they are developed to a stage where the risks around unintended and unwanted effects are understood and minimised to an acceptable level (and assuming agreement can be reached on that). Returning to the three distinctions commonly used to justify MRT is useful here to understand what may happen. First, justifying permitting MRT because of distinctions based on a comparison of nDNA with mtDNA and/ or the lack of impact on the resulting child's personal characteristics will, as Ludlow has argued in work outside this volume (Ludlow, 2020), inevitably strengthen calls to allow corrective genome editing of mtDNA and also to allow genome editing of nDNA involved in the operation of genes on mtDNA. Turning to the second distinction, for countries that consider that if changed DNA is not inherited then there has not been a heritable genetic modification (i.e., the United States and its attitude to male-only embryo selection), then HHGE used to prevent defective mtDNA being carried over to a new entity would also not cause a heritable genetic modification. Indeed, Doxzen (Chapter 10) records that some experts have argued that the intergenerational therapeutic value of HHGE is precisely the reason why, if proved safe, HHGE should be used to extend its benefits beyond a single patient. This is unlike MRT, where the focus is placed on the impact on the resulting child, and some have suggested limiting use to male embryos to avoid replaced mitochondria being passed to descendants. The third distinction though, is likely to pose problems for those advocating for legalisation of HHGE. The ability to make selected and targeted changes to an embryo is, as concluded above, the most powerful concern around MRT. Nevertheless, and importantly, despite MRT being considered by some to be a germline change, Dimond and Stephens (Chapter 4) note that it was still legalised in the United Kingdom (and now in Australia as well), and it is available in other countries because, amongst other things, it avoids inheritance of a serious disease. HHGE is likely to also be able to do the same as science advances.

Doxzen's contribution in Chapter 10 raises thought-provoking issues around another cutting-edge ART, the development of artificial wombs. This technology, offering a potential solution for those unable to gestate as well as saving extremely premature infant lives, offers a further way to create alternative biological family structures. Doxzen observes that countries will need to re-evaluate the rights given before and after birth, including whether transfer to an artificial womb is birth for the purposes of countries where legal personality is endowed only upon live birth. In light of the learnings from the MRT debate, it is important here that artificial wombs may assist in the creation of genetically related children without the use of a third party given that this justification has driven much of the push to allow MRT (and other ARTs before it). However, as with MRT, it is expected that countries will respond in very different ways to the use of this technology. The contribution by Cohen et al. (Chapter 6) puts MRT in the United States against the context of abortion and foetal personhood. Ishii (Chapter 9) also raises the issue of the moral status of human embryos and foetuses in his discussion of the role of religion in the Asian jurisdictions considered in his contribution. Ishii describes three different sets of beliefs with regard to that status: the 'all,' 'none,' and 'gradualist' positions with respect to the development of rights from conception to birth. In contrast, these issues are not explicitly raised in contributions regarding other jurisdictions, although the destruction of fertilised eggs as an objection to at least some forms of MRT is discussed in the Australian context (Ludlow, Chapter 5).

11.8 CONCLUSION

The human genome is no longer considered untouchable. Nevertheless, distinctions to separate MRT from other technologies continue to be made, and these inevitably impact the reception of other reproductive advancements. However, respect for humanity's genetic heritage remains fundamental, meaning that, as the MRT debates show, caution is needed to consider the voices of all stakeholders as medical and scientific advances are made.

The responses to MRT discussed in this volume show that it is unlikely that international agreement on MRT will be reached, particularly given its place as a reproductive technology, a matter on which multilateral agreement has never been reached. It may even be too late for such agreement around HHGE. Nevertheless, discussions between jurisdictions and between stakeholders are important because they add to our understanding of the values that do and should matter to us all. They also may drive the development of best practice, even if implementation must occur through the cooperation or coordination of individual jurisdictions with one another, through non-state actors such as professional medical bodies, or through transnational mechanisms such as the international registry for human genome editing clinical trials being established by the WHO. Reproduction is an intimately personal matter, but society's responses to techniques used to assist reproduction show that the global community needs to be involved in deciding the direction of emerging reproductive technologies.

REFERENCES

Australia House of Representatives. Supplementary Explanatory Memorandum 2021: *Mitochondrial Donation Law Reform (Maeve's Law) Bill 2021*, Amendments to be moved on behalf of the Government.

Berg, Paul, David Baltimore, Sydney Brenner, Richard O. Roblin III, and Maxine F. Singer. 'Asilomar conference on recombinant DNA molecules.' *Science* 188, no. 4192 (1975): 991–994.

Brown, W. Miller. 'On defining "disease."' *Journal of Medicine and Philosophy* 10, no. 4 (1985): 311–328.

Cohen, I. Glenn, Eli Y. Adashi, Sara Gerke, César Palacios-González, and Vardit Ravitsky. 'The regulation of mitochondrial replacement techniques around the world.' *Annual Review of Genomics and Human Genetics* 21 (2020): 565–586.

Committee on Science, Technology, and Law; Policy and Global Affairs; National Academies of Sciences, Engineering, and Medicine; Olson, Steven (Ed.), and National Academies of Sciences, Engineering, and Medicine. 'International summit on human gene editing: A global discussion.' Washington, DC: National Academies Press, 2016. https://www.ncbi.nlm.nih.gov/books/NBK343651/.

Demack Report. 'Report of the special committee appointed by the Queensland government to enquire into the laws relating to artificial insemination, in vitro fertilisation and other related matters.' Queensland Government, 1984.

Edwards, Robert G., Barry D. Bavister, and Patrick C. Steptoe. 'Early stages of fertilization in vitro of human oocytes matured in vitro.' *Nature* 221, no. 5181 (1969): 632–635.

Fakih, Michael H., Mohamad El Shmoury, Julia Szeptycki, Dennis B. dela Cruz, Caroline Lux, Suleman Verjee, Colleen M. Burgess, et al. 'The AUGMENTSM treatment: Physician reported outcomes of the initial global patient experience.' *Journal of Fertilization: In Vitro, IVF-Worldwide, Reproductive Medicine, Genetics & Stem Cell Bilogy* 3, no. 3 (2015).

Greely, Henry T. 'CRISPR'd babies: Human germline genome editing in the "He Jiankui affair."' *Journal of Law and the Biosciences* 6, no. 1 (2019): 111–183.

Herbrand, Cathy. 'Mitochondrial replacement techniques: Who are the potential users and will they benefit?' *Bioethics* 31, no. 1 (2017): 46–54.

Isa, Noor Munirah, Nurul Atiqah Zulkifli, and Saadan Man. 'Islamic perspectives on CRISPR/Cas9-mediated human germline gene editing: a preliminary discussion.' *Science and Engineering Ethics* 26, no. 1 (2020): 309–323.

Johnson, Walter G., and Diana M. Bowman. 'Inherited regulation for advanced ARTs: Comparing jurisdictions' applications of existing governance regimes to emerging reproductive technologies.' *Journal of Law and the Biosciences* 9, no. 1 (2022): lsab034.

Kolata, Gina. 'Birth of baby with three parents' DNA marks success for banned technique.' *New York Times* 27 September 2016. https://www.nytimes.com/

2016/09/28/health/birth-of-3-parent-baby-a-success-for-controversial-proced
ure.html.

Labarta, Elena, Maria José de Los Santos, Sonia Herraiz, Maria José Escribá, Alicia
Marzal, Anna Buigues, and Antonio Pellicer. 'Autologous mitochondrial
transfer as a complementary technique to intracytoplasmic sperm injection
to improve embryo quality in patients undergoing in vitro fertilization: A
randomized pilot study.' *Fertility and Sterility* 111, no. 1 (2019): 86–96.

Liu, Zitao, Zaher Merhi, John Zhang, and Taosheng Huang. 'Response: First birth
following spindle transfer-should we stay or should we go?' *Reproductive
Biomedicine Online* 35, no. 5 (2017): 546–547.

Ludlow, Karinne. 'Genetic identity concerns in the regulation of novel reproductive
technologies.' *Journal of Law and the Biosciences* 7, no. 1 (2020): lsaa004.

Marchant, Gary E. 'Global governance of human genome editing: What are the rules?'
Annual Review of Genomics and Human Genetics 22 (2021): 385–405.

National Academies of Sciences, Engineering, and Medicine. 'Second
International Summit on Human Genome Editing: Continuing the global
discussion: Proceedings of a workshop: In brief.' 2019. https://nap.nationalac
ademies.org/catalog/25343/second-international-summit-on-human-genome-
editing-continuing-the-global-discussion.

New Hope Fertility. 'About: John Zhang, MD, MSc, PhD.' 2022. https://www.newho
pefertility.com/about-us/fertility-doctor/john-zhang/.

Normile, Dennis. 'Shock greets claim of CRISPR-edited babies.' *Science*
(2018): 978–979.

Perry, Anthony C. F. 'Nuclear transfer cloning and the United Nations.' *Nature
Biotechnology* 22, no. 12 (2004): 1506–1508.

Reardon, Sara. '"Three-parent baby" claim raises hopes—and ethical concerns.' *Nature
News* (2016). https://www.nature.com/articles/nature.2016.20698

Seng, Esther. 'Human cloning: Reflections on the application of principles of
international environmental and health law and their implications for the
development of an international convention on human cloning.' *Oregon Review
of International Law* 5 (2003): 114–138.

Sobek, Ales, Emil Tkadlec, Eva Klaskova, and Martin Prochazka. 'Cytoplasmic
transfer improves human egg fertilization and embryo quality: An evaluation
of sibling oocytes in women with low oocyte quality.' *Reproductive Sciences* 28,
no. (2021): 1362–1369.

United Kingdom Department of Health. 'Stem cell research: Medical progress with
responsibility: Executive summary.' June 2000.

United Nations. 'General Assembly adopts United Nations declaration on human
cloning by vote of 84-34-37.' Press Release GA/10333 8 March 2005. https://
www.un.org/press/en/2005/ga10333.doc.htm

World Health Organisation (WHO). 'Human genome editing: Position paper.' 2021a.
https://www.who.int/publications/i/item/9789240030404.

World Health Organisation (WHO). 'Human genome editing: A framework for
governance.' 2021b. https://www.who.int/publications/i/item/978924
0030060.

World Health Organisation (WHO). 'Human genome editing: Recommendations.'
2021c. https://www.who.int/publications/i/item/9789240030381.

INDEX

For the benefit of digital users, indexed terms that span two pages (e.g., 52–53) may, on occasion, appear on only one of those pages.

Note: Tables, figures, and boxes are indicated by t, f, and b following the page number. Footnotes are indicated by "n" following the page number.

Printed in the USA/Agawam, MA
January 26, 2023

804967.026